W9-BLF-760

THE
ROVING
EDITOR

THE
ROVING
EDITOR,

—————— OR ——————

TALKS WITH SLAVES IN THE SOUTHERN STATES, BY JAMES REDPATH

EDITED BY
JOHN R. MCKIVIGAN

THE PENNSYLVANIA STATE UNIVERSITY PRESS
UNIVERSITY PARK, PENNSYLVANIA

Library of Congress Cataloging-in-Publication Data

Redpath, James, 1833–1891.
  The roving editor, or, Talks with slaves in the southern states /
  by James Redpath ; edited by John R. McKivigan.

      p.   cm.
  Includes bibliographical references and index.
  ISBN 0-271-01532-2 (cloth : alk. paper)
  ISBN 0-271-01533-0 (paper : alk. paper)
  1. Slaves—United States—Social conditions. 2. Southern States
—Description and travel. I. McKivigan, John R., 1949– .
II. Title.
E443.R43   1996
306.3′62′0973—dc20   95-31729
                                             CIP

It is the policy of The Pennsylvania State University Press to use acid-free
paper for the first printing of all clothbound books. Publications on uncoated
stock satisfy the minimum requirements of American National Standard for
Information Sciences—Permanence of Paper for Printed Library Materials,
ANSI Z39.48–1992.

FRONTISPIECE: James Redpath. Courtesy The Kansas State Historical Society,
Topeka

CONTENTS

ACKNOWLEDGMENTS

As is the case for many important milestones in my career, I owe a large debt of thanks to John Blassingame of Yale University, my longtime senior in editing the Papers of Frederick Douglass. John was the first person I told of my discovery that the "John Ball, Jr." letters published in the abolitionist press in the mid-1850s were by the same James Redpath who had written *The Roving Editor; or, Talks with Slaves of the Southern States* (1859). He immediately saw the potential in using Redpath's published letters to validate the *Roving Editor*'s numerous firsthand interviews with southern slaves. Without Blassingame's encouragement, this book would never have been prepared.

I also would like to thank another Douglass Papers colleague, Peter Hinks, for guiding me to the Pennsylvania State University Press as a publishing house with an interest in bringing back into print key documents in African American history. Peter Potter of the Press was of enormous assistance as a sounding board on editorial policy decisions. Peter Ripley of Florida State University supplied valuable suggestions about how to explain the *Roving Editor*'s place among African American historical documents to the reader. Brent Tarter of the Virginia State Library and Archives provided me with a crucial clue to discovering Redpath's source for much of his information on the early history of slavery in the Old Dominion.

A number of current and former students at West Virginia University enthusiastically assisted in various tasks connected with editing the *Roving Editor*. Kathleen McKenny oversaw the optical scanning and preliminary proofreading of the text of the book. Erica Gruver demonstrated great skill in uncovering obscure sources for the annotation of the text. Jane Holtan also proved herself a skilled researcher for the annotation— but most of all, she provided me with a congenial partner to orally proofread the text.

I am deeply indebted to my wife, Pat Barnes, for numerous suggestions on ways to improve this volume but most of all for her unflagging emotional support over the years of its preparation. Our young son, "Jeb," also needs to be thanked for allowing his dad to find the spare moments to complete his editing tasks.

INTRODUCTION

Both antebellum Americans and contemporary historians have vehemently debated the condition of blacks under slavery in the southern United States. Reliable evidence about the treatment of slaves and their degree of contentment within that institution has always been in short supply. The voluminous records of plantation owners are rightfully suspected of ideological bias. The writings of northern abolitionists are not only biased but based upon little firsthand observation. The accounts of northern and European travelers in the South relied primarily upon the planters for information regarding the treatment of slaves. A growing awareness of such deficiencies led historians in recent decades to become skeptical of analyses of slavery that relied exclusively on these traditional white-authored sources.

In the 1970s, historians such as George P. Rawick, John W. Blassingame, and Herbert G. Gutman pioneered efforts to utilize the testimony of slaves as a new means to study slavery.[1] These and other historians uncovered a significant body of interviews, speeches, letters, and autobiographies by former slaves that portray the South's "peculiar institution" in a strikingly different light than that found in earlier studies. Today the scholar has available a wide and varied range of primary documents produced by African Americans with which to explore the history of American slavery.

One seriously underutilized source for such firsthand testimony by slaves about their treatment is James Redpath's *The Roving Editor; or, Talks with Slaves in the Southern States.* The largest portion of the *Roving Editor* is a series of interviews that the British-born abolitionist Redpath secretly conducted with slaves during three journeys through the South

---

1. George P. Rawick, ed., *The American Slave: A Composite Autobiography,* 19 vols. (Westport, Conn., 1972–); John W. Blassingame, *The Slave Community: Plantation Life in the Antebellum South* (New York, 1972); Herbert G. Gutman, *The Black Family in Slavery and Freedom, 1750–1925* (New York, 1976).

in the 1850s. After first publishing many of them pseudonymously in the antislavery press, Redpath gathered these interviews together, edited them slightly, and published them using his own name in a book-length collection in 1859. Redpath supplemented the interviews with auto-biographical sketches by former slaves and with eyewitness testimony on the institution from both southern whites and northern visitors to the slave states. Redpath was himself a perceptive traveler who added many personal observations on southern life to the volume.

Thanks to its varied makeup, Redpath's *Roving Editor* is an extraordi-narily valuable addition to the primary sources available to students of slavery. As in the case of other sources that purport to reveal the slaves' perspective on the southern institution, however, scholarly use of the *Roving Editor* requires circumspection. By employing the same tests for reliability that historians have applied to traveler's accounts, runaway narratives, and slave interviews, the special value of Redpath's *Roving Editor* can be demonstrated.

Redpath's volume was one of hundreds of accounts of the slave experi-ence written by travelers through the American South in the decades before the Civil War. These visitors from Europe and the American North came from diverse walks of life, including missionaries, teachers, scientists, and entrepreneurs. Many of their accounts are flawed as historical sources be-cause of the travelers' preconceptions, the brevity of most observers' stays, and the limited contact most travelers had with slaves. Of the few travelers who did attempt to record conversations with slaves, almost none was a trained stenographer. A few of these travel accounts, however, possess ele-ments that enhance their reliability. For example, Henry Chase and Charles W. Sanborn's 1856 volume, *The North and South: A Statistical View of the Free and Slave States,* attempts to corroborate its observations by citing supporting statistical evidence. The best known of all these travel accounts, Frederick Law Olmsted's multivolume account of a series of southern jour-neys in the mid-1850s, while full of anecdotes on slave life, was primarily an economic critique of the slave system, intent on demonstrating how free labor had been degraded in the region.[2]

Redpath's *Roving Editor* compares well to the best of the traveler's ac-counts. He dwelt for many months in several southern cities as he worked as a reporter for local newspapers. At that time, he mixed freely with resi-dents of all stations. Redpath strove to win the confidence of slaves in his

2. Max Berger, "American Slavery as Seen by British Visitors, 1836–1860," *Journal of Negro History* 30 (April 1945): 181–202; Eugene H. Berwanger, *As They Saw Slavery* (Min-neapolis, 1973); Thomas D. Clark, ed., *Travels in the Old South: A Bibliography,* 3 vols. (Norman, Okla., 1956–59); Broadus Mitchell, *Frederick Law Olmsted: A Critic of the Old South,* Johns Hopkins University Studies, ser. 42, no. 2 (Baltimore, 1924), 71–72, 127–28.

numerous conversations with them and, when he had the opportunity, recorded his interviews stenographically. Like Chase and Sanborn and Olmsted, Redpath utilized economic and demographic sources to validate his observations about slavery. Although Redpath professes to report objectively on what he witnessed in the South, he quickly became a biting critic of the institution in the series of newspaper articles that eventually became the core of the *Roving Editor*. Redpath's pronounced abolitionist biases require readers to evaluate his personal commentary on slavery cautiously.

Another important feature of the *Roving Editor* is a number of autobiographical narratives by former slaves that Redpath includes. Historians have discovered and cataloged more than six thousand such published narratives. These vary in length from accounts of a few hundred words to full-length autobiographies. Almost two hundred of the latter were published in the United States and Great Britain before the Civil War.[3]

Historians have encountered problems with the testimony found in the runaway slave narratives. The geographic breadth of the works is limited because the authors mainly had resided in states close to the North, and so the experiences of the Deep South slaves are underrepresented. Likewise few of the published slave narratives had female authors. Because they were written by runaways, suspicion arises that the authors' treatment as slaves had not been typical.[4] A few of these works were proven fraudulent, and others are suspected of abolitionist coaching and editing. Such shortcomings led most early historians of slavery and many later ones to dismiss the historical value of the narratives.[5] Careful examination of these works by recent scholars, however, has found all but a small number to be remarkably reliable in their factual descriptions of slave life.[6]

In a latter section of the *Roving Editor,* Redpath reproduces an autobiographical narrative by an ex-slave from Missouri and the Kansas Territory. Redpath had befriended the female former slave, Malinda Noll, while

3. Frances Smith Foster, *Witnessing Slavery: The Development of Antebellum Slave Narratives,* 2d ed. (Madison, Wis., 1994), 21–22; John W. Blassingame, *Slave Testimony: Two Centuries of Letters, Speeches, Interviews, and Autobiographies* (Baton Rouge, 1977), 364.

4. Blassingame, *Slave Testimony,* xli–xlii; Thomas Fiehrer, "Slave Narratives," in *Dictionary of Afro-American Slavery,* edited by Randall M. Miller and John David Smith (Westport, Conn., 1988), 517–18.

5. Ulrich B. Phillips, *Life and Labor in the Old South* (Boston, 1929), 219; Stanley Elkins, *Slavery: A Problem in American Institutional and Intellectual Life* (Chicago, 1968), 3–4; David T. Bailey, "A Divided Prism: Two Sources of Black Testimony on Slavery," *Journal of Southern History* 46 (August 1980): 382.

6. Charles T. Davis and Henry Louis Gates, Jr., *The Slave's Narrative* (New York, 1985), xxxii; Foster, *Witnessing Slavery,* xviii–xx; Blassingame, *Slave Testimony,* xi–xii, xvi–xli; C. Vann Woodward, "History from Slave Sources," *American Historical Review* 79 (April 1974): 470–81.

he was a reporter in Kansas. Besides his personal endorsement, Redpath supplies corroborative details and documents to attest to the reliability of her account of slavery. Noll's story is a valuable addition to the canon of the slave narrative. Redpath also includes in the *Roving Editor* a number of secondhand runaway narratives as well as anecdotes from white sources about various aspects of slave life. While the sources for these stories usually can be identified, unlike the Noll narrative they lack sufficient detail to verify their accuracy.

Probably the most valuable feature of the *Roving Editor* is the interviews that Redpath conducted with slaves during his southern travels. Historians have access to only a few hundred antebellum interviews with slaves, and those are mainly with runaways. Like Redpath's, most of these interviews originally were published in newspapers or magazines. Some of the interviews also appeared in published volumes such as *The Refugee; or, The Narratives of Fugitive Slaves in Canada* (1856), which contained brief sketches of four hundred fugitive bondmen and bondwomen drawn from interviews conducted by Boston journalist Benjamin Drew in 1855. Drew's admission that he had made "verbal alterations" and "studiously omitted" certain categories of comments undermines the reliability of this source.[7] More care was taken in the interviews conducted in 1863 by the American Freedmen's Inquiry Commission headed by abolitionist Samuel Gridley Howe. The commission took pains to record stenographically the answers of newly emancipated slaves to questions about their past treatment. Unfortunately the commission interviewed only forty-eight former slaves. Its report devoted far more attention to the testimony of white teachers, missionaries, and army officers.[8]

Many more interviews with former slaves took place earlier in this century. These were conducted by both amateur and professional historians. Pioneer scholars in this field, including sociologists and folklorists as well as historians, interviewed several hundred aging ex-slaves mainly in the 1920s. A much bigger effort was undertaken during the Great Depression by the Federal Writers' Project (FWP), part of the Works Progress Administration. Its field staff of nearly three hundred conducted approximately three thousand interviews in 1936 and 1938.[9]

---

7. As quoted in Blassingame, *Slave Testimony*, 369.

8. Blassingame, *Slave Testimony*, lix–lx, 369–70; Foster, *Witnessing Slavery*, 20; Paul D. Escott, "Slave Interviews," in Miller and Smith, *Dictionary of Afro-American Slavery*, 366–67.

9. Among the earliest interviewers of the ex-slaves were Lawrence D. Reddick, Thomas Moore Campbell, John Trotwood Moore, and Orland Kay Armstrong. Blassingame, *Slave Testimony*, xlii–xliv; Paul D. Escott, *Slavery Remembered: A Record of Twentieth-Century Slave Narratives* (Chapel Hill, 1979), 3–6; Escott, "Slave Interviews," 366–67; Norman R. Yetman, "Ex-Slave Interviews and the Historiography of Slavery," *American Quarterly* 36 (Summer 1984): 181–85; Woodward, "History from Slave Sources," 470–72.

Historians have questioned how well the twentieth-century interviews describe the slave experience. Most of the subjects were in their eighties and had been mere children while slaves. Occupationally, the interview subjects were disproportionately from the ranks of house slaves and their children. Another problem lies in the geographic representation of the interview subjects. Texas and Arkansas provided nearly 45 percent of the total, while the border states and Mississippi were significantly under-represented.[10]

As Yale University historian C. Vann Woodward has observed, "The most serious sources of distortion in the FWP narratives came not from the interviewees but from the interviewers—their biases, procedures, and methods—and the interracial circumstances of the interviews."[11] The predominantly southern white interviewers generally asked leading questions and often edited the answers they received. The racial etiquette of the 1930s raises serious doubts about the candor of the interviewees. The interviewers' condescending tone likely offended the subjects. The aged blacks might have censored their responses to ingratiate themselves.[12] Unfortunately the record of most interviews has survived in a narrative form rather than a stenographic transcription, so evidence of such distorting factors is often masked.

Despite these problems, the interviews with former slaves are among the most valuable historical sources available because they provide a voice for the largely inarticulate slave class. What is required to counteract the inherent flaws in these recorded oral sources is for historians to exercise the same type of caution as when handling written documents such as diaries, correspondence, or published speeches. For example, cliometricians have developed statistical techniques to minimize many of the demographic distortions in the former slaves' testimony. Other historians have carefully screened the interviews for internal evidence of distortion and devised additional tests for reliability. Therefore, Woodward and others have concluded, these ex-slave interviews are no more difficult for historians to use than most other primary sources.[13]

All of the internal tests devised by historians are useful in evaluating

10. Escott, *Slavery Remembered*, 6–7, 12–17; Jerrold Hirsch, "Federal Writers' Project (FWP)," in Miller and Smith, *Dictionary of Afro-American Slavery*, 235–36; Fiehrer, "Slave Narratives," 517–18; Yetman, "Ex-Slave Interviews," 182, 187–89; Woodward, "History from Slave Sources," 472–73, 474–75.

11. Woodward, "History from Slave Sources," 473.

12. Ibid., 473–75; Bailey, "Divided Prism, " 381–404; Yetman, "Ex-Slave Interviews," 187–89; Hirsch, "Federal Writers' Project," 234–35.

13. Robert William Fogel, *Without Consent or Contract: The Rise and Fall of American Slavery* (New York, 1989), 175–80; Escott, *Slavery Remembered*, 7–11; Escott, "Slave Interviews," 367; Yetman, "Ex-Slave Interviews," 185, 193–210; Woodward, "History from Slavery Sources," 475–81; Bailey, "Divided Prism," 382–83, 402–4.

Redpath's *Roving Editor* interviews. A geographic bias exists in his interviews because his subject pool was heavily rural and largely from East Coast states, especially Virginia. While Redpath attempted to choose his subjects randomly, his fear of detection by southern white authorities as an abolitionist questioning slaves also influenced that selection. What distinguishes Redpath's interviews most from the others regularly studied by scholars is that they were conducted with current, not former, slaves. No distortion in recollections caused by the passage of time therefore is present in his interviews. However, the peculiar circumstance of an abolitionist interviewing actual southern slaves naturally raises concerns about the candor of the slave interviewees and Redpath's faithfulness in recording them accurately. To evaluate these interviews, the next step is to examine Redpath's personal background and biases, his reliability as a reporter, and the manner in which he approached and interacted with his interviewees.

James Redpath was a prototype for subsequent generations of journalists who combined reporting with participation in reform movements. Born in Scotland in 1833, Redpath emigrated to the United States in 1849 and soon found work as a reporter for Horace Greeley's *New York Tribune.* While working at the *Tribune,* he had been assigned responsibility for compiling a regular feature article, entitled "Facts of Slavery," composed of clippings from southern newspaper exchanges.[14] As a result of this assignment, Redpath developed a strong curiosity about slavery. He later recalled: "My object in travelling was, in part, to recruit my health, but chiefly to see slavery with my own eyes, and personally learn what the bondsmen said and thought of their condition."[15]

Redpath set off for the South in March 1854 and traveled by railroad, boat, and foot through Virginia, North Carolina, South Carolina, and Georgia. After three months in the South, he returned to New York but set off again in September for a journey through Virginia, North Carolina, South Carolina, Georgia, Alabama, and Louisiana. On this second trip, he resided for several months both in Augusta, Georgia, and New Orleans, Louisiana, where he worked as a reporter on local newspapers. In June 1855 Redpath traveled to St. Louis and gained employment on the *Daily Missouri Democrat,* which sent him to Kansas to report on the violent feuding there between free state and slave state settlers. Between 1855 and 1858

14. Some examples of the "Facts of Slavery" column can be found in the *New York Daily Tribune,* February 15 and 16, 1854.
15. James Redpath, *The Roving Editor: or, Talks with Slaves in the Southern States* (New York, 1859), 3.

Redpath resided in Kansas, where he reported for the *Missouri Democrat,* the *New York Tribune,* and other newspapers and briefly edited his own newspaper, the *Doniphan Crusader of Freedom.* In Kansas he also encountered a paramilitary band led by John Brown that was engaged in the struggle to make the territory a nonslaveholding state. Redpath and Brown discovered that they shared the belief that the slaves would rebel if encouraged and armed by abolitionists.[16] Brown acted on this conviction when he attempted to incite a slave insurrection at Harpers Ferry, Virginia, in October 1859. After Brown was executed for treason, Redpath became his first biographer and helped win for him the lasting reputation of a "Martyr for Freedom."[17] During his years in Kansas, Redpath made several visits back to the East. While on one of them, in spring 1857, he conducted a third tour of the South, this time limited to Virginia.[18]

Although Redpath kept a diary on his first trip to the South in spring 1854, he had not originally planned to write about his experiences. In fact he claimed later that "my object was to aid the slaves. If I found that slavery had so far degraded them, that they were comparatively contented with their debased condition, I resolved, before I started, to spend my time in the South, in disseminating discontentment. But if, on the other hand, I found them ripe for a rebellion, my resolution was to prepare the way for it, as far as my ability and opportunities permitted."[19] Despite his desire to participate in the violent overthrow of slavery, Redpath's chief contribution to that cause was as a journalist.

On returning to New York after his first journey, Redpath decided to recount his experiences for sympathetic readers of the abolitionist press. Preparing five letters that described his contact with southern slaves, Redpath took them first to the offices of the *New York National Anti-Slavery Standard,* where they were ignored.[20] In a hurry to depart for his second southern tour, he retrieved the letters and mailed them to William Lloyd Garrison, the editor of the Boston *Liberator.* Redpath requested

16. Jeffrey Rossbach, *Ambivalent Conspirators: John Brown, the Secret Six, and a Theory of Slave Violence* (Philadelphia, 1982), 175–77.

17. James Redpath, *The Public Life of Capt. John Brown, With An Auto-Biography of His Childhood and Youth* (Boston, 1860); James C. Malin, *John Brown and the Legend of Fifty-six,* Memoirs of the American Philosophical Society, vol. 17 (Philadelphia, 1942), 293–309; John R. McKivigan, "James Redpath, John Brown, and Abolitionist Advocacy of Slave Insurrection," *Civil War History* 37 (December 1991): 293–313.

18. An itinerary of Redpath's three southern tours can be found in appendix 1.

19. Redpath, *Roving Editor,* 300.

20. Redpath's letters had not been evaluated for publication in the *National Anti-Slavery Standard* because that newspaper's editor, Sydney Howard Gay, had been preoccupied with the illness of one of his children. James Redpath to William Lloyd Garrison, July 26, 1854, William Lloyd Garrison Papers, Boston Public Library (hereafter cited as Garrison Papers).

that Garrison publish the letters under the pseudonym "John Ball, Jr." rather than his own name. To further camouflage his identity, Redpath supplied Garrison with what he called a "blind," a short letter purportedly from Ball to relatives in Iowa to be published at the start of the series, supplying false biographical information about the correspondent.[21] Redpath told Garrison that he feared that "if it were to become known that I am an 'ultra' abolitionist, my life would not be considered a profitable investment at any insurance."[22] Garrison and later editors of Redpath's writings under that pen name kept his secret so well that the true authorship of the John Ball, Jr. letters has never been disclosed in historical scholarship. The first series of John Ball, Jr. letters appeared in the *Liberator* in August and September 1854 while Redpath journeyed again in the South.[23]

During this second tour, Redpath entered into an arrangement with Sydney Howard Gay, editor of the *National Anti-Slavery Standard,* to send that paper a new series of John Ball, Jr. letters.[24] Fifteen of these letters appeared in the *National Anti-Slavery Standard* between October 1854 and April 1855.[25] The *Standard* paid Redpath $2.50 for each of the letters. Redpath told Gay that that salary did not even meet his traveling expenses but boasted, "As I am 'a fanatic' or an Enthusiast at least—I gladly gave my time to promote so desirable a Revolution!"[26]

Redpath also sent the *National Anti-Slavery Standard* numerous clippings describing the mistreatment of slaves and free blacks from newspapers in the cities he visited.[27] In addition he wrote occasional pseudonymous reports for publication in the *New York Tribune,* but he signed these with other pen names than John Ball, Jr.[28]

An abolitionist risked his well-being and perhaps even his life to enter the South to interview slaves and record their opinions about slavery for

---

21. Boston *Liberator,* 4 August 1854. The original John Ball was a fourteenth-century English priest executed by King Richard II for seditious preaching that encouraged the peasants' insurrection led by Wat Tyler. *Dictionary of National Biography,* 21 vols. (London, 1921–22), 1:993–94, 19:1347–48 (hereafter cited as *DNB*).

22. Redpath to Garrison, July 26, 1854, Garrison Papers.

23. Boston *Liberator,* August 4 and 11 and September 1 and 8, 1854.

24. James Redpath to Sydney Howard Gay, November 6 and 17, 1854, Sydney Howard Gay Papers, Columbia University Library (hereafter cited as Gay Papers).

25. *New York National Anti-Slavery Standard,* October 14, 21, and 28, November 11 and 25, December 2, 9, 16, and 23, 1854, January 27, February 10, March 17 and 31, and April 7 and 14, 1855.

26. Redpath to Gay, November 6, 1854, Gay Papers.

27. *New York National Anti-Slavery Standard,* January 20, February 3 and 17, March 3 and 17, 1855.

28. Articles definitely written by Redpath while in the South can be found in the *New York Daily Tribune,* April 13, 15, 16, 17, and 18, 1854, February 16 and March 24, 1855.

the northern press. Redpath remained in fear that some unfriendly northern colleague would recognize his writing style and identify him as the author of the John Ball, Jr. letters. He warned Gay to "never mention my name to any one—above all not to the *Times*-servers. Never let it appear in the Stand*d* in *any* connection."[29] To avoid having his frequent correspondence with the abolitionist newspaper editor traced, Redpath arranged an elaborate system of third parties, including New York City friends and Michigan relatives, to forward mail to and from him. Redpath also instructed Gay to discontinue the exchange of the *National Anti-Slavery Standard* with newspapers published in the cities where he was residing in order to prevent unwanted local publicity for his reporting.[30] In case copies of his John Ball, Jr. articles nevertheless reached the South, Redpath supplied false itineraries in the letters to throw the suspicious off his track.[31]

After moving to Kansas in mid-1855, Redpath occasionally sent the abolitionist press letters signed John Ball, Jr. describing slavery as he observed it in Missouri and Kentucky as well as Kansas.[32] During a final tour of the South in 1857, Redpath published another series of travel letters in the *Boston Daily Traveller* using the pen name Jacobius.[33] Accompanying Redpath on this third southern tour was a young Boston abolitionist named Francis Jackson Merriam, who later would become one of John Brown's followers at Harpers Ferry.

After this third trip, Redpath began to conceive the idea of publishing his letters in the form of a book. Such a step had already been taken by such travelers through the South as Frederick Law Olmsted, whose reports had originally appeared in the *New York Times.*[34] While the *Roving Editor* differs significantly from Olmsted's work in its concentration on slave interviews, Redpath occasionally cites the latter's writing to corroborate his observations.[35]

A second important influence on Redpath's composition and publication of the *Roving Editor* was William T. Thompson, the editor of the *Savannah Daily Morning News.* Redpath had worked for more than two months for Thompson while living in Savannah in the late spring of

29. Redpath to Gay, November 17, 1854, Gay Papers.

30. Redpath to Gay, November 6 and 17, 1854, and January 23, 1855, Gay Papers.

31. *New York National Anti-Slavery Standard,* December 16, 1854, and February 10, 1855.

32. Boston *Liberator,* March 20, 1856, and February 20, 1857; *New York National Anti-Slavery Standard,* March 22, 1856, and March 7, 1857.

33. *Boston Daily Evening Traveller,* May 23 and June 6 and 13, 1857.

34. Frederick Law Olmsted, *The Cotton Kingdom: A Traveller's Observations on Cotton and Slavery in the American Slave States,* edited by Arthur M. Schlesinger (1860; New York, 1954), ix–xxvii.

35. Redpath, *Roving Editor,* 142–43.

1854. Thompson had built a reputation as a humorist by publishing several collections of his newspaper columns purporting to be letters from "Major Jones," a Georgia tourist on a world tour.[36] Redpath copied Thompson's pseudonymous style in articles for the *Daily Morning News*. Redpath created the character "Berwick," a southerner "by temperament and self-adoption," who regularly wrote Major Jones lengthy letters while purportedly on a visit to New York City. Using his old skills as an exchange editor, Redpath manufactured a chatty series of reports on cultural and political events in New York by scanning and reproducing items from that city's newspapers mailed to the *Daily Morning News*. These letters were filled with news of sensational court trials, descriptions of exhibits at Barnum's American Museum, accounts of the latest novels, and biting gossip about the inner workings of New York's newspapers.[37] While Thompson's Major Jones articles and books had a mildly proslavery undertone, Redpath's John Ball, Jr. letters and the book they were transformed into used the travel-letter format to proclaim a vehement antislavery credo.[38]

Determined to bring out his John Ball, Jr. letters in book form, Redpath approached the New York City publisher Asher B. Burdick with his proposal. Burdick indicated interest in the idea but requested that Redpath give him a bond to cover the costs of setting the book's type. A cautious man, Burdick had previously imposed the same requirement on Hinton Helper, whose *Impending Crisis of the South* became a runaway best-seller for the firm.[39] To raise this printing subvention Redpath turned to Gerrit Smith, a leading New York abolitionist, who gave freely of his vast personal fortune to various antislavery causes. Redpath confided his belief that Burdick regarded the proposed book as "too bloody" and that the "difficulty is to get a publisher for a work of a decidedly antislavery cast, which shall advocate—as I do—the right of slave-theft (from their masters) & Slave Insurrections & also speak of Kansas politics without fear-

36. Charles C. Jones, *History of Savannah, Ga.* (Syracuse, N.Y., 1890), 519–20; F. D. Lee and J. L. Agnew, *Historical Record of the City of Savannah* (Savannah, Ga., 1869), 194–96; *Dictionary of American Biography*, 20 vols. (New York, 1928–36), 9:479–80.

37. *Savannah Daily Morning News*, May 12, 13, 15, 16, 17, 22, 23, 24, 26, 27, and 30 and June 2, 5, and 7, 1854.

38. In the *Roving Editor*, Redpath admitted that his residence in Savannah and association with Thompson had influenced his thinking about slavery. About slaveholders, he reported that "I saw so much that was noble, generous and admirable in their characters; I saw so many demoralizing pro-slavery influences—various, attractive, resistless—brought to bear on their intellects from their cradle to their tomb, that from hating I began to pity them." Redpath, *Roving Editor*, 82.

39. Hugh T. Lefler, *Hinton Rowan Helper: Advocate of a "White America"* (Charlottesville, Va., 1954), 19–20.

ing to offend the dominant parties whether in or out of office."[40] Thanks to Smith's generosity, Burdick agreed to publish Redpath's book.

The final text of the *Roving Editor* was not the one that Redpath had desired to publish originally. Redpath wrote Smith that he had learned that the manuscript was considered too short by publishers for a "large volume."[41] Redpath made up for this deficiency in length in several ways. First, he added several new sections to the original letters explaining his current views on slavery and abolition. He also added a number of chapters with material written by other authors. The latter included stories about slave insurrection plots by other journalists and a personal letter from Samuel Gridley Howe to Charles Sumner describing southern prisons for slaves.

The most important addition to the manuscript was a number of chapters supplying what Redpath told Smith was "a sketch of Kansas history— a true account; giving honor to whom honor, discredit to whom discredit is due. Nothing of the kind has been attempted yet."[42] These chapters drew upon Redpath's career as a journalist in the Kansas Territory on and off from 1855 to 1858. One chapter, reproduced with minimal changes, is his own firsthand report of a mob in Parkville, Missouri, that tarred and feathered a white man accused of attempting to free a slave.[43] Redpath noted that many of these lawless Missourians were the same "Border Ruffians" involved in attacks on free state settlers in Kansas. Redpath also published a lengthy interview, which he had never before published, with Malinda Noll, reputedly the first slave brought to Kansas. The longest of the new chapters was Redpath's history of the slavery controversy in Kansas. As he promised Smith, he heatedly denounced the proslavery activities of every important federal appointee, settler, and "Ruffian" in the territory. He also criticized the Republican party and moderate antislavery leaders in Kansas for believing that political rather than military means would ultimately secure the territory as a free state. The final chapter contained two anonymous accounts of antislavery guerrilla skirmishes with Missourians in Kansas. It appears that Redpath was told of these incidents by another journalist, John Henri Kagi, who later accompanied John Brown in the raid on Harpers Ferry in 1859.

As well as making these additions, Redpath decided not to reproduce eight of the original John Ball, Jr. letters in the *Roving Editor.*[44] Several of these letters intentionally had been written with considerable false infor-

---

40. James Redpath to Gerrit Smith, November 1858, Gerrit Smith Papers, George Arents Research Library, Syracuse University.

41. Redpath to Gerrit Smith, November 1858, Smith Papers.

42. Ibid.

43. *St. Louis Daily Missouri Democrat,* October 24, 1855.

44. A complete list of all of the John Ball, Jr. letters can be found in appendix 2.

mation about Redpath's travel itinerary, and their inclusion in the book would have required more editing than Redpath apparently could justify. The remainder of the omitted letters were written during Redpath's second tour but pertained to reviews of recent books or controversies with other abolitionists that Redpath felt were extraneous to the book's focus on the opinions of southern slaves. Three letters published in 1856 and 1857 concerned issues of slavery in Kentucky, Missouri, or Kansas that also must have been regarded as too specific to blend gracefully with the themes of the included letters. These other John Ball, Jr. letters have been reproduced in appendixes 3–10.

Dedicated to John Brown, the *Roving Editor* was published by the Burdick firm. It was promoted as "the most searching, thorough, and reliable investigation of American Slavery ever published." Its advertisements noted the oral testimony of slaves in the book but avoided any allusion to the question of slave insurrection. The company reprinted endorsements of Redpath's veracity and writing skills from political friends and foes in Kansas. The most insightful of these came from John C. Vaughan, who in 1859 operated his own free state newspaper in Leavenworth: "Redpath could not be dull, or tame, or slavish, if he were to try; he has not an idle bone in him—and if eccentric and humorous it is all for Humanity."[45]

There is no record of the sales of the *Roving Editor*. It had a market among abolitionists, of course. Frederick Douglass promoted Redpath's book by publishing excerpts from it.[46] But not everyone was so impressed. Bronson Alcott, for example, felt the *Roving Editor*'s portraits "are overdrawn, and tempered with prejudices unjust to all parties."[47]

Together the John Ball, Jr. letters and the *Roving Editor* provide a highly enlightening resource for studying slavery. In their correspondence, Redpath told Gerrit Smith that he had interviewed nearly a thousand slaves during his travels.[48] Only a fraction of these appeared in published form; the actual number of full-scale interviews recorded in Redpath's articles includes twenty-nine slaves, five free blacks, and seven slave owners. Redpath took great pains to record the responses of slaves to his questions accurately. In the *Roving Editor,* he described his method: "My conversations with the slaves were written down as soon after they occurred as was convenient; occasionally, indeed, in stenographic notes, as the negroes spoke to me. It will be seen that I do not aim at a literary reputa-

---

45. *New York Tribune,* March 5, 1859.
46. *Rochester Frederick Douglass' Paper,* April 8, 1859.
47. Odell Shepard, ed., *The Journals of Bronson Alcott* (Boston, 1938), 323.
48. Redpath to Smith, November 1854, Smith Papers.

tion. I have only plain truth to tell—only plain words to tell them in. My mission was a humble one—to report. I claim no other merit than fidelity to that duty."[49] Earlier, in the *National Anti-Slavery Standard,* Redpath answered contemporary critics of the veracity of his reports: "I defy the united slaveocracy of the South to prove that I have spoken falsely. Many facts that I have advanced will be doubted or denied; but whoever will follow in my footsteps and speak with the slaves as I spoke to them, and as frequently as I did, will find that I have been a most truthful chronicler."[50]

In his interviews, Redpath usually questioned the slave about topics of interest to his northern readers such as work patterns, living conditions, family life, and religious practices. When Redpath asked for evidence of mistreatment by masters or by other whites, he received some exceptionally graphic replies.[51] The interviews also contain considerable slave testimony regarding violations of the sanctity of their marriages and the involuntary separation of their families.[52] Redpath quotes black complaints about white controls over their churches, but he showed little respect for the religious practices of slaves.[53] Eugene Genovese attacks Redpath for his castigation of slave religion: "Some northern abolitionists and southern slaveholders alike doubted the depth of the slaves' Christian commitment. . . . for some northern critics, the slave system was so vicious that no one could possibly expect the slaves to be capable of understanding the Christian message. Thus James Redpath, whose youth may excuse his insufferable self-righteousness."[54] True to his promise to report positive as well as negative aspects of slavery, Redpath related the testimony of several slaves who, while hired out by their masters, had managed to earn money toward their eventual manumission.[55]

In response to his questioning, the slaves frequently asked Redpath for information about the condition of free blacks in the North and in Canada and about the prospects of the abolition movement. Redpath admitted that free blacks in the North faced heavy discriminatory laws and customs and reproved his readers for not abolishing them.[56]

49. Redpath, *Roving Editor,* 2; also see Boston *Liberator,* September 1, 1854.
50. *New York National Anti-Slavery Standard,* March 17, 1855.
51. Boston *Liberator,* September 1 and 8, 1854; *New York National Anti-Slavery Standard,* December 2, 1854.
52. Boston *Liberator,* September 1 and 8, 1854; *New York National Anti-Slavery Standard,* October 14 and 28, 1854; Redpath, *Roving Editor,* 27, 42, 49, 63, 66, 94, 117.
53. Boston *Liberator,* August 11, 1854; Redpath, *Roving Editor,* 18–20.
54. Eugene D. Genovese, *Roll, Jordan, Roll: The World the Slaves Made* (New York, 1976), 214.
55. *New York National Anti-Slavery Standard,* October 28, 1854, and February 10, 1855; Redpath, *Roving Editor,* 119, 174.
56. Boston *Liberator,* August 11 and September 8, 1854; Redpath, *Roving Editor,* 33, 57–58.

Invariably Redpath inquired if any of the slaves were contented with their status. The answers to this last question were quite revealing. *"Not more than one-tenth.* As few as has good masters doesn't think about freedom so much; but if they could get the offer, *all* of them would be free," replied a North Carolina slave. "Well, I never met but one. *He* said he would rather be a slave than a freeman; he, I guess, was a liar. . . . What slave-man wouldn't rather work for himself than for a boss, mass'r?" was the response from a Virginia field hand.[57]

Redpath noticed interesting variations in the degree of discontent voiced by his slave confidants. After interviewing a free black in Wilmington, North Carolina, Redpath concluded: "In the city [blacks] are more intelligent, and the discontented sentiment is stronger, because the colored people have more chance of talking to one another about their feelings."[58] Likewise, Redpath discovered the slaves of Georgia and Alabama equally discontented but more resigned to slavery than their counterparts in Virginia and the Carolinas because the means of escape seemed too remote to them.[59] Despite Redpath's disclaimer of racial prejudice, his comments revealed a belief that mulattoes were more unhappy under slavery because they possessed a large degree of "Saxonic restlessness."[60]

An important feature of Redpath's interviews was the number of slaves who expressed a willingness to escape or even fight for their freedom, especially if assisted by sympathetic whites. For example, a Charleston slave told Redpath that "all [slaves] that I does know *wants to be free very bad,* I tell you, and *may be will fight before long if they don't get freedom somehow."*[61] In the John Ball, Jr. letters, Redpath encouraged northern abolitionists to assist slaves to escape. More than a year before he met John Brown in Kansas, Redpath was publicly advocating a plan historians associate with the older abolitionist. Redpath predicted that "A GENERAL STAMPEDE OF THE SLAVES" could involuntarily make North Carolina and Virginia into free states "if the Abolitionists would send down a trustworthy Band of 'Liberators' provided with compasses, pistols, and a little money for the fugitives."[62] Redpath claimed to have personally given advice on ways to escape to more than a dozen slaves.[63]

In addition to the slave interviews, the John Ball, Jr. letters and the

57. Redpath, *Roving Editor,* 31, 57, 93.

58. Boston *Liberator,* August 11, 1854.

59. *New York National Anti-Slavery Standard,* January 27, 1855.

60. Boston *Liberator,* September 1, 1854; Redpath, *Roving Editor,* 30, 38, 171.

61. Boston *Liberator,* September 8, 1854; Redpath, *Roving Editor,* 57.

62. *New York National Anti-Slavery Standard,* December 2, 1854. See also Boston *Liberator,* September 1, 1854; Redpath, *Roving Editor,* 125, 136.

63. Boston *Liberator,* September 1, 1854; *New York National Anti-Slavery Standard,* January 27, 1854; Redpath, *Roving Editor,* 34.

Roving Editor contain Redpath's reports on many other aspects of his southern travels. He relates numerous conversations with free blacks, nonslaveholding whites, and planters about the institution of slavery. For example, Redpath reports finding the nonslaveholding artisans and small merchants of southern cities and towns, especially immigrants from Britain or Germany, to be "secret abolitionists."[64] On the other hand, Redpath describes conversations with slave owners who revealed a determination to crush all criticism of their peculiar institution, not just in the South but nationwide.[65] Redpath also recounts with a keen reportorial eye his visits to slave auctions, political meetings, and religious services in various parts of the South. When he does halt his narrative to interject antislavery arguments, they draw upon his personal observation of the system of slavery rather than abstract concepts. As a combination of a documentary account of conditions under slavery given by the slaves themselves and a travelogue of the antebellum South by a perceptive critic, Redpath's reports of his southern travels in the 1850s are a very rare historical resource deserving much greater scholarly attention.

Redpath's interest in the conditions of black Americans continued after publication of the *Roving Editor*. Following the Harpers Ferry raid, Redpath's notoriety as an outspoken apologist for John Brown scuttled his plans for a fourth reportorial journey through the South, this time down the Mississippi River. Instead he toured Haiti in 1860 as a reporter and returned as the official Haitian lobbyist for U. S. diplomatic recognition of the Caribbean republic, a status he secured within two years.[66] During the Civil War, he was a publisher of inexpensive books designed for distribution to the troops and was a frontline war correspondent in Tennessee, Georgia, and South Carolina. In March 1865 the Union army appointed Redpath the first superintendent of public schools in South Carolina under federal military occupation. During Reconstruction, Redpath loudly denounced actions first by Andrew Johnson and later by Rutherford B. Hayes that surrendered the freedmen to the mercies of southern white "Redeemers." His support for efforts to assist black Americans and other oppressed groups continued throughout the rest of his active life.[67]

While some historians over the years have utilized Redpath's book in

64. Boston *Liberator,* August 11 and September 1, 1854; *New York National Anti-Slavery Standard,* December 9, 1854; Redpath, *Roving Editor,* 47.

65. Boston *Liberator,* September 8, 1854; Redpath, *Roving Editor,* 156–59, 183–84.

66. Walter D. Boyd, "James Redpath and American Negro Colonization in Haiti, 1860–1862," *The Americas* 12 (October 1955): 169–82; John R. McKivigan, "James Redpath and Black Reaction to the Haitian Emigration Bureau," *Civil War History* 69 (October 1987): 139–53.

67. The only full-length biography of Redpath is Charles Horner, *The Life of James Redpath and the Development of the Modern Lyceum* (New York, 1926).

their studies of slavery, they have basically treated it as just one more in the large series of traveler's accounts of the antebellum South. It is noteworthy that most of the historians who have relied on the *Roving Editor* for information regarding slavery have ignored its slave interviews and dealt only with Redpath's personal observations.[68] This last fact indicates skepticism among scholars regarding Redpath's ability to have conducted authentic interviews with southern slaves and elicited candid answers about their physical well-being and contentment. It is among the purposes of this modern edition of the *Roving Editor* to certify the authenticity of these slave interviews for historians.

For example, this edition alerts the historian to the discovery of Redpath's correspondence with Garrison and Gay, which links the material in the *Roving Editor* to the original John Ball, Jr. letters in the Boston *Liberator* and the *New York National Anti-Slavery Standard.* The original newspaper articles supply the places and times of many of the slave interviews, which Redpath had edited out of the book. Surviving correspondence and Redpath's published articles in other newspapers also are used to verify Redpath's residence in specific southern communities at the times these interviews were reported to have taken place.[69] Through the presentation of such corroborative evidence, the new edition of the *Roving Editor* should prove to be a valuable and compelling source of the slaves' own testimony regarding their treatment in the late antebellum period.

One other historically important feature of the *Roving Editor* is the evidence it gives of some abolitionists' support in the late 1850s of violent slave insurrection. While Redpath's views might not be representative of those of most northern abolitionists in the late antebellum era, publication of the *Roving Editor* was indicative of a growing body of opinion ready to endorse and even assist the violent plots of antislavery militants such as John Brown. Redpath's revisions and additions to the John Ball, Jr. letters in the text of the *Roving Editor* reveal a significant evolution in his thinking about abolitionist tactics between 1854–55 and 1858. In the *Roving Editor,* Redpath essentially dismissed his 1854 plan for aiding

68. A few studies of slavery have utilized Redpath's personal description of conditions in the South, including Herbert Aptheker, *American Negro Slave Revolts* (New York, 1943), 114–16; Kenneth M. Stampp, *The Peculiar Institution: Slavery in the Antebellum South* (New York, 1956), 121, 422; Genovese, *Roll, Jordan, Roll,* 214, 410, 437, 484, 554; Gutman, *Black Family,* 63, 82, 202, 238. Only the first work, however, treats Redpath's slave interviews as a reliable source.

69. In the *Roving Editor,* Redpath corrects some of the false addresses and dates he had originally used in the John Ball, Jr. letters to conceal his identity. *New York National Anti-Slavery Standard,* December 16, 1854; Redpath, *Roving Editor,* 142.

slave escapes with pocket compasses and pistols and instead professed: "I now believe that the speediest method of abolishing slavery, and of ending the eternal hypocritical hubbub in Congress and the country, is to incite a few scores of rattling insurrections—in a quiet gentlemanly way—simultaneously in different parts of the country, and by a little wholesome slaughter, to arouse the conscience of the people against the wrong embodied in Southern institutions. . . ."[70] Redpath noted that events in Kansas in the mid-1850s had hastened the coming of slave insurrections. He declared that "the Second American revolution has begun. Kansas was its Lexington. . . . The South committed suicide when it compelled the free squatters to resort to guerilla warfare, *and to study it both as a mode of subsistence and a science.*" Redpath also derided the leadership of the Republican party for counseling the antislavery guerrilla bands to disband before Kansas had won admission as a free state. Redpath predicted that these well-trained former fighters would provide the leadership that the slaves needed to revolt.[71]

Redpath dedicated the *Roving Editor* to John Brown, with words that strongly hinted at the latter's plans for Harpers Ferry: "You, Old Hero! believe that the slave should be aided and urged to insurrection, and hence do I lay this tribute at your feet."[72]

The modern edition of the *Roving Editor* republishes the original 349-page text together with editorial apparatus to facilitate the reader's comprehension of the work. For example, the editor has provided annotations that disclose the original sources in the John Ball, Jr. letters for the various chapters of the *Roving Editor* and that analyze the textual differences between the original newspaper reports and the subsequent book. In addition to the edited original text of the *Roving Editor,* this volume also provides the text of the eight John Ball, Jr. letters that Redpath did not utilize for materials in that book. Reproduced in appendixes, these letters supply further information about Redpath's observations of the South and his views on contemporary political issues.

Great pains have been taken to reproduce the text of the *Roving Editor* exactly as it appeared in the 1859 first edition. Spelling, capitalization, and punctuation have been kept as close as practicable to the original style. The reader is alerted to a small number of significant errors through endnotes. Because Redpath used occasional footnotes to verify or elaborate on key points, the editor has employed endnotes for his

70. Redpath, *Roving Editor,* 129.
71. Ibid., 299, 300, 306.
72. Ibid., iii–iv.

annotation. Furthermore, using the Ball letters and Redpath's unpublished correspondence, the editor has supplied considerable information regarding the exact place and date of incidents described in the *Roving Editor.* Likewise, people, places, events, and literary allusions appearing in Redpath's writing that would be unfamiliar to a modern reader have been identified in notes following each section. The editor also uses annotations to verify the accuracy of Redpath's descriptions. In several cases it even has been possible to identify the individuals whom Redpath interviewed despite his effort to disguise them.

James Redpath's *The Roving Editor; or, Talks with Slaves in the Southern States* is a significant document in the history of slavery in the United States. Its full value has never been comprehended by historians because they have lacked sufficient evidence confirming the reliability of Redpath's interviews with southern slaves. This new edition has reproduced those interviews as well as supplying documentation of their accuracy. With the addition of these editorial features, the *Roving Editor* makes an important contribution to the documentary history of nineteenth-century African American life.

THE
ROVING
EDITOR

"He went to the cell. The slave-felon and the man of God confronted each other." (see page 234)

THE

ROVING EDITOR:

OR,

TALKS WITH SLAVES

IN

THE SOUTHERN STATES.

BY

JAMES REDPATH.

"With the strong arm and giant grasp, 'tis wrong
To crush the feeble, unresisting throng.
Who pities not the fallen, let him fear,
Lest, if he fall, no friendly hand be near:
Who sows ill actions and of blessing dreams,
Fosters vain phantasies and idly schemes.
Unstop thy ears! thy people's wants relieve!
If not, a day shall come when all their rights receive."
Sadi.

New York:
A. B. BURDICK, PUBLISHER,
8 SPRUCE STREET.
1859.

DEDICATION.

To CAPTAIN JOHN BROWN,[1] Senior, of Kansas:

To you, old Hero, I dedicate this record of my Talks with the Slaves in the Southern States.

To you is due our homage for first showing how, and how alone, the gigantic crime of our age and nation can be effectually blotted out from our soil forever. You have proven that the slaver has a soul as cowardly as his own "domestic institution;" you have shown how contemptible he is as a foe before the rifle of the earnest freeman. With your sword of the Lord and of Gideon[2] you met him face to face; with a few ill-clad and ill-armed footmen, you routed his well-mounted and well-armed hosts.[3]

I admire you for your dauntless bravery on the field; but more for your religious integrity of character and resolute energy of anti-slavery zeal. Rifle in hand, you put the brave young men of Kansas to shame; truth in heart, you rendered insignificant the puerile programmes of anti-slavery politicians.

You have no confidence in any man, plan or party that ignores moral principle as the soul of its action. You well know that an Organized Iniquity can never be destroyed by any programme of action which overlooks the fact that it *is* a crime, and is therefore to be eradicated without compromise, commiseration or delay. This, also, is my belief. Hence do I doubt the ultimate efficacy of any political anti-slavery action which is founded on Expediency—the morals of the counting-room—and hence, also, I do not hesitate to urge the friends of the slave to incite insurrections, and encourage, in the North, a spirit which shall ultimate in civil and servile wars. I think it unfair that the American bondman should have no generous Lafayette.[4] What France was to us in our hour of trial, let the North be to the slave to-day. The oppressions of which the men of '76 complained through the muzzles of their guns and with the points of their bayonets, were trifling—unworthy of a moment's discussion—as compared with the cruel and innumerable wrongs which the negroes of the South now endure. If the fathers were justified in *their* rebellion, how much more will the slaves be justifiable in *their* insurrection? You, Old Hero! believe that the slave should be aided and urged to insurrection, and hence do I lay this tribute at your feet.

You are unwilling to ignore the rights of the slave for any reason—any "constitutional guarantees"—any plea of vested rights—any argument of inferiority of race—any sophistry of Providential overrulings, or pitiable appeals for party success. You are willing to recognize the negro as a brother, however inferior in intellectual endowments; as having rights, which, to take a way, or withhold, is a crime that should be punished without mercy—surely—promptly—by law, if we can do it; *over* it, if more speedily by such action; peacefully if we can, but forcibly and by bloodshed if we must! So am I.

You went to Kansas, when the troubles broke out there—not to "settle" or "speculate"—or from idle curiosity; but for one stern, solitary purpose—*to have a shot at the South.* So did I.

To you, therefore, my senior in years as in services to the slave, I dedicate this work.

JAMES REDPATH.

MALDEN, *Massachusetts.*

NOTES

1. Connecticut-born John Brown (1800–1859) had grown up in Hudson, Ohio, where he received only a rudimentary education. His professional life was marked by failure as a tanner, wool dealer, and farmer. He made an early commitment to abolitionism and became a friend of Gerrit Smith and Frederick Douglass. Brown moved to Kansas with four sons and became a minor leader in the free state guerrilla movement there. He became notorious for his role in the massacre of five proslavery settlers in retaliation for attacks on the free state settlement of Lawrence. Redpath interviewed Brown for the *New York Tribune* shortly after that incident and eventually joined the elder abolitionist's plot to foment slave insurrection. Brown's conspiracy culminated in the unsuccessful attack by his band of twenty-one men on the federal arsenal at Harpers Ferry, Virginia, in October 1859. Stephen B. Oates, *To Purge This Land with Blood: A Biography of John Brown* (New York, 1970); *DAB*, 3:131–34; James Redpath, *The Public Life of Captain John Brown* (Boston, 1860); *New York Tribune*, June 12, 1856.

2. Judg. 7:20.

3. An allusion to John Brown's victories over proslavery "Border Ruffians" in skirmishes

and small-scale battles, such as that at Black Jack Creek in 1856. Daniel W. Wilder, *The Annals of Kansas* (Topeka, Kans., 1875), 199–200.

4. French aristocrat Marie-Joseph-Paul-Yves-Roch-Gilbert du Motier, marquis de Lafayette (1757–1834) volunteered his services to the Continental Army during the American Revolution. *DAB,* 10:535–39.

MY CREED.

In order that no man, or body of men, may be injured or misrepresented by unfair presentations or perversions of my creed, or induced to peruse the pages that follow, under false impressions or pretenses, I will here briefly state my political, or rather, my revolutionary Faith:

I am a Republican—and something more. I am inflexibly opposed to the extension of slavery; but equally do I oppose the doctrine of its protection in States where it already exists. Non-intervention[1] and protection are practically synonymous. Let slavery alone, and it lives a century. Fight it, and it dies. Any weapons will kill it, if kept ever active: fire or water—bayonets or bullion—the soldier's arm or the writer's pen. To prevent its extension merely, will never destroy it. If it is right that slavery should exist in Georgia, it is equally right to extend it into Kansas. If the inter-state traffic in human beings is right, equally just is the demand for re-opening the slave trade.

I am an Emancipationist—and something more. I believe slavery to be a curse, which it is desirable to speedily abolish. But to Gradual Emancipation I am resolutely antagonistic. For I regard property in man as robbery of man; and I am not willing that our robbers should give notes on time—for freedom and justice at thirty days, or thirty years, or any other period: rather let them be smitten down where they stand, and the rights that they have wrested from their slaves, be wrested—if necessary—with bloodshed and violence, with the torch and the rifle, from them.

I am an American—and something more. I think it wrong to give to foreigners the rights that we deny to native-born Americans. I think it wrong and tyrannical for one class of persons—sometimes citizens of foreign birth—to vote for, disfranchise, whip, sell, buy, breed for market, and otherwise degrade the colored natives of our Southern soil. I regard the decision of Judge Taney,[2] and his brethren, as not infamous only, but insulting to our national character. I would extend to all Americans, without distinction of color or creed, the inalienable birthright of whistling Yankee Doodle, and hurrahing, with heart-felt emphasis, on the Fourth of July, and after every presidential election—unless Buchanan[3] is again a successful candidate.

I am an Abolitionist—and something more. I am in favor, not only of *abolishing* the Curse, but of making *reparation* for the Crime. Not an Abolitionist only, but a Reparationist. The negroes, I hold, have not merely the inalienable right to be free, but the legal right of compensation for their hitherto unrequited services to the South. I more than agree with Disunion Abolitionists.[4] They are in favor of a free Northern Republic. So am I. But as to boundary lines we differ. While they would fix the Southern boundary of their free Republic at the dividing line between Ohio and Kentucky, Virginia and the Keystone State, I would wash it with the warm waters of the Gulf of Mexico. "But what shall we do with the slaves?" Make free men of them. "And with the slaveholding class?" Abolish them. "And with the Legrees of the plantations?" Them, annihilate! Drive them into the sea, as Christ once drove the swine; or chase them into the dismal swamps[5] and black morasses of the South. "Anywhere—anywhere —out of the world!"

I am a Peace-Man—and something more. I would fight and kill for the sake of peace. Now, slavery is a state of perpetual war.

I am a Non-Resistant[6]—and something more. I would slay every man who attempted to resist the liberation of the slave.

I am a Democrat—and nothing more. I believe in humanity and human rights. I recognize nothing as so sacred on earth. Rather than consent to the infringement of the most insignificant or seemingly unimportant of human rights, let races be swept from the face of the earth—let nations be dismembered—let dynasties be dethroned—let laws and governments, religions and reputations be cast out and trodden under feet of men!

This is my creed. For myself, I am an earnest man. If you think proper, now, to accompany me—come on; if not, *au revoir*—and may the Lord have mercy on your soul!

NOTES

1. Radical abolitionists, such as Redpath, objected to the pledges made by many of the Republican party's leaders not to interfere with slavery in southern states where it already

was established and protected by law. David M. Potter, *The Impending Crisis, 1848–1861* (New York, 1976), 266; *New York Radical Abolitionist* 2 (October 1856): 24.

2. Former Federalist turned Jacksonian Democrat, Maryland slaveholder Roger B. Taney (1777–1864) became chief justice of the U.S. Supreme Court in 1835. In March 1857 Taney wrote the majority decision in the case of Dred Scott, a slave, versus his Missouri master. The court turned down Scott's claim to freedom on the grounds of a four-year residence in free territory. The courts also ruled that blacks were not legally citizens of the United States and that Congress could not constitutionally prohibit slaveholding in any federal territory. Don E. Fehrenbacher, *The Dred Scott Case: Its Significance in American Law and Politics* (New York, 1978); Carl B. Swisher, *Roger B. Taney* (Hamden, Conn., 1961); *DAB*, 18:289–94.

3. The fifteenth president of the United States, James Buchanan (1791–1868) quit the law to enter politics first as a Federalist and then as a Democrat. He served in the U.S. House of Representatives (1821–31) and the U.S. Senate (1834–45) and then as James K. Polk's secretary of state. Franklin Pierce made Buchanan U.S. ambassador to Great Britain (1853–56). Buchanan won the Democratic presidential nomination in 1856 on his fourth try and went on to defeat both Republican John C. Frémont and American Millard Fillmore. L. Sandy Maisel, *Political Parties and Elections in the United States: An Encyclopedia,* 2 vols. (New York, 1991), 1:100–101.

4. In May 1844 the American Anti-Slavery Society, now under the control of followers of William Lloyd Garrison, adopted a resolution calling for northern secession from the Union as a means of depriving the institution of slavery of outside support. Garrisonians found their disunionist position an extremely effective propaganda device to castigate northerners for their complicity with slavery stemming from cooperation with the South under the "proslavery" Constitution. In January 1857 Redpath had covered a Garrisonian "Disunion Convention," held at Worcester, Massachusetts, for the *New York Tribune. New York Tribune,* January 17, 19, and 21, 1857; Lewis Perry, *Radical Abolitionism: Anarchy and the Government of God in Antislavery Thought* (Ithaca, 1973), 161–66.

5. Perhaps an allusion to the Dismal Swamp, along the eastern border between Virginia and North Carolina.

6. Heavily influenced by Christian perfectionism, most Garrisonian abolitionists adopted a commitment to personal nonviolence and an opposition to all forms of coercion. Denunciation by these "Non-Resistants" of voting as wrongful submission to worldly discipline helped to produce the schism in the abolitionist movement in 1840. Aileen S. Kraditor, *Means and Ends in American Abolitionism: Garrison and His Critics on Strategy and Tactics, 1834–1850* (New York, 1967), 106, 135; Perry, *Radical Abolitionism,* 55–56, 61–62.

CONTENTS.

MY FIRST TRIP.

MY SECOND TRIP.

I.—Virginia.

Preliminary Words on Insurrection—I start again—Chesterfield County
Facts—Social Reunions North and South—The poor Whites and Slavery—

MY THIRD TRIP.

IN MY SANCTUM.

SLAVERY IN KANSAS.

I.

II.

III.

MY FIRST TRIP.

I.

A WORD BEFORE STARTING.

I have visited the Slave States several times—thrice on an anti-slavery errand. First, in 1854. I sailed to Richmond, Virginia, from New York city; travelled by railroad to Wilmington, North Carolina; and from that port by sea to the city of Charleston. I remained there two weeks—during the session of the Southern Commercial Convention. I then sailed to Savannah, where I resided three months, when I returned direct to New York city.

My second journey was performed in the autumn of the same year. It was rather an extended pedestrian tour—reaching from Richmond, Virginia, to Montgomery, Alabama.

My third journey was performed last spring, and was confined to Virginia. My letters, descriptive of this journey were published in the *Boston Daily Traveller.*[1] They are somewhat different from my previous sketches, relating chiefly to the influence of slavery on the agriculture, education, and material prosperity of a State. Reports of my talks with the slaves occupy in them a subordinate position.

In this volume alone, of all American anti-slavery or other books, the bondman has been enabled, in his own language, (if I may employ the familiar phrase of political essayists and orators), to "define his position on the all-engrossing question of the day." Almost everybody has done it. Why, then, should not he? Surely *he* has some interest in it, even if it be "subject to the Constitution;" even if his interest is unfortunately in conflict with "the sacred compromises of the federal Compact!"

My object in travelling was, in part, to recruit my health, but chiefly to see slavery with my own eyes, and personally to learn what the bondmen said and thought of their condition.

My conversations with the slaves were written down as soon after they occurred as was convenient; occasionally, indeed, in stenographic notes,[2] as the negroes spoke to me.

It will be seen that I do not aim at a literary reputation. I have only plain truths to tell—only plain words to tell them in. My mission was a humble one—to report. I claim no other merit than fidelity to that duty.

I most solemnly declare here, that in no one instance have I sought either to darken or embellish the truth—to add to, subtract from, or pervert a single statement of the slaves. There may be, scattered throughout these pages, a few minor inaccuracies; but I assure the reader, on my honor as a gentleman, that if there *are* any errors of fact, or other errors, I am totally unconscious of them. I believe this book, as it leaves my hand, to be a volume of truths, undeformed by a single falsehood, or even the most trivial mis-statement.

Let these few words suffice for a preface.

I START——MY VOYAGE.[3]

The good steamship Roanoke, after a very pleasant voyage, in the month of March, 1854, arrived at Richmond early in the morning.[4]

I landed and strolled about the city. Of the voyage and of the city I intend to say nothing. There are books enough that treat of such themes. I shall write of the slave class only, or of subjects that relate to their condition.

THOUGHTS IN A GRAVEYARD.

Therefore, one word on the cemetery, which was the first public place I visited. I wondered at the absence of all headstones to colored persons deceased. Julius Caesar, Hannibal, George Washington and Pompey, had no representatives among the citizens interred—none, at least, whose monuments proclaimed and preserved their names.

I inquired where the "slave quarter" was.

"Why," I was told, "in the nigger burying-ground. You don't suppose we allow slaves to be buried here?"

I did suppose so, in my ignorance of southern customs, but soon discovered that I greatly erred. In every southern city that I have visited since (and I believe the rule universally prevails), the whites and the slaves and free people of color have separate places of interment.

Cemeteries are separated; churches are pewed off; theatres are galleried off: I wonder now, (between ourselves and in strictest confidence), if Heaven, likewise, is constructed and arranged with special reference to this hostility of races and conditions of life? In the many mansions of the Heavenly Father, will there be sets of apartments for Africans exclusively—in the parlance of the play-bills, "for respectable colored persons?" If there are not, and if the Southern proslavery divines ever get there, we may expect a second Satanic rebellion against Authority so indifferent to the finer feelings—the refined sensibilities—of the slaveholding saints. With such a doughty champion as Mr. Parson Brownlow,[5] in the character of Beelzebub, the coming conflict must be terrible indeed, and will require as its historian, a genius more exalted by far than the author of *Paradise Lost.*[6] "May I be there to see!"

A SHERIFF'S ADVERTISEMENT.

I walked from the cemetery to the Court House, accompanied some distance by a slave, who was whistling, as he drove along, a popular line, which faithfully describes his lot in life:

"Jordan am a hard road to trabble!"

Undoubtedly, I mused; and so, too, was the Red Sea to the Egyptians![7]

I intended to attend the Mayor's Court, but when I reached the hall his honor had not yet arrived.

On the outer door of the hall, was posted a manuscript advertisement, of which I have preserved a verbatim copy. Here it is:

"SHERIFF'S SALE.

Will be sold, to the Highest Bidder, on the 2d Monday in April, next, at the City Hall, commencing at 12 o'clock noon, "Negro Boy, named Willis, to satisfy two Executions, in my hands, against Aaron T. Burton. "

"PHILLIP BLOMSTON, S.D."[8]

After transcribing this atrocious advertisement, I walked to the auction rooms in Wall street and that vicinity.

A SLAVE SALE.

The first apartment that I entered was an old, long, low, whitewashed, damp-looking room, of which the ceiling was supported by three wooden pillars. There were between thirty and forty white persons present. Seven or eight living chattels were "on sale, for cash, to the highest bidder."

The sale commenced almost immediately after I made my appearance in the shambles. The first Article offered was a girl twelve years of age. She was dressed in a small-checked tartan frock, a white apron and a light-colored handkerchief. She was mounted with the auctioneer on a wooden stand, four steps high. The audience was standing or sitting on forms in different parts of the room.

The auctioneer was a middle-aged, fair-complexioned man, with light-blue, lazy-looking eyes, who drawled out, rather than uttered his words, and chewed an enormous quid of tobacco with a patient and persevering industry that was worthy of a nobler cause.

"Gentlemen," said the body-seller, "here's a girl twelve years old, warranted sound and strong—what d'ye bid to start her?"

For at least ten minutes, notwithstanding all the lazily-uttered laudations of the auctioneer, the "gentlemen" who composed the audience did not bid a single cent to start her.

"Come here," said a dark-complexioned man of thirty, whose face mirrored a hard, grasping, unsympathetic nature, "come here, gal."

"Get down," drawled the auctioneer.

The girl descended and went to the dark man, who was sitting with his face toward the back of his chair.

"How old are you?" said the fellow, as he felt beneath the young girl's chin and pinched her arms, for the purpose probably of ascertaining for himself whether she was as sound and strong as she was warranted to be.

"I don't know how old I'm," replied the chattel.*

"Can you count yer fingers?" demanded the dark man.

"Yes," returned the chattel, as she took hold, first of her thumb, then of her forefinger, and lastly of her ring-finger, "one—three—two—five."

"You're wrong! Tut. Take care," interposed a mulatto, the slave or servant of the auctioneer, as he accompanied her hand from finger to finger. "Now try agin—one—two"—

"One," began the girl, "two—three—four—five."

"She'll do—she'll do," said the dark man, who appeared perfectly satisfied with her educational attainments.

"Gentlemen! will none o' ye make a bid to start this gal?" asked the auctioneer, in an indolently imploring tone.

"Four-fifty," said the dark man.

"Four-fifty's bid, gentlemen, for this gal—four-fifty—four hundred and fifty dollars—four-fifty—four-fifty—four-fifty—four-fifty—four hundred

---

*Slaves shall be deemed sold, taken, reputed and adjudged in law to be chattels personal in the hands of their owners and possessors, and their executors, administrators and assigns, to all intent and purpose whatsoever.—*Code of South Carolina.*

and fifty—four hundred *end* fifty dollars—four hundred *end* fifty dollars bid—going at four hundred *end* fifty dollars"——,

"Sixty," said a dirty-looking, unshaven man, with a narrow-brimmed hat on, who looked so tall and slim as to induce the belief that he must be the celebrated son of A. Gun so often spoken of in the quarrels of the Bowery boys.[9]

"Sixty!" repeated the auctioneer; "four-sixty—four-sixty—four-sixty—four hundred and sixty—four hundred *end* sixty dollars bid—going at four hundred and sixty dollars, and gone—if—there is no—other bid—four h-u-u-n-dred ende"——

"Seventy!" said the dark man.

I need not continue the report.

To induce the buyers present to purchase her, the girl was ordered to go down a second time, to walk about, and to hold up her head. She was finally knocked down to Mr. Philorifle, of the narrow-brimmed hat, for five hundred *end* fifty dollars.

The second lot consisted of a young man, who was started at seven hundred dollars, and sold for eight hundred and ninety-five dollars.

"A thousand dollar nigger"—so the auctioneer styled a strong, healthy, athletic specimen of Southern flesh-goods, was the next piece of merchandise offered for sale; but as not more than eight hundred dollars were bid for him, he was reserved for a more convenient season.

A mulatto—a kind-looking man of forty-five—was next put up; but no bids were made for him.

"That's all, gentlemen," said the auctioneer, as he descended from his Southern platform—this truly "national" and "democratic platform"—"I don't think I can offer you any *thing* else to-day."

"This way—over the way, gentlemen!" tolled a strong, iron-toned voice at the door.

We went over the way into another auction-room (at the corner of the streets), and saw two young female children sold into life-long slavery; doomed to forego, whenever and as often as their masters willed it, all true domestic happiness in this world; condemned to total ignorance of the pleasures of knowledge, of home, of liberty; sentenced to be whipped, imprisoned, or corrupted, as the anger, the caprice, or the lust of their buyers deemed proper; forced to see their husbands lashed, their daughters polluted, their sons sold into distant States. "God bless you, Mrs. Stowe!"[10] I involuntarily ejaculated in the slave shambles, as I saw these children sold, and thought of their sad prospective fate.[11]

I entered a third room. One man, about twenty-five years of age, "warranted sound and strong," was sold for seven hundred dollars. He was a captured runaway. The owner, or rather the trustee of this slave, cut quite a conspicuous figure in the room. A little, Dutch-built, blue-eyed man, very limber indeed both of limb and tongue. He strutted about, with a little stick in his hand, now here, now there; talking incessantly and to everybody: his light-colored overcoat, like the white plume of Henry of Navarre,[12] always visible in the thickest of the crowd.

It would express but a faint idea of his state of mind, were I to say that he was somewhat agitated. Very faint, indeed. Angry is equally inexpressive. "Mad to the bung and boiling over," although it has not the sanction of classical usage, is the only phrase which is at all appropriate to the little man's mental condition.

"Would you believe it, sir!" he snapped at me; "he actually ran away; I offered one hundred dollars reward, too, and I didn't hear tell of him for two years and three months!"

I could hardly suppress a smile at the little man's ludicrously angry expression, as I thought of the very virtuous offence that the cause of his indignation had committed. As I saw that he expected me to say something, I exclaimed:

"Really! Two years and three months. Where did you find him finally?"

"In a saloon at Petersburg!" he said; "where"—here he raised his voice so that every one could hear him—"where, I dare say, the fellow made as good mint juleps as anybody need drink!"

I saw that the slave was standing behind the platform—which in *this* room was about five feet high—and that he was surrounded by a crowd of spectators. I left the little man angry and went up to the crowd.

Perhaps, my readers, you may be disposed to doubt what I am about to add—but it is a God's truth, notwithstanding its obstinate non-conformity with some Northern "South-side" views of Slavery.[13]

The slave was dressed in his pantaloons, shirt and vest. His vest was removed and his breast and neck exposed. His shoes and stockings were next taken off and his legs beneath the knees examined. His other garment was then loosened, and his naked body, from the upper part of the abdomen to the knees, was shamelessly exhibited to the view of the spectators.

"Turn round!" said the body-seller.

The negro obeyed, and his uncovered body from the shoulders to the calves of his legs was laid bare to criticism.

Not a word, not a look of disgust condemned this degrading, demoralizing and cowardly exhibition.

"You see, gentlemen," said the auctioneer, "he's perfectly sound and a very finely formed nigger."

He was sold for $700—about two-thirds only of the price he would have brought, if his masters could have given him that certificate of soulless manhood which the Southrons[14] style, when they refer to the existence of the passive-obedience spirit in a slave, "a good character."

A good name is a very unfortunate thing for a negro to possess. I determined, then and there, in my future intercourse with slaves, to urge them to cultivate as a religious duty all the habits which would speedily brand them as men of bad morals![15]

These scenes occurred on the 30th of March, 1854.

NOTES

1. The itinerary of Redpath's three southern tours can be found in appendix 1. A list of the names and dates of the newspapers originally publishing Redpath's John Ball, Jr. letters can be found in appendix 2.

2. Redpath had received training in an early form of stenography while a teenage reporter for the *Berwick-on-Tweed Advertiser* in his hometown in Scotland in the mid-1840s. Charles F. Horner, *The Life of James Redpath and the Development of the Modern Lyceum* (New York, 1926), 12.

3. The first John Ball, Jr. letter, as published in the Boston *Liberator* on August 4, 1854, began in quite different fashion than this chapter in the *Roving Editor*. What follows is the beginning of that letter up to the point in the chapter, at the subheading "A SHERIFF'S ADVERTISEMENT," where the two texts become nearly identical:

A JOURNEY TO CHARLESTON

BY THE WANDERING GENTILE

————VILLE, Iowa, July 20.

WILLIAM LLOYD GARRISON:

DEAR SIR,—I have just reached home, after a long excursion abroad, undertaken for the benefit of my health. From New York I travelled to South Carolina, and from thence I sailed for Boston—on my way to Europe. I had hardly seen the smoke of the Great Metropolis, before the news of a domestic calamity recalled me to Iowa.

The following letters were written to the 'old folks at home,' during my sojourn in the Southern States. Of course, they were never intended for publication! The carelessness of the style, the frequent occurrence of colloquial phrases in them, and their allusion to topics that are always avoided by elegant writers, will serve to convince you of this fact.

My friends think that I owe it to the cause of freedom to publish the facts of slavery that my letters contain. Be it so. I enclose you my letters, either for publication or— conflagration. I have no time to alter the phraseology of them. If you deem them worthy of publication, I hope that you will make all necessary corrections.

Yours ever,
JOHN BALL, JR.

A JOURNEY TO CHARLESTON.

AMERICAN HOUSE, RICHMOND, Va.

March 30, 1854.

MY DEAR PARENTS AND FRIENDS:

I think I see the stare of surprise that will follow the announcement of the date of this letter. Doubtless, you expected that I should write to you from Old England instead of from the Old Dominion. So did I! I will inform you how I came to change my original resolution. I hate cold,—whether it be moral or physical frigidity. Now, it came to pass, that for several days after my arrival in New York, the weather was intensely cold, and in every street, saharas of dust were to be seen and *felt.* I could not endure this double nuisance. I seized a newspaper, and read that the 'Roanoke' would sail for Richmond that afternoon. 'Inquire,' said the advertisement, 'of Messrs. Ludham & Pleasants.'

I ordered a carriage, and called on Mr. Pleasants—who deserves his name, *entre nous*—and procured a ticket, and—sailed.

After a very pleasant voyage, then, on the rapid-sailing steamship 'Roanoke,' I arrived in this city. At Norfolk—of which I have only to say, that it deserved Tom Little's satire—we stayed for an hour.

I arose at an early hour this morning, and have just concluded a day's laborious idleness. I have seen all the sights here—the Cemetery, the Slave Shambles, the Police Court, and the Theatre. I will employ the few hours that remain before I start again, in rendering you an account of my ramble in Richmond.

As I was ascending one of the hills on which the city is situated, I heard a negro teamster singing a stanza that embodies what appears to be a very popular doctrine in Virginia at present—that, namely,

'Jordan am a hard road to trabble.'

I heard this sublime truth announced by at least a score of persons during the day.

Very few of the stores were opened when I entered the city. I walked along the private streets, read the morning papers, and proceeded to the Cemetery. A shower of rain descended. I took shelter in the doorway of a handsome house, and was invited to enter. I took a chair, looked at a copy of the Potipher Papers, which lay on the table, near an old English Bible, and other books 'all of the olden time,' and then made the subjoined memorandum in my note book:—

'*For an Essay on Early Rising.*—Among the manifold advantages of early rising, may be mentioned the saving it effects in the printer's expenses. The Early Riser need not purchase a single newspaper: he can read them every morning at the doors of rich men.'

This morning, at the doors of the rich men of Richmond—of the professors of the creed of Him who said, 'Love one another, as I have loved you'—in the daily papers of the metropolis of a State which boasts of having produced the Father of the First Free Land—I read that human beings—men, women and children—were to be sold (for cash) to the highest bidder!

THE CEMETERY.

The Cemetery of Richmond is pleasantly situated, well laid out, and ornamented with elegant marble tombstones. I noticed one curiosity. In an upright marble slab was ingeniously inserted the daguerreotype of the youth to whose memory it was erected. A beautiful custom.

Slaves, and even freemen of color, are not buried in the white man's cemetery. I wonder if heaven and hell will be partitioned off, as our own planet is, to suit the prejudices of 'our Southern brethren'!" [Boston *Liberator,* August 4, 1854]

4. In his first John Ball, Jr. letter, Redpath indicated that he had arrived in Richmond, on board the *Roanoke,* on either March 29 or 30, 1854. Boston *Liberator,* April 4, 1854.

5. Methodist minister William Gannaway Brownlow (1805–77) became known first in Tennessee and then nationally for his disputatious nature. He frequently engaged in pamphlet debates over religious topics with Baptist and Presbyterian rivals. He also owned and edited Whig party newspapers in several Tennessee communities. A Civil War Unionist,

Brownlow first became governor and then a U.S. senator during Reconstruction. In September 1858 Brownlow engaged in a three-day debate with New York abolitionist minister Abram Pryne in Philadelphia, which was stenographically reported and published as *Ought American Slavery to Be Perpetuated?* (Philadelphia, 1858). E. Merton Coulter, *William G. Brownlow: Fighting Parson of the Southern Highlands* (Chapel Hill, 1937); *DAB,* 3:177–78.

6. An allusion to English poet John Milton (1608–74), who published *Paradise Lost* in 1667. *DNB,* 13:471–88.

7. An allusion to Exod. 14:21–30.

8. This sale was not advertised in the Richmond newspapers on this day. In his John Ball, Jr. letter, Redpath identified the advertiser's initials as "D.S." rather than "S.D." Boston *Liberator,* August 4, 1854.

9. An allusion to young working-class rowdies who frequented saloons and other inexpensive amusements in New York City's Bowery neighborhood. Mitford M. Mathews, *A Dictionary of Americanisms on Historical Principles,* 2 vols. (Chicago, 1951), 1:173.

10. The daughter of Congregationalist minister and educator Lyman Beecher, Harriet Elizabeth Beecher Stowe (1811–96) married theology professor Calvin Ellis Stowe and lived an essentially private life until 1851–52 when the Washington (D.C.) *National Era* serially published her first novel, *Uncle Tom's Cabin; or, Life Among the Lowly* (Boston, 1852). This work, which criticized slavery and endorsed African colonization, quickly became an international best-seller. Forrest Wilson, *Crusader in Crinoline* (Philadelphia, 1941); Joan D. Hedrick, *Harriet Beecher Stowe: A Life* (New York, 1994); Edward T. James, ed., *Notable American Women, 1607–1950: A Biographical Dictionary,* 3 vols. (Cambridge, Mass., 1971), 3:393–402.

11. In the John Ball, Jr. letter, Redpath ended the paragraph in the following fashion:

> "God bless thee! Mrs. Stowe," I ejaculated in the slave shambles, "and may thy name forever be a hallowed household word in the cabins and cottages of the lowly and oppressed; and may the curses of the slave, and the contempt of all true men forever blast thy prospects, O Douglas, thou son of Iscariot; and may thy name be forever associated with all that is ignoble, as thy memory will be classed with those men whom the nations loathe, as Arnold the traitor, Louis Napoleon the liberticide, and John Mitchel the "patriot," who defended tyranny. [Boston *Liberator,* August 4, 1854]

12. Unlike most of the aristocrats of his age, Henry of Navarre (1533–1610), who ascended to the French throne in 1589 as Henry IV, the first of the Bourbon line, avoided affectations in clothing except for a long white plume of Navarre that he wore in his wide-brimmed hat. Desmond Seward, *The First Bourbon: Henri IV, King of France and Navarre* (Boston, 1971), 164–65, 184–85.

13. An allusion to the proslavery travel account, *A South-Side View of Slavery; or, Three Months at the South, in 1854* (Boston, 1854) by the Boston Congregational minister Nehemiah Adams (1806–78). *DAB,* 1:93–94.

14. A substitute for southerner, traceable to the 1820s, that first was popular among early southern sectionalists and nationalists but later was also used by abolitionists to deride those same groups. Mathews, *Dictionary of Americanisms,* 2:1602.

15. Redpath concluded the first John Ball, Jr. letter with the following short section:

> "Richmond is a very quiet city; its streets are clean, and generally well paved; its first-class houses are good, without being either splendid or the reverse. In my letters to you, however, it is of the living South, not of the natural or artificial South, that I purpose to write.
>
> FIVE, A.M. The breakfast and the train wait. I shall leave this city within an hour; so, friend Joseph,

'You may give my respects to all the pretty girls—
I am going off to Charleston before break of day!'

J.B."

Boston *Liberator*, August 4, 1854.

II.

TALK WITH A FREE NEGRO.[1]

IN walking along one of the streets of Richmond, I was suddenly over-taken by a shower. I went into the store of a fruiterer and confectioner. He was a free man of color. I soon entered into a conversation with him, ascertained his history, and learned many valuable facts of the condition of the slaves of Richmond and vicinity.

A COLORED LIBERATOR.

He was a mulatto of about thirty-five years of age. His eyes and his conversation showed him to be a person kind hearted yet resolute of purpose. The tone of his voice, the expression of his face, bespoke a man familiar with sorrow and cares. He was very intelligent and used exceed-ingly few negro phrases. He had been a slave, but had bought his free-dom; and since that time had purchased his wife, brother, sister-in-law, with *her* husband and their two young children.[2] He had been rather fa-vored as a slave. He had had a kind proprietor, who had permitted him to hire himself—that is to say, to pay to his master a certain sum monthly for the use of his own bodily strength and mental faculties, retaining as his own funds whatever he might make "over and above" the sum thus agreed upon between them. He had been a porter at a popular hotel, and was lucky enough to soon save sufficient with which to purchase his free-dom from his owner. The next money he got was expended on articles of traffic. He prospered in his small retail trade, and with its earliest profits he purchased his wife.

What a low state of morals, by the way, does it indicate, when a robber, *in fact,* of the lion's share of a poor man's wages is spoken of as a kind and indulgent master! How unspeakably mean, too, to live on money thus ungenerously taken from the hard hands of lowly, unprotected toil!

"You have acted nobly," I said to him, "in buying seven persons from slavery, and you must have been very lucky to be able to do it, as well as to buy this house." (He had told me that he owned the house and shop we were in.)

"Ah, sir!" said the good man, in a sad tone, "I wish I could do something more effectual. It's all I live for. No one," he added, "can have any idea of how our people are persecuted here, only on account of their color."

OPPRESSIVE LAWS AND ORDINANCES.

"Indeed!" I said, "I wish you would tell me some of the methods employed by the whites in persecuting your people. I will publish them."

He named a host of them, from which I selected at the time the following particulars:

1. The oath of a colored man, whether free or a slave, is not admissible in courts of justice. Therefore,

If a white man owes a debt to a person of color, and refuses to pay it, it is impossible for the creditor to resort to legal remedies in order to collect it.

If a white man, from any cause or motive—for the purpose, for example, of extorting money—chooses to swear before a court that any colored person, whether free or slave, has been insolent to him, he can cause the unfortunate object of his malice to be whipped by the public officers.

If a worthless vagabond, with a white skin, however black his heart may be, enters the store of a free man of color, and steals, *even before the owner's eyes,* any articles from it, the unfortunate merchant has no legal remedy, unless a white man saw the property thus feloniously appropriated—for the fear of the municipal lash restrains him from entering a public complaint or resenting the robbery on the spot.

Thus the blacks are always at the mercy of the whites—a position which no *un*colored person, I am sure, would be willing to occupy.

In stating these facts, my informant related an incident which I shall narrate here, as it is at once a most striking illustration of the injustice sometimes practised by "our Southern brethren" toward their colored fellow creatures, and serves to show the practical workings of the laws relating to the oaths of persons of the subjugated race.

A few weeks before this interview, a white man went to the green market and was putting some vegetable—parsley, I believe—in his basket, when the colored woman in attendance asked him if he had measured it? He turned round fiercely and asked what she meant by insulting him! Next day he took out a warrant, had the market woman brought before the mayor, and swore positively, as did his son also, that she had used insolent and abusive language to him. She would have been whipped, as usual, and had her sentence chronicled in the papers as the punishment of a "worthless free negro," if several white persons, who were present at the time and knew her to be an honest inoffensive soul, had not promptly stepped up and swore that she was innocent of the offence charged by the plaintiff. She was therefore discharged; but the cowardly perjurers were not even reprimanded.

2. Although free men of color pay the same municipal taxes levied on white citizens, they are not only prohibited from exercising any influence in elections, but from entering the public square or the white man's cemetery.

3. They are prohibited from carrying any offensive or defensive weapons.

4. They are not allowed to go abroad after sunset, without a written permit from their owners or carrying their papers of freedom.[3]

5. If they violate these regulations they are imprisoned until claimed by their masters, if slaves, or visited and liberated by their friends, if free. If they are free but without friends to attend to their interests—hear this and defend it if ye can, ye "Northern men with Southern principles"—they are kept in jail for a certain time, and then—God help them—they are sold into slavery to pay the expenses incurred by the city by keeping them incarcerated. Not many years ago, a *free* girl from the opposite side of the river, incautiously entered the city of Richmond without her certificate of freedom. She was arrested, kept in prison forty days, and then sold into perpetual bondage, for the Southern crime known as "being at large!" "How long, O Lord, how long?"[4] How long, O North, how long?

6. All assemblages of colored men, consisting of more than five persons, are illegal, and severely punished by the administrators of Southern *in*-justice. This ordinance is strictly enforced.

7. Women of color are compelled to endure every species of insult. White boys often spit on their dresses as they are going to chapel; and when they meet a colored female out of doors after sunset, they conduct themselves still more grossly.

These are a few—a very few—of the outrages which the colored freeman is expected to endure and does submit to in the civilized, theologized, church-studded city of Richmond, in the middle of the nineteenth century. Strange—is it not? Yet, in the free States of the North, the name of Abolitionist is frequently used as a by-word of reproach. Stranger still—is it not?

HOW VERY CONTENTED THE SLAVES ARE.

In the course of the conversation in which these facts were mentioned, I stated to my companion that I had frequently heard the defenders and apologists of Southern crime in the Northern States, confidently declare that the slaves were perfectly contented with their lot, and would not willingly exchange it for freedom. I asked him if the slaves of Richmond were contented with their condition?

"No, sir," said the merchant with unusual energy, "they are *not.* I know the most of them. I've lived here for thirty years. First, in a hotel where I used to meet dozens of them every day, and in my store, here, where I see hundreds from every part of the city and the country all the time. *They are as discontented as they can be.* There's a few of them, though, who are poor ignorant creatures, and have good masters, don't care anything about freedom."

"How many do you suppose?" I asked; "one quarter of them?"

"No, sir," said the storekeeper, energetically; "not more than one-tenth."

"What! you don't mean to say that not more than over one-tenth of the slaves have good masters?"

"No, sir," he answered; "but I do say that *those who have good masters are as little contented as those who have bad masters.*"

"Why so?"

"Kind treatment is a good thing, but it isn't liberty, sir; and *colored people don't want that kind of privileges; they want their rights.*"

"Do you think," I asked, "that this feeling of discontent is as strong in the country as in the city?"

"No; not so strong," he returned. "In the city they are more intelligent, and the discontented sentiment is stronger, because the colored people have more chance of talking to one another about their hardships."

"Do you think," I inquired, "that the feelings of discontent have increased during your recollection?"

ABOUT RUNAWAYS.

"Oh, yes, sir," he rejoined, "it has increased a hundred times, especially within the last eight years. When I was a boy, the colored people didn't think much about freedom, because they were allowed a great deal of liberty; but now it seems as if the laws were becoming worse and worse for us every day; we can't enjoy anything now; we can't have the social meetings as we used to have; and now I tell you, sir, the colored people do think about it a good deal. They run away every good chance they can get. I know about a hundred that's gone North since last New Year; most of them got away altogether, and plenty's ready to follow them."

"Do any of them return?"

"No, sir," said the freeman, "they've too much sense for that! You can't tell anything at all about the colored people from what the papers say. Whenever one comes back any whar', they make a string of remarks about it *so* long." He measured about half a yard with his right hand on his left arm. "But," he added, "they don't say nothing about them that run away—hundreds—and never come back agin! And jist look at the paragraphs about the trials at the courts here. It's always 'a worthless negro,' or 'a worthless free negro.' They allers say that, no difference what his character is, or what the character of the white man who appears against him is."

He pointed to a paragraph of this kind in the *Dispatch,* and gave me a proof that the white accuser of the "worthless free negro" named in it, was a man of the most disreputable character.

THE AFRICAN CHURCH.

"I was advised," I said, "by a pro-slavery man to visit the African Church.[5] Is it a splendid concern?"

"Yes, sir," he rejoined, "it's a very fine church. I thought they would tell you to go there! They allus do. That's an old game of theirs—'Go to the African Church' they allus say to strangers, 'and see how happy our slaves are, and how well they dress.' When I was living at the hotel, I've of'en heerd them say so to strangers. Once a gentleman from the North said to me, 'Well, you people of color seem very happy. I was at your church to-day, and I really never did see a better dressed, or a happier-looking congregation.' Them was his words.

"'Yes, massa,' I said, 'but appearances is deceitful. You don't see their hearts. Many of them that you saw there with happy-looking faces had *heavy hearts and raw backs.* They're not all slaves either, as they tell you they are; one half of them's free people.'

"'But they look happy,' the gentleman said.

"'Very true massa,' says I, 'so they do; Sunday's the only happy day they have. That's the only time they have a chance of being all together. They're not allowed to 'sociate on any other day.'"

"By whom," I asked, "is this African Church supported?"

"By the colored people."

"You have a colored preacher, of course?"

"Oh, no;" said the storekeeper, "colored people are not allowed to enter the pulpit in Virginia. ____ ____ (I have forgotten the name), a colored clergyman, once attempted it, but they put him in jail."

"How much do you pay your preacher?"

DEITY VINDICATED AGAINST A DIVINE.

"Six hundred dollars a year," he replied; "but we don't elect him. We have nothing to do with the church but to go there, pay all the taxes, and listen to sermons 'bout submission to the will of God."

"Does he often expatiate on that duty?"

"Very often—very often. One day I heard him say that God had given all this continent to the white man, and that it was our duty to submit."

"Do the colored people," I inquired, "believe all that sort of thing?"

"Oh, no, sir," he returned; "one man whispered to me as the minister said that,

"'He be d——d! God am not sich a fool!'"

"Who elects your minister?"

He explained at considerable length, but I lost the greater part of his answer in thinking about the skeptical negro's vindication of the ways of Providence in its dealings with the colored children of men. I understood him to say that the church was governed by a board of trustees elected by all the churches in the city. Certain it is, that the people who pay the church expenses have neither part nor lot in the government of the church.

"Some time since," said the storekeeper, "they told us we might have the church for —— thousand dollars. (I have forgotten the sum he named.) Well, we raised it somehow or other, and got the building; but then we didn't get the right of choosing our own minister, as we expected."

"Does your white minister *always* preach to suit the slaveholders?"

"Yes, sir," he said, "*always*. He wouldn't be allowed to preach at all if he didn't."

HOW DO UNTO OTHERS, ETC., FARED.

The wife of the storekeeper hitherto had taken no part in the conversation. She interrupted her husband, and told me the history of a Northern preacher at present officiating in the city of New York, who was forced to leave Richmond because he once selected as a text, "Do unto others as ye would that others should do unto you."[6] He is devotedly loved by the colored people of the city, and has cause to be proud of the hatred of the traffickers in human kind. When this clergyman first came to Richmond, he said nothing offensive to the human-property-holders. He paid a visit to New England, and came back what hitherto he had only nominally been—a Christian minister. The first text he selected, after his return to the city, was the Golden Rule. He commenced his sermon by saying that he had recently visited the scenes of his childhood and his early love; had knelt once more in the Christian church where he first experienced the spirit of religion; had looked upon the walls of the college where he had been trained to fight the good fight of faith; and had stood at the grave of his sainted mother. He had felt there, he said, that hitherto he had not done his duty as a Christian clergyman, but he was determined now, with the aid of the Holy Spirit, to atone, by his future zeal, for his shortcomings in by-gone days. He then spoke of the free colored girl who had been sold into slavery for having unfortunately forgotten to carry her certificate of freedom: (the instance that I have already cited). It had just occurred. "Brethren," he exclaimed, in the enthusiasm of his newly-awakened zeal, "*that* was not 'doing unto others as we would that others should do unto us!'" Before retiring to rest that night, he received *forty* letters of remonstrance from as many different members of his congregation. He was obliged to leave the city. Richmond, with true old Virginia pluck, would not submit to be reproved for her "peculiar" sins by a Northern Christian preacher.

The wife asked me if I was acquainted with the minister.

"I am not," I said, "but perhaps I may have seen him in New York."

She went up stairs, and brought down a lithographic portrait of him, which she handled with a loving care, and looked at with an admiring regard, of which any public man might well have been proud.

"Such a testimonial," I said, "oh! Douglas,[7] prince of demagogues— breaker of sacred compacts for the sake of slavery—is more to be desired than ten thousand Presidencies. Such a testimonial—nay thousands of the like—you, during your life-time, might easily have earned, if, regardless of morality, duty, self-respect, you had not basely sold your soul for the chance of an office!"

THE POOR WHITES AND SLAVERY.

I asked the storekeeper whether the poorer white population of Richmond were in favor of Slavery or against it?

"That's a question," he replied, "that can't be answered very easily. Hundreds have said to me, when they came into the store, that they detested slavery; but they never talk about it to white people: *they're afraid to do so!*"[8]

"*Afraid to do so!*" Think of that, ye New England sons of revolutionary sires! In America, "the land of the free and home of the brave;"[9] free white men of the haughty Saxon race are "afraid" to express their opinions. Ah! Southern rights are human wrongs!

NORTH AND SOUTH——RECIPROCAL AMENITIES.

The abolitionists of the North are often accused of malignantly misrepresenting the sentiments and the character of the people of the South. I was informed by the storekeeper, whose conversation I have been reporting, that the citizens of Richmond very zealously inculcate on the minds of their slaves that all that the Northern abolitionists want with them is to sell and cruelly treat them. The North is pictured to them as a place of punishment—a terrestrial hell—where negroes are abused, starved, and kicked about for the amusement of the white race. Abolitionist with them is the synonym for all that is vile and odious in human nature.[10]

The freeman then asked me the true character of the people of the North?

I answered as an admirer of her character, principles and institutions might be expected to reply.

He asked if there was any disrespect shown to people of color?

I love the North, but I worship truth. Why will you, men of the North, seal the lips of your southern friends by your conduct to the free men of color among you? Ah! if you knew what affectionate natures, what noble aspirations, what warm, pure, loving hearts beat beneath the bosoms of the negroes of the North, you would not, you could not harbor much longer the disgraceful and relentless prejudices that now keep you aloof like national enemies during the prevalence of a temporary truce.

I will not extend this report of our conversation any further. I will merely mention that I was advised by my colored friend to associate as much as possible with the free colored people, if I wished to ascertain the real sentiments of the slave population on the subject of slavery.

"Some of the slaves," he said, "will distrust you; so will some of the free people; but don't form your opinion until you ask lots of them. You'll soon see, sir, how discontented they all are."

I have followed his advice: with what result will be seen.

Of this man, let me add all that I now know. The next time that I visited Richmond, I found him in great distress: he had recently lost his wife. On my third visit, I found that he had sold out and gone to Philadelphia.[11]

THE CONTENTED SLAVE.

In Richmond I found *one* contented slave. As I was going to the theatre (as I was ascending Monument street), I overtook a negro boy of about eight years of age.

"Come here, Bob," I said.

I had almost passed him. As he did not come immediately I turned round. He was leaning on the rails of the public park, grinning from ear to ear—looking, in fact, like an incarnate grin.

"He-he-he-e-e-e-he-eh-eee!" grinned Bob.

"Come here, Bob," I repeated.

Bobby approached and took hold of my extended hand.

"What's your name, Bob?"

"Bill," he grinned.

"What's your other name?"

"Hain't got none!" said Bill.

"Are you a free boy?"

"No I'se a slave."

"Have you a father and a mother?"

"Yes, he-he-e-e-he!" grinned Bill.

"Who do you belong to?"

"Mrs. Snooks,"* said Bill.

"Would you like to be free and go North?"

"No!" he said, "I wouldn't go North; I don't want to be free; he-he-he-ee-e!"

"Were you ever sold?" I asked.

"No," he returned, "Mrs. Snooks never sold her slaves all her life. *I don't see what good sellin' slaves does,*" he added.

"Nor I! . . . 'Never sold a slave in her life' . . . Bill?" I asked with appropriate solemnity; "will you tell your mistress that a Northerner said she was a trump?"

"Yes," grinned Bill, "I'll tell her: he-he-he-e-e-e,"[12] and he ran away trilling off his grins as he went along.

So much for the Old Dominion.

A CORROBORATION.—"They (the blacks) invariably give way to the white people they meet. Once, when two of them, engaged in conversation, and looking at each other, had not noticed his approach, I saw a Virginian gentleman lift his cane and push a woman aside with it. In the evening I saw three rowdies, arm in arm, taking the whole of the sidewalk, hustle a black man off it, giving him a blow as they passed that sent him staggering into the middle of the street. As he recovered himself he began to call out to, and threaten them—'Can't you find anything else to do than to be knockin' quiet people round? You jus' come back here, will you? Here! you! don't care if you is white. You jus' come back here and I'll teach you how to behave—knockin' people round!—don't care I does hab to go to der watch house.' They passed on without noticing him further, only

---

*He gave her real name: of course, I adopt instead a generic title.

laughing jeeringly . . . I observe in the newspapers complaints of growing insolence and insubordination among the negroes, arising, it is thought, from too many privileges being permitted them by their masters(!) and from too merciful administration of the police laws with regard to them. Except in this instance, however, I have not seen the slightest evidence of any independent manliness on the part of the negroes towards the whites . . . Their manner to white people is invariably either sullen, jocose or fawning."

T.L. OLMSTED.[13]

Dec. 3, 1851.

NOTES

1. Redpath began the second John Ball, Jr. letter with the following preamble that preceded the material found in this chapter:

COLORED CONTENTMENT IN VIRGINIA.

WASHINGTON HOTEL.
WILMINGTON, N.C. April 1, 1854.

WILLIAM LLOYD GARRISON:

SIR:—I will devote this letter to the narration of a few facts in relation to the subject of contentment 'with slavery,' in Virginia, which will, I earnestly hope, disabuse the minds of many Northern men of the belief, that the majority of the colored citizens of the South prefer their present bondage to the freedom enjoyed by the African population of the Northern States and the British Provinces. I will relate, with equal willingness, whatever I see of evil or of good in slavery as it exists here; because I regard the question of slavery as a moral question, and therefore to be determined by pure reason, and neither by social nor historical considerations, nor by the deductions of experience. If Slavery is right, then are the sufferings of the slaves—and sufferings exist—of no moment whatever; and if, on the other hand, it is a wrong, then, also, are the contentment and happiness of the slaves—if they *are* happy and content—of no importance whatever, as far as the settlement of the question of slavery is concerned." [Boston *Liberator,* August 11, 1854]

2. The text of the original John Ball, Jr. letter differs substantially from the *Roving Editor* text from this point until the subheading "OPPRESSIVE LAWS AND ORDINANCES." The letter describes this portion of the conversation as follows:

"You've done very well, indeed," said I, "to buy seven persons besides this property"—the house he lived in was his own property—"you're an Abolitionist of the first water!"

"Ah! sir," said the good man in a sad tone, "I wish I could do something more effectual. It's all I live for."

Before proceeding farther, I may state that, before questioning any of the slaves, or free men of color whom I have hitherto spoken with on the topic of slavery, I have invariably informed them that I am a Northern abolitionist, travelling in the South for the purpose of ascertaining the real sentiments of the African population on the subject of involuntary bondage. By showing myself to be their friend, I have elicited replies that could have been obtained by no other method.

"No one," said he, "has any idea of how our people are persecuted here, only on account of their color." [Boston *Liberator,* August 11, 1854]

3. The following paragraph was not given a separate number in the original John Ball, Jr. letter. Boston *Liberator,* August 11, 1854.

4. Redpath paraphrases Pss. 13:1, 79:5, and 89:46.

5. Redpath probably alludes to Richmond's First African Baptist Church. It was originally part of the city's First Baptist Church, which included both white and black members. Among the latter were a number of both exhorters and preachers until blacks were forbidden to hold those posts by state legislation passed in 1832 in the wake of the Nat Turner rebellion. In 1841 blacks were allowed to purchase the building at the corner of Broad and College Streets and found their own congregation, the First African Baptist Church. While the blacks were permitted to select their own deacons, the white Reverend Robert Ryland, president of Richmond College, presided over services in the African church until after the Civil War. Marie Tyler-McGraw and Gregg D. Kimball, *In Bondage and Freedom: Antebellum Black Life in Richmond, Virginia* (Chapel Hill, 1988), 37–40; Stanley Kimmel, *Mr. Davis's Richmond* (New York, 1958), 109; Virginius Dabney, *Richmond: The Story of a City* (1976; Charlottesville, Va., 1990).

6. The biblical Golden Rule found in Matt. 7:12 and Luke 6:31.

7. Born in Brandon, Vermont, Stephen Arnold Douglas (1813–61) migrated to Illinois where he practiced law. Democrats elected him to the U.S. House of Representatives in 1843 and to the U.S. Senate in 1847. Douglas played a crucial role in floor-managing the passage of the Compromise of 1850. As chair of the Senate Committee on the Territories, Douglas authored the Kansas-Nebraska Act, whose passage in 1854 greatly intensified political sectionalism. Robert W. Johannsen, *Stephen A. Douglas* (New York, 1973); *DAB,* 5:397–403.

8. The following paragraph from this point in the original John Ball, Jr. letter is omitted in the *Roving Editor* text:

(I may state, that, as far as I have had an opportunity of judging hitherto, I am of opinion that the majority of the Southern people in the cities of Richmond and Wilmington are secret abolitionists.) [Boston *Liberator,* August 11, 1854.]

9. Redpath quotes from the final lines of the first stanza of Francis Scott Key's lyrics for the "Star-Spangled Banner" (1814).

10. The following paragraph at this point in the John Ball, Jr. letter is omitted from the text of the *Roving Editor:*

Southrons! no good ever came of a lie! Desist from giving us false characters; for the slaves, be assured, do not believe you; and, perhaps, by continuing to misrepresent us, you may annihilate that party in whom is your only hope of safety—the Northern men with the Southern *want of* principles. [Boston *Liberator,* August 11, 1854]

11. Redpath returned to Richmond in September 1855 and again in May 1857. His description of this Richmond free black confectioner makes the latter's identification possible. A check of business directories for Richmond and Philadelphia reveals that the name "Thomas Atkinson" was the only one listed in the confectioner trade in both communities at the dates indicated by Redpath. Atkinson conducted a confectioner's business in Richmond at 119 Main Street in 1855 and in Philadelphia at 1107 Pine Street in 1859. *Butters' Richmond Directory for 1855* (Richmond, Va., 1855), 19; *Boyd's Directory for Philadelphia . . . 1859–60* (Philadelphia, 1859), 116; *Cohen's Philadelphia, Pa. City Directory for 1860* (Philadelphia, 1860), 1031.

12. The original John Ball, Jr. letter ended at this point. Boston *Liberator,* August 11, 1854.

13. This misdated quotation is from Frederick Law Olmsted, *A Journey in the Seaboard Slave States in the Years 1853–1854: With Remarks on Their Economy* (1856; New York, 1904), 1:33–34.

III.

NORTH CAROLINA.

MY next communication is dated from Charleston, April 4.[1] I transcribe as much of it as relates to the North Carolina slaves.

I left Richmond on Friday morning, and arrived at Wilmington about nine in the evening.[2] On Saturday forenoon I took a stroll into the pine-tree forests by which the city is surrounded. After walk[ing][3] a few miles I came upon a rice plantation. About half a dozen old wooden shanties, a neat frame house, recently erected, and a large barn in the yard, formed what in the free States would be termed the homestead, but probably has another name here, as the buildings were all intended to hold the owner's property—to wit: rice and negroes.

SOVEREIGNTY OF THE INDIVIDUAL.

I was extremely thirsty, and extremely curious to know something about the place, too; and so, to satisfy both cravings, I climbed over the fence—a rather disagreeable task as well as dangerous, in the present style of gents' nether garments—and then knocked at the door of the new wooden cabin. It was of no use knocking at the door. Dar was no one in.

"Massa, you needn't knock dar: open it."

I turned round and saw—let me see (I am a judge of the price of colored Christians now)—say 'a 'leven hundred dollar nigger'—standing between me and the fence, with his hat in his hand, and a very obsequious face on his shoulders.

"Look'e here, old boy," I said, suiting my language to my company—the way to get into favor with it—"what d'ye take me for: a woman?"

"Oh-eh-eh! Oh! No, no, no, no, massa! Oh! no!" said the chattel timorously.

"You don't, eh? Then put your hat on as quick as a mice. Never lift your hat to any one but a lady, and never do that if your wool isn't all fixed slick."

The slave at once dismissed his dismal expression of countenance, and grinned rather than laughed aloud:

Ah! massa! he! he! he! you isn't a *slave;* you kin do as you like; but ah can't do dat," said Sambo.

"Are you a married man?"

"Oh, yes! massa; ah was married, but ah didn't like my old woman, and ah lives wid anoder now."

"Is your wife living?"

"Yes, oh, yes, massa."

"You believe in the sovereignty of the individual—eh? old boy?"

"Dusseno, massa, what dat am," rejoined the black.

(Stephen Pearl Andrews! do you hear that? Here is a colored persona-tor of your doctrine of individual sovereignty,[4] who "dusseno what dat mean, massa" Stephen. Enlighten him, pray!)

CONTENT OR NOT?

"Have you ever been at the North?" I asked.

The eye that had looked frivolous but a moment before, now suddenly flashed with earnestness—it paid, I thought, a very eloquent eulogium on the institutions of the North.

"No, massa, no!" he responded in a sad tone of voice, "neber, and I neber 'specks to be dar."

"You would like to go there?" I remarked.

It is very easy to ascertain the opinions of simple people, from the peculiar expression of their eyes: I saw at once that my colored compan-ion was struggling with the suspicion that he might be speaking to a spy.

"You come from de North?" he asked cautiously.

"I am a Northern abolitionist: do you know what that means?"

"Oh, yes, massa," said Sambo, "you's for the slave. Do you tink, massa, dat we'll all get out of bondage yet?"

"I hope you will, my boy—very soon."

"Dunno, massa; I's feared not. I's allus heerd dem talking 'bout freedom comin', but it amn't comed yet."

"*You* wish you were free?"

"Oh, yes, massa—*we all does.*"

"Do all the colored people you know wish to be free?"

"*Yes, massa, they all does indeed.*"

I spoke with him a little longer; looked into the barn where about a dozen persons, of both sexes, were thrashing rice with cudgels, and then I addressed another man of color.

"This man," I soliloquized, as I cast my eyes upon the mulatto, "if he were an educated gentleman, would be a secret skeptic in religion but an orthodox professor; he would naturally prefer the practice of the law as a profession; but if he took to politics he would be as non-committal as our democratic aspirants to the presidential chair, or even, perhaps, as the editor of a northern national religious paper on the crime of slavery, and its numerous brood of lesser sins.

"How do you do?" I began.

He instantly took off his hat. All colored persons "away down South," excepting in large cities, do so when addressed by a white man.

He was very well!

I was very glad to hear it—and how did his folks do?

I forget how he answered—you're not particular I hope? I talked irrelevantly for a time, for I knew it would be useless to throw away my frankness on him. So I put him through a course of Socratic questions.

He admitted dat freedom am a great blessin'; dat de collud pop'lation in general—in fact, nine-tenths of those whom he knew—would like berry much to be free; but as for himself *he* allus had had good masters; *he* didn't see how he could better himself by being free. No—no—no—he didn't car about freedom, he didn't. He admitted, however, with ludicrously hasty expression of it, his willingness to accept freedom for himself if he were offered the boon.

"My friend," I said, " will you tell me *why* you would take it if freedom would not 'better you' as you call it?"

He was puzzled. Burton's acting[5] never afforded me one-half so much amusement as I derived from watching the bewildered and cunning expression of this non-committal negro's eyes.

"Why, massa," he stuttered, "I meaned that—a. If—I *had* to take my freedom—eh—if I'se '*bleeged* to, why, I'd—I'd—*have to take it!*"

I offered him my hat in token of my admiration of this truly resplendent feat of logic.

"Your answer is perfectly satisfactory," said I; "I only beg pardon for having caused you to act against your principles by telling the truth."

I left him amazed at my answer. As I shook hands with the other negro on departing, he said:

"I's a slave, massa; that's what I is, and I neber 'specks to be free."

"Keep up your heart, my boy," I answered, "I hope I shall see you in the North yet."

"Feared not, massa," he returned, "feared not. I only hope to be free when I gets to Heaben."

THE MULATTO.

In returning to my hotel I met a mulatto—an intelligent looking man with a piercing dark eye. I saw that he had not a single spark of servility in his spirit; that if his skin made the middle passage, his soul came over in the Mayflower.[6]

"What are these birds?"

I pointed to a couple overhead.

"Buzzards," said the black man.

A few more trivial remarks and I asked:

"Are you a free man?"

"No, sir, I am a slave."

"Who owns you?"

"—— ——; but he hires me out."

"Have you ever been North?"

"No, sir, I never was."

"You would like to go there and be free, I suppose?"

He gave me a penetrating look before replying. I seem to have stood the test; for he prefaced his reply by a remark which three others have made, after closely inspecting my physiognomy:

"I know you're honest, sir. I'll say to you what I wouldn't say to plenty who'd ask me, as you've done. *Yes, sir; I would like to go North.* What man of color would not?"

"I've often been told," I remarked, " by the slave-holders' friends in the North, that you colored people are perfectly satisfied, and rather prefer slavery, indeed. Is that so? I always thought the colored people loved slavery"—a pantomimic gesture concluded the sentence.

"Yes, massa," said the slave, "I knows what you mean. They does love it. Over the left."

"Are the majority of colored people of your acquaintance satisfied or dissatisfied with slavery?"

"*I know hundreds and hundreds,*" he replied, "*and almost all of them are as dissatisfied as they kin be.*"

"Are one-third satisfied, do you think?"

"No, sir. *Not more than one-tenth.* As few as has good masters doesn't think about freedom so much; but if they could get the offer, *all* of them would be free."

"Are you a married man?"

"Yes, sir," said the slave.

"Were you married by a clergyman?"

"Yes, sir."

"Have you any children?"

"Yes, sir. I've had thirteen."

"E-e-eh?" I ejaculated; "you don't mean that?"

"Yes, massa; I's had thirteen, but they all died, 'cept four; it's an unhealthy place this."

I confess that I was rather astonished at finding so resolute a family man in bondage; for I thought that the energy he had thus exhibited in the "heavy father line" of endeavor, might also have effected his escape, or at least his self purchase.

"Did you ever read 'Uncle Tom's Cabin?'"[7]

"No, massa; what is it?"

Explanations followed—but you've read it of course? It's truly a fiction without fiction.[8]

On leaving, he shook hands, and said, with emotion:

"God bless you, massa! God bless you! I hope de abolitionists will win de battle, and bring us all out of bondage."

I may state here that the word bondage is very frequently used by the colored people to express their condition. More frequently, I think, than slavery.

I walked on, and at length came near an unpainted wooden house, occupied exclusively by colored people.

A COLORED PREACHER'S FAMILY.

The family consisted of eight persons—the mother, four sons and three daughters. One son is twenty-one years old; the eldest daughter is nineteen, the other two female children are under ten years of age.

They are the children of a colored Methodist "Bethel" preacher, in New York or Brooklyn, of the name of Jacob Mitchell.[9] He has, it appears, been struggling a long time to get money enough to buy his wife, eldest daughter, and three youngest children. Come! my Methodist friends of New York, I want you to redeem this lot—to convert them from chattels into human beings. Here they are, for sale for cash—five immortal beings, all church members, and good moral people, too! Assist Mr. Mitchell without loss of time! He has already saved about two thousand dollars; another, thousand, they say, would buy the "whole cargo, and their blessing into the bargain." Let the three sons escape for themselves; they are not fit to be free if they make no effort to escape from slavery.

Mr. Mitchell is a freeman by gift. This family are from Maryland. Some time ago, knowing that they were all to be sold to the South, they made their escape into the semi-free State of Pennsylvania, but were captured, and brought back, and sold to North Carolina. What a celestial gratification must it be to Mr. Millard Fillmore,[10] and the friends of the Fugitive Slave Law,[11] to know of such triumphs of the true spirit of nationality— such pleasing proofs of inter-national, or rather of inter-state courtesy! Great Heavens! it must be overpowering, overwhelming, overshadowing! Ah! little do our sectional and fanatical souls know of the bliss that awaits the Conqueror of his Prejudices in favor of humanity and freedom! Very little, alas![12]

Mr. Mitchell's family can read.

A CHRONIC CASE OF RUNAWAYISM.

A man of twenty-three, or thereabouts, was laboring, might and main, as I entered the room, at mastering the mysteries of the first lesson-book.

"Hullo!" I exclaimed, "do they allow colored people to learn to read in this city?"

"No, massa!" said the sable student, " dey don't 'lows it: but they can't help themselves. I'll do as I please!"

"Oh! you're a freeman?"

"No, massa, I's a slave; but I won't stand any bad treatment. I's run away six times already, and I'd run away agin, if they tried to drive me," he exclaimed with emphasis.

"Six times!" I repeated. "Why, you must have been very unfortunate to have been recaptured so often. How far north did you ever get?"

"Oh, massa, I never tried to get North. I never ran more than thirty miles, and then I worked, and staid dare."

"What did your master do to you when he caught you?"

"I ketched it," said the fugitive, " dey lashed me; but I doesn't care—*I won't be druv.*"

He looked as if he meant what he said, too. I advised him, as I have advised at least a dozen darkeys already, to run away to the North at the very earliest opportunity.

A BOY'S OPINION.

I had five other conversations with slaves in Wilmington. I will briefly state the result of each interview.

"How old are you, Bob?"

"Thirteen, sir."

"Are you free?"

"No; I'm a slave."

"Would you like to go North?"

"Yes, sir. I would like to—very much."

"What! don't you like to be a slave?"

"No, sir; I don't," he said with savage emphasis, " I HATE it."

"Do all the boys you know hate to be slaves?"

"No, sir; *but all the smart boys do.* There's only a few, and them's stupid devils, who don't care about it."

"Then, you're one of the smart boys?" I said, smiling, as I placed my hand on his head.

But the boy was in no mood for smiles. His face exhibited signs of the most poignant grief, as he replied:

"Well, sir, I wish I was a free boy—and away from this darned mean country."

The boy was a mulatto.

A SIGN OF THE TIMES. [13]

Parson Brownlow, in his recent challenge to the North,[14] reserved the right to refuse to accept any offer to discuss the Slavery Question with a person of color. This fact may yet be cited as a sad and significant indication of our inveterate blindness to danger. For, is it not quite probable or possible, that the colored race alone may yet decide this question, both for themselves and us, and reciprocate the parson's compliment, by refusing to permit the uncolored man to have anything to say about it? When we find that "all the smart boys" of the subjugated race *hate* slavery with a deadly animosity, it surely is not unreasonable to believe in such a terrible, *but desirable* result. Terrible to the tyrant, but desirable for the sake of our national honor.

ADVANTAGES OF A NATIONAL CREED.

Freedom of speech (this passage I wrote at a later period),[15] the freeman's great right of public utterance of thought, even in conversation—for exceptions, however numerous, do not disprove the fact—is a luxury of which the Northerner has the exclusive monopoly, and that only in his own Free States, if he cherishes a radical anti-slavery creed, or any Christian sympathy for the negro bondman. How insufferable, therefore, the insolence, or the intended insolence, which taunts the Republican party with being sectional—with having no nationality—with not daring to maintain any political organization in the Southern States! The ebon oligarchy, having effectually crushed out the essential elements of Republican freedom, exult over the damnable disgrace—throw their harlot taunts at the decencies and virtues which, having outraged, they affect to despise and try to make odious by glorying in their own deep shame.

I regret that the great Republican party is not more worthy of these laudatory taunts. I deeply lament that it should tolerate in its ranks any but the deadliest, the most earnest enemies—not of the mistake merely, but the cowardly crime of American Slavery.

I regret to see the anxiety its prominent politicians so often and so unnecessarily display, to quiet the apprehensions of the traffickers in humanity, by announcing their fixed determination never, under any circumstances, to interfere with the infernal institutions where it already exists.[16] Ah! gentlemen! if such be your creed, God send us another Democratic President! The best friend of the slaves I have often thought, is his worst enemy. Legree[17] hastens the day of emancipation more rapidly than St. Clair.[18] Atchison[19] has done more for the slave by his brutality than Garrison[20] by his humanity. I hope to see the day when the Republican party will glory in its hostility to slavery *everywhere* and always. Until then, its mission must be fulfilled by individual effort and underground transit companies.

Yet that there *are* advantages in a national creed I saw, and thus stated, after reading a speech by Senator Douglas,[21] in which he used in substance the expression here attributed to him:

DOUGLAS.

The Dropsied Dwarf of Illinois,
　By brother sneaks called "Little Giant"
He who made so great a noise
　By being to the Slave Power pliant,
Upon the Senate floor one day
"Rebuking" Freedom's friends, did say:
　"Republicans must stay at home,
Or hide their creed, so none can find 'em,
　The Democrat alone can roam.
Nor leave his sentiments behind him!"
"Pray why?" asks Freedom, in surprise,
"Because" (the Dropsied Dwarf replies),
"Your 'glittering generalities'
Are odious in St. Legree's eyes,
While *we* such 'self-apparent lies'
Reject, and in his favor rise."
Ah! then," said Freedom, "in my rambles,
I'll keep away from negro-shambles,
Yet you (I see), your creed suits well,
'Twill serve you here—and when in Hell."

SLAVERY IN NORTH CAROLINA.—The aspect of North Carolina with regard to slavery is, in some respects, less lamentable than that of Virginia. There is not only less bigotry upon the subject, and more freedom of conversation, but I saw here, in the Institution, more of patriarchal character than in any other State. [Very patriarchal, in the old slave mother's case! —J.R.] The slave more frequently appears as a family servant—a member of his master's family, interested with him in his fortune, good or bad. . . . Slavery thus loses much of its inhumanity. It is still questionable, however, if, as the subject race approaches civilization, the dominant race is not proportionably retarded in its onward progress. One is often forced to question, too, in viewing slavery in this respect, whether humanity and the accumulation of wealth, the prosperity of the master and the happiness and improvement of the subject, are not in some degree incompatible."—OLMSTED.[22]

NOTES

1. Redpath used the same information in the heading of his third John Ball, Jr. letter. This probably is accurate because Redpath reported on the commercial convention that began in Charleston the following week. Boston *Liberator,* September 1, 1854; *New York Tribune,* April 13, 1854.

2. Redpath gave the same facts in his third John Ball, Jr. letter. According to information in his letter published in the Boston *Liberator,* September 1, 1854, the date of his trip from Richmond to Wilmington would be March 31, 1854. Redpath began his third John Ball, Jr. letter with the following heading and introductory paragraph that supply some additional details on his trip to Charleston:

A JOURNEY TO CHARLESTON. NO. IV.

BY THE WANDERING GENTILE.

Talks with the Slaves in South Carolina—the Sugar House.

Charleston Hotel, S.C., April 10.

FELLOW-GENTILES—I arrived in this, the chosen land of the chivalry of the South, on last Tuesday morning, in the steamer Gladiator, from Wilmington, which made her last trip 'on this occasion only'; and, by doing so, caused the regular line of steamships between that port and this city to make its exit, with great eclat, from that vast theatre of which the celebrated and venerable Mr. Neptune is the able stage manager. The Gladiator paddled well her part, and arrived two hours earlier than the steamer of the same line, which started from the same port on the same hour that we did. Alas! like other faithful servants of the public, Away Down South, she is to be sold "by auction, (for cash,) to the highest bidder." [Boston *Liberator,* September 8, 1854]

3. In the *Roving Editor,* the word "walk" followed by a hyphen appears at the end of a line, with the next line beginning with "a few miles. . . ." In the original John Ball, Jr. letter, the word appears as "walking." Boston *Liberator,* September 1, 1854.

4. Massachusetts-born Stephen Pearl Andrews (1812–86) practiced law in Texas from 1839 to 1843, when a mob drove him from the state on account of his antislavery views. He later settled in New York City, where he vigorously advocated phonetic language. He also attracted notoriety for his propagandizing for an anarchistic utopia that he called "Pantarchy," which included free love ("individual sovereignty") among its practices. Madeleine

Stern, *The Pantarch: A Biography of Stephen Pearl Andrews* (Austin, Tex., 1968); *DAB*, 1:298–99.

5. An allusion to the London-born comedic actor William E. Burton (1804–60), who migrated to the United States in 1834. He worked as both an actor and a publisher in several East Coast cities in the 1830s and 1840s. Beginning in 1848, he operated "Burton's Theatre" on Chambers Street in New York City and starred in many of the comedies performed there. He then moved uptown to Broadway to manage "Burton's New Theatre" from 1856 to 1858, thereafter shifting his energies to organizing touring theatrical companies. Joseph N. Ireland, *Records of the New York Stage from 1750 to 1860*, 2 vols. (1866–67; New York, 1968), 2:235–38; Gerald Bordman, *The Oxford Companion to American Theatre* (New York, 1992), 114–15; Mary C. Henderson, *The City and the Theatre: New York Playhouses from Bowling Green to Times Square* (Clifton, N.J., 1973), 83, 87, 107.

6. An allusion to the ship *Mayflower* that carried a party of English religious dissenters, known as Separatists, from their initial place of refuge in Holland to a colony at Plymouth, Massachusetts, in 1620. Owen Chadwick, *The Reformation* (Harmondsworth, Eng., 1964), 203–8, 220–21.

7. Harriet Beecher Stowe's *Uncle Tom's Cabin* (1851).

8. This paragraph read differently in the original John Ball, Jr. letter:
> Explanations followed; but, as my reader has most probably read or seen Uncle Tom's Cabin, it will be unnecessary for me to narrate them here. [Boston *Liberator*, September 1, 1854]

9. No black minister by this name appears in either the New York or Brooklyn city directories in the mid- or late 1850s. These directories list two Bethel African Methodist Episcopal churches in Brooklyn at this period, but other individuals are listed as their ministers. *Brooklyn City Directory for the Year Ending May 1st, 1858* (Brooklyn, n.d.), 258.

10. Veteran New York politician Millard Fillmore (1800–1874) was nominated for vice president in 1848 by the Whig party to add sectional balance to its ticket headed by Zachary Taylor of Louisiana. Following Taylor's death in July 1850, Fillmore ascended to the presidency and vigorously supported passage of the compromise legislation of that year. Denied the presidential nomination by the Whigs in 1852, he unsuccessfully ran for that office in 1856 as the candidate of the nativist American party. *National Cyclopaedia of American Biography* (New York, 1898–), 6:177–78 (hereafter cited as *NCAB*); *DAB*, 6:380–82.

11. Part of the Compromise of 1850, the Fugitive Slave Act authorized appointment of commissioners to hear cases concerning the rendition of accused runaway slaves. Normal rules of evidence were suspended in these hearings, and the commissioners received an extra five dollars for ruling that the accused was a runaway. Federal marshals were empowered to assist in these renditions, and heavy fines could be imposed on anyone impeding the law's enforcement. Stanley W. Campbell, *The Slave Catchers: Enforcement of the Fugitive Slave Law* (1968; New York, 1972), 23–25.

12. In the original John Ball, Jr. letter, this paragraph read:
> Mr. Mitchell is a free by gift. The family came from Maryland. Knowing that they were to be sold to the South, they made their escape, but were captured in Pennsylvania by that infernal 'instrument,' the Fugitive Slave Law. They can read. [Boston *Liberator*, September 1, 1854]

13. The remaining paragraphs in this chapter did not appear in the John Ball, Jr. letter in the Boston *Liberator*, September 1, 1854. The following chapter resumes the republication of interviews from this letter.

14. An allusion to William G. Brownlow's challenge to debate slavery that the Reverend Abram Pryne accepted.

15. This passage did not appear in any of the known John Ball, Jr. letters.

16. While some Republicans, such as Salmon P. Chase, condemned the Fugitive Slave Act of 1850 as unconstitutional, most party leaders in the late 1850s acknowledged its legality while vowing to repeal it if they gained control of Congress. Eric Foner, *Free Soil, Free Labor, Free Men: The Ideology of the Republican Party before the Civil War* (New York, 1970), 83–34, 136–37.

17. A reference to the fictional character Simon Legree, an extremely inhumane slave owner in Harriet Beecher Stowe's novel *Uncle Tom's Cabin.*

18. A fictional character in *Uncle Tom's Cabin,* Augustine St. Clare was an easygoing slaveholder who felt guilty over the institution of slavery but lacked the energy to oppose it.

19. A native of Kentucky, David Rice Atchison migrated to Missouri in 1830 and practiced law there. He quickly rose in local politics until he was appointed to a seat in the U.S. Senate in 1840. He held that post until 1855 and made a name as a friend of western land grants to railroads and the expansion of slavery. After being defeated for reelection, Atchison led several raids by Missourians on the free state settlements in Kansas Territory in 1856 and 1857. Theodore C. Atchison, "David R. Atchison: A Study in American Politics," *Missouri Historical Review* 24 (July 1930); *DAB,* 1:402–3.

20. The nation's best-known abolitionist, William Lloyd Garrison (1805–79) had apprenticed as a printer in his youth in Newburyport, Massachusetts. Converted to the antislavery cause by Quaker Benjamin Lundy, Garrison founded a weekly abolitionist newspaper, *The Liberator,* in Boston in 1831. Garrison's advocacy of other controversial reforms, especially women's rights, precipitated a heated schism in abolitionist ranks in 1840. He remained highly active in the antislavery cause until closing *The Liberator* in 1865. James B. Stewart, *William Lloyd Garrison and the Challenge of Emancipation* (Arlington Heights, Ill., 1992); John L. Thomas, *The Liberator: William Lloyd Garrison* (Boston, 1963).

21. Stephen A. Douglas.

22. This passage originally appeared in Olmsted, *Journey in the Seaboard Slave States,* 1:408.

IV.

THE next slave with whom I talked was also mulatto—one-third white blood.[1] The mulattoes are invariably the most discontented of the colored population.

SLAVERY OR MATRIMONY——A COLORED CALCULATION.

"I've five children," he said, "but my wife is a free woman, and they are free, although I am a slave."

Of course the reader knows that by American law the child follows the condition of its mother. Mother free, children free; mother slave, slave children.[2] Perhaps the speediest method of peaceably abolishing slavery would be to change (by reversing) this law. Under its beneficent operations the chivalry would be transformed into manifold liberators![3]

"How old are you?"

"I'm thirtymseven."

"How do the colored people feel about slavery?"

All the colored people of my acquaintance (and I know them all here), *would gladly be free if they could get their liberty.* Say about a third have good masters, and they are not so discontented, of course, as the rest, but ask them at the ballot, or some other way, so that they could express their sentiments without fear, and then you would hear such a shout for liberty as never was raised before."

I will omit my questions.

"My owner hires me out to hotels. He gets twenty dollars a month for me. I clear besides that about two hundred dollars for myself. About ten years since I took up with this woman."

He is speaking of the wife of his bosom!

"Were you married?"

"Oh yes," he continued, "I was regularly married by a minister. They always do it here. The slaves will be married, and their owners make a fine wedding of it, but it doesn't amount to anything, because they are liable to be separated for life at any moment, and often is. I've often thought this subject over."

"What subject?"

"About marrying," he said.

"Most men do."

"Well, but I mean different. I see, if I hadn't married, I would have been free now; bekase I would have had a thousand dollars by this time to have bought myself with. But it took all I could make to get along with my family. Well, they're all free, my sons ar'; and I'm giving them as good an education as we dare give them; so that, if the time does come when I'm going to be sold, they may buy me."

He sighed, and added:

"When I'm an old man."

I asked if he did not think of escaping before that time?

"No," he said, "I wouldn't run the risk now of trying to escape. It's hardly so much an object, sir, when a man's turned the hill. Besides, my family. I might be sold away from them, which I won't be, if I don't try to run away—leastways till I'm old."

"Are the whites very hard on you here?"

"Yes, sir, they are very hard on us here. We dare not say anything about being discontented."

This was the statement of one man, fully confirmed in its general particulars by another slave, of whose domestic relations I asked nothing and know nothing.

THE OLD SLAVE MOTHER.

I entered a cabin on the roadside. A little child, a slave, with a future as dark as its own face before it (as the poet might have observed, but didn't), was sitting quietly playing on the doorstep.

"Will you have the kindness, madam," I said, "to give me a glass of water?"

"Oh yes, massa," said the old woman I had spoken to, as she set herself about getting it. I did not want it—I only asked for it as an excuse for entering the house."

"Are you a free woman, madam?"

"No, massa; I's not. I's not likely to be," said the old lady.

"Were you ever at the North?"

"No, massa."

"Would you like to go there!"

She gave a funnily scrutinizing glance:

"We-ll, massa, I ca-n't say dat, for I neber was dar," she returned, in a slow and very peculiar tone.

"How old are you?"

(Wasn't that popping a rather delicate question in a rather summary manner, my fair sisters of the North?)

"I's sixty-two," said the venerable slave.

(Ladies, lovely, of the North! would you believe it? She actually appeared to be of the age she mentioned—no, not even a single day older.)

She had had eleven children, but—

"I's only three I kin see now, massa," she added, mournfully.

"Have any of your children been sold?" I inquired.

"Yes," she said, sobbing, the tears beginning to trinkle down her furrowed cheeks, "three on 'em. Two boys were sold down South—I don't know where they is; and my oldest son was sold to Texas three years since. There was talk about him coming back, but it's bin talked about too-oo-oo"—her sobs interrupted her speech for a few seconds—"too-oo-oo long to be true, I's afeerd."

Her maternal affections were strongly moved; I knew she would answer any questions now.

"It must have been very hard with you to part with your boys; almost as hard as when your other children died?" I said.

"Almost, massa?" she rejoined, "far wuss. When they're dead, it seems as if we knowed they was gone; but when they're sold down South uh!—ah!—massa"—

She did not finish the sentence in articulate words, but the tears that raced down her wrinkled face, the sighs that heaved her bereaved maternal breast, concluded it more eloquently than her tongue could have done.

"It almost broke my heart, massa," she said, "but we cannot complain—*we's only slaves.*"

A curious wish entered my mind as she uttered these words. I wished that I had the right of selecting the mode of punishing the Southern pro-slavery divines in the world to come. I would give each of them, what not one of them has, A CHRISTIAN HEART, capable of compassion for human sorrow and suffering; and then I would compel them to look, throughout all eternity, on the ghost of the face of this poor miserable mother, whose childreri had been sold by their inhuman masters far away from her, and far distant from each other.

"Oh! God!" I ejaculated as I gazed on her grief-furrowed face, which was wet with heart-sad tears, "this slavery is the most infernal institution that the sun looks down upon."

I did not address this remark to the old woman; I did not, indeed, intend to utter it at all; but I did speak it aloud, and she heard it.

"Yes, massa," she said, "it am infernal; but we's no choice but to submit."

"Would you believe it, my old friend," I said, "that your masters, and their white serfs at the North, say you are all happy and contented with slavery?"

"Well, massa," she replied, "we has often to say so to people that ask us; I would have said it to you, if you hadn't talked about my childer; we's afeerd to complain."

"Yes, I suppose so; not half of you are contented?"

"A half on us, massa!" she exclaimed, energetically, "*no not one quarter.*"

I talked with the old mother for a few minutes longer, and then took her by the hand.

"Good bye, old lady," I said, "I hope that you will die a free woman with all your children around you."

A deep sigh preceded the slave-mother's answer.

"I hope so, massa, I hope so; but it seems as if this life was to be a hard trial to colored people. I's no hopes of seeing my boys agin this side the Land."

"Good bye," I repeated, as I retreated hastily—for, to say the truth, I could no longer restrain my tears, and I hated to let a woman see me weep—"good bye."

"Goodbye," said the slave-mother. "God bless you, massa, God bless you! Yes, massa, and God *will* bless you, if you is the friend of the slave."[4]

I find, in a recent number of the *Boston Saturday Express,* a simple narrative, in rhyme, of another North Carolina slave-mother's reply. I subjoin it here:

THE SLAVE-MOTHER'S REPLY.

"All my noble boys are sold,
Bartered for the trader's gold;
Where the Rio Grande runs,
Toils the eldest of my sons;
In the swamps of Florida,
Hides my Rob, a runaway;
Georgia's rice-fields show the care
Of my boys who labor there;
Alabama claims the three
Last who nestled on my knee;
Children seven, seven masters hold
By their cursed power of gold;
Stronger here than mother's love—
Stronger here, but weak above;
Ask me not to hope to be
Free, or see my children free;
Rather teach me so to live,
That this boon the Lord may give—
First to clasp them by the hand,
As they enter in THE LAND."[5]

THE CHUCKLING NEGRO.

I was walking along the river side. A colored man passed me. He could hardly move along. It was evident that no auctioneer could have warranted him to be "sound and strong."

Two other negroes were walking along. One of them pointed to the slow man, and said, grinning as he said it:

"Dat dare fellow am as ill as if he were one of de white pop'lation."

Now this was very far from a compliment to "de white pop'lation," as the cause of the fellow's lameness was evident enough, and said nothing very flattering for his moral character.

I went up to the chuckler.

"Now, old follow, what were you saying?"

The negro grinned, laughed, and chuckled alternately for several minutes before answering:

"Oh, er-r-er-he-he-he-eee!" he laughed, "I was saying dat de white pop'lation would be makin' some remarks on dat 'ar nigger."

"Oh! oh!" I answered, "old fellow, how can you lie so?"

"Oh no, I isn't massa," said the old jolly-looking slave, as he relapsed into a fit of chuckling, interspersed by ejaculations of very broken English.[6]

"Are you a slave, old fellow?"

"Oh, yes, massa," said the chuckler.

"How old are you?"

"Sixty, massa," he replied. "I's eighteen when Jefferson war President, and dat war in 1812;[7] I mind 'bout de war. De regiments camped on dat hill. I carried de wood for dem."

"Have you been a slave ever since?"

"Yes, massa, and long afore dat."

"Would you like to be free?"

The chuckling laugh was again put in full blast. He seemed to use it for the purpose that young ladies reserve their swoons for—to avoid continuing disagreeable conversation; or, that Senator Douglas[8] uses footpad language[9] on the stump for—to avoid the answering of disagreeable questions.

"No, massa,"—a long chuckle—"I'd not like to be free. In de North, de free colored pop'lation isn't able to get 'long widout eating one anoder."

"Who told you that?" I inquired.

"De masters of de ships from dar." (He was a stevedore.)

"You wouldn't like to be free, eh?" I replied, in a jovial tone, as I poked him in the ribs, "what a lying scamp you are, old fellow!"

Hardly had I done so, before I had a realizing experience of the profundity of Shakspeare's philosophy:

> "One dig i' th' ribs, good, my lord,
> Makes white and colored men akin."
> *Julius Caesar Hannibal's edition.*[10]

He threw off his dissimulation, dismissed his grins and his chuckles, looked grave, and said,

"Well, massa, you's a funny man—dat am a fact. I's *would* like to be free; but it's no use, massa—it's no use. I's a slave, and I's been one sixty years, and I 'specs to die in bondage."

"Do all the colored people you know want to be free?"

"*Oh, yes,* massa," he said firmly, "*they all does,* OF COURSE."

I had a long conversation with him: he spoke seriously, gave direct and explicit answers to all my questions, and God-blessed me at parting.

In North Carolina, then, I have had long and confidential conversations with at least a score of slaves. They all stated, with one exception, that not only they, but all their acquaintances, were discontented with their present condition. He that hath slaves let him think! Negroes have all the fierce passions of white men, and there is a limit set by Deity Himself to human endurance of oppression.[11]

TALKS WITH WHITES.

"How do you think the negroes feel on the subject of slavery?" I asked of a carpenter in Wilmington. "Contented?"

"Oh,"—a very long oh—"yes, they're all content. How could they better themselves? I know what the North is. I've travelled all over York and the New England States. All that abolition outcry is only interest. What does the North care for niggers? Look at them in New York, the poor, scourged, driven, kicked, and cuffed wretches."[12]

I had a talk also with a German who had lived in Wilmington five years. He was an abolitionist.

"At Richmond," I said, "I was told that many of the poorer citizens—those who did not own slaves—were secret abolitionists. Is it so here?"

The reply was very decided.

"Yes, sir. Look there," he said—it was Sunday—"look at that girl walking a long way behind her master and mistress, who're going to church, just exactly as if she was a dog."

"Do you think that the majority of the classes I mentioned, in this city, are secret abolitionists?"

"Oh, YES," he said, with excessive emphasis.

A SLAVE PEN.

I visited one *very* peculiar institution in Wilmington—a house where negroes, or rather slaves, of both sexes are kept for sale.[13] There were dozens of the poor wretches squatting or walking about the yard.

As I entered it, I saw a colored girl go up to a young male chattel, put her arms, in the most affectionate manner, around his neck, stand unsteadily on tiptoe, and salute his lips with the long lingering kiss of a lover. I mention this incident for the benefit of Northern gentlemen, whose sweethearts, to use a newspaper phrase, are "respectfully requested to please copy" this admirable fashion. That it is of lowly origin is no reason for rejecting it.

The Articles on sale at this establishment were of every shade of color, from the almost white to the altogether black. Yet—"Christ died for all?"[14]

There was one man with sharp features, fine blue eyes, and a most intelligent-looking face. He was what I have heard called a saddle–leather-colored negro. He asked me if I would buy him?

Poor fellow! I hadn't quite change enough to change his condition.

There was a black girl, with an infant nearly white, having blue eyes and straight hair. I learned the mother's history. She had lived in a family at Richmond, Virginia. She there became acquainted with a young American, to whom, in time, she bore a daughter. Her master was so enraged, when he discovered her condition, that he swore he would sell her South. The author of her misfortune offered to buy her; but the master of the woman, under whose quivering heart the young man's child was beating, with demoniacal sternness rejected the proffered reparation: and he sold both the mother and the unborn babe to the dreaded Southern Traders.

Defend the institution that caused this most infernal outrage, ye "national" ministers of the Most Just God—struggle priestfullly, hand in hand, against its philanthropic assailants, and, verily, you shall have your reward.

Stir up the fires, Beelzebub![15]

NOTES

1. This chapter appeared as the second half of the same third John Ball, Jr. letter that was the source for chapter 3. The first sentence of the original source differed slightly from that in the *Roving Editor*. It read:

> The next two individuals may be classed together, as both gave me the same answers, and as both manifested the same Saxonic restlessness under wrong. [Boston *Liberator,* September 1, 1854]

2. The colony of Virginia in 1662 was the first to declare that all children would inherit the status of their slave mothers. This rule, eventually established in all slave states, substituted the ancient Roman legal practice in place of the opposite principle of English common law. Miller and Smith, *Dictionary of Afro-American Slavery,* 393.

3. This paragraph did not appear in the original John Ball, Jr. letter.

4. In the third John Ball, Jr. letter, this exchange ended somewhat differently, and Redpath added an interesting observation:

> "Good bye," said the slave mother, as she shook my hand; "God bless you, massa! God bless you!"
>
> John Mitchell! I have associated with hundreds of your countrymen from my childhood; I know how affectionate they are by nature; alas! also, how heartless they are when they are taught that it is their duty to feel no compassion. Desist, for dear Liberty's sake, from teaching them to be stony statues in Irishmen's apparel! The majority of the "fat negroes," believe me, whom you spoke of so contemptuously, have as warm hearts, ay, and as strong intellects, too, as the majority of the inhabitants of your own Emerald Isle. Reserve, I pray you, the vitrol of the vial of your wrath for that tyrannical aristocracy, whose "bloody hoof" is so often spoken of in the prophecies and phillipics of Young Ireland! The slave is miserable enough already; if

you cannot act as the good Samaritan did, do not, for Humanity's sake, pour your "vitriol" or thrust your "pikes" into his bleeding body! [Boston *Liberator*, September 1, 1854]

5. This poem did not appear in the original third John Ball, Jr. letter. Boston *Liberator*, September 1, 1854.

6. In the John Ball, Jr. letter, Redpath added a footnote at this point to discuss the language skills of southern blacks:

Many of the colored people speak excellent English—a few words and phrases excepted. In relating conversations, I have given their own language, as often as I remembered it; but I have never attempted to translate what I remembered of their answers in the proper dialect into Ethopian-English. I have, no doubt, made many *verbal* errors in writing their answers after a few hours had elapsed; but I have been VERY careful to preserve the *spirit* of them. [Boston *Liberator*, September 1, 1854]

7. Thomas Jefferson (1743–1826) served as the third president of the United States from 1801 to 1809. Another Virginian, James Madison, was president in 1812. *DAB*, 10:17–35.

8. Stephen A. Douglas.

9. In medieval England, the term "footpad" designated a highwayman who robbed on foot. *Oxford English Dictionary*, 12 vols. (Oxford, 1978), 4:408.

10. These lines do not appear in William Shakespeare's play *Julius Caesar*. A roughly similar passage occurs in his *King Lear*, act 3, scene 6, line 69.

11. At this point in the third John Ball, Jr. letter, Redpath supplied the following short description of Wilmington, North Carolina:

THE CITY OF WILMINGTON.

The town or city of Wilmington contains about eight or nine thousand inhabitants during the winter months, and about one thousand fewer in summer.

Its principal features are sandy streets, tar, pitch and turpentine barrels, and lumber and timber. It supports two daily and one tri-weekly newspaper. The Whig party, I believe, is represented by two of these three journals.

During the year 1853, the chief exports were—of spirits of turpentine, 115,174 barrels, of forty-two gallons each, estimated at $2,660,519.40; of rosin, 380,459 barrels, worth about $525,573; of tar, 26,130 barrels; of pitch, 7823 barrels; of timber, P.P., 1,115,798 feet; of lumber, P.P., 88,157,950 feet; of rice, 7,976 1/2 casks; of pea nuts or ground peas, 69,811 bushels; of corn, 2950 bushels; and of flour, 1485 barrels. [Boston *Liberator*, September 1, 1854]

12. Redpath has omitted the following paragraph that appeared at this point in the John Ball, Jr. letter:

Reader! did you ever see any colored men miserable, kicked, scourged and cuffed in New York? I never did. The answer of the mechanic, however, is an embodiment of an opinion entertained very extensively in Virginia and North Carolina—perhaps throughout the entire South. [Boston *Liberator*, September 1, 1854]

13. Although it lacked the large slave market of cities such as Richmond and Charleston, Wilmington still conducted a noteworthy interstate slave trade. The firm of D. J. Southerland and James C. Coleman, with a second office in Mobile, Alabama, was the leading slave trading company in the city in the 1850s. Frederic Bancroft, *Slave Trading in the Old South* (1931; New York, 1959), 237–38; 38; Guion Griffis Johnson, *Ante-Bellum North Carolina: A Social History* (Chapel Hill, 1937), 473–74.

14. A close paraphrase of 1 Cor. 15:3 and 1 Pet. 3:18. This biblical passage did not appear in the third John Ball, Jr. letter. Boston *Liberator*, September 1, 1854.

15. In place of this short paragraph, Redpath concluded the third John Ball, Jr. letter with the following section, which is not reproduced in the *Roving Editor:*

I visited yet another institution—the Ladies' Benevolent Society. The Constitution of this philanthropic association is similar to its sister societies in New York. Its object is, 'the relief of the sick poor in the vicinity and in the city of Wilmington.'

They also aid poor persons by giving them work. Thus: A poor woman applies for sewing at the office; the materials are furnished her, and the work paid for when finished. The ladies obtain the orders for work from rich families and planters from the country. The work is sold at their store, which is attended, by the way—this is a good custom, too—by the prettiest young lady in the State.

This plan is a very praiseworthy one, as it at once abolishes absolute able-bodied poverty, and does not break up households by making it necessary—as in English workhouses, and even in some American philanthropic institutions—for the pauper to become an inmate of the establishment.

The Maine Law is likely to gain a victory in this State. Strong efforts are being made by the friends of Temperance, who are aided, singularly enough, but for a very apparent reason, by precisely the antetheses of its adherents in the North—the slaveholders. They want the negroes to be sober men!

I remain,—rather exhausted from writing so much, but in excellent health, strength, and spirits,—

Yours, in hatred of the bonds of the slave,

                                                    JOHN BALL, JR.

Boston *Liberator,* September 1, 1854.

V.

IN SOUTH CAROLINA.

I LOVE Charleston! I spent a fortnight there—one of the happiest periods of my life.[1] Perhaps it was the aspect of the city—its thoroughly English appearance and construction, its old-time customs, its genial climate—for there were roses in full bloom in its public gardens when there were snow storms at the North; perhaps it was the English architecture, the merry peal of bells, the watchman chaunting the time of night, the uniformed patrol[2]—which I soon learned to hate—all of them reminding me of my boyhood days, that cast a spell around my spirit during my sojourn there, and which now casts a spell over my recollections of the city of Calhoun;[3] but, be this as it may, in spite of my stern and inflexible anti-slavery zeal, I would rather to-day be a sojourner in Charleston than a resident of any other city on the Continent.

Did I say a spell? Not of idleness, however. I attended to my business. Here is an extract from a letter that I wrote at the time:[4]

"The city jail is an old brick building, of the Scotch Presbyterian style of architecture.[5]

"Close beside it is another massive building, resembling a feudal castle in its external form—the infamous Bastile or the Spanish Inquisition[6] in its internal management—an edifice which is destined to be levelled to the earth amid the savage yells of insurgent negroes and the shrieks of widowed ladies, whose husbands shall have been justly massacred by wholesale; or else amid the cheers of true chivalry of the age, the assailants of slavery and the friends of the bondmen, and the applause of the fair daughters of the Southern States. God grant that the beautiful women of the South may be the first to demand the demolition of this execrable edifice; God grant that they may be spared the misery of seeing their husbands and their children slaughtered by their slaves; but God grant, over and above all, that the Sugar House of Charleston,[7] by some means, or at any costs may speedily be levelled to the earth that it pollutes by its practices and presence.

"The first of man's natural rights is the right to live: without liberty there is no life, but existence only. If any man unjustly deprived me of my liberty, and I had it in my power to kill him, it would, I conceive, be a very grave crime to permit him to live and enslave me."

BULLY BROOKS AND COLORED CONTENTMENT.

"And such," I wrote—"let the howling Mr. Preston S. Brooks,[8] and the Northern sycophants of the slaveholders, say as they will—*such are the sentiments of the majority of the slaves in the city of Charleston.*"

Mr. Brooks was a nobody at that time. But I had just read, in the *Charleston Mercury,* a speech of his, wherein he stated, with an audacity which is peculiar to the Southern politicians, that the slaves were happy and eminently contented with their unfortunate condition. The *Mercury,* on the strength of this speech, predicted a glorious future for him! The eulogist has since fallen in a duel,[9] and the eulogized is lying in an assassin's grave. Fit future for a liar, a despot, and a coward! But let us not linger here. Let us spit upon his grave and pass on, leaving his soul in the custody of the infernal gods!

At Richmond and at Wilmington, I continued, I found the slaves discontented, but despondingly resigned to their fate. At Charleston I found them morose and savagely brooding over their wrongs. They know and they dread the slaveholder's power; they are afraid to assail it without first effecting a combination among themselves, which the ordinances of the city, that are sternly enforced, and the fear of a traitor among them, prevent. But if the guards who now keep nightly watch were to be otherwise employed—if the roar of hostile cannon was to be heard by the slaves, or a hostile fleet was seen sailing up the bay of Charleston—then, as surely as God lives, would the sewers of the city be instantly filled with the blood of the slave masters. I have had long and confidential conversations with great numbers of the slaves here, who trusted me because I talked with them, and acted toward them as a friend, and I speak advisedly when I say that they are already ripe for a rebellion, and that South Carolina *dares not* (even if the North was willing to permit her) to secede from this Union of States. Her only hope of safety from wholesale slaughter is THE UNION. Laugh the secessionists to scorn, ye Union-loving sons of the North, for the negroes are prepared "to cement the Federal compact" once more—and really it needs it—with "the blood of despots," and their own *then* free blood, too, if the "resistance-to-tyrants"[10] doctrine in practice shall call for the solemn and voluntary sacrifice.

The Sugar House of Charleston is a building created for the purpose of punishing and selling slaves in. I visited it. It is simply a prison with a treadmill, a work yard, putrid privies, whipping posts and a *brine barrel* attached. There are, I think, three corridors. Many of the cells are perfectly dark. They are all very small.

What, think you, is the mode of conducting this peculiar institution?

If a planter arrives in the city with a lot of slaves for sale, he repairs to the Sugar House and places them in custody, and there they are kept until disposed of, as usual—"by auction for cash to the highest bidder."

If any slaveholder, from any or from no cause, desires to punish his human property, but is too sensitive, or what is far more probable, too lazy to inflict the chastisement himself—he takes *it* (the man, woman or child), to the Sugar House, and simply orders *how* he desires it to be punished; and, without any trial—without any questions asked or explanations given, the command is implicitly obeyed by the officers of the institution. A small sum is paid for the board of the incarcerated.

If any colored person is found out of doors after ten o'clock at night, without a ticket of leave from its owner, the unfortunate wanderer is taken to the Sugar House and kept there till morning; when, if the master pays one dollar fine, the slave is liberated; but, if he refuses to do so, the prisoner is tied hand and foot and lashed before he or she is set at liberty. For women are whipped as frequently as men.

And yet the city which supports these official Haynaus,[11] regards itself as one of the burning lights of our modern civilization! Miserable race of woman-whippers—worthy constituents of the assassin Brooks—fit men to celebrate his memory and to revile, with worse than fiendish glee, the sufferings of his pure-hearted victim, Charles Sumner!*[12]

*I never spoke to any poor whites of this State, in order to learn their feelings towards slavery and slaveholders. Yet it may be interesting to the friends of the greatest of Massachusetts' Senators to know, as an indication of sentiment, that there is a native-born child of

STORY OF A SLAVE.

The concluding portion of the narrative that I subjoin, related to me by a slave, whose answers I took down in short hand as he uttered them, will serve to show how the name of the Sugar House has become a word of terror to the colored race in South Carolina and the adjoining slave States. I first heard of it and its horrors at Richmond, from the colored storekeeper of whom I have spoken at considerable length. Of course I alter the real names of the different parties mentioned in the statement. I omit, also, many of my questions:

"My name is Pete Barclay.[13] I was born in Newberg, South Carolina. I'm 'bout tirty years old now."

"Why don't you know your exact age?"

"No, sah," said the slave. "Let me see. I'll tell you 'xactly how old I'm now. I've bin two years here—not quite two years till nex' month—and I know Nicholas Smith—I seen him only de oder day; he says I's 'xactly de same age as he is. I'm 'xactly thirty-two years old. Dat's his age."

"Is he free?"

"Yes, sah, he's a free man. He was *raised* where I *growed.*"**

"Is he a white man?"

"Oh, yes, sah, he's a white man, he's not a colored man at all. He knows everytin'—more dan I do—he kin read and write, and all dat sort o' thing, you know. I' a sister and a mother in Carolina, 'bout 130 miles on the cars, as I'm told. I was *raised* by Mr. Kenog. He's bin dead for years; I wish I was wid him now. Dat was de first man dat *raised* me."

"Did you ever know your father and mother?"

"Oh, yes; I knowed dem like a book. Mother died four years afore I came to Columbus—I've bin here two years—four and two is six isn't it, sah?"

I assumed the responsibility of answering in the affirmative.

"Well, she has been dead about dat time. It may not be quite so long, though."

"Who's Kenog, sir?"

"He was a farmer in Newberg," said the slave.

"Did your father belong to him?

"No, sah."

"Was your father a slave?"

South Carolina parents, who reside in the capital, named after our torch-tongued orator, Charles Sumner.

**Long after this sentence was spoken, I found a world of sad histories in this accidental utterance. Raised—and growed!

"Yes, sah, and my moder too."

"Was your mother ever sold?"

"No, sah, my mother neber was sold; she was raised dere and died dere."

"How many children had she?"

"I can't say 'xactly," replied the slave, "let me count jist how many she had."

He commenced with his thumb to count the number of his brothers and sisters on his fingers.

"Maria," he said, "dat's my sister dat I got a letter from home, the other day; Alice—she's dead—dat's two; Lea—I never seen her—she's dead—dat's three; I've three sisters. Wash, dat's one; Hannibal, dat's two; Major and Jackson, dat's—let me, me—aint it four, sah?"

"Yes."

"Den, I've dree sisters and four broders—dat's—dat's a"——

He could not finish the sentence. The intricate problem was beyond his arithmetical ken.

"Yes," he continued, in reply to my questions, "sometimes slaves has got two names, and sometimes only one. My fader belonged to a widow woman, named Lucy Roberts. I knowed him as well as I know dat candle.

This conversation occurred in a house occupied partly by colored people, during candle light.

"Dat's how I came to be called Roberts," he said, "he took her name. After I left Roberts I belonged to Richardson. I was about six years old when I went to Mr. Richardson. I was a present from Roberts to him; dat's how I came to belong to him. I stayed wid him till 'bout two years since—not quite two years; it's not two years till May. Den I was sold to dis ole man, my boss now."

It is unnecessary to say "dat dis ole man, my boss now," was not present at this nocturnal meeting of Southern colored and Northern uncolored woolly-heads.

"What sort of a boss is he?" I inquired.

The answer was brief enough, and as bitter as brief:

"He's de meanest ole scamp goin'."

"Are the colored people of your acquaintance all discontented with their present condition?"

"Yes, sah," he replied, "all on 'em; I knows lots and lots on 'em since I came here, and I's a stranger in the city: I's not bin quite two years yet—not two years till nex' month, sah—and all dat I does know *wants to be free very bad,* I tell ye, *and may be will fight before long if they don't get freedom somehow.* Dis country is de meanest country in de world."

"Did you ever live outside of South Carolina?"

"No, sah," he said, nothing abashed by his recent decision, "I never has bin out on it, but I knows dat nothin' could be worse. I's been knocked about five or six years now very bad; but I won't stand it much longer; I'll run away the firs' chance I gets. Massa, is a colored man safe in the State of New York?"

I replied that I believed that it now would be impossible, without a desperate and bloody contest between the municipal authorities and the people of New York, for a Southron to rethrust a slave as a brand *into* the burning, after he had once trod the soil of Manhattan Island. I thought that perhaps he could have done so as late as a year ago, but that he could not do it since the recent anti-slavery revival. (Abolitionism, at that time, had penetrated the theatres, and even the pulpits were belching forth anathemas against it.)[14]

He spoke of one John Bouldon,[15] an intimate friend of his, who had been legally kidnapped from New York city after successfully effecting his escape from slavery.

"Dey brought him back," he said, "but he looked brave and game. Oh, he looked well, sah," he added, with enthusiastic energy. "Dey wouldn't let us talk to him; we only see him through de grating of de jail. Dey took him away one morning—he came wid de sheriff of New York—and I heerd tell of somebody havin' raised $1,500 or $15,000 to buy him—yes, I believe it *was* $1,500—but it wasn't a high price, sah; he was a first-rate tailor."

"Do you know anything," I asked, "about the Sugar House here? A colored man at Richmond advised me to go and see it. I've been there, but the officer who showed me round seemed to think that my absence would be as much for the good of the house as my company. He showed me all of the cells, because he could n't well help himself; but he did n't give me any information."

(On entering the yard of this Inferno—the day was excessively sultry—I was almost suffocated by the first inhalation of its atmosphere. The odor arising from the privies, *which were in close proximity to the treadmill,* rendered the atmosphere insufferably corrupt. There were eight persons on the treadmill at the time inhaling the poisonous air.)[16]

"You could n't have axed a better person, sah," said the slave, "dan me. I's bin twice dere. De first time dat I was dere I was put in by my master for playin' at cards. He came up one night and caught us—a few boys and myself—playin' in a room."

"'I don't want my boys to do that,' he said, and den he went down stairs.

"Three days passed, and I thought it war all over. But it warn't. On de fourth day, he came into my bedroom afore I got up and put a pair of handcuff on me and tuk me to de Sugar House. I was kept dare in a dark cell—de only light I had came through five gimlet holes—for four days, and I was paddled twice."

"Paddled!" I repeated, "What do you mean?"

"Oh," he said, "dey whip us with a paddle."

"What's that?" I asked.

"A paddle," he rejoined, "is a piece of board 'bout three fingers wide and half an inch deep wid holes in it. I got twenty de firs' day and twenty de last. Dey put in a kind of drawer wid hominy in it, nothing else, once a day, and dat was our vittals. I couldn't taste any de firs' day at all."

"What was your second offence?" I asked.

"Nothin', massa, nothin' at all. I got leave to go to the races, and I met some friends dare, and when I came back I was half an hour too late. He put me to the Sugar House agin. I was kept dar two days and got twenty-five lashes."

"How many at each time?"

"Fifteen bof times, massa."

"Two fifteens make thirty, not twenty-five," I ventured to suggest.

"Does it, massa?"—he pondered for a few seconds with a gravity becoming the importance of the subject—"so it does. Well, I got thirty. *Den after dey paddle dem,* you know, *dey wash their backs with salt water.*"

I astonished my colored friend by starting from the chair in which I had been lounging.

"Great God!" I exclaimed, "you don't mean to say that in earnest!"

"Massa," he repeated, "it am as true as I'm sitting here."

"Will you swear that!" I asked.

"Massa," he repeated slowly and solemnly, "it am God's truth; I'll swear it wherever you like; dere's hundreds beside me who would do it if you axed them. De colored people here know it too well, sah."[17]

POSTSCRIPT.—Hon. Humphrey Marshall,[18] of Kentucky, in his defence of Matt Ward,[19] thus describes another efficient means of saving grace invented for the maintenance of the blessed "Missionary Institution:"

"The strap, Gentlemen, you are probably aware, is an instrument of refined modern torture, ordinarily used in whipping slaves. By the old system, the cow-hide—a severe punishment—cut and lacerated them so badly as to almost spoil their sale when brought to the lower markets. But this strap, I am told, is a vast improvement in the art of whipping negroes; and, it is said, that one of them may be punished by it within one inch of his life, and yet he will come out with no visible injury, and his skin will be as smooth and polished as a peeled onion!"

The paddle is a large, thin ferule of wood, in which many small holes are bored; when a blow is struck, these holes from the rush and partial exhaustion of air in them, act like diminutive cups, and the continued application of the instrument has been described to me to produce precisely such a result as that attributed to the strap by Mr. Marshall.

NOTES

1. Redpath's visit to Charleston to attend a southern commercial convention in April 1854 is described in chapter 7.

2. In the 1850s Charleston employed a force of one hundred armed and uniformed guards to patrol the city in the evenings in two watches. The memory of the 1822 Vesey uprising conspiracy remained strong in Charleston, and the main duty of the night watch was to control the city's black population. William H. Pease and Jane H. Pease, *The Web of Progress: Private Values and Public Styles in Boston and Charleston, 1828–1843* (New York, 1985), 100–101.

3. The leading defender of southern political interests for most of his lifetime, John Caldwell Calhoun (1782–1850) of South Carolina served as a U.S. congressman, senator, vice president, secretary of war, and secretary of state. *DAB*, 3:411–19.

4. The material for this chapter originally appeared in the fourth John Ball, Jr. letter, published in the Boston *Liberator*, September 8, 1854. That letter, however, contained the following opening paragraphs:

A JOURNEY TO CHARLESTON. NO. IV.

BY THE WANDERING GENTILE.

Talks with the Slaves in South Carolina—the Sugar House.

CHARLESTON HOTEL, S.C., April 10.

FELLOW-GENTILES—I arrived in this, the chosen land of the chivalry of the South, on last Tuesday morning, in the steamer Gladiator, from Wilmington, which made her last trip "on this occasion only"; and, by doing so, caused the regular line of steamships between that port and this city to make its exit, with great eclat, from that vast theatre of which the celebrated and venerable Mr. Neptune is the able stage manager. The Gladiator paddled well her part, and arrived two hours earlier than the steamer of the same line, which started from the same port on the same hour that we did. Alas! like other faithful servants of the public, Away Down South, she is to be sold "by auction, (for cash,) to the highest bidder."

Charleston is a pleasant city; its streets, if not spacious, are well paved and clean; its public buildings are numerous and massive, and many of its private "palace-mansions," like Jacob's loved Rachel, are very good for the eyes to look upon. Its theatre is much superior, as an edifice, to either the National, Barnum's, Burton's, or Wallack's of New York.

The Irish have a splendid building here—the Hibernian Hall.

5. Located on Back Street, adjacent to the Marine Hospital, the Charleston jail was located near a swampy marsh along the Ashley River in the western section of the city. Pease and Pease, *Web of Progress*, 6, 8.

6. Popularly regarded as a symbol of monarchal tyranny, the Bastille was a fortified Parisian prison that was captured by a revolutionary mob on July 14, 1789. The Inquisition was an ecclesiastical court created by the Spanish monarchs in the late fifteenth century to

enforce religious conformity in their far-flung territories. William Langer, *Political and Social Upheaval* (New York, 1969), 346–50; Arthur G. Dickens, *The Counter Reformation* (London, 1968), 104, 118–19.

7. This term for the official place of detention and punishment for Charleston's slaves had been in usage at least as early as the end of the American Revolution. An actual sugar factory before becoming a house of correction, the building was located at the west end of Broad Street. Thomas Petigru Lesesne, *Landmarks of Charleston; Including Description of an Incomparable Stroll* (Richmond, Va., 1939), 96; Mathews, *Dictionary of Americanisms,* 2:1674.

8. Redpath refers to U.S. congressman Preston Smith Brooks (1819–57) of South Carolina. He had served as a captain in the Mexican War before winning election to Congress in 1852. Brooks's infamous attack on Massachusetts senator Charles Sumner on May 22, 1856, had not occurred at the time the original John Ball, Jr. letters were published. *DAB,* 2:88–89.

9. In 1856 William Robinson Taber, editor of the *Charleston Mercury,* died in a duel with Edward Magrath, whose brother had been attacked in a *Mercury* article by Taber's first cousin, Edmund Rhett, Jr. Edmund's brother, Robert Barnwell Rhett, Jr., became the editor of the *Mercury.* C. Vann Woodward and Elisabeth Muhlenfield, eds., *The Private Mary Chesnut: The Unpublished Civil War Diaries* (New York, 1984), 50.

10. Thomas Jefferson used the motto "Rebellion to tyrants is obedience to God" on his personal seal. Jefferson believed Benjamin Franklin to have authored the line. Julian P. Boyd, ed., *The Papers of Thomas Jefferson* (Princeton, N.J., 1950–), 1:667–79, 16:xxxii.

11. Redpath perhaps refers to the biblical figure Haman, a Greek in the hire of the Persians, infamous for his persecution of all Jews. David Noel Freedman, *The Anchor Bible Dictionary,* 6 vols. (New York, 1992), 3:33.

12. Originally a Whig, Boston lawyer Charles Sumner (1811–74) joined the Free Soil party in 1848 and won election to the U.S. Senate in 1851. An uncompromising critic of slavery and slaveholders, Sumner's personal attack on South Carolina senator Andrew P. Butler provoked a brutal physical assault on the floor of the Senate by Representative Preston Brooks in 1856. During his three-year convalescence, Sumner became a martyr to the young Republican party. After returning to his Senate seat, Sumner was a strong advocate of emancipation during the Civil War and black rights during Reconstruction. David Donald, *Charles Sumner and the Coming of the Civil War* (New York, 1960); *DAB,* 18:208–14.

13. In the fourth John Ball, Jr. letter, Redpath originally identified this slave by the name Peter Roberts. He apparently forgot this editorial change in the *Roving Editor,* because he refers to the slave by his last name later in this chapter. Boston *Liberator,* September 8, 1854.

14. In the fourth John Ball, Jr. letter, Redpath described the abolitionist revival in New York City in greater detail:

> I replied that I believed it would now be impossible, without a desperate and bloody contest between the municipal authorities and people of the city of New York, for a slaveholder to pluck a slave "as a brand *into* the burning," after he had once trod the soil of Manhattan Island, and that no attempt would ever be made to execute the Fugitive Slave Law in our commercial metropolis. I said that perhaps a slaveholder might have succeeded in catching his "property," as late as a year ago, but that he certainly could not do so since "Uncle Tom," Purdy, and Nebraska Bill, and the Bowery (stage) Boys, and "Eva" Howard, and "Topsy" Dawes, and the dramatic Aitkens, and Stevens, and the scenic artist Rogers, and Free Soil Phineas, with his compromised "Cabin," had commenced their anti-slavery campaign. [Boston *Liberator,* September 8, 1854]

15. The individual to whom this slave probably refers was John Bolding, a young black

tailor from Poughkeepsie, New York. In August 1851 Bolding was arrested on the charge of being a runaway slave from South Carolina, and a Fugitive Slave Act commissioner ordered that he be remanded to his owners. Wilburt H. Siebert, *The Underground Railroad from Slavery to Freedom* (1898; New York, 1968), 241; Campbell, *Slave Catchers,* 200.

16. Redpath omitted the following paragraph from this point in the John Ball, Jr. letter:

I dropped my pencil as I gave my description of it, and did not lift it up again—for the very first sentences he uttered filled me with such horror of the Sugar House, that I forgot the writer in the man. [Boston *Liberator,* September 8, 1854]

17. Redpath's John Ball, Jr. letter here included the following paragraphs not reprinted in the *Roving Editor:*

I had just returned from the Theatre, where I had seen at least one hundred lovely ladies—many of them models of womanly beauty—looking all so happy and so good, and laughing so merrily, as the pit roared loudly at the comic gestures of Gabriel Ravel and his troupe of dancers, that a misanthrope in gazing at them would undoubtedly have felt the spirit of old Simon going out of him. For the ladies of Charleston, although they have a rather haughty look, are a noble race of women.

An alarm of fire gave me an opportunity of suddenly leaving my colored companions. I went out to walk and to ponder.

How is it, I asked myself, that this infernal institution exists, when surrounded by so much nobility of nature? At Wilmington, a philanthropic lady told me, mildly, that Northern abolitionists had no idea how many and how friendly the bonds were that united the slave to his master. As she said so, I felt inclined to reply, that perhaps Southern slaveholders had no idea of how many and how revolutionary the reasons are that are daily tending to array them one against the other. I did not say so, however, for the lady was a slaveholder, and I was in her house.

I obtained, I think, a correct solution of this question in the conduct of the little stout man with the white coat on, whom I mentioned in my description of the slave holders of Richmond. I read it in his indignant eye.

A Puritannical mind, on seeing a man angrily complaining of the conduct of a human being, to whose persons or services he had no right whatever, in running away from his prison-farm to nature's liberty, would have knit his brows, and openly or secretly anathematized and loathed him. A humorist would have laughed at the comicality of such conduct. But a philosopher would have tried to trace the source of such an evil. I adopted the latter mode of procedure. This man, I soliloquized, is not by any means a bad man: he appears to be a hospitable, trustworthy and generous person. His conduct, viewed in one light, is virtuous: he is indignant, as every man should be, at one who he supposes to be a criminal. If the man was a real instead of a mere conventional criminal, his indignation would be just. But as the runaway was merely a breaker of Southern society's laws, and may not a violator of Nature's, the error of his master consisted in regarding them as one and inseparable.

Thus, although I say that I wish to see slavery abolished at any cost, even at the cost of a black St. Bartholomew's night, I do not say that even the majority of the slaveholders are depraved men. But the negroes have the right to that liberty to which their masters, who deprive them of it, have none: and if their owners resolutely refuse to set them free, then—let them, without mummering, endure *the approaching massacre.* Men of Carolina! that event, if you continue to oppress the poor as you have hitherto done, is much nearer at hand than you ever imagined.

An owner, who is a St. Clair to his slaves, lately said to me that his negroes *could not* be discontented, because they had no cause of complaint, as he was as kind to them as it was possible for any master to be.

"What right have you to be kind (as you call it) to the slaves?" I asked.

"Sir!" he ejaculated, with an expression of surprise.

"That's my title," I replied. "My dear sir, you don't see that you speak of your kindness as of a possession you had a right to dispense or retain at pleasure. You forget at the outset that the negro is a man—your equal. Now, wouldn't you be very apt to call me out if I were to go about and say, in a condescending tone, that I had always been very kind to you?"

"I don't forget—I deny that the negro is my equal," said the Southron; and thus the conversation dropped.

But I have forgotten, I see, that I intended to write a letter descriptive of effects, and not to investigate their cause.

As my letter is long enough already, I must be brief. I have spent six days now in conversing with colored people here, and I have never yet met *one* who professed to be even contented with, far less to prefer, slavery to freedom. Many, many have I met, who are panting for liberty; *and several who are prepared to risk the chance of failure in an insurrection.* [Boston *Liberator,* September 8, 1854]

18. Scion of a prominent Kentucky family, Humphrey Marshall (1812–72) graduated from West Point in 1832 but resigned his Army commission the following year to pursue a legal career. He was active in the Kentucky state militia and led a volunteer cavalry regiment in the Mexican War. He served in Congress as a Whig from 1849 until President Millard Fillmore sent him as a special U.S. envoy to China in 1852. Marshall returned to Congress from 1855 to 1859 as a "Know-Nothing." After serving as a brigadier general in the Confederate army, he was elected to the southern Congress in 1864. *DAB,* 12:310–11; Mark Mayo Boatner III, *The Civil War Dictionary* (New York, 1959), 513–14.

19. Kentucky native Matt Flournoy Ward (1826–62) gained some minor fame as a travel writer in the early 1850s. In 1854 Ward and his brother Robert were tried for the shooting of Louisville schoolteacher W.H.G. Butler, who allegedly abused their younger brother, William, a student. A defense team led by John J. Crittenden and Thomas F. Marshall—not Humphrey Marshall, as Redpath asserts—defended Ward in a nationally publicized trial and won an acquittal. *Appleton's Cyclopaedia of American Biography,* 6 vols. (New York, 1888–89), 6:352; *New York Daily Times,* April 24, 27, and 29, May 18 and 24, June 26, 1854; Boston *Liberator,* May 26, 1854.

VI.

SALT WATER PHILANTHROPY.

THE last revelation of the slave was so revolting that I hesitated to believe it, until it was confirmed by a cloud of colored witnesses, many of whom had been subjected in their own persons to the horrible and heathenish punishment. It shocked me beyond anything that I had ever heard.

This shows, I found, how Northern people will persist in seeing Southern institutions and Southern customs from a false and unfriendly point of view! Bless you! to wash the lacerated backs of the slaves with brine is *not* by any means an indication of a cruel disposition!

This is how I found it out:

I was talking with a Southron about slavery, and told him, in reply to his statement that the negro bondmen were the happiest of human beings, that I had heard that sometimes after they were whipped their backs were immediately washed with salt water.

"I know it," he said; "what of it?"

"I think it is infernal barbarity—that's all."

"Why, no, sir," he said, "it's *philanthropy* to do it."

I turned round. He was perfectly grave. He was not speaking ironically. I was amazed, but said nothing.

"Don't you know," he asked, "that in this warm climate, if the master were to leave his slave's back just as it is after being whipped, that mortification would ensue and the nigger die?"

Oh, philanthropy! how lovely art thou even to the tyrant when thy ways are the ways of—selfish interest! I was satisfied.

THE ANTI-GINGER GIRL. [1]

One morning, in walking up Calhoun street, I saw a pretty colored girl standing at a garden-gate, and of course went over and had a talk with her on "things in general and slavery in particular." She was a finely formed, Saxon-faced girl, with a sparkling, roguish-looking eye. Her hair was black and glossy, and all her features were Caucasian; but her complexion was yellow, and therefore she was a slave.

Did you ever try to escape?" I asked her.

She answered, but I did not hear her distinctly.

"Oh, you did," I said, in reply to her supposed remark. "In Virginia, eh? Did you come from that State?"

"No, sir," returned the yellow girl, with a merry glance and a laugh, "I did not say dat; I said I never tried, 'kase dey would catch me agin, and den *I'd get ginger.*"

From the manner in which she uttered the dissyllable ginger, I inferred that she did not relish that article of commerce.

After a few further remarks, during the course of which she hinted that her mistress *might* be induced to sell her, and that she would have no objection—in point of fact, rather the reverse—to become my property, I bade the pretty, lively female slave farewell.[2] She, like nearly all her class, was evidently the mistress of a white man. Evangelizing institution!

THE GOOD UN AND NICE OLE GAL.

I was leaning on the outside of the fence of a garden, a few miles from Charleston, in which an old man of color was working.

"Then you've had—how many masters in all?" I asked.

"Five, massa, al'degeder," said the slave, touching his cap politely, as he had done a dozen times at least during the preceding three or four minutes.

"Never mind touching your hat," I said. "How many children have you had?"

"I's had eight by my firs' wife, and five by de second, and five by dis ole woman."

He pointed to a negress who had just entered the garden. Her wool was grey, but she appeared to be twenty years, at least, her husband's junior. I saluted her.

"You ever been married more than once?"

"Oh! yes, massa," said the silver-grey woolly-head. "I's bin married once before."

"Had any children?"

"Yes, massa," she said, "I's had five by dis ole man, and seven by de last un."

"You are both Christians?" I asked.

"Yes, massa," she said, "we goes to de church; we's not members ob de church, kase we's colored people, and dey won't let us be."

This statement does not hold everywhere. It may be true, however, of South Carolina.[3]

"That's not a great misfortune," I remarked, as I recalled to my recollection a long editorial article that I had lately read in the *North Carolina Baptist Recorder,* entitled, "The Fanaticism of the New England Clergy;"[4] which was written by a professed minister of the gospel of love, for the purpose of proving that Jesus Christ, the friend of oppressed humanity, was a Southern Rights man; and that God, the Father of our race, "whose name is love," had revealed it to be his will that the negro should be, and should be kept as a bondman; and consequently, of course—this was the inference—that sugar houses, treadmills, whips, paddles, brine-barrels, bloodhounds, Millard Fillmores, and "sound national men" should exist to keep them in that debased condition.

"Is it *not* massa?" asked the woman, laughing, "well, I s'pose we kin be Christians widout bein' members ob de church."

"If you have kept all the commandments as well as you have kept the first," I rejoined, in a jocular tone, "multiply, and so forth, you know, you must be Christians of the A No. 1 sect. Eight and five are thirteen, thirteen and five are eighteen; you've had eighteen children, old man, have n't you?"

"Yes, massa," said the old slave, grinning.

"Seven and five are twelve; that's the old woman's share. You've done very well between you, I declare!"

The colored Replenishers roared with laughter.

MARRIAGE AND DIVORCE AMONG SLAVES.

"How long has your first husband been dead?" I asked the woman.

"He isn't dead yet, massa," said the mother of a dozen darkies, "he's livin' yet. I didn't like him, and I neber did; so I tuk up wid my ole man."

"And you like him, do you ?"

"Oh, yes, massa," she said as a prelude to a peal of chuckles." "I's a great deal younger dan he is, but I wouldn't change agin."

"Rather flattering to you, old boy," I said, addressing the male article of traffic; "do you return the compliment?"

"Yes, massa," he said with a laugh, and a loving look at her, "she's a nice ole gal. I's knowed her since she was dat high"—he levelled his hand to within two feet of the ground—"and I knows," he added, "dat she's a good un."

Chuckles, expressive of gratification, followed from the good un, which was succeeded by a history of the ole man's life, but it was uttered in such elaborately broken English, that I could not understand a word of it.[5]

SURPRISING IGNORANCE OF THE SLAVE.

"You say you were owned by an Englishman," I repeated, affecting an ignorance of southern geography, "and that you lived at St. Helena. Was St. Helena an island?"

"Yes, massa."

"The island that Napoleon Bonaparte lived at?"[6]

"Napol'on Bonapard!" he repeated.

"Did you never hear of Napoleon Bonaparte?" I asked.

"No, massa," he returned, "who was him?"

"It is the name of a gentleman, who did a thing or two in Europe," I returned. "But do you know what Europe is?"

"No, massa," said the slave, "*I never heerd on him!*"

I explained that Europe was a State annexable to the United States, and, therefore, destined to be one of them in the good time coming, boys.[7]

CONTENTMENT AND MORALITY.

"Were you married," I continued, "to your present wife by a minister?"

"No, massa, dey neber does de like of dat wid colored people."

(He was mistaken in this particular; for slaves are very often married by the preachers.)

"Then you live together," I suggested, "until you quarrel, and then you separate?"

"Oh, no, not allus," said the woman; "we sometimes quarrels in de day-time, and make all up at night."

Thus is the system of slavery a practical defiance of the Christian doctrine of marriage and divorce.

"Are you content with being in bondage?"

"No, no, massa, indeed," said the old man, "but we can't help ourselves. I neber 'xpects to be free dis side DE LAND."

I turned to the good un:

"The slave-masters," I said, "when they go North, say that you are all contented, and do n't want to be free—is that so?"

" Oh, J—S, NO!" she exclaimed, with a fervency of emphasis, which both amazed and amused me.

WHAT THE BOYS SAY.

I had four confidential conversations with colored mulatto youths in different parts of the city. All of them were very discontented with their condition, and said that all the boys they knew were equally dissatisfied.

I asked one boy—a free boy:

"Do you think that *any* boys, who are slaves, are content?"

"There may be one or two," he answered, "but *they* haven't got any sense."

THE WILLING EXILE.

I rode one day several miles with a free man of color, and conversed with him all the way.

At the age of thirteen he was liberated by his owner, a Quaker gentleman, who sold his estates, and manumitted all his slaves before going to the North. He had six children by his first wife, but, as she was a slave, they were born into bondage also. He said that he had done well in a pecuniary way here, but that, before three years were over, he and all his children would sail for Liberia.[8]

"No, sir," he said in reply to a question, "I wouldn't leave a child of mine in a country where they may be sold into slavery, even if they are free, if they cannot pay their taxes."

"You don't mean to say "—

"Yes, sir," he continued, interrupting me, "they does that here."

Hold! enough!—

Thus abruptly terminates the last letter that I wrote to my Northern anti-slavery friends during my first trip South.[9]

I have omitted the purely didactic passages, as my object is to furnish *facts,* rather than to advocate theories, or to philosophize. Among these portions, however, I find two paragraphs which it may be well to preserve.

PRO AND CON.

At Wilmington, a philanthropic lady, a woman evidently of pure character and kindly nature—told me, mildly, that the Northern Abolitionists had no idea how numerous and how friendly the bonds were that united the slave to his master. As she said so I felt inclined to reply that perhaps Southern slaveholders had no idea how many and how insurrectionary the reasons were that are daily tending to array them one against the other. I did not say so, however, for the lady was a slaveholder, and I was in her house. Such an assertion would have been regarded as an insult. It isn't always etiquette to speak the truth![10]

And again:

Thus, therefore, although I say that I wish to see slavery abolished at any cost—even at the cost of a social Black St. Bartholomew's night[11]—I do not say that all, or even the majority of the slaveholders, are depraved or heartless men. Far from it. Among them are the kindliest natures, the most hospitable, generous and honorable souls. They have been conceived in the sin and born in the iniquity,[12] so to speak; on the slavery problem they never think with a desire to ascertain the truth; they regard the wrong as an established right; they hear it praised and defended from their youth up; and look on it, from habit, as the true social condition of the negro. They would as soon think of inquiring into the sentiments of their horses on *their* position, as to interrogate the slaves as to *their* ideas of bondage. There are many good men in the slaveholding ranks, who support the iniquity by their influence and their character, without suspecting that they are the pillars of a gigantic crime.

Are they, then, excused? No! Ignorance of the laws of humanity excuseth no man.[13] They are the pillars of a huge Temple of Sin, and should perish with it when it falls.

A gentleman who, as I had every reason to believe, is a St. Clair[14] to his slaves, lately said to me that his negroes *could not* be discontented, because they had no reason of complaint, as he was as kind to them as it is possible for a master to be.

"What right have you to be kind, as you call it, to your slaves?"

"Sir!" he ejaculated, in surprise.

"You do not see," I continued, "that you speak of your kindness as of an exclusive possession which you had the right to dispense or retain at your pleasure. You forget at the outset that the negro is a man—your equal. Leave him alone—let him be free and he will be kind to you, I have no doubt *without* making you his slave, and not boast of it either, I will warrant. This patronizing kindness is an insult to a freeman. Would you not be very apt to call me out if I went about, and said, in a condescending tone, that I had always been very kind to you? Kindness is very well in its way—but it is not freedom. Such is the view I should take of it if I were a slave."

"I don't forget—I deny that the negro is my equal," said the Southerner, cooly; and thus the conversation dropped.[15]

I concluded my fourth letter from Charleston in these words:

"I have spent six days now in conversing with colored people here, and I have never yet met *one* who professed to be contented with slavery—far less to prefer it. Many, many have I met who are panting for liberty, and several slaves who are prepared to risk the chance of failure in a servile insurrection."

Having done my work, I left Charleston.[16]

SAVANNAH.

I spent three months at Savannah.[17] My friends have often asked me how it was, that, when I dared to talk so freely with the slaves, I was never once discovered or betrayed? I reply, by remembering that the wisdom of the serpent is as necessary to a reformer as the harmlessness of the dove. I did not think it wrong to use stratagem to serve the slave. I have the talent of silence, the talent of discreet speech—and also—and I use it quite as often as the others—the talent and virtue of *indiscreetness*. The friend of the slave needs all three!

I found that the slaves of Georgia were without hope—passively resigned. It was requisite, in the first place, to arouse their hope. To effect that result, it was indispensably necessary to let them know of the anti-slavery battle waging throughout the Union—of which, unfortunately they were totally ignorant and likely to remain uninformed.

How I went to work to enlighten them, I do not deem it prudent to say. It might close that avenue of power to the abolitionists.

Suffice it to say that I seldom spoke to the city slaves. I never cared to run the risk of being betrayed, excepting when I was travelling on a journey. Hence, when I intended to reside in a city, I never spoke confidentially to the slaves *until I was prepared to depart.*

I had only one conversation with a slave in Savannah, of which I have preserved the record.[18]

In walking along the beautiful road—one of the most charming in the Union—which leads from the city to the Catholic cemetery, I met an aged negro slave. It was on a Sunday.

"Good morning, uncle."

"Good mornin', mass'r."

"Who do you belong to?"

He told me.

"Hired out?"

"No, mass'r, I works on de boss's plantation."

"What's your allowance?"

"A peck of meal a week, mass'r."

"What else?"

"Nothin' mass'r, at all. we has a little piece of ground dat we digs and plants. We raises vegetables, and we has a few chickens. We sells them (vegetables and eggs), on Sundays and buys a piece of bacon wid de money when we kin, mass'r."

"That's pretty hard allowance," I said.

"Yes, mass'r, it is dat; but we can't help dat."

* * *

"Did you ever know a slave who would rather be in bondage than be free?"

"I neber *did,* mass'r."

Savannah is a city of 20,000 souls.[19]

How many policemen do you suppose it requires to keep the peace there?

Eighty-one mounted guards.

There are larger cities in the Northern States with but *one* constable, and he engaged occasionally only in performing his official duties!

Who pays the expenses of this guard—the salaries of the men, and for the purchase money, the feed and accoutrements of the horses?

Chiefly the non-slaveholding population.

Let the Democratic supporters of the "constitutional" crime of American slavery reflect on this unpalatable fact!

In all slaveholding cities—excepting the great seaports, and St. Louis, Louisville and Baltimore, which are practically free—the lawyers form the richest and most influential class.

Let the people think of this fact; let them remember too, that lawyers are the leeches of the body politic.

NOTES

1. At this point Redpath resumes the text of the John Ball, Jr. letter, published in the Boston *Liberator,* September 8, 1854, that he quoted in chapter 5.

2. In the original letter, Redpath omitted the sentence that here follows and instead concluded this section with the following paragraph:

> (*Honi soit que mal y pense:* there was a third party present. Shame on you, oh reader!) [Boston *Liberator,* September 8, 1854]

3. This short paragraph was not part of the letter in the Boston *Liberator,* September 8, 1854.

4. Redpath probably is quoting from the *Biblical Recorder,* a weekly Baptist periodical published in Raleigh, North Carolina. H. G. Jones and Julius H. Avant, eds., *Union List of North Carolina Newspapers, 1751–1900* (Raleigh, N.C., 1963), 81.

5. In the original John Ball, Jr. letter this paragraph appeared in the following form, which reveals a little of Redpath's earlier life:

> Chuckles expressive of gratification followed from the good un, which was succeeded by a history of the ole man's life, spoken in such broken English that the wandering Gentile, although he had drunk enough of lager bier in German cellars to have drowned Governor Seymour and all his hosts, and had dined at "down-town Taylor's," and consequently spoken with the loquacious waiters there often enough to have enabled him to talk with 'the finest peasantry in the world,' without the aid of an interpreter—notwithstanding all this, his familiarity with incorrect pronounciation he could make absolutely nothing of the old man's history. [Boston *Liberator,* September 8, 1854]

6. In 1815, after his second expulsion from the throne, the French emperor Napoleon Bonaparte (1769–1821) was exiled by the allied powers to the small, isolated South Atlantic island of Saint Helena, where he died six years later. Colin Jones, *The Longman Companion to the French Revolution* (London, 1988), 323–28.

7. Redpath alludes to the hymn "The Good Time Coming," by Charles Mackay. Charles Mackay, *Voices from the Mountains and from the Crowd* (Boston, 1853), 202.

8. Founded in 1816, the American Colonization Society settled free black volunteer emigrants in its colony of Liberia on Africa's west coast. Most free black leaders and later the abolitionists condemned the racist premises behind the colonization effort. Although endorsed by many prominent whites, the society managed to transport only a few thousand to Africa before the Civil War. Philip J. Staudenraus, *The African Colonization Movement, 1816–1865* (New York, 1961).

9. The fourth John Ball, Jr. letter concluded as Redpath indicated. Boston *Liberator,* September 8, 1854.

10. This paragraph originally appeared in Redpath's fourth John Ball, Jr. letter, following his description of the Sugar House. Boston *Liberator,* September 8, 1854.

11. The St. Bartholomew's Day massacre occurred in Paris on August 24, 1572, when Catholic forces killed more than four thousand French Protestants invited to the city to celebrate the wedding of Henry, king of Navarre, into the French royal family. Marvin R. O'Connell, *The Counter Reformation: 1559–1610* (New York, 1974), 170–71.

12. A paraphrase of Ps. 51:5.

13. Redpath adapts the saying of John Selden in *Table Talk* (1689).

14. A reference to the fictional character Augustine St. Clare from *Uncle Tom's Cabin.*

15. This segment appeared almost immediately preceding the description of the "Ginger Girl" in the John Ball, Jr. letter in the Boston *Liberator,* September 8, 1854.

16. This paragraph appeared immediately preceding the description of the "Ginger Girl" in the John Ball, Jr. letter in the Boston *Liberator,* September 8, 1854. After reporting on the southern commercial convention, Redpath had departed Charleston, South Carolina, in mid-April 1854.

17. Redpath traveled from Charleston to Savannah, Georgia, shortly after the conclusion on April 15, 1854, of the commercial convention in the former city. He almost immediately began work as a reporter for the *Savannah Daily Morning News,* edited by William T. Thompson. In mid-June 1854, Redpath left Savannah to return to New York City. *Savannah Daily Morning News,* April 17 and June 19, 1854; "James Redpath Interview," American

Freedmen's Inquiry Commission Report, National Archives, Washington, D.C.; *DAB*, 9:479–80.
18. Redpath adapted the concluding portion of a later John Ball, Jr. letter, published in the *New York National Anti-Slavery Standard*, December 16, 1854, for the final segment of this chapter. That letter, otherwise omitted from the *Roving Editor*, has been reproduced in its entirety in appendix 4.
19. The population of Savannah, Georgia, in 1850 was 15,312, including 6,231 slaves and 686 free blacks. *DeBow's Review* 17 (September 1854): 244–45.

VII.

THE COMMERCIAL CONVENTION.[1]

EVERYBODY, North and South, has heard of the great Commercial Conventions, which regularly assemble, now here, now there, but always in the Slave States, to discuss the interests, and "resolve" on the prosperity—immediate, unparalleled, and unconditional—of slaveholding trade, territory, education, Legree-lash-literature, and "direct commerce with Europe!"[2] These assemblies are generally regarded, in the Slave States, as the safety-valves of the Southern Juggernaut-institution, without which, for want of ventilation, that political organization would speedily explode, and scatter death and destruction to the ends of the earth. All the politicians of the third order, and the second class (occasionally, perhaps, of the upper circles, also) assiduously attend them, to publicly renew the unmanly assurances of their unwavering loyalty to the overshadowing disgrace of the American nation, and the blighting and devastating curse of their own unhappy section. These exhibitions would be more amusing than a farce, if they were not, to thoughtful men, more tragic than a tragedy. For what is more sorrowful than to see men of talent the willing and enthusiastic eulogists of so very foul a crime as the system of American slavery?

The ridiculous aspect of these assemblies has been admirably portrayed, again and again, by the prominent journalists of the North and South, without respect of political party. The other aspect has never yet been fully noticed, even by the New York *Tribune,* whose sarcastic and merciless presentations of these Southern absurdities were keenly felt and resented by their perpetrators—nay, even, honored by a five hours' debate in the commercial convention which assembled in Charleston in 1854.[3]

I beg pardon of the chivalry! I had closed up the record of this, my first trip, without deeming them and their Convention as worthy even of a passing notice. It would have been very unfair to have treated them so cavalierly. It would not have been rendering like for like. They did not serve me in that way. Let me render them, therefore, the courtesy of a chapter.

This was how it happened, that anti-*Tribune* debate:

I determined to remain in Charleston during the session of the Convention, to report its proceedings for the metropolitan press. Previous to my departure from New York city, I had been a member of the *Tribune's* editorial staff.[4] So I entered the Commercial Convention, and announced myself as the reporter of that paper.

I was very courteously treated. I had the distinguished honor of a self-introduction to the illustrious Parson Brownlow,[5] who, seemingly having taken a fancy to me, patronized me in his original and extraordinary way. He went with me to the principal dry goods stores, and showed me the glories thereof, invariably introducing me to strangers in this way:

"You've heerd of Horace Greeley?"[6]

They had, in every case, heard of that celebrated editor. They sometimes, even—probably to prove the exactness of their knowledge—volunteered to express their conception of his character. One or two, indeed, to use their own expression, "made no bones" of uttering what they thought of him, without waiting for a special invitation to that effect. These estimates of Mr. Greeley were seldom offensive to his friends on the score of excessive or extravagant eulogy. The answer of one Palmetto counter-jumper will abundantly prove this assertion:

"You've heerd of Horace Greeley?" asked the grinning parson, as the usual prelude to his excellent joke.

"Yes: damned rascal—what about it?" said the young, laconic, counter-jumping judge.

"This is him!" quoth the parson.

Of course, on a minute inspection, the startling effect thus suddenly produced as suddenly vanished. That spotless linen, hair elaborately dressed, moustache carefully trimmed and scientifically curled: those pantaloons, and coat, and vest, well brushed and white not one, but each of the gravest black; of the finest and most costly material too; and fitting albeit so exactly to the figure, that they seemed to have been plastic moulds, into which, in a melted physical condition, I had been cautiously poured: that superb Genin hat, those daintiest of French boots, glittering diamond ring, and no less brilliant breastpin: Did you ever see Horace Greeley, Mr. Zachariah Smith,[7] and if you have, do you wonder that I was not immediately arrested?

The parson, in convention, delivered an irregular speech, or out-of-pulpit sermon, whose moral and practical application, as he stated it, was this celestial injunction, *"Never put your arm inside of a jug handle."*

The advice was more especially addressed to the young lady spectators. By a bold license of speech, which men of genius are privileged to employ, the jug-handle of this more than celestial moral indicated the arm of every young man who would not, at his clerical command, sign the temperance, or rather the total abstinence pledge.[8]

The parson introduced me to a Southern editor, whose style of thought and conversation greatly amused me. He was from Chattanooga, Tennessee.[9] Full to overflowing, was the Tennessee journalist, of loyalty to slavery (which, down South, they often euphonize as "the South!"), and loyalty to venerable rye; and of the most friendly feelings, too, toward Parson Brownlow, Virginia short-cut, and the Honorable Mr. Jones, his representative in Congress.[10] He praised Mr. Jones first and foremost: Jones was bound to be President, he said, and had come down here (but I mustn't tell nary one about it) to put himself right with the South Carolina fire-eaters,[11] who were offended at a Union speech that he had recently delivered in New York city! Couldn't I help him out of his fix by giving him a good notice—right kind, you know, of pitchin' into him, eh? That was a d—d good fellow! Wouldn't I take a chaw? No? Was it possible I never chawed? Well, suppose we liquored then? Oh, curse it now—that was piling on the agony altogether too loud—neither chaw nor drink? That came of being in the *Tribune* office. Damn such isms, *he* said.

But when he found that I was a willing and delighted listener to his stories of Tennessee, he seemed to forgive my unfamiliar isms. He told me that he had often seen Parson Brownlow, in the pulpit, before opening his Bible to read the text of his sermon, first take out a couple of loaded pistols and lay one of them on each side of the holy volume. This precaution, he said, he was obliged to take, in order to defend himself, if suddenly assailed, by ruffians whom he often denounced. The anecdotes, admiringly told, that he related of the parson, proved him to be, of all living Americans—not even Stephen A. Douglas excepted—the most indecent and unscrupulous of speech.*

The editor knew Greeley too. Greeley, upon the hull, was a clever fellow *personally;* but a d——d rascal, no two ways about it, politically. Worst man in the country: he would be d——d if he wasn't. Perhaps, I suggested, mightn't that follow even if he *was?* He didn't see the point! He had bin to New York. Had called on Greeley, and had been told by him that he might examine his exchanges. His impressions, therefore, were favorable to Greeley.

As the Tennessee editor, with eyes half shut from the effects of

---

*Let it be remembered that Parson Brownlow is still the pastor, in good standing, of an orthodox Southern Church, although he endorsed and eulogized the conduct of a mob, who publicly burned a negro to death, without form of law.

whisky—his feet, higher than his head, resting on a table—was garrulously muttering his opinions of the New York journalist, I thought of a plan by which, if it succeeded, I might somewhat enliven the proceedings of the Convention, and hear the Southern lions roar.

"Now," I said, " since Greeley was so 'clever,' it is no more than fair that you should try to reciprocate?"

"That's a fact," mumbled the editor, "I'll be happy to serve you in any way, Mr. R. How kin I?"

"Introduce a resolution into the Convention tomorrow morning, constituting the representatives of the New York press honorary delegates."

"I'll do it," he said: and he kept his word.

The motion was put—and carried![12] The truth is, that it was not rightly understood. But, before the Convention re-assembled next morning, it was evident that there had been brains in birth-pang labor, in view of the extraordinary vote. The *Standard* and "a planter" remonstrated publicly. This gentleman, they said, may be both a Chesterfield[13] and a Howard[14] (it was not the blooded family they meant—only the English philanthropist), but in the Commercial Convention, they argued, we can recognize him merely and solely as the representative of the New York *Tribune!*[15] As such——

It is unnecessary to me to say what treatment I merited "as such."

When the Convention was called to order, a gentleman, in a shrewd and courteous speech, moved that the resolution be rescinded *without discussion.* He hoped there would be no debate. It was unprecedented to admit reporters as honorary delegates into *any* convention. The dignity invested them with the right of voting and participating in debate. Gentlemen had not thought of these facts in voting for the resolution which conferred such unusual honors on the representatives of the New York press. There were *other* reasons: which he would not name here. It was unprecedented. That was enough!

He sat down.

Shrill and loud, and in ringing tones came the sentence through the theatre:

"And if it is not enough, Mr. President, *I* have other reasons to give!"

I turned round, and saw, in the Georgia delegation, a tall, lank, bony, red-headed man, with his thin wiry finger stretched out *a la* Randolph—his body more than half bent over the gallery.[16]

Unpre-re-cedented!" he shrilly shouted, quivering with indignation, "unpre-re-cedented, why! sir, it's unparalleled, outrageous and insufferable. What, sir! have we come here to tolerate in our midst, and not only tolerate, no sir, not only that, but honor, sir, HONOR, sir, an emissary of that infamous abolition sheet, the New York *Tribune!*"

I chuckled! The poker was stirring; the lions and lesser beasts were beginning to roar!

For five mortal hours (called mortal, I suppose, because they are very short-lived) the politicians belched forth their denunciations of the *Tribune.* Never before, probably—never to my knowlege—was so splendid a tribute paid to any journal.

It was impossible to stem the current of their fanatical rage. It was in vain that one old man, grey-haired and feeble, appealed to them—for God's sake to vote at once, and not debate; not to furnish capital to their enemies—not to advertise the organ of abolitionism.

With a rush, and a roar, and a sweeping force, on came the filthy flood of speech again, all the fouler, and stronger and wilder, from that attempted check. The chance was too good to be lost. Probably many of them had never seen an abolitionist before, and never again would have such an opportunity of unburdening their minds in such a presence. I was astonished at the contempt with which they spoke of the press. I did not know then, what I soon learned, that the press South is a greater slave than the negro, and is treated by the planters and politicians who rule it, exactly as it deserves to be—like a serf.

The motion was rescinded.

I rose up at once, took my delegate ribbon from its button-hole, threw it on the ground, and walked out of the reporters' seat. This act was noticed by great numbers, as it was done in front of the audience, and was an exhibition of independence which, I discovered, made me many friends. I thought it due to the press to reciprocate the contempt of the politicians, and when gentlemen who introduced themselves after this episode, were informed of this reason of my conduct, many of them endorsed it in the usual fashion:

"*Let's liquor.*"

I went to the upper gallery (it was in the theatre), and entered a private box as spectator. I took no further notes. There were three young ladies in the box. One of them, I noticed (after I had been there some time), was playing with the stem of her parasol. I looked at it, and saw that it was a dagger, as well as a handle; like a sword cane, it was hollow, and secretly contained a glittering deadly weapon! I had never before either seen, or heard, or read of such a fashion: nor since. From before what a beneficent condition of society did that dagger-parasol-stem lift up the thick curtain! It was an irresistible argument, I thought, for the extension of slavery, and for "respecting" the "rights"—the *State* rights, not human rights—of our "Southern brethren!" Oh! eloquent parasol-stem! potent preacher! graphic painter and historian! your lesson is ever present with me, whenever, as a citizen, I am called on to act in public affairs; and long will be remembered after the faintest shadow of the eloquent orations of the Commercial Convention are utterly obliterated from my recollection.

Faint, indeed, are my present recollections. I remember only endless resolutions denouncing the North, and creating a new South; and a discourse by a Rev. Mr. Marshall, of Kentucky or Mississippi, I think, on the Importance of Planting Potatoes for Posterity;[17] which, in a defence of men of insight and foresight, he declared to be the mission of the visionary as contrasted with the lower and grosser work of the practical intellect—that only hoes its row for the present generation. It was very funny—for the preacher was in earnest. Dean Swift,[18] in jest, could not have composed a keener satire on the Southern Commercial Conventions.

NOTES

1. The material in this chapter was not part of the John Ball, Jr. letters. Redpath apparently wrote it from his recollections of attending this convention and from his reports on the gathering for the *New York Tribune* and the *Savannah Daily Morning News.*

2. First held in 1837, the southern commercial conventions were revived in 1852 and held annually throughout the remainder of the decade. These meetings promoted the development of southern manufacturing and transportation enterprises in order to give the region greater economic self-sufficiency. As the 1850s progressed, these meetings evolved more into political forums for exponents of southern nationalism and secession. Herbert Wender, *Southern Commercial Conventions, 1837–1859* (Baltimore, 1930), passim.

3. Delegates from thirteen states attended the southern commercial convention held in Charleston in April 1854. Redpath describes the debate over his own presence at this gathering as a reporter for the *New York Tribune* later in this chapter. Wender, *Southern Commercial Conventions,* 119, 144–46.

4. Redpath had worked as a reporter and a junior editor for the *New York Tribune* from approximately 1851 to the time of his departure for this southern tour. Horner, *James Redpath,* 17–24; *DAB,* 15:443–44.

5. William G. Brownlow.

6. New Hampshire–born Horace Greeley (1811–72) migrated to New York City where he entered the field of journalism in the early 1830s. In 1841 he launched the *New York Tribune,* which grew into the nation's largest circulation newspaper by the next decade. Greeley used the *Tribune* to champion a wide range of reform causes including free trade, Fourierism, and opposition to the extension of slavery. Despite the *Tribune*'s support for the Republican party from its start, Greeley ran for president in 1872 as the candidate of a Liberal Republican–Democratic coalition that was prepared to abandon Reconstruction. Glyndon G. Van Deusen, *Horace Greeley: Nineteenth-Century Crusader* (Philadelphia, 1953); *DAB,* 7:528–34.

7. The name Zachariah Smith does not appear in the Charleston directories for this period and might have been a pseudonym created by Redpath.

8. In his report for the *New York Tribune,* Redpath had caricatured this speech by William G. Brownlow as "a scientific exposition from Parson Brownlow of Tennessee,—informing the world why 'young gentlemen chew cloves and cinnamon'—which is to disguise the smell of liquor when they sit next their sweethearts in pews,—and also, a story from the same politico-commercial orthodox expounder of a young lady who would not put her arm through a jug handle, as she called a certain Young America who was intemperate." *New York Tribune,* April 19, 1854; see also Boston *Liberator,* May 12, 1854.

9. A small, isolated community, Chattanooga had only one newspaper, the pro-Whig *Chattanooga Gazette,* until 1853 when the rival *Advertiser* was founded. Owned by W. I. Crandall and H. F. Cooper, the *Advertiser* championed the completion of the Memphis and Charleston Railroad, whose president was former governor James C. Jones. Opening of this railroad helped to make Chattanooga a significant transportation hub. Gilbert E. Govan and James W. Livingood, *The Chattanooga Country, 1540–1962: From Tomahawks to TVA* (Chapel Hill, 1952), 140–41, 150–51.

10. Tennessee Whig politician James Chamberlain Jones (1809–59) came to national attention when he defeated Democrat James K. Polk for the governor's seat in 1841 and again in 1843. After a term in the U.S. Senate (1851–57) he retired to manage railroads. Robert Sobel and John Raimo, *Biographical Dictionary of the Governors of the United States,* 4 vols. (Westport, Conn., 1978), 4:1473–74; *DAB,* 10:177.

11. In the late antebellum period, the term "fire-eater" referred to proslavery southern politicians who used extreme states-rights principles to protect their regional interests. David C. Roller and Robert W. Twyman, eds., *Encyclopedia of Southern History* (Baton Rouge, 1979), 434–35.

12. On April 12, 1854, the Charleston press denounced a resolution passed by the commercial convention granting honorary membership in the gathering to reporters from the *New York Express, Herald,* and *Tribune. New York Tribune,* April 17, 1854; *New York Daily Times,* April 17, 1854.

13. The allusion was to the prominent English noble family of the Stanhopes, heirs to the title of earl of Chesterfield—specifically, to Philip Dormer Stanhope, fifth earl of Chesterfield (1694–1773). He served as a Whig in the House of Commons before his father's death in 1726 elevated him to the family title and a seat in the House of Lords. Unsuccessful in politics, he devoted much of his energies in later life to patronizing the arts. Chesterfield is perhaps best remembered for posthumously published witty letters of advice on the education of his son. *DNB,* 18:911–24.

14. Probably English reformer John Howard (1726–1790), who campaigned for the abolition of the practice of prisoners paying their jailer's fees. He inspected prisons all across Europe and wrote reports, calling for improvements in sanitary conditions there. *DNB,* 10:44–48.

15. On the morning of April 13 a delegate introduced a motion to deny Redpath, as the representative of the antislavery *New York Tribune,* access to the floor of the convention. A reporter for the *New York Herald,* whose paper had a reputation for friendlier coverage of slavery, reported a "spicy debate" over the motion and observed that Redpath's "conduct there is unexceptionable." *New York Herald,* April 16, 1854; *New York Tribune,* April 17, 1854; *Savannah Daily Morning News,* April 17, 1854.

16. Redpath alludes to Virginia politician John Randolph of Roanoke (1773–1833). Originally a supporter of Thomas Jefferson, Randolph became the leader of a small faction of independent-minded Republican members of the House of Representatives. An early southern sectionalist, Randolph opposed the Bank of the United States, protective tariffs, and federally financed internal improvements. A lifelong hormonal disorder gave Randolph a gaunt appearance and a high-pitched voice. Russell Kirk, *John Randolph of Roanoke: A Study in American Politics* (New York, 1964); Maisel, *Political Parties and Elections,* 2:907; *DAB,* 15:363–67.

17. Records of the Charleston commercial convention indicate the attendance of both C. K. Marshall and T. A. Marshall from Mississippi. However, neither man is reported to have delivered the speech on potatoes described by Redpath. Wender, *Southern Commercial Conventions,* 122, 126, 144; *New York Tribune,* April 15, 1854.

18. Redpath alludes to Irish Anglican clergyman Jonathan Swift (1667–1745), best remembered for his novel *Gulliver's Travels* (1726). *DNB,* 19:204–27.

"There, on a coffin, sat a wrinkled old negro, holding a broken piece of mirror close to his nose, and scraping his furrowed face, might and main, with a very dull razor which he held in his right hand." (see page 134)

MY SECOND TRIP.

I.

PRELIMINARY WORDS ON INSURRECTION.

MY opinion of the slaveholders, and my feelings toward them, were greatly modified during my residence in Savannah. I saw so much that was noble, generous and admirable in their characters; I saw so many demoralizing pro-slavery influences—various, attractive, resistless—brought to bear on their intellects from their cradle to their tomb, that from hating I began to pity them. It is not at all surprising that the people of the South are so indifferent to the rights of the African race. For, as far as the negro is concerned, the press, the pulpit, the bench, the bar, and the stump, conspire with a unity of purpose and pertinacity of zeal, which is no less lamentable than extraordinary, to eradicate every sentiment of justice and brotherhood from their hearts. They sincerely believe Wrong to be Right, and act on that unhappy conviction. They know not what they do.[1] Preachers tell them that slavery is a God-planted institution; lawyers, that it is the apple of the eye of the Federal Constitution; jurists, that it is the key and corner-stone of a rational and conservative Freedom; politicians, that it is the prolific source of our national greatness and the surest guaranty for the continuance of a stable prosperity—while the press, by its false and perverted record of passing events, represents every enemy of pro-slavery domination as a foe to the South—as seeking to rob and to subdue the people of the slaveholding States—and thus teaches that fidelity to their "peculiar," "patriarchal," "domestic" *iniquity* is the sum and substance—the alpha and omega of a man's duty to his country.

Thus taught—interest prompting also—they have gone on, year after year, supporting the extravagant demands of their politicians; until now, no longer content with their first demand—toleration, or their second claim—equality with freedom, they boldly insist on absolute and undisputed supremacy in every State.

They are sincere. Far less criminal are they therefore, in my opinion, than such moral outcasts as G—— S——,[2] who once publicly uttered the revolting declaration, that, if every slave in America could be instantly liberated by a single prayer, he—for one—would not offer it up! The Southern church has been a very ponderous millstone around the neck of the slave—the clergy having vied, apparently, with each other to see which of the conflicting denominations, South, could keep the negro the longest and the deepest under water.

But sincerity is not enough, in the eye of the moral law. It is necessary, also, to be RIGHT; to abstain from violating the law. How then, shall we compel the slaveholder to understand that his treatment of the negro is wrong—to show him that it is demanded, by every principle of justice and humanity, that he shall liberate his slaves? Not by propagating the popular theology—for the South has churches enough, far too many preachers, and might even spare a Tract Society! The more the worse—for the slave. Preaching even undefiled Christianity would have no universal immediate effect, and even if it would have, and could have, there is this objection to it—it cannot be carried into operation! The slaveholders will not listen to it—it is illegal—dangerous to attempt—in one word "impracticable" in the Southern States. Besides, if possible, it would be absurd. You might as well preach to buffaloes! Our duty to the slave, I think, demands that we shall speedily appeal to the taskmaster's *fear*. Let us teach, urge, and encourage insurrections, and the South will soon abandon her haughty attitude of aggression. Then it will be time enough to advocate schemes of compensation;[3] then it will be time enough to ascertain whether or not the Constitution gives us the power to abolish slavery everywhere. Until then, I confess, I regard all such labors as unnecessary, or, at best, but an awkward mode of fighting a powerful and defiant foe. If we want to make good terms with the Slave Power, let us bring it on its knees first! And there is but one way of doing that: by attacking it where it is weakest—at *home*. The slave quarter is the Achilles' heel[4] of the South. Wound it there and it dies! One insurrection in Virginia, in 1832,[5] did more for the emancipation cause, than all the teachings of the Revolutionary Fathers. What if, in such rising, a few lives are lost? What are a few hundred lives even, as compared with the liberties of four millions of men? I have no ill-feeling to slaveholders as a class. Yet I could hear of the untimely death of ten thousand of them without a sigh, or an expression, or a feeling of regret, if it resulted in the freedom of a single State.

I dismiss the argument that we have no right to encourage insurrections, the dreadful punishment of which, if unsuccessful, we are unwilling or do not propose to share, by replying that I am *not* unprepared to hazard the danger of such a catastrophe, and the chances of speedy death or enduring victory with the revolutionary slaves. To still another objection urged against my plan, I answer that, in an insurrection, if all the slaves in the United States—men, women and helpless babes—were to fall on the field or become the victims of Saxon vengeance, after the event, if one man only survived to relate how his race heroically fell, and to enjoy the freedom they had won, the liberty of that solitary negro, in my opinion, would be cheaply purchased by the universal slaughter of his people and their oppressors.

I START AGAIN.

Let us travel again!

After a detention of some months in New York city, prostrated on a sick bed, I once more departed for the Southern States.

About the middle of September, 1854, I travelled by railroad from Richmond to Petersburg.[6] I made no notes of the intervening country at the time, but will insert here what I wrote on a subsequent pedestrian journey over the same route.[7]

CHESTERFIELD COUNTY FACTS.

Nearly the entire road runs through woods. Land, from $6 to $8 an acre.

This county, a few years ago, had a population of 17,483, an increase of thirty-four only during the ten preceding years. It had 8,400 whites, 8,616 slaves, and 467 free persons of color. It had neither colleges, academies, nor private schools. Five hundred and sixty-seven pupils only attended the public schools. Three thousand and ninety-five white persons, over five and under twenty years of age, and one thousand and eight white adults, could neither read, write nor cipher![8] Add the stupidity of the black population to this amazing mass of ignorance, and then you may judge of the beneficent influence of slave institutions on the mind and morals of a rising generation, and on the social life of the Southern States. Notwithstanding, and carefully concealing this stupendous influence of evil, Mr. De Bow,[9] the compiler of the United States Census, in his official report, has the audacity to say that "the social reunions of the Southern

States, in a great measure, compensate for their want of the common schools of the North!" I wonder if he never heard of social reunions at the North! Was he never at a husking, a soiree, a lecture, a sewing, or a spiritual circle, a bee, a surprise party, a "social"—or at any other of the innumerable "reunions" which are everywhere so uncommonly common in the Free States?

Chesterfield county, by the latest census, had five hundred and sixty-four farms; 87,180 acres improved, and 108,933 unimproved acres; the total value of which, with improvements and implements, was estimated at $1,562,286. The farms supported 2,441 horses, 5,655 neat cattle, 6,020 sheep, and 24,814 swine. They produced 95,875 bushels of wheat, 116,965 of oats and rye, 33,938 of Indian corn, 22,113 of Irish and sweet potatoes, 3,646 of peas and beans, 73,044 pounds of butter and cheese, 2,892 tons of hay, 96 pounds of hops, and 608 bushels of clover and other grass seeds.[10] These figures, subdivided by the number of farms, will give the agricultural reader a better conception than I could give, or any description of their style of farming could give, of the manner in which slaves and slaveholders mutually assist each other in rejecting and wasting the wealth which Nature lies passively willing to bestow.

THE POOR WHITES AND SLAVERY.

I met and conversed with many of the poorer class of whites in my journey. All of them were conscious of the injurious infuence that slavery was exerting on their social condition. If damning the negroes would have abolished slavery, it would have disappeared a long time ago, before the indignant breath of the poor white trash. But—it won't.

I KNOW NOTHING.

I slept at night at the house of Mr. S——n, a planter and Baptist preacher. He has a farm of six hundred acres overlooking the Appomattox River. He has some thirty slaves, old and young.[11]

I rode down with one of his slaves to Wattron Mill—a mile or two.

He had lived seven years with his master; did n't know how old he himself was; did n't know how many acres there were in his master's farm; did n't know what land was worth, or how mules, horses and other farm stock sold; could not read nor write; had never been at City Point, which was only three miles distant, according to his own account, although, in point of fact, it was nearer six; did not know how many slaves his owner had, or the name of the county we were in!

One item of information, however, not generally known by slaves, nor always by whites, he did possess: he did know who his father was! So he was a wise boy after all—or the proverb is rather too liberal in its scope.[12]

FARMING UTENSILS.

Mr. S. walked down his farm with me in the morning. I noticed a hoe, which was heavier, at least, than half a dozen Northern ones, and asked why he made them so clumsy.

He said they were obliged to make everything heavy that negroes handled. If you gave a slave a Northern hoe or cradle in the morning, he would be sure to break it before night, and probably in less than two hours. You couldn't make them careful. Besides, he said, they preferred heavy implements; you could not get them to use an axe that was less than six pounds weight. They said that it tired them more to use a light axe or hoe.

I remembered, somewhere, to have heard of a slave who objected to the use of a light hoe, "'kase" he grumbled, "you has to put out your strength every time you puts it down, and in a 'Ginny hoe it goes into the ground, jest *so,* by its own weight."

Mr. S. said, he believed that this was the real objection which the negro had to the Northern hoe.

I noticed the great size of his fields—one was over fifty acres. He said they called that a small field here.

GUANO AND NIGGERS.

He had used guano, but did not like it. It was too great a stimulant, unless you put enough on to raise both a wheat and a clover crop; but the farmers here could not afford to do it at the present rate of guano, and the uncertainty of the wheat crop.

He thought niggers should be the happiest beings in the world. He believed his slaves made more money than he did. All he made was a living. They made that, or he made it for them; and then he allowed them that wanted, to keep a pig, to fish after their work was over, and hunt. They sold their fish and game, and poultry and eggs. They had no care of the morrow; all their thinking he did for them.

He admitted that Virginia would have been better off if never a negro had come there.

Nearly all the slaveholders admit that fact. How to get rid of it—that is the mountain they all see, without industry or genius—alas! also, without even the desire to remove it.

But it must be removed, or it will fall—"and great will be the fall of it!"[13]

THE SLAVEROCRACY AND THE POOR.

SEPT. 23.[14]—I slept at the house of a petty farmer, a few miles from Petersburg. We talked about slavery. He has no slaves. He is a Virginian by birth. He owns about two hundred acres of land, which he cultivates with his family's assistance. In this State, or in this section of it, two hundred acres are hardly accounted a farm. Five thousand and six thousand acre farms are very common. The farmer, his wife, his daughter and son-in-law agreed in saying, that the poor people of Virginia are "looked down upon" by the slaveholding class as if they belonged to an inferior race. The old man said, also, that the majority of the non-slaveholders here are secret abolitionists.

I walked as far as Weldon, North Carolina, from Petersburg, and there I took the cars for Wilmington.[15]

On the road I had a talk with a Virginia slave, which I reserve for another chapter.

NOTES

1. Luke 23:24.

2. Redpath probably alludes to Presbyterian minister Gardiner Spring (1785–1873) of New York City, who had publicly condemned northern resistance to the Fugitive Slave Act. Spring declared that disobedience to the government's law was the equivalent of disobedience to God. The same principles led Spring to encourage his denomination to support the Union cause in the Civil War. Gardiner Spring, *Personal Reminiscences of the Life and Times of Gardiner Spring* (New York, 1866); *DAB,* 17:479–80.

3. Public interest in the concept of compensated emancipation of slaves received a brief revival in 1857, the year before Redpath probably wrote the introductory material for this chapter. That summer a convention in Cleveland, called by abolitionists Gerrit Smith and Elihu Burritt among others, led to the formation of the short-lived National Compensation Society. While some politicians showed interest in the idea, the large majority of both abolitionists and slaveholders condemned compensation proposals. Betty L. Fladeland, "Compensated Emancipation: A Rejected Alternative," *Journal of Southern History* 42 (May 1976): 183–86.

4. In Homer's *Iliad,* the Trojan Paris killed Achilles with an arrow shot into the Greek's single vulnerable spot, his right heel. *Funk & Wagnall's Standard Dictionary,* 2 vols. (New York, 1974), 1:12.

5. Redpath alludes to the slave insurrection led by Nat Turner in Southampton County, Virginia, from 21 to 23 August 1831, not 1832. Turner's band of seventy rebels killed fifty-seven whites before being overwhelmed by local militia. Turner and seventeen of his followers were executed, and dozens of other blacks died in the panicked retaliation. Stephen B. Oates, *Fires of Jubilee: Nat Turner's Fierce Rebellion* (New York, 1975); Herbert Aptheker, *Nat Turner's Slave Rebellion* (New York, 1966).

6. Redpath's John Ball, Jr. letters report his presence in Richmond, Virginia, on September 20 and in Petersburg on September 23, 1854. *New York National Anti-Slavery Standard,* October 14 and 21, 1854.

7. No earlier published source for Redpath's account of Chesterfield County, Virginia, has been located.

8. With a few discrepancies, these statistics on Chesterfield County, Virginia, correspond with those found in Richard Edwards, ed., *Statistical Gazetteer of the States of Virginia and North Carolina* (Richmond, Va., 1856), 207.

9. South Carolina–born editor James Dunwood Brownson DeBow (1820–67) gained a national reputation for his popular New Orleans–based political magazine the *Southern Quarterly Review* and later *DeBow's Review.* He was a fervent defender of slavery but also advocated southern industrialization. The first head of the Louisiana Bureau of Statistics, DeBow was appointed superintendent of the U.S. Census by President Franklin Pierce and conducted the seventh census in 1850. *DAB,* 5:180–82.

10. These statistics closely approximate those found in J. D. B. DeBow, *The Seventh Census of the United States: 1850* (Washington, D.C., 1853), 273, 275, 279, 281.

11. Redpath probably describes the Reverend John Alexander Strachan (?–1874), who owned the Points of Rocks estate along the Appomattox River. A descendant of one of the oldest families in the county, Strachan was a Baptist minister. Francis Earle Lutz, *Chesterfield: An Old Virginia County* (Richmond, Va., 1954), 210.

12. Versions of this proverb appear in Prov. 10:1 and Shakespeare's *Merchant of Venice,* act 2, scene 2, line 83.

13. Possibly a paraphrase of Matt. 7:27.

14. This paragraph, with the date September 23, 1854, originally appeared in the John Ball, Jr. letter in the *New York National Anti-Slavery Standard* on October 14, 1854.

15. This pedestrian trip is described in the second series of John Ball, Jr. letters. *New York National Anti-Slavery Standard,* October 14, 21, and 28 and November 14, 1854.

II.

TALK WITH A VIRGINIA SLAVE.

SEPTEMBER 25.—Thirty-three miles south of Petersburg.[1] In walking near the railroad, I met a man of color.

ƒWhat time do you think it is ?" I asked.

"The sun is up 'bout half an hour," he said, politely touching his hat.

"At what hour does the sun rise just now?"

"Dunno, mass'r."

"How old are you?"

"Forty-five year old, mass'r."

"Are you married?"

"Yes, mass'r, I is."

"Have you got any children?"

"Yes, mass'r, I's got five."

"Did you ever try to run away?"

"No, mass'r, I neber did."

"Would n't you like to go to the North?" I asked, closely watching the expression of his eye. He hesitated. I knew, from experience, why. I therefore added:

"I come from the North."

"Does you, mass'r?" said the slave, as he eyed me semi-suspiciously.

"Yes," I replied, "would n't you like to go there?"

CONTENTMENT WITH SLAVERY.

"Yes, mass'r," he answered promptly, "I would like bery much to go dar, but I neber 'spects to be dar."

"Have you been a slave all your life?"

"Yes, mass'r."

"Do you know of any slaves round about here, who are contented with being in bondage?"

"No, mass'r," he answered with emphasis, "not one of dem. How could dey, mass'r? Dere's no man wouldn't sooner work for hisself dan for a boss, dat kicks and knocks us 'bout all day, and neber 'lows us anyding for oursel's."

"Do you work for your boss, or are you hired out?" I asked.

"I works for de boss."

"What kind of time do you have with him?"

"Bery hard mass'r, bery hard. He works us all day, and neber 'lows us anyding for oursel's at all from Christmas to Christmas."

"What! don't he give you a present at Christmas?"

"No, mass'r, not a cent. Some bosses do 'low someding at Christmas; but not my boss. He doesn't even gib us 'bacca to chaw."

He was carrying a bag in which his day's provisions and his tools were. He took out four apples, and offered them to me.

"Will you gib me a piece of 'bacca for dem, mass'r?"

Dozens of times, in Virginia, the Carolinas, and Georgia, have the slaves, working in the fields, come up to the fence, and obsequiously begged from me a piece of tobacco. There is no speedier way of getting into their confidence than by asking them when you meet them—"If they want a *chaw?*" and offering them a plug to take a bite off.

As I did n't use tobacco, I could not give him a chew.

"You think, then," I resumed, "that there is no slave who would not rather be a freeman?"

"I'm sartain on it, mass'r."

"Well," said I, "I never met but one. He said he would rather be a slave than a freeman; but he, I guess, was a liar."

"Yes, mass'r," returned the slave, emphatically, "he war a big liar, and you ought to hab slapped him on the mouth for sayin' so. What slave-man wouldn't rather work for hisself dan for a boss, mass'r?"

TREATMENT OF FEMALE SLAVES.

"Does your wife work all day as hard as you do?"

"Yes, mass'r," he replied, "and all my childer, too. De boss takes dem when dey is not so high"—he levelled his hand within four feet of the earth's surface—"and keeps dem at work till dey die."

"Are the wives of slaves respected as married women?"

"No, mass'r, dey don't make no diff'rence wedder de colored women is married or not. White folks jest do what dey have a mind to wid dem."

His tone was bitter as he spoke these words. There was an ominous light in his eye—the precursor, probably (I thought), of a terrible conflagration which is destined yet to burn up the oppressor and his works.

"Do white people—I mean the bosses—ever act immorally to colored women on the plantation?"

"Yes, mass'r, *bery of'en indeed.*"

"I should think, then," I said, "that colored people who are married, and are parents, would be the most discontented with slavery?"

"I dunno, mass'r," said the slave, with a heavy heart-born sigh, "I knows *I's* tired on it. I's seen my daughter—treated so dat"——

He hesitated, looked savagely gloomy, muttered something to himself, and added:

"Well, mass'r, *I's* TIRED on it. Mass'r, is it bery cold at the North?"

This question was asked by almost every slave with whom I conversed in Virginia and North Carolina. To each of them I made the same reply. In the winter, I said, it is a great deal colder than it is here; but not half so cold as the white people try to make you believe. Besides, people wear more clothes there than you do here, and do not feel the cold more than you do in Virginia. In Canada, in winter, it is very cold; a great deal colder than in the free States. In the free States a man may be taken back into bondage, if his boss discovers him:

AN UNBELIEVING NEGRO.

"No, oh, no, massa; dey can't do dat," said the slave, emphatically.

"Yes, they can," I rejoined, "but they are getting rather afraid to do it now."

"*No,* massa, dey *can't* do it," returned the slave in a still more emphatic tone, and with that peculiar smile which uneducated people involuntarily assume when instructing others on subjects with which they suppose themselves to be thoroughly familiar, and their companion misinformed.

I did not try to disabuse him of his error, for I knew that, perhaps before he escaped, the people of the North might refuse, with one accord, to act the degrading *role* of bloodhounds any longer. Indeed how could I have undeceived him? How could I have begun to convince an uncorrupted mind of the existence, or even the *possibility* of such a creature as a doughface?[2]

"In Canada," I resumed, "if a colored man once gets there, he is safe for life. Canada belongs to the British, and they never deliver up a fugitive."

"Yes, massa," said the slave, "I belieb dat. A great many white folks has told me dat, and I belieb it."

"Although it is very cold in Canada," I continued, "I never found a negro there—and I saw great numbers of them[3]—who would return, if he could, to his old home and condition in the South."

TREATMENT OF FREE NEGROES.

"I bliev dat," said the slave, "I know if I could get away, I would n't come back. Mass'r," he added, "I's heerd dat in England, a colored man is treated jest as well as dey do white folks. Is dat true, mass'r?"

"I believe so," I replied.

"Is colored people treated as well as white folks at de North?"

"Why, no," I was forced to reply, "not quite. There is a little prejudice everywhere, a great deal in some places, against them. But still, at the North, a colored person need never be insulted by a white man, as he is here, unless he be a coward, or a non-resistant Christian. He may strike back. It would not do to strike back here, would it?"

"Oh Lor', no! mass'r," said the slave, looking as if frightened by the mere idea of such a thing; "dey would shoot us down jest as soon as if we was cats."

"Well," I resumed, "a colored man at the North may strike back, and *not* be shot down."

I then related an incident, of which I was an eye witness. The last time that I travelled from Albany to Buffalo, a few months ago,[4] there was a colored man in the cars with us.* A white bully, "exquisitely" dressed, with gold chain, and brooch, and diamond pin—in the height of the blackleg[5] fashion—entered it at one station, and said to the African, in a loud domineering tone:

"Get out, you d——d nigger, and go to the South where you belong to."

The colored man arose, approached him, and applied every abusive epithet he could think of, interspersed with oaths, to his cowardly "Cir-

---

*In the South, I may state here, "the servants," as the slaves are frequently styled, and the free persons of color, are put in the first half of the foremost car by themselves, unless they are females travelling with their mistress, when they sit by her side. The other half of the negro car is appropriated for smokers, and is always liberally patronized.

cassian"[6] opponent. And I must admit, in justice to the negro's memory and knowledge, that he did remember an extraordinary number of uncomplimentary phrases, and showed a genealogical fund of information which was surprising to every one present, and seemed perfectly to stagger the dandy. He told him, for example, that he knew his family; that his mother was a member of the canine race; and several other equally rare and entertaining facts of his personal history. All snobs are cowards; so the negro remained unanswered.

"Lor', mass'r," said the slave, after I had told him this incident, "it wouldn't do to do dat here; dey would kill us right away."

CONCERNING LINEN.

"How many suits," I asked, "are you allowed a year?"

"Two, mass'r."

"Of course, you have two shirts?"

"No, mass'r; only one at a time."

"How do you get it washed?"

"I washes it at night, and sleeps naked till it's dry."

(The slaveholders, doubtless, hold to the Western boy's philosophy of living, as illustrated in his answer to the gentleman who, seeing him naked, asked him where his shirt was. "Washing." "Have you only one?" "Only one!" said the boy; "do you expect a feller to have a thousand shirts?")

We had some further talk about the country, and then went each our own way.

He told me that he would risk the chance of flying at once, *if he knew how to go.*

NOTES

1. The following conversation, dated September 25, 1854, originally appeared as part of the John Ball, Jr. letter published in the *New York National Anti-Slavery Standard* on October 14, 1854.

2. A derisive term used to describe northern politicians deemed by their opponents to be excessively sympathetic to the South. Mathews, *Dictionary of Americanisms,* 1:513.

3. Redpath's family emigrated from Scotland to Kalamazoo County, Michigan, in the late 1840s. In the early 1850s Redpath had worked as a reporter on the *Detroit Advertiser,* opposite Hudson, Ontario. It is likely that Redpath visited Canada while residing in Michigan or on a later visit to his family there. Horner, *James Redpath,* 12–18.

4. The date of this trip is unknown. Redpath might have made such a trip in connection with his employment by the FlNew York Tribune or while on a visit to his family in Michigan. Horner, *James Redpath,* 17–24.

5. In the nineteenth century, to "black-leg" was to return to work before a strike had been settled. Eric Partridge, ed., *A Dictionary of Slang and Unconventional English* (New York, 1937), 88.

6. Circassia is a region on the northeastern shore of the Black Sea, north of the Caucasus Mountains, whose inhabitants are noted for their striking physical beauty. Leon E. Seltzer, ed., *The Columbia Lippincott Gazeteer of the World* (New York, 1952), 412.

III.

IS SLAVERY A CURSE?——VOICE OF OLD VIRGINIA.[1]

MODERN Virginia denies that slavery is a curse. It is not very long ago since she adopted this opinion.

When at Richmond I purchased a little volume of "Speeches on the Policy of Virginia in Relation to her Colored Population."[2] It is a very rare book now; it has long been out of print; and it is not likely to be speedily republished. It consists of a number of pamphlet speeches, bound together; most of them, as the title-page tells us, published by request. It is a genuine Virginia volume, as the names of the authors, printers, publishers, and the amazingly clumsy appearance of it, prove. These speeches were delivered in the House of Delegates of Virginia, in 1832, by the leading politicians of the State, shortly after the celebrated insurrection, or massacre (as the slaveholders style it) of Southampton—a period of intense excitement, when abolition was the order of the day, even in the stony-hearted Old Dominion.[3]

Is slavery a curse? Listen to the answer of Thomas Marshall, of Fauquier,[4] then, as yet, one of the distinguished politicians of Virginia:

THOMAS MARSHALL'S OPINION.

"Slavery is ruinous to the whites; it retards improvement; roots out our industrious population; banishes the yeomanry of the country; deprives the spinner, the weaver, the smith, the shoemaker, the carpenter of employment and support. The EVIL admits of no remedy. It is increasing, and will continue to increase, *until the whole country* will be inundated by one black wave, covering its whole extent, with a few white faces, here and there, floating on its surface. The master has no capital but what is invested in human flesh; the father, instead of being richer for his sons, is at a loss how to provide for them. There is no diversity of occupations, no incentive to enterprise. Labor of every species is disreputable, because performed mostly by slaves. Our towns are stationary, our villages almost everywhere declining; and the general aspect of the country marks the curse of a wasteful, idle, reckless population, who have no interest in the soil, and care not how much it is impoverished. Public improvements are neglected, and the entire continent does not present a region for which nature has done so much and art so little. If cultivated by free labor, the soil of Virginia is capable of sustaining a dense population, among whom labor would be honorable, and where the busy hum of men would tell that all were happy, and all were free."[5]

JOHN A. CHANDLER'S OPINION.

The second speech was delivered by John A. Chandler, of Norfolk county:[6]

"The proposition, Mr. Speaker," said he, " is not whether the State shall take the slaves for public uses, but this: *Whether the Legislature has the right to compel the owners of slaves, under a penalty, within a reasonable time, to remove the future increase* out of the country."

His speech is devoted to the discussion of this proposition, and in it he takes the most ultra positions. The Virginia slaveholder out-Garrisons Garrison. He even introduces the golden rule[7] as an argument! In the opening paragraph, he says:

"It will be recollected, sir, that when the memorial from Charles City, was presented by the gentleman from Hanover, and when its reference was opposed, I took occasion to observe that I believed the people of Norfolk county would rejoice, could they even in the vista of time, see some scheme for the gradual removal of this *curse* from our land. I would have voted, sir, for its rejection, because I was desirous to see a report from the committee declaring the slave population an evil, and recommending to the people of this commonwealth the adoption of some plan for its riddance."[8]

The words italicized are so marked by the orator.

HENRY BERRY'S OPINION.

The third speech, delivered by Henry Berry, of Jefferson,[9] opens in these words:

"Mr. Speaker: Coming from a county in which there are 4,000 slaves, being myself a slaveholder—and I may say further, that the largest interest in property that I have, lies about one hundred miles east of the Blue Ridge, and consists of land and slaves. Under these circumstances, I hope I shall be excused for saying a few words on this important and deeply interesting subject.

"That slavery is a *grinding* curse upon this State, I had supposed would have been admitted by all, and that the only question for debate here would have been the possibility of removing the evil. But, sir, in this I have been disappointed. I have been astonished to find that there are advocates here for slavery with all its effects. *Sir, this only proves how far—how very far—we may be carried by pecuniary interest;* it proves what has been said by an immortal bard:

> 'That man is unco' weak,
>   And little to be trusted;
> If self the wavering balance shake,
>   'Tis rarely right adjusted.'[10]

Sir, I believe that no cancer on the physical body was ever more certain, steady, and fatal in its progress, than is this cancer on the political body of the State of Virginia. It is eating into her very vitals."

DANGER AHEAD.

And again:

"Like a mighty avalanche, the evil is rolling towards us, accumulating weight and impetus at every turn. And, sir, *if we do nothing to avert its progress, it will ultimately overwhelm and destroy us forever.*"

And again:

"Sir, although I have no fears for any general results from the efforts of this class of our population *now,* still, sir, the time will come when there will be imminent general danger. Pass as severe laws as you will to keep these unfortunate creatures in ignorance, it is in vain, unless you can extinguish that spark of intellect which God has given them. Let any man who advocates slavery examine the system of laws that we have adopted (from stern necessity, it may be said) toward these creatures, and he may shed a tear upon that; and would to God, sir, the memory of it might thus be blotted out forever."

A DAMNING CONFESSION.

"Sir, *we have, as far as possible, closed every avenue by which light might enter their minds: we have only to go one step further—to extinguish the capacity to see—and our work would be completed. They would then be then reduced to the level of the beasts of the field, and we should be safe; and I am not certain that we would not do it,* if we could find out the necessary process, and that under plea of necessity. But, sir, this is impossible; and can man be in the midst of freedom and not know what freedom is? Can he feel that he has the power to assert his liberty, and will he not do it? Yes, sir, with the certainty of the current of time will he do it, whenever he has the power. Sir, to prove that that time will come, I need offer no other argument than that of arithmetic, the conclusions from which are clear demonstrations on this subject. The data are all before us, and every man can work out the process for himself. Sir, *a death-struggle must come between the two classes, on which one or the other will be extinguished forever.* Who can contemplate such a catastrophe as even possible, and be indifferent and inactive ?"[11]

CHARLES JAMES FAULKNER'S OPINION.

"If slavery can be eradicated," said Charles James Faulkner,[12] "in God's name let us get rid of it."

Again:

"An era of commercial intercourse is thus fondly anticipated, in the fancy of these gentlemen, between the east and the west [of the State]. New ties and new attachments are now to connect us more closely in the bonds of an intimate and paternal union. Human flesh is to be the staple of that trade, human blood the cement of that connection. And in return for the rich products of our valleys, are we to receive the nicely measured and graduated limbs of our species?

"Sir, a sagacious politician in this State, on the evening of the debate upon the presentation and reference of the Hanover petition, remarked to me, 'Why do you gentlemen from the west suffer yourselves to be fanned into such a tempest of passion? The time will come, and that before long, when there will be no diversity of interest or feeling among us on this point—when we shall all equally represent a slaveholding interest.'

AN ELOQUENT PROTEST AGAINST SLAVERY EXTENSION.

"Sir, it is to avert any such possible consequence to my country, that I, one of the humblest, but not the least determined of the western delegation, have raised my voice for emancipation. Sir, tax our lands, vilify our country, carry the sword of extermination through our now defenceless villages, but spare us, I implore you, spare us the curse of slavery, that bitterest drop from the chalice of the destroying angel.

"Sir, the people of the west, I undertake to say, feel a deep, a lively, a generous sympathy for their eastern brethren. They know that the evils which now afflict them are not attributable to any fault of theirs; that slavery was introduced against their will; that we are indebted for it to the commercial cupidity of that heartless empire, which has never failed to sacrifice every principle of right and justice, every feeling of honor and humanity, to the aggrandizement of her commerce and manufactures. Sir, we have lands, we have houses, we have property, and we are willing to pledge them all, to any extent, to aid you in removing this *evil.* Yet we will not that you shall extend to us the same evils under which you labor. We will not that you shall make our fair domain the receptacle of your mass of political filth and corruption. No, sir, before we can submit to such terms, violent convulsions must agitate this State."

INFLUENCE OF SLAVERY ON FREE WHITE LABOR.

"Slavery," he continued, "it is admitted, is an evil which presses heavily against the best interests of the State. It banishes free white labor; it exterminates the mechanic, the artisan, the manufacturer; it deprives them of occupation; it deprives them of bread; it converts the energy of a community into indolence—its power into imbecility—its efficacy into weakness. Sir, being thus injurious, have we not a right to demand its extermination? *Shall society suffer that the slaveholder may gather his crop of flesh?* What is his mere pecuniary claim compared with the great interests of the common weal? Must the country languish, droop, die, that the slaveholder may flourish? Shall all interests be subservient to one? all rights subordinate to those of the slaveholder? Has not the mechanic— have not the middle classes their rights—*rights incompatible with the existence of slavery?*"[13]

Lest the reader should imagine that I am quoting from the files of the *Liberator*[14]—and in order that he may again peruse these extracts, and remember that they are culled from the speeches of Virginia slave-holders—I will reserve the remaining extracts for another chapter, and conclude by quoting from a letter of my own, which accompanied the little volume above alluded to, from the city of Richmond to a friend in New York.

TREATMENT OF FREE NEGROES IN VIRGINIA.

A free person of color told me to-day (Sept. 20th) that it is an offence in Richmond, punishable with imprisonment and stripes on the bare back, for a negro, whether free or bond, male or female, to take the inside of the sidewalk in passing a white man! Negroes are required "to give the wall," and, if necessary, to get off the sidewalk into the street. Rowdies take great pleasure, whenever they see a well-dressed colored person with his wife approaching, to walk as near the edge of the pavement as possible, in order to compel them to go into the street, or to incur the extreme and barbarous penalty of the law. Gentlemen of course would not do so; but in Richmond, as elsewhere, the majority of the male sex are neither gentlemen nor men.

In walking in the Southern cities, I have very often been annoyed at seeing an old man or a woman, as I approached them, getting off the sidewalk altogether. Another custom of the colored people down South has frequently irritated my democratic nerves. Excepting in the business streets of the far Southern cities—or in such a place as New Orleans, where there is no time to spare, and too much of the old French gentility to tolerate so despicable a practice—whenever a slave meets a Saxon— "ivin, be jabers, if he's a Cilt"—he touches his hat reverentially. In Georgia, Florida, and South Carolina, and even in some parts of Virginia and North Carolina, if you enter into a conversation with a colored man, and keep looking at him as you speak, he touches his cap every time that he answers your interrogatories, unless you expressly command him to desist. Perhaps this custom is the consequence of a legal enactment, also; but it is certainly the result of the imperious *lex non scripta* of the Southern States.[15]

NOTES

1. Redpath introduced the material in this chapter in a substantially different manner in his John Ball, Jr. letter. There he wrote:

For the National Anti-Slavery Standard.

EXTRACTS FROM THE DIARY OF AN ABOLITIONIST
DOWN SOUTH.

Sept. 20.—At Richmond, Virginia. I called to-day on the coloured man, the fruiterer, with whom I held a long conversation some months ago, on the condition and 'contentment' of the African population of Richmond and its vicinity. [An account of this conversation was published by our contributor in Mr. Garrison's *Liberator*, a short time since.—ED.] He was sadly altered. His wife was dead. The event had almost proved fatal to him. He had been married to her for more than twenty years, and had known and loved her from childhood. He had *bought* her out of bondage, before he married her. He proposes to migrate and settle in Philadelphia, in Spring. When he does so, I will publish his name and demand of my fellow-woolies of Philadelphia to be his patrons and friends. He told me that it was an offence in Richmond, punishable with imprisonment and stripes on the bare back, for a coloured person, whether bond or free, male or female, to take the *inside* of the sidewalk in passing a white man. Negroes are required to "give the wall," and, if necessary, to get off the sidewalk into the street. Rowdies take great pleasure, whenever they see a well-dressed coloured person with his wife approaching, to walk as near the edge of the pavement as possible, in order to compel them to go into the street—or to incur the extreme penalty of the law. Gentlemen, of course, never enforce this brutal law. But, alas! the majority of the male sex, in Richmond as elsewhere, are neither men nor gentlemen. In walking in Southern cities, I have very often been annoyed at seeing an old man or woman getting off the sidewalk as I approached. Another custom of the coloured people Down South has frequently irritated my democratic nerves. Except in the business streets of Southern cities, whenever a negro in the slave States meets a Saxon, he touches his hat reverentially. In Georgia, Florida and South Carolina, and even in Virginia and North Carolina, if you enter into a conversation with a coloured man and keep looking at him as you speak, he touches his cap every time he answers your question, unless you *command* him to desist. Perhaps this custom is the consequence of a legal enactment also; but it is certainly a result of the *lex non scripta* of every Southern State. None but petty tyrants would tolerate such degrading customs.

In Virginia, if the mother be a slave, her off-spring are born into bondage, even although they may be the children of a freeman. If the mother be free, then also are her children free, even although their father be a slave.

IS SLAVERY A CURSE? MITCHEL VS. VIRGINIA

Before making any extracts from entries in my diary, kept during my stay in Northc⅖₂₇ Carolina, I wish to enable your readers to see in what light slavery is regarded by the leading statesmen and politicians of Old Virginia. The revival of the Slave Trade has recently been discussed by the Richmond papers. The Southern press has talked magnificently about the scheme. John Mitchel, I see, has endorsed it, and has eulogized the foolish Mr. Wise for his flunkeyism to Southern fanaticism on this subject.

Mr. Wise, surnamed the Foolish, denies that slavery is a curse to a country. The Voice of Vitriol also ridicules the notion that negro servitude is productive of evil to a State. The envier of fat Alabama negroes actually pities Thomas Jefferson for having admitted that slavery was a national wrong! It is really amusing to see a demagogue and parole-breaker pitying such statemen as Thomas Jefferson, Benjamin Franklin and George Washington; but still more ludicrous is it to see Southern editors, who know, and in private acknowledge, that slavery is a curse, encouraging the foul creature in expressing such sentiments as he has lately propagated on the subject of involuntary servitude.

Is slavery a curse?

John Mitchel answers—No.

Is slavery a curse?

Listen to the voice of Virginia in reply.

New York National Anti-Slavery Standard, October 21, 1854.

2. This volume contained a collection of ten pamphlets bound together. The first nine were the texts of speeches delivered in the Virginia House of Delegates during the session of 1832 and originally published in the *Richmond Enquirer.* The tenth pamphlet was a pseudonymous letter on the slavery issue, signed "Appomatox." A copy of this undated volume has survived in the Virginia State Library and Archives. Letter to the editor from Brent Tarter, April 19, 1994.

3. Following the suppression of the bloody slave uprising led by Nat Turner in Southampton County in the summer of 1832, Virginia underwent an unprecedented debate over the future of slavery in the state. In mid-January 1832 the Virginia House of Delegates considered and rejected immediate emancipation proposals but pledged eventual gradual

emancipation for the state's slaves. No subsequent action was taken to fulfill that pledge. Miller and Smith, *Dictionary of Afro-American Slavery,* 787–88.

4. The son of Chief Justice John Marshall, Thomas Marshall (1784–1835) graduated from Princeton University and briefly practiced law in Richmond. He devoted great attention to restoring the ancestral plantation of Oakville in Fauquier County. Marshall was sent to the state constitutional convention of 1829–30 and then to the House of Delegates. Lyon G. Tyler, *Encyclopedia of Virginia Biography,* 5 vols. (New York, 1915), 5:760–61.

5. Making only minor changes, Redpath quotes from the first pamphlet in the bound collection, *The Speech of Thomas Marshall, (of Fauquier) in the House of Delegates of Virginia, on the Policy of the State in Relation to Her Colored Population: Delivered Saturday, January 14, 1832,* 2d ed. (Richmond, Va., 1832), 6.

6. From Portsmouth, Virginia, John A. Chandler (c. 1795–1848) had made a living as a merchant until around 1820 when he began a successful legal practice. He represented Norfolk County for just one term in the House of Delegates. *Norfolk Daily Southern Argus,* April 1, 1848; *Norfolk American Beacon, and Norfolk and Portsmouth Daily Advertiser,* April 1, 1848.

7. The New Testament's Golden Rule is stated in Matt. 7:12 and Luke 6:31.

8. Redpath quotes out of sequence two passages from the second document in the collection, *The Speech of John A. Chandler, (of Norfolk County,) in the House of Delegates of Virginia on the Policy of the State with Respect to Her Slave Population* (Richmond, Va., 1832), 6, 3–4.

9. Born in King George County, Virginia, Henry Rose Berry (c. 1792–1867) studied law in Alexandria before opening a practice in Shepherdstown in 1820. Later a prominent local Whig party leader, Berry represented Jefferson County in the Virginia House of Delegates from 1831 to 1836. A. D. Kenamond, *Prominent Men of Shepherdstown During Its First 200 Years* (Shepherdstown, W.Va., 1963), 39.

10. Not a quotation from William Shakespeare.

11. Redpath quotes three segments of *The Speech of Henry Berry, (of Jefferson,) in the House of Delegates of Virginia, on the Abolition of Slavery* (n.p., n.d.), 2, 3.

12. The fourth reprinted speech in the collection was by Charles James Faulkner (1806–84) of Berkeley County. Son of a War of 1812 hero, Faulkner graduated from Georgetown University in 1822. He practiced law in Martinsburg, now in West Virginia, before serving in the Virginia legislature and then the U.S. House of Representatives. He freed several of his slaves and sent them to Liberia. In 1859–61 Faulkner held the post of American ambassador to France. He later served in the Confederate army. John E. Findling, *Dictionary of American Diplomatic History* (Westport, Conn., 1980), 168; Helper, *Impending Crisis,* 98, 175; *DAB,* 6:198–99.

13. These quoted passages are from *The Speech of Charles Jas. Faulkner, (of Berkeley) in the House of Delegates of Virginia, on the Policy of the State with Respect to Her Slave Population* (Richmond, Va., 1832), 4, 10, 17. The original John Ball, Jr. letter continued the quotation from Faulkner's speech. In the *Roving Editor,* this material has been moved into the next chapter. *New York National Anti-Slavery Standard,* October 21, 1854.

14. An allusion to the weekly abolitionist newspaper *The Liberator,* founded in 1831 by William Lloyd Garrison. Stewart, *William Lloyd Garrison,* 49–53.

15. Redpath probably refers to Sydney Howard Gay, the editor of the *New York National Anti-Slavery Standard,* which published the original version of this material in the John Ball, Jr. letter series. These paragraphs are similar to those found in the *New York National Anti-Slavery Standard,* October 21, 1854, as transcribed in note 1, above.

IV.

SLAVERY AND FREEDOM COMPARED.

YOU feel sure that you were not reading from the *Liberator's* files?[1]

If you do so, let us quote, once more, from the speech of Charles James Faulkner, of Virginia:

Sir, I am gratified to perceive that no gentleman has yet risen in this hall the avowed advocate of slavery. The day has gone by when such a voice could be listened to with patience, or even with forbearance. I even regret, sir, that we should find those amongst us who enter the lists of discussion as its *apologists,* except alone upon the ground of uncontrollable necessity. And yet who could have listened to the very eloquent remarks of the gentleman from Brunswick without being forced to conclude that he, at least, considered slavery, however not to be defended upon principle, yet as being divested of much of its enormity as you approached it in practice?

"Sir, if there be one who concurs with that gentleman in the harmless character of this institution, let me request him to compare the condition of the slaveholding portion of this commonwealth—barren, desolate and seared, as it were, by the avenging hand of heaven—with the descriptions which we have of this same country from those who first broke its virgin soil?

"To what is this change ascribable?

"*Alone to the withering and blasting effects of slavery.*

"If this does not satisfy him, let me request him to extend his travels to the Northern States of this Union, and beg him to contrast the happiness and contentment which prevails throughout that country—the busy and cheerful sound of industry—the rapid and swelling growth of the population—their means and institutions of education—their skill and proficiency in the useful arts—their enterprise and public spirit—the monuments of their commercial and manufacturing industry; and, above all, their devoted attachment to the government from which they derive their protection, with the division, discontent, indolence and poverty of the Southern country.

"To what, sir, is all this ascribable?

"*To that vice on the organization of society, by which one half of its inhabitants are arrayed, in interest and feeling, from the other half—to that unfortunate state of society in which freeman regard labor as disgraceful, and slaves shrink from it as a burden tyrannically imposed upon them*—to that condition of things in which half a million of your population can feel no sympathy with the society in the prosperity of which they are forbidden to participate, and no attachment to a government at whose hands they receive nothing but injustice.

"If this should not be sufficient, and the curious and incredulous inquirer should suggest that the contrast which has been adverted to, and which is so manifest, might be traced to a difference of climate, or other causes distinct from slavery itself, permit me to refer him to the two States of Kentucky and Ohio. No difference of soils no diversity of climate, no diversity in the original settlement of those two States can account for the remarkable disproportion in their natural advancement. Separated by a river alone, they seem to have been purposely and providentially designed to exhibit in their future histories, the difference which naturally results from a country free, and a country afflicted with the curse of slavery. The same may be said of the two States of Missouri and Illinois."[2]

Surely this is satisfactory testimony?

Thomas J. Randolph[3] spoke next, and in the same strain as the preceding speakers.

Is slavery a curse?[4]

Marshall, Barry, Randolph, Faulkner, and Chandler answer in the affirmative; and thus replies Mr. James McDowell, junior,[5] the delegate from Rockbridge:

SLAVERY A LEPROSY.

"Sir, if our ancestors had exerted the firmness, which, under greater obligations we ourselves are called on to exert, Virginia would not, at this day, have been mourning over the legacy of weakness, and of sorrow that has been left her; she would not have been thrust down—down—in a still lowering relation to the subordinate post which she occupies in the Confederacy, whose career she has led; *she would not be withering under the leprosy which is piercing her to her heart.*"

Again:

"If I am to judge from the tone of our debate, from the concessions on all hands expressed, there is not a man in this body, not one, perhaps, that is even represented here, who would not have thanked the generations that have gone before us, if, acting as *public* men, they had brought this bondage to a close—who would not have thanked them, if, acting as private men, on private motives, they had relinquished the property which their mistaken kindness has devolved upon us? Proud as are the names, for intellect and patriotism, which enrich the volumes of our history, and reverentially as we turn to them at this period of waning reputation, that name, that man, above all parallel, would have been the chief who could have blotted out this curse from his country; those above all others would have received the homage of an eternal gratitude who, casting away every suggestion of petty interest, had broken the yoke which, in an evil hour, had been imposed, and had transplanted, as a free man, to another continent, the outcast and the wretched being who burdens ours with his presence, and who defiles it with his crimes."

DANGEROUS PROPERTY.

In another part of his speech he says:

"Slavery and danger are inseparable."

Such, indeed, appears to have been the unanimous opinion of the numerous delegates who spoke on this occasion, as well as of those who were silent. Says Mr. McDowell:

"In this investigation there is no difficulty—nothing has been left to speculation or inquiry; for however widely gentlemen have differed upon the power and the justice of touching this property, they have yet united in a common testimony to its character. It has been frankly and unequivocally declared, from the very commencement of this debate, by the most decided enemies of abolition themselves, as well as by others, that this property is an *evil*—that it is dangerous property. Yes, sir, so dangerous has it been represented to be, even by those who desire to retain it, that we have been reproached for speaking of it otherwise than in fireside whispers—reproached for entertaining debate upon it in this hall; and the discussion of it with open doors, and to the general ear, has been charged upon us as a climax of rashness and folly which threatens issues of calamity to the country."

Before concluding, he reiterates the assertion: *"No one disguises,"* he says, *"the danger of this property—that it is inevitable, and that it is increasing."*

("The slaveholder in the Carolina forests," truly said the *New York Times,* "trembles at his fireside every time that he hears the report of a solitary rifle in the woods.")

A BEAUTIFUL DOMESTIC INSTITUTION.

Mr M'Dowell proceeds to unfold the exceeding beauty of slavery as a domestic institution:

"It is quaintly remarked by Lord Bacon,[6] that 'liberty is a spark which flieth into the face of him who attempteth to trample it under foot.' And, sir, of all conceivable or possible situations, that which the slave now occupies in the domestic services of our families is precisely the one which clothes this irrepressible principle of his nature with the fearfullest power—precisely the one which may give that principle its most fatal energy and direction. Who that looks upon his family, with the slave in its bosom, ministering to its wants, but knows and feels that this is true? Who but sees and knows how much the safety of that family depends upon forbearance, how little can be provided for defence? Sir, you may exhaust yourself upon schemes of domestic defence, and when you have examined every project which the mind can suggest, you will at last have only a deeper consciousness that nothing can be done. No, sir, nothing for this purpose can be done. The curse which, in combination with others, has been denounced against man as a just punishment for his sins—*the curse of having an enemy in his household, is upon us.* We have an enemy there, to whom our dwelling is at all times accessible, our persons at all times, our lives at all times, and that by manifold weapons, both visible and concealed.

"But, sir, I will not expatiate further on this view of the subject. Suffice it to say, that the defenceless situation of the master, and the sense of injured right in the slave, are the best possible preparatives for conflict— a conflict, too, which may be considered more certainly at hand whenever and wherever the numerical ascendency of the slave shall inspire him with confidence in his force."

SLAVERY A NATIONAL EVIL.

Mr. McDowell regards slavery as a national as well as a State and domestic calamity. With this passage from his speech, I will close the little volume of Truths by Taskmasters:

"The existence of slavery creates a political interest in the Union, which is of all others the most positive; an interest which, in relation to those who do not possess it, is adversary and exclusive; one which marks the manners of our country by a corresponding distinction, and is sowing broadcast amongst us, both in our official and private intercourse, the seeds of unkindness and suspicion. On this interest geographical parties have been formed; on its maintenance or restriction the bitterest struggles have been waged in Congress; and, as it contains an ingredient of political power in our Federal Constitution, it will always be the subject of struggle; always defended by the most vigilant care, and assailed by the most subtile counter action. Slaveholding and non-slaveholding must necessarily constitute the characteristic feature of our country—must necessarily form the broad and indivisible interest upon which parties will combine, and will and does comprehend, in the jealousies which now surround it, the smothered and powerful, but, I hope, not the irresistible causes of future dismemberment. To all of its other evils, then, slavery superadds the still further one of being a cause of national dissension—of being a fixed and repulsive element between the differeńt members of our Republic—itself impelling with strong tendency, and aggravating all smaller tendencies to political distrust, alienation and hostility."[7]

Let no man accuse me of unfriendliness to the slaveholders. See how willing I have been to put their honorable and patriotic sentiments on record![8]

NOTES

1. The remainder of this chapter is drawn from the second half of Redpath's John Ball, Jr. letter published in the *New York National Anti-Slavery Standard,* October 21, 1854.

2. Altering the paragraph structure and adding italics to the original, Redpath continues to quote from the *Speech of Charles Jas. Faulkner,* 20.

3. The fifth speech in the collection, described as "on the Abolition of Slavery," was delivered by Thomas Jefferson Randolph (1792–1875) of Albemarle County, the favorite grandson and literary executor of Thomas Jefferson and son of Martha Jefferson Randolph and Virginia governor Thomas Mann Randolph. After brief service in the House of Delegates, Randolph largely avoided the political arena. Instead he devoted himself to editing his grandfather's writings and to serving the University of Virginia. *Harper's Encyclopaedia of United States History from 458 A.D. to 1909,* 10 vols. (New York, 1901–5), 7:379; Helper, *Impending Crisis,* 202; *DAB,* 15:369–70.

4. Redpath characterizes the sentiments in *The Speech of Thomas J. Randolph, (of Albemarle,) in the House of Delegates of Virginia, on the Abolition of Slavery: Delivered Saturday, Jan. 21, 1832,* 2d ed. (Richmond, Va., 1832).

5. Continuing to quote from the speeches in the order the pamphlets were bound together, Redpath reproduces remarks by James McDowell, Jr. (1795–1851), the delegate from Rockbridge, Virginia. After graduating from the College of New Jersey (now Rutgers University), McDowell migrated to Kentucky where he failed as a planter. He returned to Virginia and established a legal practice in Lexington. In this speech favoring gradual emancipation McDowell denounced slavery as a cause of dangerous national dissension, but he later moderated these views substantially. The Democratic party elected him as governor of Virginia (1843–46) and as a congressman (1846–51). Sobel and Raimo, *Biographical Directory of United States Governors,* 4:1641; *DAB,* 12:30–31.

6. English philosopher, jurist, and statesman Sir Francis Bacon (1561–1626). *DNB,* 1:800–832.

7. With only minor alterations in sentence structure, Redpath quotes passages from the *Speech of James M'Dowell, Jr. (of Rockbridge,) in the House of Delegates of Virginia, on the Slave Question: Delivered Saturday, January 21, 1832,* 2d ed. (Richmond, Va., 1832), 8, 10, 12, 16, 20, 21.

8. In place of this last paragraph, Redpath ended the original John Ball, Jr. letter as follows:

> These extracts will suffice, I think, to convince every impartial mind that slavery is regarded as a curse by the most enlightened politicians of the Old Dominion. I hope that the friends of freedom in the North will avail themselves of them to crush in the bud the last assertion of the sycophants of the Slave Power—that, namely, the pecu-

liar Institution of the South is *not* a curse to the country which supports it. It is so outrageous a falsehood that, if once tolerated, it will soon be advanced as an incontrovertible axiom by the allies of the oppressor. Kill it, then, at once!

—In my next communication, I will unfold a new scheme of Emancipation, and give an account of several conversations with slaves in the State of North Carolina.

JOHN BALL, JR.

New York National Anti-Slavery Standard, October 21, 1854.

V.

NORTH CAROLINA.

WELDON, North Carolina, is a hamlet, or town, or "city "—I do n't know what they call it—consisting of a railroad depot, a hotel, a printing-office, one or two stores, and several houses.[1] Whether it has increased in population or remained stationary since my visit to it—September 26, 1854[2]— I have now no means of ascertaining.*

TALK WITH A YOUNG SLAVE.

In returning from a walk in the woods, by which Weldon is surrounded, I came up to a young negro man who was lying on the ground in the shade of a tree, holding a yearling ox by a rope.

"Is that all you have got to do?" I asked.

"No, mass'r," said he; "I's waitin' for a waggon to come 'long."

I entered into a conversation with him. He answered all my questions without hesitation. He said that he would run the risk of capture, and try to reach the North; and he believed that dozens—"yes, mass'r, lots and lots" of the slaves in this neighborhood—would fly to the North, *if they knew the way.* It was not the fear of being captured, he said, that prevented them from running away, but ignorance of the proper route to the Free States.

Several slaves had told me so before, but I had never been able to devise a plan to remedy this ignorance, and thereby give to every brave bondman a chance of escaping from slavery. The north star is like the white man, "too mighty onsartin" for the majority of the slaves to rely on: they need a guide, which will serve them both by day and night—when-

---

*Mr. Helper, author of that valuable anti-slavery volume—"The Impending Crisis of the South"—informs me that it is now a town of 700 inhabitants.

ever they can see it. Dark and cloudy nights, too, when the north star is invisible, are the most propitious for the purpose of the runaway.

As this slave replied to my questions, I thought that POCKET MARINER'S COMPASSES might be made most effective liberators of the African race.

MAGNETIC LIBERATORS.

I pondered on this subject for a few seconds, and then resumed the conversation:

"Did you ever see the face of a watch?" (The question may seem absurd, but there are thousands of slaves who never saw a watch.)

"Yes, mass'r," said the slave.

"Do you know how the hands of it go round?"

"Yes, mass'r."

"Well, *we*"—I spoke as a member of the human race—"we have invented a thing somewhat like a watch; but instead of going round and round, its hand always points to the North. Now, if we were to give you one of these things, would you run away?"

"Yes, mass'r," said the slave with emphasis; "I would go to-night—and dozens on us would go too."

I described the perils of a runaway's course as vividly as I could. He answered it by saying:

"Well, mass'r, I doesn't care; I'd try to get to de Norf, if I'd one of dem dings."[3]

THE OLD BAPTIST SLAVE.

At the same place, early one morning (for I was detained here several days), I saw an old colored man sitting on a pile of wood near the railroad crossing. Beside him lay his bag of carpenter's tools. I went up to him. He touched his cap.

"Good morning, old man," I said.

"Good mornin' to you, mass'r," he rejoined.

"Are you a carpenter?" I asked.

"Yes, mass'r; in a rough way."

"How old are you?"

"Sixty-two year ole, mass'r."

"You stand your age very well, old man, I returned. I hardly thought you were more than fifty. But I have often noticed that colored people looked much younger than they are. What is that owing to, do you know?"

"Well, mass'r," said he, "I dink it's kase dey's 'bliged to live temp'rate. White folks has plenty ob money, and da drinks a good deal ob liquor;

colored people kent drink much liquor, kase da hasn't got no money. Drinkin', mass'r," remarked the negro, with the air of a doctor of divinity, "drinkin', mass'r, 'ill bring a man down sooner'n anyding; and I dink it's kase de colored people doesn't drink dat da look younger dan de white ole folks."

I have said that I had often noticed this peculiarity, but had never been able to account for it. The old man's solution satisfied me. Negroes in the country, however, sometimes procure liquor from the small groceries, by stealing fowls and other farm produce from their masters. Hence I found, on my previous visit to North Carolina, that the slaveholders were warm advocates of the Maine liquor law.[4]

"Are you a free man?"

"No, mass'r," he replied; "I's a slave."

"I come from the North," I returned; "would you like to go there?"

"Yes, mass'r," he said; "I *would* like to go dare very much."

"Of course, you are a married man?"

"I's been married twice, mass'r."

"Have you any children?"

SEPARATION OF FAMILIES.

"Yes mass'r," said the slave. "I had twelve by my firs' wife. I got her when she was seventeen, and I lived wid her twenty-four years. *Den da sold her and all de chil'ren.* I married anoder wife 'bout nine years since; but I had her little more dan tree years. *Da sold her, too.*"

"Had you any children by her?"

"No, mass'r; and I hasn't had anyding to do wid women since. I's a Baptist; and its agin my religion to have anyting to do wid anybody 'cept my wife. I's never bothered anybody since my last wife was sold away from me."

"It's too bad," said I. Not with a smile—for I never smile when I hear of men, from any motive, whether religious or social, deprived by other men of the God-implanted necessities of their natures. If slavery had no other evils, the fact that it so often separates families, forever, and causes men to lead unnatural lives, and commit unnamed and unnatural crimes, would make me an abolitionary insurrectionist.[5]

"It's too bad," I repeated.

"Yes, mass'r," said he, "it *is* too bad; but we has to submit."

COLORED CONTENTMENT.

"Do you know," I asked, "whether there are any slaves who would rather remain in bondage than be free?"

No, mass'r, not one," he replied emphatically. *"Dare's not one in this county."*

"Did you ever see *one* man," I asked, "in all your life, who would rather be a slave than a freeman?"

"No, mass'r."

Remember his age, reader—sixty-two years—and then believe, if you choose, that the slaves are contented.

"Old as you are," I said, "I suppose you would like to be free?"

"Yes, mass'r"—sadly, very sadly—"I should like bery much to spend de very few years I's got to live in freedom. I would give any man $20 to $30 down, if he could get me free."

"How much do you think your master would sell you for?"

"$200, I tink, mass'r."

"Do you work for your boss, or are you hired out,"[6] I inquired.

"I works," he rejoined, "wharver I kin get work. I gives my boss $50 or $60 a year—jest as I happens to make well out—and I works anywhars in the State. I's got a pass dat lets me go anywhar in de State—but not out on it."[7]

"How much can you make a year?"

"Well, mass'r, if I could get constant work all de time, I could make $160; but I generally makes 'bout $80 or $90."

"Why," I said, musing, "if anybody were to buy you—I mean, if an abolitionist were to buy you—you could repay the money in a couple of years if you were to get constant work."

"Yes, mass'r," he promptly added, "I could—and I would be glad to do it too."

"You said you never knew a colored person who preferred slavery to freedom?"

"No, mass'r, I neber knew one."

"Well, but did you ever know a colored person who *said* he preferred slavery?"

"Oh, yes, mass'r," said the slave. "I's knowed plenty dat would say so to white folks; kase if the boss knowed we wanted to be freemen, he would kick and knock us 'bout, and maybe kill us. *Dey of'en does kill* dem on de plantations."

MURDER WILL OUT.

"Did *you* ever *see* a slave killed on a plantation?"

He replied that he did once see a girl killed on a plantation in Georgia. He said that he heard his boss, a person of the name of Rees, tell his overseer to take some slaves down to Brother Holmes in (I think) Gainsborough county—or from Gainsborough to Hancock county—for I have forgotten which of them the old man named first—and, said the brute, "with what niggers I have got there and these, I think I can raise a crop. If you kill two niggers and four horses and do n't raise a crop, I'll not blame you; but if you do n't, and still do n't raise a crop, I'll think you have n't drove them at all." The monster added—"You need n't be afraid of killing that many; I can afford to lose them."

One day this overseer came up to a girl who was rather lagging behind. Naming her, he said:

"I say, I thought I told you to mend your gait."

"Well, mass'r," she said, " I'se so sick I kin hardly drag one foot after the other."

He stooped down—he was a left-handed man—and laid down his lash. He took up a pine root and made a blow at her head. She tried to avoid the blow, and received the weight of it on her neck. The old man—then a stripling—was obliged, he said, to stand aside to let her fall. She was taken up insensible, and lingered till the following morning. Next day she was buried. This wretch killed another slave during the same season, but my informant did not see the fatal blow struck.

PLANTATION LIFE.

The old man told this story in such'a manner that no one could have doubted its truth. I cross-examined him, and his testimony was unimpeachable.

"How long is it since this happened?" I inquired.

"Forty-two years since," said the slave.

After some further conversation on this event, I asked him:

"How much could you make by carpentering when you were young?"

"I did n't work at de carpenterin' trade, mass'r, when I was young," he replied; "I worked on a plantation. I was de head man.[8] I had twenty or thirty niggers under me"—rather proudly spoken—"but," he added, the Baptist overcoming the carnal man, "dat's no place for a man dat has religion."

"Why?"

"Oh, mass'r, *kase a man dat has religion shouldn't rule over anybody.*"

"Why?" I again asked. "What do you mean?"

"Oh, kase, mass'r," he replied, "a man dat has religion cannot bear to whip and kick de people under him as dey has to do on plantations."

"Are colored people treated *very* badly?" I asked.

"Oh, yes, mass'r," he answered, "very bad indeed; it's hard de way dey *ar* treated."

We talked of several other subjects. He said that if the colored people in this district were to be provided with compasses—the nature of which I explained to him—hundreds of them would fly to the Free States of the North.

"God bless you, mass'r!" he said heartily, as we parted.[9]

It is a good thing, I thought, to be an abolitionist! However apparently alone and neglected the abolitionist may be, he has at least the consolation of knowing that he has four millions of warm-hearted friends in the Southern States![10]

Ah! but has the pro-slavery man no equal consolation?

"It is a good thing to be a Democrat in these days," said the *Washington Union*—the organ of the Cabinet—quite recently, after publishing ten mortal columns of the most profitable kind of government advertisements.[11]

Well, be it so; every man to his taste!

NOTES

1. Weldon was the market center for a peanut-growing district. It was the junction point for a rail line running south from Petersburg, Virginia, the Wilmington and Weldon Railroad, and the Raleigh and Gaston Railroad. Blackwell P. Robinson, ed., *The North Carolina Guide,* rev. ed. (Chapel Hill, 1955), 329.

2. When the following material originally appeared in the John Ball, Jr. letters, Redpath confirmed the date of his visit but left the community unidentified for the following reason explained in a footnote:

> *For obvious reasons, I omit the name of the town. I do not wish either to have human bloodhounds on my tracks or my black friends to be discovered. [*New York National Anti-Slavery Standard,* October 28, 1854]

3. In the newspaper account of this interview, Redpath had the following concluding paragraph:

> We had a long talk on different subjects; and he told me his history—but, in thinking of the *magnetic* Liberator after leaving him, I forgot several particulars of it. [*New York National Anti-Slavery Standard,* October 28, 1854]

4. The Maine legislature adopted the nation's first statewide alcohol prohibition law in 1858. Maisel, *Political Parties and Elections,* 2:889.

5. Significantly, Redpath revised the last sentence of this paragraph when preparing the *Roving Editor* to indicate the evolution in his attitude toward abolition:

> If slavery had no other evils, the fact that it so frequently causes men to lead unnatural lives would make me a Garrisonian Abolitionist. [*New York National Anti-Slavery Standard,* October 28, 1854]

6. Modern historians estimate that approximately a tenth of all slaves and a third of urban slaves were rented by their owners to other employers for periods ranging from a day to a year. Slaves were rented to perform tasks ranging from field and domestic work to highly skilled trades. In cases, slaves even were allowed by their masters to seek out their own employers. Although some southern whites worried that hiring out weakened control over the slaves, the profits from the practice caused it to become increasingly common. Miller and Smith, *Dictionary of Afro-American Slavery,* 321–26.

7. Southern states passed laws that required all slaves, when away from home, to carry on their persons written passes from their masters indicating specific permission for their travels. Larry Gara, *The Liberty Tree: The Legend of the Underground Railroad* (Lexington, Ky., 1961), 46–47.

8. Drivers were slaves given responsibilities for supervising the labor of fellow bondsmen. Usually these drivers supervised small field gangs, but on some plantations thay had significant control over many facets of management. Miller and Smith, *Dictionary of Afro-American Slavery,* 196–98.

9. Redpath ended the original John Ball, Jr. letter at this point with a different parting toast from the slave:

> "God bless you, mass'r; yes, mass'r, and God *will* bless you if you is the friend of the Slave."
>
> JOHN BALL, JR.

New York National Anti-Slavery Standard, October 28, 1854.

10. The U.S. Census of 1860 reported the population of slaves at 3,953,760. U.S. Bureau of the Census, *Historical Statistics of the United States, Colonial Times to 1970* (Washington, D.C., 1975), part 1, series A59–70.

11. During the presidencies of Democrats Franklin Pierce and James Buchanan, the *Washington Union* received the lucrative federal government printing patronage in the District of Columbia and functioned as the journalistic "mouthpiece" for those administrations. Larry Gara, *The Presidency of Franklin Pierce* (Lawrence, Kans., 1991), 52, 69, 81, 94; Roy F. Nichols, *The Disruption of American Democracy* (1948; New York, 1967), 71–72, 103.

VI.

IN NORTH CAROLINA.

I CONTINUE my extracts from my Diary:

September 28.—At Weldon.[1] This morning I took a walk in the woods. A colored man, driving a horse and wagon, was approaching. I accosted him and got into the wagon.

We soon began to talk about slavery.

AFRAID OF THE ABOLITIONISTS.

He said that he had often seen me within the last few days, and that the people in this district were very much afraid of the abolitionists coming down here and advising the negroes to run away. Whenever a stranger came here, they asked one another who he was, and used every means in their power to discover his business. He advised me not to trust the free colored population, because many of them were mean enough to go straight to the white people and tell them that a stranger had been talking to them about freedom. He advised me also to be cautious with many of the slaves, because there were many of them who would go and tell. But there were many, too, who would rather die than betray an abolitionist.

THE WAGONER.

He said that he would run the risk of capture if he had a compass or a friend to direct him to the North. Ignorance of the way, he added, was the chief obstacle in preventing the slaves in this district from escaping to the North. Dozens, he said, were ready to fly.

We came up to a colored man who was chopping in the woods.

"Now there," said the wagoner, " is a man who would not tell what you said to him, and would like very much the chance of being free."

We had previously met a boy driving oxen that were drawing logs to town. This man was chopping the trees for him. They both belonged to the same master, who is described by his slaves, as well as by other colored people, as a type of the tribe of Legrée.[2]

We met, also, two wagons laden with cotton. "These," said the wagoner, "these come from right away up the country, and very likely these boys—the drivers—have travelled all night."

I bade the wagoner farewell, and went up to the axeman.

THE AXEMAN.

He was a powerful, resolute-looking negro. A cast in one of his eyes gave him an almost savagely dogged appearance.

"Good day, friend."

"Good day, mass'r."

"You are a slave?"

"Yes, sah."

"Who do you belong to?"

"Mr. D——."

"I am told he is a pretty hard master?"

A pause. I was under examination.

"I come from the North," I said.

"Yes, sah," said the slave, who seemed to be satisfied with my appearance, "he *is* a very hard master."

"Have you ever run away?"

"Yes; I have run away twice."

"Did you run North?"

"No," he replied; "I am told no one kin get to de North from here without being taken. Besides, I do n't know de way."

"How far did you run?"

"I just went round to de next county," he said.

"If you knew the way to the North, would you try to get there?" I inquired. "Would you run the risk of being captured and brought back?"

"Yes, mass'r," said the slave, in a manly tone, "I would try; *but dey would never bring me back again alive.*"

I explained the nature and uses of a compass.

"If I gave you one of these things," I added, "would you risk it?"

ARM THE SLAVES.

"Yes, mass'r, I would; but I would like to have a pistol and a knife, too."

He said that he did not care about the hardships a runaway must endure, for they could not be greater than the hardships he endured with his present owner.

"Would you be afraid," I asked, "or would you hesitate for a moment to shoot a man if he tried to capture you?"

"No, sah," he said, as if he meant what he said, "I would shoot him rather dan be taken agin; for dey would kill me any how if dey got me back agin."

"Good," I said; " you deserve to be free! Has your boss ever killed any of his slaves?"

MURDER AND TORTURES.

"*He killed one.* The boy ran away, and when they got him back they lashed him and kicked him about so that he only lived a week."

"Does he often lash them?" I inquired.

"Oh, very often," said the slave.

"How many does he give them at a time?"

"Fifty," he replied, "and seventy-five and a hundred sometimes. I saw three men get seventy-five apiece last Sunday. He drives dem very hard, and if dey do n't work like beasts, he lashes dem himself, or if he is too tired to do it, he gets his son or a colored man to do it for him."

"I should think," I said, "that seventy-five lashes would be enough to kill a man."

"Oh!" said the slave, "it is very bad; but dey have to go to their work again the same as ever. He just washes their backs down with salt water, and sends them to work again."

"Washes their sore backs with salt water!" I ejaculated; for although I knew that this infernal operation is frequently performed in South Carolina, still I cannot hear of it without a shudder of disgust. "What do they do that for?"

"To take the soreness out of it, dey say."

(It is to prevent mortification.)

"But," I continued, "is it not very painful to be washed in that way?"

"Yes, sah, *very*," said the slave, "*dat* does n't make any difference. He (the boss) does not care for dat."

WORK——WORK——WORK.

"What are your working hours?" I asked.

"From two hours before daylight till ten o'clock at night."

"Do you think that the slaves are more discontented now than they used to be?"

"Yes, sah," said he, "dey are getting more and more discontented every year. De times is getting worse and worse wid us 'specially," he added, "since dese engines have come in here."

"What difference do they make?" I asked, supposing that he alluded to the Indians.

"Why," said he, "you see it is so much easier to carry off the produce and sell it now; 'cause they take it away so easy; and so the slaves are druv more and more to raise it."

"I see. Do you think that if we were to give the slaves compasses, that 'lots' of them would run away?"

"Lots an' lots on dem," he replied, emphasizing every syllable.

"Would you run away even without a pistol?"

"Yes, sah," he said, "I would risk it; but I would rather have a pistol and knife, too, if possible."

"How did you live before when you ran away?"

"I walked about at night, and kept mighty close all day."

"Where did you find food?"

"I went," he said, "to de houses of my friends about here, and they gave me something to eat."

"I suppose you would like to have some money, too, if you were going to the North?"

"Yes, mass'r," said he, "I *would* like to; 'cause if a man has money he can get food easily anywhar; and he can't allus without it. But I would try it even without money."

"Are you married?"

"Yes, sah."

"Any children?"

"No, sah."

CLOTHING, ETC.

"What would you do with your wife, if you were to run away?" I asked.

"I would have to leave her," he said; "she would be very willing, 'cause she knows she can't help me, and I might help her if I was once free."

"How old are you?"

"Thirty-five."

"How many suits of clothing do you get in the year?"

"Two."

"Only one shirt at a time?"

"Yes."

The shirt of the slaves in this State—of course I allude to rural slaves—appears to be a cross between a "gent's under-garment" and an ordinary potato-bag. The cloth is *very* coarse.

"Does the boss allow you anything for yourself?"

"Nothing," he said, and looking at his used-up boots—

"He hardly keeps us in shoes," he added.

"Now, when would you run away if you had a compass?"

"I will run away to-night," he replied firmly, "if you will only give me one of them things."[3]

PLAN OF EMANCIPATION.

In a public letter, published at this time in an anti-slavery journal—dated at Weldon, or posted there[4]—I offered the following programme of action for the abolition of slavery in the Northern Slave States.

Although I believe now that the speediest method of abolishing slavery, and of ending the eternal hypocritical hubbub in Congress and the country, is to incite a few scores of rattling insurrections—in a quiet, gentlemanly way—simultaneously in different parts of the country, and by a little wholesome slaughter, to arouse the conscience of the people against the wrong embodied in Southern institutions, still, for the sake of those more conservative minds, who are not yet prepared to carry out a revolutionary scheme, I will quote it, as I wrote it, and insert it here:

"If I had a good stock of revolving pistols"—thus this peaceful programme opens—" and as many pocket-compasses, I would not leave this State until I had liberated, at least, a hundred slaves. Already I have spoken to great numbers of them—negroes and mulattoes—resolute and bold men, who are ready to fly if they knew the route, and had the means of defending themselves from the bloodhounds, whether quadrupeds or bipeds. . . .[5]

"Let not the Abolitionists of the North be deceived. The South will *never* liberate her slaves, unless compelled by FEAR to do so; or unless the activity of the abolitionists renders human property so insecure a possession as to be comparatively worthless to its owner.

"Abolitionists of the North! Would you liberate the slaves of the South as speedily as possible? I will tell you how to do it within ten, or, at furthest, twenty years.

"*First.* Fight with all your hearts, souls and strength, until the Fugitive Slave Law be repealed. As soon as the Northern States are as secure against the invasions of the slaveholder as Canada is to-day, three-fourths of our coming victory will be won.[6] We need a sterner public sentiment at the North. When the people shall believe that the corpse of a tyrant is the most acceptable sacrifice that we can offer to the Deity—when juries shall find a verdict of Served Him Right on the body of every kidnapper, or United States Commissioner, who shall attempt to return a slave to bondage, and may be shot, as he deserves to be, for the cowardly crime; then, we will hear of no more attempts to extend the area of Human Bondage—only plaintive appeals for the toleration of the iniquity in States where it already exists.

"*Second.* Let us carry the war into the South. We have confined our27selves too long to the Northern States. We have already, in a great measure, won the battle there. The public defenders of slavery are rapidly retreating to the Southern States. Let us follow and fight them until the last man falls!

"In the South there are three great parties—the slaveholder, the pro-slavery non-slaveholder, and the anti-slavery non-slaveholder. Great numbers of the slaveholders secretly believe slavery to be a curse, and some of them would liberate their slaves now, if appealed to in the 'proper spirit.' Let arguments in favor of abolition—especially arguments extracted from the writings of Southern statesmen—be diligently circulated among this class of slaveholders. It is useless to argue with the other class of slaveholders; for it is impossible to convince them of their crime: for them let the deadly contents of the revolver and the keenest edge of the sabre be reserved.[7]

"Appeals should be addressed to good men; proofs that slavery is a curse to the non-slaveholding population—by increasing their taxes, driving away commerce, manufactories and capital from the State—which can easily be done—should be furnished to the pro-slavery non-slaveholders who are invulnerable to all ideas of justice.

"Let the *anti-slavery* population of the South be associated by forming a secret society similar to the Odd Fellows, or the Masons, or the Blue Lodges of Missouri,[8] and let this union be extended over the entire country. The societies could circulate tracts, assist slaves in escaping, and direct the movements of the agents of the Grand Lodge.

"*Third.* Begin at the borders. In every free border town and village, let an underground railroad be in active operation. Appoint a small band of bold but cautious men to travel in the most northern Slave States for the purpose of securing the cooperation of the free colored population in assisting fugitives; of disseminating discontent among the slaves themselves, and of providing the most energetic of them, who wish to escape, with pocket compasses and pistols, and reliable information of the safest routes. Such agents must be consummate men of the world, 'wise as serpents'[9] though formidable as lions. An incautious man would soon be betrayed either by free blacks or sycophant slaves, and a man incapable of judging character by physiological indexes would waste both his time and his stock. Ten or twelve such Apostles of Freedom could easily, in one year, induce five thousand slaves, at least, to fly to the North; and of this number, if they were properly equipped, three-fourths, at the lowest calculation, would escape forever. Unarmed and without any money with which to purchase food, at least one-half of the fugitives would probably be captured by the bloodhounds *of both breeds.*

"There are many methods of enabling fugitives to escape rapidly, and by a direct route, to the Free States, which these agents could employ; but they must be carefully kept a secret from the slaveholder and his friends."[10]

To show my faith in this scheme, I offered my services free, for three months, if any anti-slavery man or society would provide me with the stock. I had no offer.

NOTES

1. As in the previous chapter, Redpath failed to disclose the identity of Weldon, North Carolina, in the fourth article in his second series of John Ball, Jr. letters. *New York National Anti-Slavery Standard,* November 11, 1854.

2. An allusion to the character Simon Legree in Harriet Beecher Stowe's *Uncle Tom's Cabin.*

3. Significantly, Redpath omitted a promise he made to this slave at the conclusion of the original John Ball, Jr. letter:

> You will see me again in a few months: I will get you one: good bye, old boy. [*New York National Anti-Slavery Standard,* November 11, 1854]

4. The quoted material that follows was dated September 29 and came immediately after the interview reproduced above (at the beginning of the chapter) in the *New York National Anti-Slavery Standard,* November 11, 1854.

5. Redpath here omitted the following brief paragraph from the original John Ball, Jr. letter:

> If I could for one year command the resources of the Anti-Slavery Society, I believe that I could make it the most formidable Emancipation Society that the world ever saw. [*New York National Anti-Slavery Standard,* November 11, 1854]

6. The remainder of this paragraph did not appear in the original John Ball, Jr. letter. *New York National Anti-Slavery Standard,* November 11, 1854.

7. The final sentence in the John Ball, Jr. letter read somewhat differently:

Argue not with the other class of slaveholders—for you cannot convince *them* of the sin of slavery. [*New York National Anti-Slavery Standard,* November 11, 1854]

8. Redpath added the phrase "Blue Lodge of Missouri" to the *Roving Editor* text. Variously named "Sons of the South," "the Social Band," and "the Self-Defensives" but generically called the "Blue Lodges," these groups of Missourians functioned to support the adoption of slavery by the Kansas Territory. Redpath probably observed these organizations firsthand while a reporter in Kansas. The term originally referred to a third-degree lodge of master masons. *New York National Anti-Slavery Standard,* November 11, 1854; Alice Nichols, *Bloody Kansas* (New York, 1954), 24, 26.

9. An allusion to the behavior of the devil while disguised as a serpent in Gen. 3.

10. The original letter concluded with the following paragraphs:

Schemes seldom command much respect: and every bold plan is at once pronounced impractical by the Gradgrinds of this world.

For example, in this my scheme of emancipation, it will be objected that few properly qualified agents could be found to go upon so *dangerous* a mission. The anticipated success, also, would be doubted.

Now, so confident am I of the practicability of this plan, that I offer to carry it into effect, in the Spring of 1855, if the Anti-Slavery Society or any wealthy Abolitionist will provide me with *stock.* I will give all that I have to give—for silver and gold have I none—*my time, for three months.* I am certain that at least seven-eights of the pistols, compasses and dollars I gave the slaves would be surrendered to our agents in the Free Cities of the North.

I would try to carry my scheme into effect immediately—but private business, of an imperative nature, requires my presence in the West India Islands this Winter.

You will hear from me again. Meanwhile, let us fight with ardour the good fight of Abolitionism! Remember, brothers! that "Southern Rights are Human Wrongs."

JOHN BALL, JR.

New York National Anti-Slavery Standard, November 11, 1854.

VII.

NORTH AND SOUTH CAROLINA.[1]

I REMAINED at Weldon about a week—every day making new excursions into the surrounding country—every day holding long and confidential conversations with the slaves. The preceding two chapters are accurate indications of my experience, and of the sentiments, aspirations and condition of the negro population.

I walked, after the expiration of the week, about fifty miles southward, but without increasing my knowledge of the workings of "the peculiar institution," or seeing anything noteworthy in the manners or in the scenery of the country to repay me for my journey. So I jumped into the cars and rode to Wilmington.[2]

A LONG WALK.

I staid there four or five days in the expectation of receiving a draft from Philadelphia which a debtor had promised to forward from that city to my address at Wilmington.[3] He failed to fulfill his promise. Here was a pretty "fix" to be in—only a few dollars in my purse—among strangers—no prospect of getting money—no hope of being befriended, and no inclination to make friends with anybody. I had not enough to pay my fare to Savannah, where I intended to go; but a little trifle of that kind did not discourage me. I resolved to walk to Charleston; and, as I did not know a foot of the way, to follow the railroad track.[4]

I had no adequate conception of the nature of the tour I thus carelessly resolved on. If I had known, I should have shuddered to have thought of it. Those who follow in my footsteps will find out the reason when they come to the interminable and everlasting black swamps; see the height of the rough, long timber bridges or scaffoldings that are erected across them; the yawning widths between the cross-beams which must be leaped, and their accursedly uneven shape, which often makes it almost impossible—difficult always—to secure a foothold; and when they discover, further, that a single false step, or a fit of nervous dizziness, endangers your life! It has taken me a couple of hours, several times, to travel one mile. If, in those days, there had been any manner of despair in my heart, I know that I should have abandoned this trip as hopeless. But as there was n't, I trudged on—only losing my temper on one occasion, when I came to a horrible piece of work over a horrible swamp. My carpet bag incommoded me so much in walking, and once or twice, in leaping, so nearly caused me to lose my balance, that in a mild and genial temper, and with soft words of valedictory regret, I pitched it (with an unnecessarily extravagant expenditure of energy) at the flabby black bosom of the swamp, and then and there entertained the sinful desire that some person of profane habits were present, as I would willingly have given him half of my cash to have done a little swearing on my private account—a mode of relief which my habits and taste would not permit me to indulge in. I suppose this sentence shocks you very much; but judge me not until you have attempted the same dreary journey that I successfully accomplished! Probably *you* will swear—and *not* by proxy.

I walked nearly or quite to Manchester, and then, changing my mind, took the branch to Columbus, the capital of South Carolina.[5] I walked from there to Augusta—sixty miles. I kept no notes during this trip; but in a letter written shortly after my arrival in Augusta, I have preserved and recorded the anti-slavery results of it.[6]

I was ten days on the trip, I find; but whether ten days to Columbus, or ten days from Wilmington to Augusta, I cannot now recall. I walked from Columbus to Augusta in two days: that I remember—for I slept one night in a barn, and the next in a flax house.

Here is the sum total of my gleanings on the way.

DISCONTENTMENT.

I have spoken with hundreds of slaves on my journey. Their testimony is uniform. They all pant for liberty, and have great reason to do so. Even a free-soil politician, I think, if he had heard the slaves speak to me, would have hesitated in again advocating the non-extension doctrine of his party,[7] and been inclined to exchange it for the more Christian and more manly doctrine of *non-existence!*

Wherever I have gone, I have found the bondmen discontented, and the slaveholders secretly dismayed at the signs of the times in the Northern States.

NORTH CAROLINA A FREE STATE.

North Carolina, *nolens volens,*[8] could be made a member of the Free States, if the abolitionists would send down a trusty band of liberators, amply provided with pistols, compasses, and a little money for the fugitives. I believe that Virginia is equally at our mercy; but I am ready to vouch for North Carolina. I questioned the slaves of that State on this subject almost exclusively. Christmas is a good season for the distribution of such gifts; as, at that time, the Virginia and Northern Carolina slaves, who are hired South during the year, are nearer to the North by being at their owner's residence. If the abolitionists of the North could secure the coöperation of the captains of vessels that sail to the Southern seaports, several hundreds of the slaves could easily be liberated every year in that way.

RAILROAD HANDS.

The Manchester and Wilmington Railroad owns the majority of the hands who work on that line.[9] What do the Irish Democrats think of that plan?

Their allowance varies, as it depends on the overseers. The average allowance is one peck of Indian meal, and two pounds and a half of bacon a week; two suits of clothes, a blanket, and a hat, a year. No money.

This road runs through the most desolate looking country in the Union.

Nothing but pine trees is seen on both sides of the track until you enter South Carolina, when a pleasant change is visible.

ALLOWANCE OF SLAVES.

In the pine tree country the boys are engaged (I mean away from the railroad) in manufacturing turpentine.[10] The allowance of "the turpentine hands," varies on different plantations and in different localities. Slaves everywhere in the rural districts of Virginia, the Carolinas, and Georgia, receive one peck of Indian meal per week. On the turpentine plantations some "bosses" allow, in addition, one quart of molasses and five pounds of pork; others, one quart of molasses and three pounds of pork; others, again, two or two and a half pounds of pork, minus the molasses. On many plantations the slaves are allowed one peck of meal a week without any other provisions. In such cases, I believe, they are generally permitted to keep poultry, whose eggs they dispose of on Sundays or at night, and with the money buy pork or vegetables. They bake the meal into cakes or dumplings, or make mush with it. One peck of meal is as much as any one person can consume in a week. No slave ever complained to me of the *quantity* of his allowance. Several who received no pork, or only two pounds a fortnight, complained that "We's not 'nuf fed, mass'r, for de work da takes out on us;" and others, again, said that the sameness of the diet was sickening. Everywhere, however, the slaves receive one peck of meal a week; nowhere, except in cities, and on some turpentine plantations, do they receive any money. I heard of one man—a hard taskmaster too, it was said—who gave his hands fifty dollars a year, if they each performed a certain extra amount of labor. This is the only instance of such conduct that I ever heard of. The only money ever given to rural slaves—plantation hands never have money—is at Christmas, when some owners give their hands ten or fifteen dollars. The majority, however, do not give one cent.

"EVERY COMFORT IN HEALTH."*

The railroad hands sleep in miserable shanties along the line. Their bed is an inclined pine board—nothing better, softer, or warmer, as I can testify from my personal experience. Their covering is a blanket. The fireplaces in these cabins are often so clumsily constructed that all the heat

---

*"They are happy. They have a kind and generous master; every comfort in health; good nursing when ill; their church and Bible, and their Saviour, who is also ours."—ALONE: *by Marion Harland.*

ascends the chimney, instead of diffusing itself throughout the miserable hut, and warming its still more miserable tenants. In such cases, the temperature of the cabin, at this season of the year (November), is bitterly cold and uncomfortable. I frequently awoke, at all hours, shivering with cold, and found shivering slaves huddled up near the fire. Of course, as the negroes are not released from their work until sunset, and as, after coming to their cabins, they have to cook their ash-cakes or mush, or dumplings, these huts are by no means remarkable for their cleanly appearance. Poor fellows! in that God-forsaken section of the earth they seldom see a woman from Christmas to Christmas. If they are married men, they are tantalized by the thought that their wives are performing for rich women of another race those services that would brighten their own gloomy life-pathway. They may, perhaps—who knows?—have still sadder reflections.

WHITE AND NEGRO HOSPITALITY.[11]

Travelling afoot, and looking rather seedy, I did not see any of that celebrated hospitality for which the Southerners are perpetually praising themselves. They are very hospitable to strangers who come to them well introduced—who don't need hospitality, in fact; but they are very much the reverse when a stranger presents himself under other and unfavorable circumstances. The richer class of planters are especially inhospitable. The negroes are the hospitable class of the South.

One evening I travelled very late; the night was dark, too, and a storm was coming on. It was nearly ten o'clock when I went up to the house of a planter and asked to be permitted to stay there all night. I had lost my way, and did not know where I was. My request was sullenly rejected. I asked no *favor*, for I was careful always to incur no debt to the slaveholder, excepting the debt of unrelenting hostility.* I asked simply for a lodging. There was no possibility, I found, of moving him, although there were ample accommodations in his house. He directed me to the railroad track again and said that if I walked about half a mile southward, I would come to a house, where, *perhaps*, I would be accommodated for the night. I did not stir until I was warmed. When I went out it was perfectly dark. I groped down to the railroad track, and found it was impossible to see my way. I went back—offered to sleep on the floor—to sit up all

---

*I had so often seen anti-slavery travellers accused of abusing hospitality, that, when I went South, I resolved to partake of none. I never even took a cigar from a slaveholder without seizing the earliest opportunity of returning it, or giving him its equivalent in some form.

night—to pay for any kind of nocturnal shelter. The storm was beginning. No! He would not listen to me. I saw a negro hut at a distance in the woods, and adjoining the railroad track. I went up to it. It was hardly larger than an ordinary pig-sty. I went in and told the boys that I intended to stay there all night. One of them was evidently afraid, and urged me to go to his master. I told him that his master was a brute, and I would rather stay here. This remark brought me into favor. They offered me the warmest corner, and gave me a blanket to cover me. I laid down and pretended to sleep. By and by the door opened, and a mulatto woman entered, and after some talk about the white folks—not at all complimentary to their masters—she laid down at the furthest end of the hut and went to sleep. There were broad shelves round the cabin, on which, and on the floor, the negroes slept.

How many do you suppose slept in that miserable hut?

Five negroes, the mulatto woman and myself.

"Every comfort in health!"

CHRISTIAN MORALITY AND SLAVERY.

From the talk of the boys (I wrote) you would not have imagined that any woman was present. How is it that clergymen forget the fact that Slavery *cannot* exist without creating what they anathematize as crime? Adultery, fornication, and still viler acts are the necessary consequences of the domestic institution of the South.

I belong to the Ruling Race: *dare* a slave resist my criminal advances? By a false statement before a magistrate, or by a blow, I can punish her if she does. Her word is not taken in any court of justice, and she does not dare to resent my blow.

I am a rich man: the slave is without a cent. Is it likely—thus bribed— that she will refuse my request, however low, or however guilty?

Again, I am a white man, and I know that mulatto women almost always refuse to cohabit with the blacks; are often averse to a sexual connection with persons of their own *shade;* but are gratified by the criminal advances of Saxons, whose intimacy, they hope, may make them the mothers of children almost white—which is the quadroon girl's ambition: is it likely, then, that a young man will resist temptation, when it comes in the form of a beautiful slave maiden, who has perhaps—as is often the case—a fairer complexion than his own, and an exquisitely handsome figure?

It is neither likely, nor *so!* It is a crime against morality to be silent on such subjects. Slavery, *not* Popery, is the foul Mother of Harlots.[12]

A HOSPITABLE SWAMP.

Next morning I arose at an early hour—before the boss was up—and resumed my peregrinations. What, think you, did I discover? A few rods distant from the master's house, in the direction that he had advised me to take in the dark night, when he told me "to walk half a mile south-ward," lay a wide soft marsh, far beneath the railroad track, to cross which, even in daylight, required the closest attention, and steadiness of nerve. If I had attempted to cross it in the night-time I should unques-tionably have fallen, and been lost in the black slushy depths of the marsh.

Columbus is a beautiful little city; but as the letter in which I described it, and my journey to Augusta, was unfortunately lost, and as I am too faithful a chronicler to rely on my memory alone for facts, I will here close my chapter on slavery in North and South Carolina, and devote the remainder of my space to the slaves and the States of Georgia and Ala-bama.

POSTSCRIPT.—*Malden, Massachusetts, Dec. 30.*[13]—In my communications to my friends, written on this tour, I strictly confined my observations to the slave population—the colored South. The evidences that I saw daily of the injurious effects of slavery on the soil, trade, customs, social condi-tion and morals of the whites I reserved for editorial use; to advance, from time to time, to such "enlightened fellow-citizens" as are incapable of seeing or appreciating the self-evident truth that every crime is neces-sarily a curse also; that it is impossible to be a robber, either as an indi-vidual or as a race, and permanently to prosper even in material inter-ests. I saw, on this trip, and heard enough, to enable me to testify to the truth of the paragraph subjoined, by a gentleman whose writings have done much, I learn, to advance the knowledge of that sublime—aye, and terrible—truth, which the South has yet to learn or die—that you cannot fasten a chain on the foot of a slave without putting the other end of it around your own neck.

Mr. Olmsted, speaking of the turpentine plantation, says:

"SLAVES AND OTHER PEOPLE IN THE TURPENTINE FORESTS.—The negroes em-ployed in this branch of industry, seemed to me to be unusually intel-ligent and cheerful. Decidedly they are superior in every moral and intel-lectual respect to the great mass of the white people inhabiting the turpentine forest. Among the latter there is a large number, I should think a majority, of entirely uneducated, poverty-stricken vagabonds. I mean by vagabonds, simply, people without habitual, definite occupation or reli-able means of livelihood. They are poor, having almost no property but their own bodies; and the use of these, that is, their labor, they are not accustomed to hire out statedly and regularly, so as to obtain capital by wages, but only occasionally by the day or job, when driven to it by necessity. A family of these people will commonly hire, or 'squat' and build, a little log cabin, so made that it is only a shelter from rain, the sides not being chinked, and having no more furniture or pretension to comfort than is commonly provided a criminal in the cell of a prison. They will cultivate a little corn, and possibly a few roods of potatoes, cow-peas and coleworts. They will own a few swine, that find their living in the forest; and pretty certainly, also, a rifle and dogs; and the men, ostensibly, occupy most of their time in hunting. A gentleman of Fayette-ville told me that he had, several times appraised, under oath, the whole household property of families of this class at less than $20. If they have need of money to purchase clothing, etc., they obtain it by selling their game or meal. If they have none of this to spare, or an insufficiency, they will work for a neighboring farmer for a few days, and they usually get for their labor fifty cents a day, *finding themselves.* The farmers say that they do not like to employ them, because they cannot be relied upon to finish what they undertake, or to work according to directions; and because, being white men, they cannot 'drive' them. That is to say, their labor is even more inefficient and unmanageable than that of slaves. That I have not formed an exaggerated estimate of the proportion of such a class, will appear to the reader more probable from the testimony of a pious colpor-teur, given before a public meeting in Charleston, in February, 1855. I quote from a Charleston paper's report. The colporteur had been sta-tioned at ———— county, N.C.:—'The *larger portion* of the inhabitants seemed to be totally given up to a species of mental hallucination, which carried them captive at its will. They nearly all believed implicitly in witchcraft, and attributed everything that happened, good or bad, to the agency of persons whom they supposed possessed of evil spirits.' The majority of what I have termed turpentine-farmers—meaning the small proprietors of the long-leafed pine forest land, are people but a grade superior, in character or condition, to these vagabonds. They have habi-tations more like houses—log-cabins, commonly, sometimes chinked, of-tener not—without windows of glass, but with a few pieces of substantial old-fashioned heir-loom furniture; a vegetable garden, in which, however, you will find no vegetable but what they call 'collards' (colewort) for 'greens'; fewer dogs; more swine, and larger clearings for maize, but no better crops than the poorer class. Their property is, nevertheless, often of considerable money value, consisting mainly of negroes, who, associat-ing intimately with their masters, are of superior intelligence to the slaves of the wealthier classes. The larger proprietors, who are also often cotton planters, cultivating the richer low lands, are, sometimes, gentlemen of good estate—intelligent, cultivated and hospitable. The number of these, however, is extremely small."[14]

NOTES

1. The bulk of this chapter originally was published in the *New York National Anti-Slavery Standard,* of December 2, 1854. The introduction to this letter, up to the subheading "RAILROAD HANDS," read substantially differently and is reproduced below:

A LETTER FROM THE SOUTH

To the Editors of the National Anti-Slavery Standard.

LIBERTY LODGE, SLAVE STATES.

Nov. 1, 1854.

THE Wandering Gentile has at length reached his southern home, and thereby ended his journeying—for the present year! Since I copied the last extracts that I sent you from my diary, I have travelled several hundreds of miles, and have spoken with several hundreds of bondsmen on the subject of slavery. I have travelled both by land and water; by railroad and on foot. For ten consecutive days, I travelled on foot in the States of North and South Carolina—from whence I sailed to my watchtower here. I claim, therefore, the right I have sought to acquire by many long and weary journeys and innumerable conversations with persons of colour, in Maryland, Virginia, the Carolinas and Georgia, of speaking for the slaves of the Atlantic Southern States as with the voice of one having knowledge and not as the politician. I have partaken of their bread and slept in their cabins; have trusted them and been trusted by them. I have spoken, also, with the slavers, as well as with the slaves.

Brothers! Rejoice—*and work!* Wherever I have gone, I have found the bondsmen discontented, and the slaveholders secretly dismayed at our recent victories in the Northern States. Little did any of them think, as they confessed to each other in my presence, that "the fanatics" would force them to abolish slavery before many years are over—little did thay think that they were basking in the company of an Abolition Spy! of one who solemly swore, when a child, to devote his life to avenging the oppressed; and who glories in betraying tyrants. If I had recorded all the sayings of the slaves I have met with, and chronicled the confessions of all of the slavers I have talked with, it would, I am convinced, have given great delight to our good and brave friend, Mr. Garrison, who so nobly began the holy war of freedom when no cheering sign encouraged the philanthropist's exertions. Rejoice, brothers! for our labours have not been in vain; and WORK with renewed zeal for the final struggle is at hand!

For reasons that I do not think it necessary to explain, I will not, *at present,* describe the incidents of my journey. I shall merely state a few facts that I gathered in the course of my wanderings, and add a few remarks on the programme of Mr. Phillips and Mr. Seward. NORTH CAROLINA COULD BE INVOLUNTARILY MADE A MEMBER OF THE FREE STATES BY A GENERAL STAMPEDE OF THE SLAVES, if the Abolitionists would send down a trusty Band of "Liberators," provided with compasses, pistols and a little money for the fugitives. I am convinced that Virginia is equally at our mercy; but I am ready to vouch for North Carolina. I questioned the slaves of that State on this subject almost exclusively.

Christmas is a good season for the distribution of such gifts—as at that time, the Virginia and North Carolina slaves, who are hired South during the year, are near to the North, by being at their owner's residence.

If the Abolitionists of Boston and New York could secure the cooperation of the Captains of vessels that sail to southern ports, several hundred of slaves could easily be liberated every month. It would be necessary for Liberators, however, to act in concert with the Captains. Can you secure such cooperation?

2. Redpath's letters indicate that he definitely resided in Weldon, North Carolina, during September 26–29, 1854. He would have walked along the tracks of the Weldon and Wilmington Railroad and boarded it in the vicinity of Goldsboro, North Carolina. When completed in 1840, this 161.5-mile track boasted of being the longest in the world. *New York National Anti-Slavery Standard,* October 28 and November 111 1854; Allen W. Trelease, *The North Carolina Railroad, 1849–1871, and the Modernization of North Carolina* (Chapel Hill, 1991), map 2; Robinson, *North Carolina Guide,* 329.

3. Redpath had stayed at the Washington Hotel in Wilmington, North Carolina. From a letter to Sydney Howard Gay, editor of the *New York National Anti-Slavery Standard,* it appears that Redpath was waiting in Wilmington to receive a payment from Gay for John Ball, Jr. letters already published in the *Standard.* Gay's payments were to be sent through an intermediary, Henry Melrose, who had recently moved from New York City to Philadelphia. Redpath to Sydney H. Gay, November 6, 1854, Gay Papers.

4. The only railroad route between Wilmington, North Carolina, and Charleston, South Carolina, went westward on the Wilmington and Manchester Railroad to Florence, South Carolina, and then southward along the route of the Northeastern Railroad. The first segment of this route crosses swampy land drained by the tributaries of the Great Pee Dee River. Trelease, *North Carolina Railroad,* map 2.

5. Redpath, of course, meant Columbia, South Carolina. When he reached Florence, South Carolina, he apparently abandoned his plan to go to Charleston. He continued along the line of the Wilmington and Manchester Railroad until Kingville and there changed to the South Carolina Railroad leading to Columbia. Trelease, *North Carolina Railroad,* map 2.

6. Redpath supplies no other specific details of this trip in his John Ball, Jr. letter dated: "LIBERTY LODGE, SLAVE STATES. Nov. 1, 1854." *New York National Anti-Slavery Standard,* December 2, 1854.

7. Founded in 1848, the Free Soil party was committed to the support of legislative measures such as the Wilmot Proviso, which prohibited the introduction of slavery into newly organized federal territories. This "nonextension" platform also became the central principle of the Free Soilers' successor, the Republican party. Maisel, *Political Parties and Elections,* 1:409–10.

8. Redpath employs the Latin phrase "nolens, volens" for unwillingly or willingly. C. O. Sylvester Mawson, ed., *A Dictionary of Foreign Terms,* rev. ed. (New York, 1975), 245.

9. Redpath was traveling along the line of the Manchester and Wilmington Railroad. The more common practice of railroads in that region was to hire rather than to own slaves. As the cost of slaves rose in North Carolina during the 1850s, however, the purchase of slave workers by railroad companies became more common. Trelease, *North Carolina Railroad,* 62–63, 230.

10. The Wilmington and Manchester Railroad's tracks passed through the turpentine belt in eastern North Carolina where long-leaf pine trees grew in abundance. Johnson, *Ante-Bellum North Carolina,* 52–53.

11. This section did not appear in the original John Ball, Jr. letter. In its place was the short passage that follows:

One night I slept in a plantation cabin—hardly larger than a decent-sized pig-sty—in which, besides myself reposed six negroes and—a mulatto woman! [*New York National Anti-Slavery Standard,* December 2, 1854]

12. Redpath concluded this John Ball, Jr. letter at this point with the following para-graphs:

Wendell Phillips is wrong, I think, in wishing to *anchor Massachusetts* by Abolition judges. Why not anchor Maryland, Missouri and the Border Slaves States by a band of Liberators? *They could be added to the Free States in less time than it would take to anchor Massachusetts.*

William H. Seward is wrong, I think, in saying "No more Slave States." I would vote for the admission of Cuba, even with the Institution of Slavery. It would be open to the labours of our Agents if one of the United States: at present it is a closed port to all Garrisonian goods.

Yours, in the hatred of slavery,

JOHN BALL, JR.

New York National Anti-Slavery Standard, December 2, 1854.

13. This postscript would have been prepared by Redpath at his Malden, Massachusetts, home in 1858.

14. This passage appeared in Olmsted, *Seaboard Slave States,* 1:388.

VIII.

A PLAGUE STRICKEN CITY.[1]

I WELL remember my first entrance into the city of Augusta. The yellow fever was raging there, as well as in the cities of Charleston and Savannah. Everybody was out of town![2]

The nearer I approached Augusta, the more frequently was I asked, as I stopped on the way to talk to the people, or entered their houses to get water or food, where I was bound for and how the yellow fever was?

When I answered that I was bound for Augusta, a stare of surprise, a reproof, or ejaculation of astonishment, was very sure to follow. Two gentlemen were even kind enough to tell me that I looked as if I had caught the yellow fever already. I was not surprised at their startling statement when I came to view my image in a mirror. I was indeed quite ill from unaccustomed fatigues, and the incessant enjoyment of "every comfort in health," which I had shared during my trip with the Carolina slaves.

"God help me!" I said; "a few more 'comforts'—say the comforts of sickness—and I would soon be a tenant of that blessed habitation, to which worthy members of the African race, like the good old Uncle Edward,[3] are accustomed to repair to immediately after their decease on earth."

A CRABBED OLD MAN.

I well remember, too, when within ten miles of the plague-stricken city, that I astonished every one whom I met, in walking along the road, by a long and hearty roar of laughter, in which, without interruption, I continued to indulge for nearly an hour.

I came up to a gate. A crabbed looking old man was working inside of it in a sort of kitchen garden. I asked him if I might come in and get a drink of water at the well.

"Where y' goin' to?" he snapped.

"Augusta."

"Must be a d—d fool," he jerked out, looking at me savagely. "Do n't ye know the yaller fever's there?"

"Yes, old man, I do."

"You'll die ev you-go-thar."

"I wo n't live to be uncivil then," I said.

"Hum!" he grunted.

"What o'clock is it?"

"'Bout twelve."

"Can't you sell me something to eat, or get me a dinner?"

"No," he snapped, talking so rapidly that his words often ran together; "old-woman's-busy; we-do n't-get dinners for Tom-Dick-en-Harry.[4] Need n't ask us."

"Curse your insolence!" I said. "I asked you a civil question. I want no favors. I'll pay you for all I get. May I have a drink?"

"Guess-you-kin-get it," he said, looking as if he meant to fight; but, seeing that I was angry in earnest, he merely added—"there's-the-well."

I went in and was going straight to it.

"Hello! good-God-STOP!" he shouted in a trembling, earnest tone; "yev-got the yaller-fever—let me-get from between you-en-the-wind!"

I roared. But the little Vitriol Vial was evidently in earnest, for he ran away as if the very devil was after him.

His wife—a quiet, dignified personage—in spite of his frequent, shrieked warnings to her, came kindly forward and gave me a glass.

AUGUSTA.

Opposite Augusta, on the other side of the Savannah River, is the town of Hamburg, in South Carolina.[5] Although the pestilence had raged in Augusta with terrible fatality for more than a month, no case of yellow fever had as yet occurred in the town of Hamburg. The wind, fortunately for the town, had blown in the opposite direction ever since the plague broke out. They expected to be stricken as soon as the wind should veer about. Yet they escaped; no single case occurred there; for the wind was friendly to them to the end.

I walked down to the river side. It was sad to see Augusta—apparently deserted—not a human being anywhere visible! When the people found that I intended to cross, they earnestly remonstrated with me. But I went up to the bridge—and stepped on it. It is rather a solemn thing to do at such a time; it requires either courage or a blind faith in Fate. I believed in destiny; and therefore never hesitated to run any risk of any kind anywhere. So I went over.

I met no one. When I landed on the opposite side, the first sight that I saw, far away up the street, was a black hearse standing at a door. One or two negroes were working on the bank of the river. I walked along the street that runs parallel with it. Everything was as still as a calm midnight at sea; no living creature was astir—neither men, women, children, horses, nor dogs! I turned up another street; and, in doing so, suddenly caught a glimpse of a lady, dressed in deepest mourning, as she quickly disappeared into a doorway, which was immediately closed behind her. I continued to walk through the deserted streets: for more than an hour I travelled about the city in every direction. The houses were all closed. I saw no sign of life, excepting, in all, four or five negroes, in different places, and a gentleman in the principal street, walking very rapidly and clad in mourning. Perhaps the utter desolation of Augusta may best be inferred from the fact, that this city of at least twenty thousand inhabitants,[6] was estimated, when I entered it, to contain only from one hundred and fifty to two hundred whites, who were dying at the rate of six, eight, and ten a day!

I bent my steps to the burying-ground. I had become very sombre by the desolation everywhere so apparent; but when I entered the little dead-house at one corner of the cemetery, I could not refrain from a hearty laugh.

THE NEGRO OF THE CEMETERY.

It was the coolest thing I ever saw! There, on a coffin, sat a wrinkled old negro, holding a broken piece of mirror close to his nose, and scraping his furrowed face, might and main, with a very dull razor which he held in his right hand. The contrast between his sombre seat and its pallid tenant, his extraordinary contortions of countenance, and his employment, was so great (and such a ludicrous picture of life withal), that I startled him by a sudden laugh and complimentary salutation.

He told me that the coachman, who had been employed to drive the dead to the burying-ground, was himself a corpse, and that every one who had taken the position had fallen a speedy victim to the terrible pestilence. But still, he thought, they would get another "right away," for the pay was high, and there were fools enough to jump at the chance of escaping.

"You may have noticed," I wrote at this time to a Northern friend, "the extraordinarily small number of colored people who die from yellow fever, as compared with the voluminous array of the white victims of the pestilence. Ludicrous and curious enough are the reasons advanced to account for this difference."

"No care on their minds," said some.

"Came from a hot climate!" said another.

"Two centuries ago?" I asked, ironically.

This philosophical old negro gave me the true reason. The whites are effeminate and enfeebled by idleness, debauchery, and drunkenness; while the blacks are industrious, temperate, and in every way as virtuous as their condition admits of.

THE CEMETERY.

I entered the cemetery. It is level and rather small, but finely shaded. I walked to one corner of it.

Three little graves, little more than a span long, side by side, first brought the reluctant tears to my eyes. I counted over fifty new-made graves in that melancholy corner alone, and could have stepped from one to another, and stood on each, without ever once touching the undug sod! Never before did I stand so near the Unseen Land—never since have I felt any fear or any awe of death. Everything around me was dead or dying. I felt as if I now were out of harmony with nature—the only living thing in an expiring earth. The long bent grass was yellow; the roses and the flowers were dying; the sere autumn leaves were dropping from the trees; and the sick, languid wind seemed to be spending its feeble breath in sighing a sad chant for the last of life! The leaves, the grass, and the wind united in this dying dirge, whose solemn notes were these recent clusters of untimely graves.

I sat down and listened, and wished for death. It must, indeed, I felt, be a terrible fate—to be the last man alive!

The sighing of the wind, and the sad sights around me, soon seemed to throw me in a trance—from which I awoke to fear death and the grave no more on earth. I seemed to have been dead and in the spirit land, and reluctantly returned to earth-life again.

When I opened my eyes, the tears started up unbidden and resistless. It was a simple thing that called them up. It had nothing poetical, or solemn or sacred about it. It was only a shingle! I had not particularly noticed it before, although now I saw that there was one of them on every new grave. I did not touch it; for it was on sacred soil. I drew near, and saw on it, in pencil marks, initials and a date. That was all. I put my hand over my face and wept like a girl. They were hastily written, those simple records; but how ominous and how graphic! Could any eloquence have so faithfully portrayed the condition of a plague-stricken city! Shingles for tombstones—no time for marble; for the chisel, a pencil—hastily used: and away—away—away—for dear, dear life! Poor cowardly relatives, make haste—make haste, or the shingle may yet mark where your timid corpses lie! Away! away! away!

With tears streaming down my face—no sound, save the sighing of the winds, and the grass and the leaves—no grasshopper, even, and no bird, to tell me that there was life still astir—I slowly, slowly, moved over to the opposite corner of the burying-ground.

Sixty—seventy—eighty—eighty-one—two!

An open grave!

I stopped my enumeration, and went over to it. I was sick and tired, and could count the red graves no longer.

I expected to see a coffin at the bottom of the grave; but it was empty. I looked again, and suddenly uttered an exclamation of delight.

I seized the shovel, and jumped down into the open grave.

I know that the reader will laugh at me—I know that some of you will think that I was mad; but I never before experienced a keener thrill of pleasure, never felt so sudden a love for any living thing, as when I saw, at the bottom of the open grave, and jumped into it to rescue—a mouse!

Yes, it was a poor little mouse, that, by some mischance, had fallen into the open grave. I do n't feel ashamed to confess that I *loved* it! Insignificant and ignoble seeming as it was, I hailed it a messenger from a *living* world, with which, in my sad reflections, and amid these sad scenes, I had begun to believe that I had no further business. For I was sick in body—predisposed, as people told me, to the plague—and soon expected to lie there, in the cemetery, without even a shingle for a tombstone. So I thanked God, and blessed the little captive mouse, as I rescued and set it at liberty again!

NOTES

1. The material in this chapter did not appear in the original John Ball, Jr. letters. Apparently attempting to hide the actual itinerary for his journey, Redpath published a fictional account of a visit to Charleston, South Carolina, and Savannah, Georgia, before describing

his arrival at Augusta, in a letter published in the *New York National Anti-Slavery Standard,* December 16, 1854. That letter has been reproduced in appendix 4.

2. Redpath arrived in Augusta, Georgia, in early November 1854. Newspaper reports from that city confirm that the severity of the Yellow Fever epidemic, which also had afflicted Savannah for weeks, had recently subsided. *Augusta Daily Constitutionalist and Republican,* October 20 and November 10 and 17, 1854.

3. Whites of all ages referred to older male slaves by the title "uncle." This practice was adopted by authors for stage and fictional characters. Mathews, *Dictionary of Americanisms,* 2:1793.

4. This expression for strangers or anonymous members of the working class was in popular usage in the United States by the second decade of the nineteenth century. Burton Stevenson, ed., *The Home Book of Proverbs, Maxims, and Familiar Phrases* (New York, 1948), 2338.

5. A village in Aiken County, South Carolina, along the Savannah River opposite Augusta, Georgia, Hamburg was the terminus of a railroad from Charleston. Seltzer, *Columbia Lippinott Gazeteer,* 62, 66.

6. The U.S. Census of 1850 reported Augusta's total population as 11,753. DeBow, *Seventh Census,* xcv.

IX.

GEORGIA NOTES.

As I had no hope now of receiving a remittance from the North, I doffed my coat, and went to work at a trade.

I remained in Augusta nearly two months.[1]

From letters written there during that time, I subjoin such selections as are appropriate to my purpose.

A GHOST; OR THE HAUNTED CABIN.[2]

"Haunted!" said I; "do people here really believe in ghosts?"

"Yes," said the landlord, "there are thousands, both in this State and South Carolina, who believe in them as firmly as they believe in anything. The old time people all believe in them."

"And this cabin was haunted, you say?"

The cabin referred to stood on a lonely field westward of Charleston.

"It got that reputation for years," resumed my companion. "Nobody would go near it, night nor day. On dark nights, people who rode along the highway, near the cabin, often reported that they had seen it. Hundreds saw it. I believed it myself. I'd as lief have gone into a rattlesnake's nest, as into that there field after dark."

"Is it still haunted?" I asked.

"No," said the landlord. "Not now. He was found out."

"Who?"

"The ghost!"

"The deuce! How?"

"Why, you see, there was a sort of drunken fellow lived not far off; and when he's on a spree he does n't care a fig for anything. He's a regular dare-devil. Well, one night he determined to go a ghost-hunting. He had a horse that was a very singular beast; it would stand still if he fell off, or go home of itself, if he was too drunk to guide it—which was often the case. Well, he rides up to the field, and sure enough there was the ghost."

"What was it like?" I asked.

"He said it was like a body as white as a corpse, but without either head, arms or legs."

"Was he not frightened?"

"He said he would have been frightened to death," resumed my land-lord, "if he had not been so drunk that he would as lief have met the devil as not. Well, his horse reared. He spurred it. It was no use. It would n't go one step further, although the ghost stood not more 'n a rod from his head."

"What did he do then?"

"Oh! he brought a lick at the ghost with his whip. The lash rested on it. Now, then, said he, I was sure it was something more natr'al than it got the credit for; bekase, you see, if it had been a ghost the lash would have gone through it."

"So it would," said one of the boarders, "so it would: that's accordin' to natur'."

The landlord resumed.

"As soon as the whip touched the ghost, it went backwards to the door of the cabin. He spurred his horse. It was no use agin. It would n't go a step. So he got off and tied her to a post, and then rushed at the ghost, on foot, whip in hand. As he came at it, it kept agoin' back and back, till at last it got inside the cabin, and was beginnin' to shut the door, when he gave another lick at it, and then rushed forward and seized a hold of it!"

One of the boarders drew a long breath.

"What was it?" asked another, open-mouthed and anxious.

"What do you think?" asked the landlord, he-he-he-ing heartily; "what d'ye think?"

Nobody *could* think. So the landlord relapsed again. When he had re-covered so far as to speak:

"Ha! ha! ha!" he cried. "Oh-a Lord!—ha! ha! ha!-a-a! Do you give it up?"

We gave it up.

"He! he!-e-e-e!" he began, "he-e-e-e! It was a strong buck nigger, who had run away from his boss in Georgia four years before. He had lived there ever since. He was as black as coal, and every night used to walk about in his shirt-tail, and frighten the folks round about out of their five senses!"

"But how did he live?" I asked.

"Oh!" said the landlord, "he stole at night. —— made him strike up a light in the cabin, and found it half full of provisions."

SOUTHERN AUDACITY OF ASSERTION.[3]

One of the most remarkable characteristics of conversation at the South, is the audacity with which the most flagrant falsehoods are advanced as undeniable truths, when the subject of negro slavery is under discussion. That the negroes are perfectly satisfied with slavery; that the blacks of the North are the most miserable of human beings; that all slaves are happy, and all free negroes wretched: these ridiculously false assertions are far more earnestly believed by "the public" of the South, than the "self-evident truths" of the Declaration of Independence are believed by the wildest, the most fanatical of European Democrats. From Wisconsin to Georgia, I have frequently found men who did not fear to laugh at the doctrines of Jefferson as rhetorical absurdities; but, in the Seaboard Slave States, I have yet to meet the first Southerner who believes that the condition of the Northern negroes is superior to the condition of the Southern slaves.

In a recent conversation in this city, I emphatically denied—first, that the slaves are contented with bondage; and, secondly, that their condition was enviable as compared with that of their Northern brethren. My denial was received with a simultaneous shout of derision and laughter by every person in the room.

"What privileges have they (the free negroes) at the North that the slaves have not here?"

I did not deem it expedient to utter a reply that would have silenced *them*, but probably tarred and feathered me also; but I ventured to suggest:

"Well, there's the privilege of acquiring knowledge, for example."

"I guess," said one, *"there's very few niggers in this State that can't read!"*

"I do n't believe one-tenth of them can't read," said another.

Now, as there is nothing more certain than that not one slave in five hundred can read, these assertions (and they are but types of a numerous tribe), will enable you to see how it is that Northern men, who travel South, and accept such statements without personal experience or investigation, so frequently return home convinced that the slaveholders are a much misrepresented class and the negroes a highly privileged people.

"They are *not* contented; I know it from themselves," I added, rather incautiously.

"Oh h—ll!" said one sensual-eyed fellow; "I know better than that. I've seen niggers that ran away from here to the North at New York, and they offered to work for me all their lives if I would only pay their passage back again."

The reader may guess without difficulty what I thought of this statement. In the land of pistols, bowies, and tar and feathers, however, an abolitionist, if he desires to accomplish anything, must be exceedingly prudent in his *words.* I merely rejoined:

"I should very much like to see *one* negro who would rather be a slave than free."

THE NEGRO WHO WOULD N'T BE FREE!

"Why, there," said the Southron, pointing to a negro who had just entered the room, "there's a nigger there that you could n't hire to be free."

He was asked, and replied that he would not be free.

"Now, *thar!*" Triumphantly.

I said nothing and the conversation dropped. In a few days after it, the negro came to me and we had a long conversation.

He asked me whether, on returning to New York, I would take him along with me as a servant. He offered to repay whatever expenses I might incur, both on my own account and his fare, as soon as he could obtain employment in the Free States.

"Do you know a single person of color," I asked, "who does not want to be a freeman?"

"No, sir; not one," was his decisive answer.

"When they ask you whether you want to be free, you always say no, I suppose?"

"Yes," said the slave, with a smile of contempt, "I says so *to them*—we all does—but it's not *so.*"

"Is it not amazing to see them believe such stuff?" I remarked.

"It is dat, mass'r," replied the slave whom "you could n't hire to be free," but who offered to hire me—to be free!⁴

Not one man—not even one Northerner—in ten who speaks with the slaves on the subject of bondage ascertains their sincere opinions. They never will learn what they are until they address the slaves, not as bondmen but as brothers. This is the secret of my universal success with the slaves. I have been their favorite and confidant wherever I have gone, because I never once adopted the "shiftless" policy of addressing them as if conscious of being a scion of a nobler race.[5]

THE FOREIGN POPULATION OF THE SOUTH.[6]

I am sorry to say that the Irish population, with very few exceptions, are the devoted supporters of Southern slavery.[7] They have acquired the reputation, both among the Southerners and Africans, of being the most merciless of negro task-masters. Englishmen, Scotchmen and Germans, with very few exceptions, are either secret abolitionists or silent neutrals.[8] An Englishman is treated with far more and sincerer respect by the slaves than any American. They have heard of Jamaica; they have sighed for Canada. *I have seen the eyes of the bondmen in the Carolinas sparkle as they talked of the probabilities of a war with the "old British."* A war with England NOW would, in all probability, extinguish Southern slavery forever.

A SOUTHERN REQUIEM.

It is sad to hear a slaveholder, of the less educated class, speak in eulogy of a negro who has gone to the world where the weary are at rest. It is sickening to think, as he recounts their virtues, that he never could have regarded them as *immortal souls;* that their value in his eyes consisted solely of their animal or mechanical excellences; that he measured a human servant by the self-same standard with which he gauged his horses and his cattle.

One day, after listening to a conversation of this character—not in Georgia, however, but another Slave State—I endeavored to put a slaveholder's post-mortem praises into rhyme—to write a requiem for a valued or valu*able* slave. Here it is:

I.

Haste! bury her under the meadow's green lea,
   My faithful old black woman Sue;
There never was negro more *useful* than she,
   There never was servant more true;
Ah! never again will a slaveholder own
A darky so *honest* as she who has gone.
      Gone! gone! gone!
   Gone to her rest in the skies!
      Gone! gone! gone!
   Gone to her rest in the skies!

II.

They say that I worked her both early and late,
    That my discipline shortened her days;
'Twas God and not I who predestined her fate—
    To Him be the curses—or praise!
I thanked him that one so unworthy should own
A darky so *robust* as she who has gone.
        Gone! gone! gone!
    Gone to her rest in the skies!
        Gone! gone! gone!
    Gone to her rest in the skies!

III.

My enemies say that my coffers are stained
    With the price of the fruits of her womb;
Yet what if I sold them? she never complained,
    From her cradle-bed down to her tomb.
Ah! never again will a slaveholder own
A darkey so *pious* as she who has gone.
        Gone! gone! gone!
    Gone to her rest in the skies!
        Gone! gone! gone!
    Gone to her rest in the skies!

IV.

They say that she bore me a chiid whom I sold—
    I doubt, but I do not deny;
Yet e'en if I bartered its body for gold,
    'Tis God who's to blame and not I,
For He in His wrath said that Saxons should own
The offspring of Canaan—like her who has gone.
        Gone! gone! gone!
    Gone to her home in the skies!
        Gone! gone! gone!
    Gone to her home in the skies.

V.

Haste! bury her under the meadow's green lea,
    My faithful old black woman Sue;
I'll pray to the Lord for another like she,
    As *dutiful, fruitful,* and *true!*
Yet I fear me that never again shall I own
A darkey so "likely" as her who has gone!

Gone! gone! gone!
Gone to her rest in the skies!
Gone! gone! gone!
Gone to her rest in the skies![9]

NOTES

1. Redpath remained for several weeks in Augusta, Georgia, working as a reporter for the city's *Daily Constitutionalist and Republican.* During his stay there he wrote a letter to the Boston *Liberator,* disputing published contentions of a leading Garrisonian abolitionist, Charles K. Whipple. This letter, signed John Ball, Jr., was not included in the *Roving Editor* but is reproduced in appendix 3. Redpath made a hasty departure from Augusta after the *Constitutionalist*'s editor, James Garner, inadvertently opened a letter to Redpath from his sisters back in Michigan, which contained references to the John Ball, Jr. series of letters. *New York National Anti-Slavery Standard,* November 17 and December 9, 1854; Boston *Liberator,* November 18 and December 8, 1854; Redpath to Sydney Howard Gay, November 6 and 17, 1854, and January 23, 1855, Gay Papers.

2. This tale originally appeared in a John Ball, Jr. letter published in the *New York National Anti-Slavery Standard* on December 9, 1854. It had the following title and introduction:

SOUTHERN NOTES FOR NORTHERN CIRCULATION.

LIBERTY LODGE, Slave States, November.

I am suspected here of being a lover of Liberty; and therefore—as I have an innate aversion to a costume of feathers—I am preparing to fly to another State. Under these circumstances you must pardon the sins of rhetoric, of which, in my present communication, I shall most probably be guilty.

3. The following section, with only very minor changes, immediately followed the preceding one in the John Ball, Jr. letter published in the *New York National Anti-Slavery Standard,* December 9, 1854.

4. The following short paragraph appearing in the original John Ball, Jr. letter at this point was omitted from the *Roving Editor* by Redpath:

It is from accepting the assertions of the Southerners as facts that so many Northern men return from the slave States with a friendly feeling for the accursed institutions of this land of bondage. [*New York National Anti-Slavery Standard,* December 9, 1854]

5. This revealing sentence concluded the paragraph in the original letter by Redpath:

I *could not* do so if I would: for I, for one, am a firm believer in the equality of the African race. [*New York National Anti-Slavery Standard,* December 9, 1854]

6. This section concluded the John Ball, Jr. letter published in the *New York National Anti-Slavery Standard* on December 9, 1854. In place of the final sentence here, Redpath originally wrote the following:

Some papers, I see, talk of a civil, others of a foreign, war. *We cannot engage in either without also engaging in a servile war.*

JOHN BALL, JR.

7. Although frequently the subject of virulent prejudice themselves, Irish Americans by the 1840s displayed strong racism against African Americans. Their loyalty to the Demo-

cratic party and their vulnerable economic position as unskilled laborers led many Irish Americans to oppose any movement toward emancipation. David R. Roediger, *The Wages of Whiteness: Race and the Making of the American Working Class* (London, 1991), 133–50.

8. In the late antebellum era, recent immigrants frequently were in direct competition with slaves and free blacks across the South. Many of them came to view slavery as an obstacle to improving wage and working conditions, especially in urban areas. Miller and Smith, *Dictionary of Afro-American Slavery,* 349–51.

9. Redpath had originally published this poem, with a dedication to William G. Brownlow, in the March 6, 1858, issue of the *Doniphan Crusader of Freedom,* a newspaper he published briefly in Kansas.

X.

SELF-EDUCATED SLAVES.[1]

THE population of Augusta, as I have already said, was estimated at twenty thousand. Yet it supports only two daily papers both of which have but a limited circulation.[2] The reason why the South supports so few journals in comparison to the North and the Northwest, is that there the laboring class are prohibited by law from learning to read.[3] The laborers are Africans. Yet, in spite of the law, great numbers of the *city* slaves can read fluently and well, and many of them have even acquired a rudimental knowledge of arithmetic. But—blazen it to the shame, and to shame the South—the knowledge thus acquired has been stolen or snatched from spare seconds of leisure, *in spite of their owners' wishes and watchfulness.*

"You can read—can you not?" I asked of an intelligent slave, whose acquaintance I made in Augusta.

"Yes, sir," said he.

"Write, too?"

"Yes, sir."

"Let me see you write a *pass.*"

He wrote one in a legible hand. The words were correctly spelled.

"How did you learn to write?" I asked. "Did the boss allow you to learn?"

"No, *sir,*" returned the slave. "There's no bosses would 'low their niggers to read if they could help themselves. My missus got hold of my spellin' books thrice and burned them."

"You taught yourself?"

"Yes, sir."

"How did you learn the alphabet?"

"Well, sir," he replied, "out in —— county, near where the boss's plantation is, there's a schoolhouse. The well is close by, and when I used to go for water I got the boys to teach me a letter at a time. I used to give them nuts and things to teach me. Then, after that, when I come to 'Gusta, —— ——" (he named a young white mechanic), "him that came from New Jersey, ga'en me a lesson in writing once in a while, and I learned that-a-way."

"You married?" I asked.

"Yes, sir; I's got a wife and three children."

"Where is she?" I rejoined.

"Out in —— county."

"Is she a slave?"

"Oh yes, sir; she lives with her boss out there."

"How often do you see her?"

"'Bout once every two or three months."

Great *domestic* institution that![4]

I have met several slaves in the course of my journeyings who had taught themselves to read and write, with as little instruction as the negro mentioned in the preceding conversation. I never yet met a slave who was not anxious to acquire the forbidden knowledge.

HELPLESSNESS AT TABLE.

Helplessness is as fully developed at Southern public tables as "shift-lessness" is in the Southern households, according to the statement of Miss Ophelia.[5] "Every one for himself, heaven for us all, and slops for the hindermost," is the principle that underlies the system of dining at many of the Northern, and at every Western hotel. At the South, on the contrary, it is easy to see that an opposite theory prevails: "Nobody for anybody, and the nigger for us all!" is evidently their fundamental maxim. I have seen a debilitated Southerner call a negro from the opposite side of the table, to hand him a dish that he could easily have reached without unbending his elbow!

THE CHAMBERMAID'S OPINION.[6]

"Would you like to be free?" I inquired of a colored girl at the hotel.

"Yes, sir, I would indeed," she said briskly; "and I would like to know who would n't."

"How much do you get?"

"I do n't get a cent" (she was hired out); "my mistress takes every red."

"Do n't the landlord allow you something?"

"No, sir."

"Do you never have money, then?"

"Oh yes, sometimes."

"Where do you get it?"

"Gentlemen here sometimes gives me a dollar," she said, laughing and looking boldly at me.

"Do you know any persons of color who would rather be slaves than free?"

"No, sir, I do n't know any one."

"If the colored people were free," I asked, "do you think they would work as hard as they do now? I mean the colored people of the city?"

"I guess most of them would work harder," she replied; "'cause, you see, they could live better, and dress and buy things with the money they has to give to the white folks now. I know I would work hard, and make lots of money if I was free. There's some that would n't work so hard though; they would buy liquor and loaf about—*the same as the white folks!*"

WHY SLAVES STEAL.

I have very often heard the negroes spoken of harshly in consequence of their thievish habits. In walking in the vicinity of Augusta one day, I came up to a negro, who was carrying a bag of provisions from town to his master's plantation. We talked about the patriarchal institution. He said that plantation slaves in this vicinity generally received one peck of meal, and from one to two and a half pounds of pork a week. He knew one planter who gave a very "short" allowance of meat.

"So, you see, mass'r, his slaves steal whatever dey kin lay their hands on. He's cons'ant whippin' 'em; but dey does n't stop it. My boss gives us two pounds and a half of pork a week, and *we* never takes anyt'ing. *We's above it,*" he added proudly.

Pity that the slaveholders had not as high a spirit. Pity that they should condescend to steal the negro's wages: pity that they cannot say of such disreputable theft—"*We's above it!*"

"Are you a married man?"

"Yes, sir."

"Were you married by a minister?"

"No, sir; *I was married by de blanket.*"

"How 's that?"

"Wall, mass'r," he said, "we come togeders into de same cabin, an' she brings her blanket and lays it down beside mine, and we gets married dat-a-way!"

"Do ministers never marry you?"

"Yes, mass'r, sometimes; but not of'en. Mass'r, has you got a chaw of 'bacca?"

I never yet gave a chaw of 'bacca without accompanying it with a revolutionary truth. John Bunyan, I remember, gave a *text* with *his* alms.[7]

THE FUGITIVE SLAVE ACT.[8]

The South has proclaimed the right of any Northern State to pass a Personal Liberty Law[9]—to annul the Fugitive Slave Act!

In the Resolutions of '98,[10] and in 1829, Virginia proclaimed that "Each State has the right to construe the federal compact for itself."[11] If, therefore, a Northern State believes that the Constitution does not warrant a fugitive slave act, of course it has the right, and it is its duty, to protect the panting fugitive by a Personal Liberty Law!

So, too, South Carolina. In 1830 she said:

"The government created by the Constitutional compact was not made the exclusive and final judge of the extent of the powers delegated to itself; but, as in all other cases of compact between parties, having no common judge, each party has an equal right to judge for itself, as well of infractions as of the mode and measure of redress. *Whenever any State, which is suffering under this oppression, shall lose all reasonable hope of redress from the wisdom and justice of the Federal Government, it will be its right and duty to interpose, in its sovereign capacity, to arrest the progress of the evil.*"[12]

During John Adams's administration, Virginia, through her "medium," Mr. Madison, used equally emphatic language:

"In case of a deliberate, palpable, and dangerous exercise of other powers not granted by the said compact, the States who are parties thereto have the right, and are in duty bound to interpose for arresting the progress of the evil, and for maintaining within their respective limits the authorities, rights and liberties appertaining to them."[13]

Kentucky indorsed this doctrine through the pen of Thomas Jefferson:

"The several States," so the passage reads, "who formed the instrument being sovereign and independent, have the unquestionable right to judge of the infraction, and a nullification, by those sovereignties, of all unauthorized acts done under color of that instrument is the rightful remedy."[14]

As late as 1825, Mr. Jefferson adhered to this doctrine. See his letter to William B. Giles, dated December, 1825.[15]

The *Southern Quarterly Review,* the chief organ of the slave power, has repeatedly promulgated and defended this doctrine. It is from that periodical—June No. for 1845—that these extracts are selected.[16] Of course it was not the fugitive slave law that called forth these opinions; but as what is sauce for the tariff must equally be sauce for freedom, it cannot complain of my use of its argument.

Freemen of the North! unfurl the Southern flag of Nullification! Resist the Fugitive Slave Law! "Better far," as South Carolina once humorously said of the Southern slave region, "better far that the territories of the States be the cemetery of freemen than the habitation of slaves!"

True!—very true! oh, South Carolina! Soon may the negroes utter and carry out the doctrine!

THE DRED SCOTT DECISION.

The same number of the Quarterly to which I have alluded, contains a constitutional opinion, which, in view of the Dred Scott decision, is worthy of being written in letters of gold in the legislative halls of every free Northern State. Here it is:

*"An unconstitutional decision of a judge is no authority; and even if confirmed by the highest judiciary in the land, namely, the Supreme Court of the United States, it would still be no authority: no law which any one of the States would be bound to recognize. An'unconstitutional law is no law—*IT IS NULL AND VOID—*and the same is true of a judge's decision given against the supreme law."*

Can any good come out of Nazareth?[17] Undoubtedly! There is a gospel of freedom in that one Southern word—NULLIFICATION!

IS SLAVERY A LOCAL INSTITUTION.

It does not suit the South now to admit that slavery is a local institution. It is national, and a blessing now, and claims the protection of national institutions. It may be well, therefore, to remind the South of her old opinions. Read what Governor Wilson[18] said in his message to the South Carolina legislature—opinions which were enthusiastically indorsed by the politicians and the press of the State. It was during the days of Judge Hoare's mission:[19]

"There should be a spirit of concert and of action among the slaveholding States, and a determined resistance to any violation of their LOCAL INSTITUTIONS. The crisis seems to have arrived when we are called upon to protect ourselves. The President of the United States, and his law adviser, so far from resisting the efforts of foreign ministry, appear to be disposed, by an argument drawn from the overwhelming powers of the General Government, to make us the passive instruments of a policy at war not only with our interests, but destructive also of our national existence.

The *evils* of slavery have been visited upon us by the cupidity of those who are now the champions of universal emancipation. To resist, at the threshold, every invasion of our domestic tranquillity and to preserve our independence as a State, is strongly recommended; and if an appeal to the first principles of the right of self-government is disregarded, and reasons be successfully combated by sophistry and error, there would be more glory in forming a rampart with our bodies on the confines of our territories, than to be the victims of a successful rebellion, or the slaves of a great consolidated government!"[20]

Undoubtedly! Let the North apply this doctrine to freedom, and thus preserve *its* local institutions inviolate. Truly, in such a case,

"There would be more glory in forming a rampart," etc.—!—

FORWARD. [21]

From the city of Augusta, I partly walked and partly rode to the town of Atlanta. I found the slaves in Georgia *passively* discontented. They did not hope. Hope is a white there. They were not morose. They wore their manacles without a curse and without an aspiration. A sad, very sad condition of mind!

Atlanta is a straggling business place, of about nine thousand inhabitants. I was there, I think, on New Year's Day, 1855.[22] Atlanta has no beauty that we should desire it as a residence. It feebly supports two little daily papers, and two weekly journals—a medical and a theological organ. In the Southern States the newspaper press is neither so numerous, influential, nor respected, as in the northern section of the Union.[23] It is gagged; the editor is merely the planter's oracle; and hence, being a serf, it commands no respect.

THE PEANUT SELLER'S TRIUMPH.

I heard a good story of Young America[24] at Atlanta. It shows what manner of individual that young gentleman is. I believe I have forgotten to state that I was credibly informed that boys of from twelve to sixteen years of age frequently wear bowie knives and pistols in the southern part of Georgia.

One day, at Atlanta, a peanut and candy-selling urchin, at the railroad station, was rudely pushed off the platform of the train by one of the conductors. "He was so mad," they said, "that he weighed a ton." He swore revenge. His heaving breast, contracted brow, compressed lips, flashing eyes—and, above all, his half-muttered "By golly! if I don't make you pay for that, then I'm mistaken—there now"—all these outward signs foretold that a dreadful retribution awaited the devoted conductor of the freight train; for he was a full-blooded Young American, was this candy-selling urchin, and when he swore it was the sign that there "was suthin' orful a-comin'."

He sold out his stock that day with unusual rapidity, for he sold it at half price, and was diligent at his business. He raised twenty-five cents and bought a piece of fat pork.

The "grade" at Atlanta is very steep; and heavy freight trains, when going at full speed, seldom exceed the rate of three miles an hour until they reach a considerable distance from the city.

Young America attached a piece of string to the pork, and went down with another boy to the place where the grade is steepest.

"Now, look 'ye here," said the candy seller to his comrade, as he placed the fat pork on the rail, "you take hold of that string and pull me along!"

He squatted down on the pork and was trailed up and down both rails for half an hour or more by his willing and laughing comrade. The rail, of course, was *rather* greasy. The freight train came up. Puff-uff-uff! Young America screamed with delight. It was literally as he said, "No go, no-how!"

For two days the engine vigorously puffed from morning to night in a vain attempt at progress. The conductor was finally compelled to call in the aid of another engine.

Thus concludeth the instructive history of the Peanut Seller's Triumph; or, Young America's Revenge.

NOTES

1. This and the following sections appeared in reverse order in the John Ball, Jr. letter published in the *New York National Anti-Slavery Standard* on December 23, 1854. Redpath began the original letter with the following commentary on southern traveling and dining:

A LETTER FROM THE SLAVE STATES.

In Georgia, December 3.

From Savannah to Augusta the country, as the Hoosiers say, is as flat as a pancake. The flash of the cannon, annually fired at Augusta in commemoration of the advent of Democracy in America, can be seen, it is said, at a distance of more than one hundred miles Atlantic-ward.

Travelling, in these far-southern sea-board States, is a very expensive pastime, especially by rail. The cars, too, are far less comfortable than their "Northern brethern." Hotels charge more for board; and both the attendance and cooking are inferior to what northern men are accustomed to. I must except, however, vegetables and bread. Sweet potatoes are as common here as dough-nuts are in Connecticut, or as bigots, knaves and tyrants are in Know-Nothing Lodges, or as unprincipled politicians are at Washington, when the representatives or the deceivers of the people are in Congress assembled; to wit, very common indeed. Other and still sweeter tropical fruits are furnished in great abundance in their respective seasons. I wonder that corn-bread is not more popular as an edible at the North. When properly baked and warm, it is as pleasing to the taste as it is nourishing to the frame; and that it is a "strengthening" diet, the great numbers of able-bodied negroes that are fed on it *alone,* whom one meets near the large plantations in the country South, sufficiently attests. I prophesy a great future for Corn Bread! In my mind's eye, I see it driving the "lazy root" from the Emerald Isle; oat meal, with its "parrich," alias porridge, "crowdy," bannocks and "yett-cakes," from Scotland; round-meal from England; black bread from Germany and Hunger from every Hemisphere! All the Earth shall yet rejoice because of it! Let us then eat success to corn-bread; and do what in our stomachs's power lies to enable it to fulfill its mission.

2. In the mid-1850s the two daily newspapers of Augusta, Georgia, were the pro-Whig party *Chronicle* and the Democratic *Daily Constitutionalist and Republican,* later just the *Constitutionalist.* Roller and Twyman, *Encyclopedia of Southern History,* 91.

3. Only Maryland, Kentucky, and Tennessee refrained from passage of legislation to forbid teaching slaves to read and write. In the other slave states, both slaves and masters commonly ignored such legislation. In most parts of the South, free blacks could establish schools to educate their children. Miller and Smith, *Dictionary of Afro-American Slavery,* 210–11, 264–65.

4. Instead of this brief paragraph, the following section appeared at this point in Redpath's letter:

"I should think," I replied, "———eh?"

He gave a laugh, but added—

"Oh no, sir; I would kill any man that touched my wife, and kill her, too, if she 'lowed him too; and I'd want her to kill me if I was n't the same way to her as she's to me. Course, I wish she could live with me; but we has to submit." [*New York National Anti-Slavery Standard,* December 23, 1854]

5. A fictional character in Harriet Beecher Stowe's *Uncle Tom's Cabin,* Ophelia St. Clare from Vermont was a middle-aged cousin of the slaveholding Augustine, who persuaded her to take up residence on his Louisiana plantation.

6. This and the following section originally appeared in the John Ball, Jr. letter that the *New York National Anti-Slavery Standard* published on February 10, 1854. That letter began with a passage, reproduced below, that was not republished in the *Roving Editor:*

A LETTER FROM THE SLAVE STATES.

ALABAMA, January 1, 1855.

TALES AND WALKS IN GEORGIA.

AT Augusta Georgia, on December 20, I conversed with several slaves and slavers on the subject of Bondage and Abolitionism.

"D—— me! if I don't believe you're an Abolitionist yourself."

"Why should you?"

"Wall, you say that slavery is an Evil, and none but Abolitionists talk that-a-way."

"Jefferson, Washington, Patrick Henry, and Madison believed and declared that they thought 'that-a-way,' though!"

"Now, see here—you dare not deny that you are an Abolitionist."

"I am *not* an Abolitionist—any more than if I lived in England I would be a Radical!

"What are you, then?"

"I am an Abolitionist, and *a great deal more!* I am a REPARATIONIST. I would not only *abolish* the Evil, but *repair* the Wrong. The South has acknowledged that slavery is a Curse; I recognise it as a crime, also."

"You're d—— explicit, I be sworn! You had better not talk that-a-way in these parts. Suppose I was to tell on you?"

"You dare not."

"Why dare n't I?"

"I would blow your brains out. That's why."

7. English Puritan John Bunyan (1628–88) wrote his allegorical masterpiece *Pilgrim's Progress* while imprisoned for his religious beliefs. Stanley J. Kunitz, *British Authors before 1800: A Biographical Dictionary* (New York, 1952), 64–66. In the original John Ball, Jr. letter, Redpath ended this section with a different final paragraph:

(This question has been asked me dozens of times by plantation slaves—in fact, every time that I have gone into the country, negroes with an humble air and with hand touching hat, have asked me for it. A chaw o' 'bacco has seldom failed to be the "instrument" of conveying Republican ideas. When I was a boy, I was very much impressed with one sentence in John Bunyan's works. The divine Dreamer says, that whenever he gave a penny to a pauper, he accompanied it with a text. John has had imitators in that respect among the Abolitionists in the Southern States.) [*New York National Anti-Slavery Standard,* February 10, 1854]

8. The next three sections of this chapter were drawn from a John Ball, Jr. letter that began with the following introduction, omitted from the *Roving Editor:*

SOUTHERN NOTES FOR NORTHERN CIRCULATION.

To the Editors of the National Anti-Slavery Standard.

LIBERTY LODGE, SLAVE STATES, Nov. 10.

I HAVE had several notes in my portfolio for some time past; which, *because* they are not counterfeits, but true bills, are uncurrent in this truth-forsaken section of this Land of Liberty, &c. The first you will please to forward to Charles Sumner; the others are for general circulation.

I..... WHO SHALL JUDGE OF UNCONSTITUTIONAL LAWS?

I have lately read, in the *Evening Post,* Charles Sumner's masterly reply to the *National Intelligencier.* It showed either a disgraceful ignorance of history or the spirit of a bad bold man, for the Editor of a metropolitan journal to assume that the doctrine of Constitutional Interpretation promulgated by the distinguished Senator from Massachusetts was a doctrine without precedent, or disorganizing in its effects. Mr. Sumner demonstrated that the doctrine was not a new one; he might have gone further and have proved that its most prominent advocates have been southern politicians and slaveholders. If the doctrine of State or Individual Interpretation of the Constitution—with which is blended the doctrine of a Higher Law—if it be destined to divide the Northern and Southern States, let 'the public' of the South remember that they were its Evangelists: they sowed the wind—let them reap the whirlwind.

I can prove that the doctrine of a Higher Law has been eloquently advocated, and, in certain States, universally adopted, at the South. At present, however, I will content myself with proving that the South has publicly and *officially* proclaimed the doctrine of State Interpretation of the Federal Compact. [*New York National Anti-Slavery Standard,* November 25, 1854]

9. One of the reasons for the passage of the federal Fugitive Slave Act of 1850 was that several northern states in the early nineteenth century had enacted laws forbidding state officials from aiding in the rendition of runaway slaves to their owners. In the 1850s, how-

ever, nine northern states passed new "personal liberty laws" that in various ways attempted to impede enforcement of the new federal law, such as by appointing state attorneys to defend accused fugitive slaves, harassing slave catchers with stringent antikidnapping legislation, and forbidding the use of public buildings for the temporary detention of runaways. Campbell, *Slave Catchers,* 10–11, 87–88, 171–72, 175–79.

10. Passed by the legislature of Virginia on December 24, 1798, this resolution had been written by James Madison. Together with a similiar resolution written by Thomas Jefferson and passed by the Kentucky legislature in 1799, these measures protested the constitutionality of the repressive federal Alien and Sedition Acts (1798). Later southern nationalists used these resolutions as a precedent for their doctrine of state nullification. John C. Miller, *Crisis in Freedom: The Alien and Sedition Acts* (Boston, 1951), 169–81.

11. Redpath takes this and a number of the following quotations from an article entitled "Carolina Political Annals" by "D." in the *Southern Quarterly Review* 7 (April 1854): 511.

12. Ibid., 512.

13. Ibid., 523.

14. Ibid.

15. Ibid., 524.

16. Redpath incorrectly cited the article, which appeared in the *Southern Quarterly Review* in April 1854, not June 1845. He concluded this paragraph in a substantially different manner in the John Ball, Jr. letter:

> Of course, the Fugitive Slave law was not the statute then under Review! Armed RESISTANCE to the Power of the Federal Government was officially recommended by the Governor of South Carolina when the Millocrats of the New England States threatened to pass their equally unconstitutional "Bill of Abominations." You know what the culinary proverb says. I will paraphrase it thus: what's truth for the Tariff Bill is truth for the Fugitive Slave law! [*New York National Anti-Slavery Standard,* November 25, 1854]

17. John 1:46.

18. John Lyde Wilson (1784–1849) served as governor of South Carolina from 1822 to 1824. A strong advocate of states rights, Wilson was active during the Nullification Crisis in the early 1830s. Sobel and Raimo, *Biographical Dictionary of United States Governors,* 3: 1396–97.

19. After South Carolina passed laws requiring the incarceration of free black sailors while their ships were in the state's ports, Massachusetts governor George N. Briggs sent Samuel Hoar (1778–1856)—a former Whig congressman (1835–37) with antislavery views— to Charleston as his agent to investigate treatment of Bay State citizens there. Hoar's visit was condemned by the South Carolina legislature. Threatened by mob violence, Hoar departed Charleston after only eight days. David Duncan Wallace, *The History of South Carolina,* 4 vols. (New York, 1934), 2:496–98; Phillip M. Hamar, "Great Britain, the United States, and the Negro Seaman's Acts, 1822–1848," *Journal of Southern History* 1 (February 1935): 3–28.

20. Redpath quotes from "Mr. Hoar's Mission" by "W." in the *Southern Quarterly Review* 7 (April 1854): 464. He completed the original John Ball, Jr. letter of November 10, 1854, with the following paragraphs not found in the *Roving Editor:*

> Slavery, then, is admitted to be a LOCAL Institution and—an Evil. Over Local Institutions the Individual States alone, and not Congress, have been invested with authority by the Federal Compact. *Ergo,* to obey the Fugitive Slave law's requirements is to violate the Constitution. Northerners! in the name of our Fathers who framed that glorious Instrument: for the sake of humanity, with whose hopes (on Fourths) we are often told it is laden; for our sacred UNION's sake, do not violate the Constitution,

then: Resist, if necessary, aye, Resist, to the death, the execution of that unconstitutional law: for if, as Cass, and Webster, and (white) Douglas & Co., have repeatedly declared—if you violate the Constitution, you dissolve the Union! Don't do that. Let our rallying cry be, 'Garrison to the Devil—our Union of States (and our breed of bloodhounds) must and shall be preserved!'

—Who, then, shall be judge of Unconstitutional Law? The States, not Congress, says the South.

Has Congress power over Local Institutions? By no manner, or means, replies the South.

Is Slavery a Local Institution? Yes, says the South—until it is convenient to cry NO!

Thus 'out of their own mouths' have Southerners recommended to the North Resistance—resistance to the death—to the Fugitive Slave law and all other unrighteous enactments.

II.....THE CHIEF OF THE LIES.

It is the right of Might to rule the weak. The institution of Slavery is an embodiment of this Lie. Like all other great falsehoods, it is supported by a Legion of lesser Lies. Slavery's body-guard is daily decreasing. *Her most powerful ally was recently swept away by the New York Tribune's articles on the Commercial Value of the Union.* The next in rank could easily be demolished as effectually as it was and to its destruction the whole force of our Society should be directed at once. Kill this Lie and Slavery will be compelled to fall back into the Realms of Cant. With Fact for us and Religion with us, who could stand against us? Nether theologism nor any other evil Power.

Since the *Tribune's* statistical articles on the value of the Union were published, the Southern press have very seldom said—what they were wont to say very often before—that it was the South which supported the finances of the country by paying the greater portion of the Federal taxes and which supported the North by consuming the greater portion of her products and manufactures. They taught the South to see sion, that the Northern "States had no motive in the Union but a commercial one. *They were able to protect it themselves. They were not afraid of external danger, and did not need the aid of the Southern States."* Now, as the South knows, *and has confessed,* that of herself she is neither able to protect herself from the external nor against domestic danger, she became very much alarmed when she saw it demonstrated that the North was the *loser* by the Federal Compact.

The *commercial* lie dead, she now chiefly relies on another—found on the condition of the coloured population of the North. You can have no idea how often it is said in the South—in the domestic circle, by the press, on the stump *and in the pulpit*—that the condition of the slaves of the South is infinitely superior to the condition of the free coloured population of the North. This lie is uttered, repeated and reechoed by hundreds every day. I have heard it wherever I have gone.

Say the *Southern Review:*

"Every day's observation proves that the condition of dependence which the African occupies at the South, and with which he is perfectly [*dis-*]satisfied, is a far better boon than the liberty, with its concomitants of poverty, degradation and crime, which the North would give him."

Now, I most earnestly petition the friends of the slave to proceed immediately and disprove this wicked but *powerful* falsehood—not by a simple denial, but by unrefutable facts; not through our own organs only, but through the general and pro-slavery press. Make it a prominent subject of discussion at the next Anti-Slavery Convention, or appoint a Lecturer to select it as a subject for discourse during the approaching season. The former course, I think, would be the most efficacious. If Mr. Garrison spoke of the condition of the coloured population of Boston; Mr. Furness of those of Philadelphia; Mr. Booth of those of Wisconsin; the *Standard*-bearer of those of New York—the thing would be done and the Anti-Slavery cause would be rolled ten years ahead. Do not think that I over-estimate the importance of this Falsehood. *It is the main pillar of the pro-slavery feeling of the South.* The publication of statistical articles or speeches on this subject, in the New York *Tribune,* the Boston *Telegraph,* or even the garbled reports of the *Herald,* would convert to our cause hundreds and probably thousands of Southerners, as well as compel the politicians who support the institution of slavery to cease their slanders.

III.....SOUTHWARD HO!

As far down as Georgia and Florida, the slaves have heard of us, and are longing to enjoy the Freedom of the North. But, alas! it is almost impossible for a fugitive to escape so many hundred miles, without meeting the bloodhounds and being recaptured. Something must be done to lessen the distance—or Slavery is destined to a long life in these Far Southern States. What shall be done?

The Florida and Georgia slaves cannot reach the North: we have, then, to choose another alternative—*we must bring the North to them.* "Southward ho!" ye friends of the bondsman.

Let us concentrate all our forces on Maryland; and, by mariners' compasses and by freemen's thoughts, by moral and material means, add that State to the North. It can easily be done; for the public sentiment—the *silent* if not the *expressed* sentiment—of that State already favours such a change. Having done so and brought the North to Virginia, let us again shout our watchword: SOUTHWARD, HO!

JOHN BALL, JR.

New York National Anti-Slavery Standard, November 25, 1854.

21. With the exception of the first paragraph, this and the next section concluded Redpath's John Ball, Jr. letter in the *New York National Anti-Slavery Standard* of February 10, 1855, minus the following salutory:

A happy New Year to you all, Standard-bearers and Standard-followers both!

Sincerely, JOHN BALL, JR.

22. To judge from the dates supplied in his John Ball, Jr. letters, Redpath probably was in Atlanta in early December 1854 and had moved on to Montgomery, Alabama, by the end of the year. *New York National Anti-Slavery Standard,* January 25, 1855.

23. The U.S. Census recorded the population of Atlanta as 2,572 in 1850. The city was home to at least twenty-eight newspapers during the 1850s, but most died within a year or two. The two principal newspapers in Atlanta at the time of Redpath's visit were the *Daily Examiner* and the *Intelligencer,* which merged in 1857. [Works Progress Administration], *Atlanta: A City of the Modern South* (New York, 1952), 94–96; DeBow, *Seventh Census,* civ.

24. Redpath is making a pun on the then well-known term "Young America," which was both the name and the slogan of a group of Democratic party journalists and politicians agitating for U.S. expansion in the 1840s and 1850s. Mathews, *Dictionary of Americanisms,* 2:1908.

XI.

ALABAMA.[1]

I WALKED the entire distance from Atlanta, Georgia, to Montgomery, Alabama. As I intend to revisit that country at the earliest opportunity, I will not here narrate my adventures on this journey. They would probably discover me—not my mere name, but personality. That I desire to avoid. Alabama, as the reader most probably is aware, is preeminently the Assassin State; for it has still on the pages of its statute book a law authorizing the payment of $5,000 for the head of Mr. Garrison, dead or alive.[2]

The results of my journey are thus recorded in a letter from Montgomery:

CONTENTMENT OF SLAVES IN ALABAMA.

I have spoken with hundreds of slaves in Alabama, but never yet met *one* contented with his position under the "peculiar" constitutions of the South. But neither have I met with many slaves who are actively discontented with involuntary servitude. Their discontent is passive only. They neither hope, nor grumble, nor threaten. I never advised a single slave either in Georgia or Alabama to run away. It is too great a responsibility to incur. The distance is too far; the opportunities and the chances of escape too few. The slaves, I found, regard themselves as the victims of a system of injustice from which the only earthly hope of escape is—*the grave!*

RAILROAD HANDS.

The shareholders of the railroad from West Point, Georgia, to Montgomery, Alabama,[3] own all the slaves who are employed in grading, pumping, wood cutting, engine firing, and in other necessary labors along the line. These men are the most favored sons of Africa *employed in the country,* in the States of Alabama or Georgia. They are hard worked from sun to sun, and from Christmas to Christmas, but they are well fed and clothed, and comfortably lodged—comfortably, that is, for negro slaves.

THEIR ALLOWANCE.

They receive five pounds of pork, a pint of molasses, and one peck of meal each per week; three suits of clothes, a blanket and a hat a year. But they have no wives. They are chiefly by birth Virginians, and were nearly all bought in the Old Dominion eleven years ago. The majority that I spoke with were married men and fathers at the time of the purchase; but, as the railroad company had no need of female servants, *their* "Domestic Institutions" were broken up, and—wifeless and childless—the poor "fellows" (as they are called), were transported south, and condemned for life to Alabama celibacy and adultery.[4] Of course, He who, amid the lightnings of Mount Sinai, uttered the command, "Thou shalt not commit adultery,"[5] was the founder of the system of slavery in America, which breeds such crimes, and many others of the same character, but far more odious in their nature! Of course? Do n't the Southern clergy and the Rev. South-Side Adams, of Instantaneous Conversion and Instantaneous Rendition notoriety,[6] announce the fact? And do n't they know?

MARRIAGE AND SLAVERY.

Several of these hands, as they frankly owned, have cohabited with plantation slaves since their arrival in Alabama. All of them, of course, resemble Napoleon in one respect—they are "no Capuchins."[7] One of them—a bachelor when sold, and who had been clerically married here—remarked to me:

"Yes, mass'r, I 'se been married; but it's no satisfaction for a man in this country."

"Why?"

"'Cause, mass'r," he replied, "you see white folks here do n't know nothin' 'bout farmin'. Dey buy a place and use it up in two or tree years, and den dey go away agin. So we's never sartin of our girls 'bove a year or two."

THE RICH SLAVE.

When about fifty miles distant from Montgomery, I saw a young man of color, well dressed—rather a dandy, in fact—walking along the road in company with a country-looking slave, near to the railroad depot. I overtook him and soon began to inquire into his history. He spoke our language as correctly as any educated man does in ordinary conversation. He was a manly looking person and very intelligent.

He was a slave; by trade a carpenter. He hired his own time—that is to say, he paid his owner $300 annually as body rent, boarded and clothed himself, and retained whatever money he made after defraying these expenses. He was twenty-eight years of age. Last year he saved $100. Altogether, since he first cherished a hope of purchasing his freedom, he had succeeded in saving $930.

"How much does your boss ask for you?"

"He said he would not sell me for less than $2,500. He was offered $2,000 cash down. I hope to buy myself for less. I was raised with him from a child, and I expect that he will let me buy my freedom for $2,400 on that account."

"$2,400!" I exclaimed, "and you have only got $900 yet. Why it will take you fourteen years to buy yourself at that rate."

"I know that, sir," he replied, "but I can't help myself; *you see he has the advantage of me.*"

"Yes," I returned, "but you have got $930 the advantage of him. Once on the road, you could travel rapidly to the North, as you could easily pay all your expenses, and would not have to run the ordinary risks of a runaway. If I was in your place," I added, "I would see your boss in a hotter climate than this, before I would pay him the first red cent. Can't you get any one to write you your free papers?"

"That's what I want, sir," he said—his eyes flashed as he looked on me and said it—"but I'm afraid to ask; I dare not trust any of the white men I know."

"I'll write them," I replied, "if you will get me free papers to copy from. I don't know how free papers are worded; but if you will show them to me, I will willingly make out yours."

He joyfully promised to furnish me with the "copy" desired, and appointed a place of meeting in Montgomery.

Alas for the poor fellow! Either I mistook the place of rendezvous, or, fearing betrayal, he was afraid to meet me.[8]

OTHER SLAVES AND SLAVE SALES.

My washerwoman in Montgomery hired her own time also. She paid her owner $200 a year; lived in a house rented by herself; was entirely self-supported in every respect.

Another man I spoke with—a plasterer—paid his owner $600 annually. He was a very intelligent and skillful mechanic. He would have sold for $4,000.

These persons never see their owners, excepting only when they pay their body-rent. Of course, this demonstrates that the negroes need a master to take care of them. And does it not prove, too, that American slavery is a *patriarchal* institution, with a vengeance and a half?

The first things that I saw on entering Montgomery were three large posters, whose captions read respectively thus:

"Negroes at auction!"

"Negroes at auction!"

"Negroes for sale!"

Three distinct sales of immortal souls within a few days were thus unblushingly announced. I saw two of them. In one instance, the auctioneer turned, as coolly as an iceberg incarnate, from the last of the negroes whom he sold, to a mule with a buggy and harness. Hardly had the word—"Gone!" escaped his lips, as he finished the sale of the "fellow," than he began:

"The next lot that I shall offer you, gentlemen, is a mule with a buggy and harness. This lot," etc.

The negroes brought very high prices. It is interesting to observe how the enlargement of commercial relations makes the interest of one nation the interest of every one with which it has extended intercourse. The Eastern war, which England was waging at the time,[9] was the immediate cause of these inhuman auctions. Cotton was selling at so very reduced a figure, that many of the planters were compelled to dispose of a portion of their human live stock, in order to provide subsistence for the others. And this, you know, is one of the beauties of this beautiful institution.

A GODLY CITY.

Montgomery is a very handsome city. It supports two churches, one weekly (temperance), one tri-weekly, and two daily papers. Population, at that time, nearly nine thousand.[10] It is the capital of Alabama.[11]

Montgomery, albeit, is a very godly city. It is true that its citizens sell human beings on week days; but then—and let it be remembered to its lasting honor—it imposes a fine of thirteen dollars for every separate offence and weed, on any and every unrighteous dealer who *sells a cigar on Sunday!*

Let us smoke!

NOTES

1. The material in this chapter was drawn from Redpath's John Ball, Jr. letter published in the *New York National Anti-Slavery Standard* on January 27, 1855. Redpath greatly revised the first two sections of this chapter. His original text is reproduced below:

A LETTER FROM ALABAMA.

MONTGOMERY, Ala., Dec. 10.

I AM sitting at the table of the public room of a hotel, surrounded by a large and loquacious host of planters, and "monthly boarders." You must pardon me, therefore, if my letter should prove to be disqualified for admission into the *Methodist* Denomination of Epistles.

My last letter, I believe, left me at the little city of Atlanta, in Georgia. A narration of my adventures since I left it, until I reached Montgomery, would make a rather interesting and exciting article. But, prudential motives counsel me to defer my description of it till a more convenient season. I will state, however, that I have travelled on foot nearly two hundred miles in Georgia and Alabama, and conversed with great numbers of city and country slaves on the subject of Bondage and Freedom. I have never yet met one slave contented with his position under the "peculiar" Constitutions of the South. But neither have I spoken with slaves in these two States who are *actively* discontented with involuntary Bondage. Their discontent is merely *passive.* They would all like to be free, but they do not *hope,* nor did they murmur sullenly as I spoke to them of Freedom. In Virginia and the Carolinas, all the slaves I spoke with were *actively* discontented. In Georgia and Alabama, in consequence, chiefly, of the almost impossibility of reaching the North from States so far distant from the Land of Freedom, they regard themselves as the victims of a system of injustice from which there is no earthly hope of escape—except by death.

2. After the Nat Turner insurrection in 1831, many southerners blamed the newly started Boston *Liberator,* edited by William Lloyd Garrison, for fomenting slave discontent. It was the legislature of Georgia, not Alabama, that authorized a five-thousand-dollar reward for anyone bringing Garrison to that state for arrest and trial. Russel B. Nye, *William Lloyd Garrison and the Humanitarian Reformers* (Boston, 1955), 54.

3. Constructed without any form of governmental assistance, the Montgomery and West Point Railroad opened in June 1840. This rail line connected Montgomery to eastern markets through the Central Railroad of Georgia. M. P. Blue et al., *City Directory and History of Montgomery, Alabama* (Montgomery, Ala., 1878), 35–36, 63.

4. In the original John Ball, Jr. letter, Redpath concluded this paragraph with the following sentences:

> Garrison! thou 'infidel' and 'fanatical demagogue'—how did'st thou ever dare to deny that God was the founder of the Institution of Slavery! or to affirm that it was of its father, the Devil, whose work it does? [*New York National Anti-Slavery Standard,* January 27, 1855]

5. Exod. 20:14.

6. An allusion to the Reverend Nehemiah Adams.

7. Napoleon Bonaparte's family had had several earlier members join the Capuchin monastic order. Bonifacio Bounaparte was beatified by the Roman Catholic church. In later life, Napoleon used the expression that he "was no Capuchin" as the equivalent of "was no saint." Gaspard Gourgaud, *Talks of Napoleon at St. Helena* (Chicago, 1903), 36, 87; William Wale, *What Great Men Have Said about Great Men* (London, 1902), 294.

8. Redpath ended this section of the original letter with a different paragraph:

> Alas! Either I mistook the name of the rendezvous, or by some accident have been unable to meet him. For three days I have sought him diligently but without success. But I have not yet abandoned all hope of meeting him. I shall devote the day that still remains to me to a search for the carpenter-slave. [*New York National Anti-Slavery Standard,* January 27, 1855]

9. Redpath alludes to the Crimean War (1854–56), which brought Great Britain, France, and Sardinia into conflict with Russia over the latter's ambitions to seize territory in the Balkans from the faltering Ottoman Empire. Incompetently managed and fought, the high point of the war was the allied nations' invasion of Russia's Crimean Peninsula. W. Baring Pemberton, *Battles of the Crimean War* (New York, 1962), 15–26.

10. Redpath accurately described Montgomery, Alabama, incorporated in 1819 and the state capital since only 1846. Blue et al., *Montgomery,* 30.

11. The final section of this chapter originally appeared as a postscript to Redpath's letter, which ended with the following:

> I have just heard of John Mitchell's fall. 'So perish all Queen' Liberty's 'enemies!'
> Amen! Selah!

Joyfully,

JOHN BALL, JR.

New York National Anti-Slavery Standard, January 27, 1855.

XII.

ABOUT SOUTHERN WOMEN AND NORTHERN TRAVELLERS CHIEFLY.

I REMAINED in Montgomery two or three weeks; sailed down the romantic Alabama to Mobile; in that place rambled for twenty-four hours; and then entered the steamer for the city of New Orleans.[1]

I passed the winter there. For reasons that I have already stated, I did not speak with the slaves on the subject of bondage during the earlier part of my sojourn; and, as I was obliged to leave the city in a hurry—to escape the entangling endearments of the cholera, which already had its hands in my hair before I could reach the Mississippi River[2]—I never had an opportunity of fully ascertaining their true sentiments and condition. I saw several slave sales; but they did not differ from similar scenes in Richmond.[3]

THE HIGHER LAW AND OLD ABRAHAM.

Let me recall one incident. In the courts of New Orleans there is an old, stout, fair-complexioned, grey-haired lawyer, of Dutch build and with a Dutch cognomen.[4] I saw a pamphlet one day—his address to a college of young lawyers—opened it, and read a most emphatic denunciation of the doctrine of a Higher Law.[5]

One day I visited the prisons of New Orleans. At one of them—a mere lock-up, if I remember rightly, for I have forgotten its name and exact location—the jailer, or an officer in the room where the records are kept, told me, in the course of a conversation, that there was "an old nigger inside," whose case, as he pathetically said in his rough way, was "rather too d—d bad." I asked to be permitted to see him. I was conducted up dark and filthy stairs, through a dark and dirty passage, and accompanied to the door of a perfectly dark cell—having an iron grating in its door.

"There," said the officer; "you call him; he's in there. I'll be back in a few minutes."

I went up to the grating and looked in. The odor of the cell was revolting. The stench could not have been more sickening if the foul contents of a privy had been emptied there. I drew back in disgust.

Again I approached the door, and, seeing no one, called aloud to the invisible inmate of the cell.

A very old negro came up to the door and put his face against the grating. His wool was silvery; his face was deeply furrowed; his eyes were filmy with disease and age. I never before saw so very frail and venerable a negro.

He told me his story. He had belonged to the lawyer who denounced the doctrine of a Higher Law; had been sold, with all the other slaves on his country estate, or on *one* of his plantations; had been purchased by a person who had hired him out to the Mississippi steamers as a deck hand; and then was put up, at a public auction, with some other negroes, who comprised one "lot." He was very sick and could not work. His new purchaser at first refused to take him; and, when he again presented himself, told him to go back to the auctioneer. He returned. The agent of the great body-selling firm there turned him with curses out of the office, and compelled him to carry his little baggage along with him. He threatened to cut his bowels out if he dared to return.

Alone—sick—a member of an outcast race—without money—without family—and without a home in his tottering old age! Where could the wretched invalid go?

He applied to the police. They took him to the jail and confined him in that putrid cell!

"How long, oh Lord! how long?"[6]

Here my talks with the slaves on my third trip end. From New Orleans I sailed to St. Louis, and from thence to Kansas, where I lived, with brief intervals, for three years, during the "civil wars" and the troubles which so long distracted that unhappy Territory.

ABOUT NORTHERN TRAVELLERS.

With two additional extracts from my Letters, I will close this record.[7]

Why is it (it has been asked) that Northern travellers so frequently return from the South with pro-slavery ideas?[8]

"Their conversion," I wrote, "has already become an argument in favor of slavery. A Yankee renegade, for example, whom I met in South Carolina, and who told me that he had once been an ultra abolitionist!—although he was now a pro-slavery politician—after failing to convince me of the beauty or divine origin of slavery, or satisfactorily reply to my anti-slavery arguments, abruptly concluded our conversation in these words:

"'Well, you'll not hold these opinions long—at least, if you stay in the South. No Northerner does. If the niggers were as badly treated as the abolitionists say they are—or if slavery were as diabolical an institution as they try to make out—*what's the reason that all the Northerners who come South with your notions, go back with different opinions?* There's Dr. Cox,[9] for instance."

"I reply:

"I. As to the treatment of the negro: it is of no sort of consequence, in my mind, whether the negro is treated ill or well, and no one, I think, should consider it for a moment in determining the right or wrong of American slavery. I deny the *right* of property in man. Property in man is robbery of man. The best of the slaveholders are cowardly thieves. They take advantage of a race who are *down,* friendless, inferior! There would be some nobility in enslaving an equal. There is a sort of virtue in extorting money from a powerful and popular enemy. But how unutterably contemptible is it to disarm, to disperse, and then to rob a race of unfortunate captives! If the Southern negroes had any chance of successfully asserting their rights by arms, I would not feel a single throb of sympathy for them. But they are carefully prevented from forming coalitions—the laws forbid them from assembling anywhere in numbers, unless white witnesses are present—they are not allowed to purchase or to carry arms—they are kept everywhere and always entirely at the mercy of the ruling race. *Then* they are robbed of their wages—often of their wives and children also! CHIVALRY, forsooth! The only true knights of the South are the runaway slaves![10]

"II. The Northern travellers fail to ascertain the true sentiments of the slaves, in consequence of retaining their prejudices of race. I have been told by Northern ladies that, during their visits to the South, they have sometimes asked the female slaves if they would not like to be free, and were astonished at receiving a reply in the negative. I have sometimes heard the same question asked of slaves, in order to convince me of their contentment, and have heard it answered as the Southron desired; and yet, within a few days, the same negroes have uttered in my presence the saddest laments over their unfortunate condition. Why? Because I did not ask the negro as if I honored him by condescending to hold a conversation with him. I did not speak in a careless or patronizing tone. This circumstance accounts for the difference of statements made by the same person. Topsy's remark about Miss 'Phelia's aversion to her is a true touch of negro nature.[11] I have already said that the slaves often told me, at first, that they did not care about freedom. I have spoken long and confidentially with several hundreds of slaves in Virginia, the Carolinas, Georgia, and Alabama, and never yet have I met with one—unless the Wilmington negro be excepted—who did not finally confess that he was longing for liberty. But I spoke to them as to men—not as to slaves.

"III. Northerners generally confine themselves to cities, and judge of the condition of country slaves from the condition of the bondmen of the town. This is a great error, and the source of unnumbered errors. Plantation slaves form the vast majority of our four millions of American chattels. They are the most degraded class of them. They either work under their 'boss' or an overseer, or are hired out for a stipulated sum per annum. The tar, pitch, and turpentine planters, or rather plantation lease-holders, of North Carolina, are principally supplied with their hands from Virginia. These masters in the Old Dominion often own no land, but live by hiring out their human stock from year to year. (I once got myself into hot water by calling a lady who lived on the hire-money of her slaves, a kept woman—kept by negroes! The epithet, although coarse, was deserved.) These negroes return regularly at Christmas to see their wives and little ones—*if not sold*—and to be hired out again.

"*Plantation slaves,* when working under their owners, are more kindly treated, on an average, than when governed by an overseer. Slaves have told me so. Cotton, tobacco, rice, and sugar plantation slaves are worked from sun to sun. Their food and lodging varies very much. They are not so well fed as, they could not be worse lodged than, the turpentine plantation and railroad hands, but in one respect their condition is vastly preferable. They have wives on these old plantations; while, from Christmas to Christmas, many of the slaves in the pineries and on the railroads of North Carolina never see theirs.

"*Country slaves,* as a class, very seldom, indeed, have any money. I once met a railroad hand who had saved $11; but he was regarded as the Rothschild[12] of the gang.

"City slaves, on the contrary, are generally well clad. They get enough to eat; they often save money. I have met slaves—remember, *city* slaves —who owned real estate and had cash in hand. They held the property under the name of another person. In the cities, the slaves—excepting the household slaves—are generally allowed to 'hire their *own* time,' as, with hidden sarcasm, the negroes term it: that is to say, they give their master a certain sum per month; and all that they make over that amount they retain. As negroes are usually a temperate and economical class of persons, the Southern city slaves sometimes save money enough to purchase their freedom.

"What, therefore, may be true of city slaves is no indication of the condition of rural bondmen. This fact, while it does not hide the cold-heartedness of such divines as South-Side Adams, vindicates their character and sacred office from the less odious offence of deliberate lying.

"IV. Northerners, also, are gradually and insensibly influenced by the continual repetition of pro-slavery arguments; the more especially as they never hear, excepting in partisan news summaries, the counter arguments of the anti-slavery party. Beattie, in his book on the formation of opinions, ably analyzes this tendency of the human mind.[13] What we hear often, we at length begin to believe.[14] In the South they hear only one side of the great slavery controversy, and are gradually, and without knowing it, brought over to the Satanic ranks of the oppressor."

WHY THE SOUTHERN LADIES ARE PRO-SLAVERY.[15]

The Southern ladies, as a class, are opposed to emancipation. They are reared under the shadow of the peculiar institution; in their nurseries and their parlors, by their preachers, orators and editors, they hear it inces-never afterwards appealed to. They seldom see its most obnoxious features; never attend auctions; never witness "examinations;" seldom, if ever, see the negroes lashed. They do not know negro slavery as it is. They do not know, I think, that there is probably not one boy in a hundred, educated in a slave society, who is ignorant (in the ante-diluvian sense) at the age of fourteen. Yet, it is nevertheless true. They do not know that the inter-State trade in slaves is a gigantic commerce. Thus, for example, Mrs. Tyler, of Richmond, in her letter to the Duchess of Sutherland, said that the slaves are very seldom separated from their families![16] Yet, statistics prove that twenty-five thousand slaves are annually sold from the Northern slave-breeding to the Southern slave-needing States. And I know, also, that I have seen families separated and sold in Richmond; and I know still further, that I have spoken to upwards of five hundred slaves in the Carolinas alone who were sold, in Virginia, from their wives and children.

Ladies generally see only the South-Side View of slavery. Yet Mrs. Douglas, of Norfolk—a comely woman—was confined in a Virginia penitentiary for the crime of teaching *free* colored children to read.[17] If the woman of the South knew slavery as it is, she would not stand alone in her memorable protest against it. For young unmarried men are not the only sinners that slavery creates in the Southern States. A majority, I believe, of the married men in South Carolina support colored mistresses also.

A FUGITIVE POEM.

I wish to conclude this record of my second trip with an anti-slavery poem, written by my noble and gifted friend, William North,[18] during the contest on the repeal of the Missouri Compromise,[19] at the time when John Mitchel,[20] of unhappy memory, gave utterance to his longings for a "plantation in Alabama, well stocked with fine fat negroes." It is indelibly associated in my memory with the recollections of my long journey; for often, when alone, I repeated it aloud in the pineries of North Carolina, and the cotton and rice fields of Georgia and Alabama. It is entitled—

NEBRASKA.

I.

There's a watchword, weak and timid,
Watchword which the gods despise,
Which in dust the poet tramples,
And that word is—Compromise!
Word of spirits, feeble, fallen,
Creed of dollars and of cents,
Prayer to the Prince of Darkness,
From a craven army's tents.

II.

Let an Irish renegado,
Born a slave of slavish race,
Bend before the Southern Baal,
In his mantle of disgrace:
He who turned his back on *honor,**
Well may cringe to slavers grim,

III.

But the poet has no pity
On the human beast of prey,
Freely speaks he, though the heavens
And the earth should pass away;
Aye, though thrones and empires crumble,
Races perish in the strife,
still he speaks the solemn warning-
Live for the eternal life.

IV.

Ye may talk, and print, and vainly
Rear a pyramid of lies,

*Alluding to Mitchel's alleged breaking of his parole of honor.

Slavery is still a fiction,
Still his lord the slave denies;
Still the mighty Institution
Is a long enduring crime:
God and devil, truth and falsehood,
Slave and freedom, never rhyme!

V.

Is the negro man or monkey?
Has he reason—yea or no?
Is the brutal Celtic peasant
Placed above him or below?
Is intelligence the measure,
Or the color of the skin?
Is the slavery of *white* men
Russia's virtue or her sin?

VI.

But I argue not; I scorn to
Make a channel of my mouth,
For the simple facts that conscience
Proves to all from North to South;
There is not a single slaver
In the land, that dares to say
That the mighty institution
Will not die and pass away.

VII.

Let it vanish! let it perish!
Let the blot on Freedom's flag
Be torn from it, and rejected
Though it leave you but a rag!
Let the prisoner and captive
Not be loosened on parole,
But released as the descendants
Of the sires your fathers stole.

VIII.

Not as foe, as man and brother
To the South I say this word:
What is past is past—the future
Frowns upon the negro's lord!
Give Nebraska, give the future
To a crime and to a lie?

Rather leave the land a desert,
Rather battle till we die!

IX.

Let the hearts of cowards wither,
Let the pale intriguers flinch
From a visionary peril,
Say we—Not another inch!
Not one forward step, oh blinded
Worshippers of slave-born gold!
Let a swift and sure destruction
Blast the little that ye hold!

X.

Who are ye, vain legislators,
That dispose of man's domain?
Who are ye, thus arrogating
Over continents to reign?
Know a truth—too long forgotten—
Earth is man's, and thought is fate:
Pause! ye reckless band of traitors
Ere ye so sell mankind's estate!

XI.

Compromises! Extraditions!
By the hope of life divine,
Rather would I howl with devils
Than such degradation sign!
Aid in capturing a negro,
Flying from the slaver's land?
Rather forge, or steal, or murder
With a pirate's lawless hand!

XII.

Let the course of reparation
Flow as gently as ye will,
Let humanity and justice
Peacefully their ends fulfill;
But, to slavery's extension,
Let one loathing voice outgo
From the heart of human nature,
No!—AN EVERLASTING—No!

NOTES

1. While in Montgomery, Alabama, Redpath arranged with the editor of that city's *Daily Mail* to become its New Orleans correspondent. He probably covered a southern commercial convention in New Orleans in mid-January but then found other employment there. Redpath to Sydney Howard Gay, January 23, 1855, Gay Papers; *New York National Anti-Slavery Standard,* January 27, 1855.

2. The more likely explanation for Redpath's hurried departure from New Orleans in mid-March 1855 was the increased likelihood of his exposure as an abolitionist. At the end of January he had sent two incautious pseudonymous letters, describing and condemning a slave auction, to his old employer, the *New York Tribune.* When copies of the *Tribune* articles reached New Orleans, the city's *Delta* denounced the reports and demanded that the police detect and punish "the sneaking Abolitionists in the pay of Northern journals, who pry about our city, hunting up pretexts for their atrocious falsehoods." Redpath might also have been afraid of cholera at this time. New Orleans had suffered a major cholera epidemic in 1849, and periodic rumors of a new outbreak were common throughout the 1850s. *New York Daily Tribune,* February 16 and March 24, 1855; *New Orleans Delta,* n.d., as quoted in the *New York National Anti-Slavery Standard,* March 31, 1855; Sarah Searight, *New Orleans* (New York, 1973), 240–41.

3. See Redpath's reports of New Orleans slave auctions in the *New York Daily Tribune,* February 16 and March 24, 1855.

4. Possibly Redpath refers to Gustavas Schmidt (1795–1877), a New Orleans lawyer who spoke and published frequently on legal issues, including slavery. Schmidt was the editor of the short-lived *Louisiana Law Journal* (1841–42).

5. This term came to characterize the view of many antislavery northerners that congressional legislation to protect slavery might be narrowly constitutional but nonetheless violated higher religious principles. Senator William H. Seward of New York employed the expression first in a congressional debate on March 11, 1850. *Congressional Globe,* 31st Cong., 1st sess., appendix, 265; Jane H. Pease, "The Road to the Higher Law," *New York History* 40 (April 1959): 131–32.

6. Variants of this phrase recur in the Book of Psalms, especially 13:1, 35:17, and 79:5.

7. The material in the remainder of this chapter originally appeared in two John Ball, Jr. letters. The first, dated March 10, 1855, from New Orleans, appeared in the *New York National Anti-Slavery Standard* on March 31, 1855. The second, dated March 15, 1855, from New Orleans, appeared in the same paper on April 7, 1855.

8. With the addition of the section now numbered as first, the remainder of this section closely approximates the John Ball, Jr. letter of March 10, 1855, that originally began as Jfollows:

> *Editors of the Anti-Standard:*
>
> IN your article on the reply of Mr. Wise, of Virginia, to the Reverend Bind-the-weak-in-chains Adams, of Massachusetts, the author of an avowedly one-sided View of Slavery, you remarked, if I rightly remember, that it was almost a profanation of human intellect to argue with slaveholders, and that men should refrain from speaking to them in any other language than in that of stern, uncompromising Denunciation. You err. Demagogues like Henry A. Wise; or the sensual-faced traitor, Nebraska Douglas; or that petty, shuffling politician, Mr. Jones, of Tennessee, whose soul is at least of fifty weather-cocks power; or James Gordon Bennett, the greatest journalist, but most contemptible public man of the country and generation—these and such as these should every Northern man allude to and address in the most fervid language of loathing, pity, or contempt. They are bad men and ought to be hurled into obliv-

ion. They should leave the Senate and sanctum for the sanctum's and the Senate's good.

Nor should other men of greater respectability, whose moral character is high in the community, in which they live, escape the denunciation which Tyranny merits, if by their ignorance and criminal carelessness in investigation, they be led to exert their influence in favour of an institution which degrades one race, distracts another, and disgraces our National name and democratic government throughout the entire world—blighting humanity's hopes as its ill-fame travels.

Denounce—denounce—but argue also. For, in spite of all your denunciation, there are thousands who will persist in believing that Adams and Cox speak truly of slavery, unless you can account for their assertions and refute them. [*New York National Anti-Slavery Standard,* March 31, 1855]

9. Probably an allusion to New School Presbyterian minister Samuel Hanson Cox (1793–1880) of Brooklyn, New York. One of the early officers of the American Anti-Slavery Society, Cox apostatized from the antislavery movement after attacks on his home and church by antiabolitionist mobs in the summer of 1834. Cox later resisted abolitionist efforts to enlist the Presbyterian church in the antislavery movement. Linda K. Kerber, "Abolitionists and Amalgamators: The New York City Race Riot of 1834," *New York History* 43 (January 1967): 28–35; *DAB,* 4:481–82.

10. This paragraph did not appear in the original John Ball, Jr. letter. *New York National Anti-Slavery Standard,* March 31, 1855.

11. In Harriet Beecher Stowe's novel *Uncle Tom's Cabin,* Topsy was a young slave girl that Augustine St. Clare purchased for his northern-born cousin Ophelia to educate. *Uncle Tom's Cabin,* chapter 20.

12. An allusion to the Rothschild family of wealthy Jewish bankers with branches in both Britain and France. Egon Caesar Corti, *The Rise of the House of Rothschild* (New York, 1928).

13. Scottish poet and philosopher James Beattie (1735–1803) was the chief proponent of the moral doctrine popularly known as the Scottish "Common Sense" philosophy. In his autobiographical poem "The Ministrel," Beattie described the formation of the mind. *DNB,* 2:22–25.

14. From this point on, Redpath ended his original John Ball, Jr. letter somewhat differently:

In the South, we hear only one side of the question of slavery, and are gradually drawn to it. During my first visit to the South, I was greatly influenced by the stream of statements and sophistries that perpetually flowed into my ear from the lips of my slaveholding friends. I believed many of their audacious assertions, and my antislavery zeal was greatly diminished by them. I never thought that slavery was right; but I did think that the slaves were happy and contented. I *don't* think so now. I *know* they are not.

In one of my letters I said that I would vote for the admission of Cuba even with the Institution of Slavery, and gave an anti-slavery reason for my intended conduct. I retract that statement. I would not vote for the admission of another slave State on any terms. *I have met the Fillibusters here!*

JOHN BALL, JR.

New York National Anti-Slavery Standard, March 31, 1855.

15. Redpath's original version of the following section, published in the *New York National Anti-Slavery Standard* on April 7, 1855, differs so greatly that that letter has been reproduced in appendix 6.

16. Redpath alludes to a public letter written by Julia Gardiner Tyler (1820–89), second

wife of former U.S. president John Tyler, to Harriet Elizabeth Georgianna Leveson-Gower, duchess of Sutherland (1806–68). A descendant of both the earl of Carlisle and the duke of Devonshire, the duchess held the appointment as Queen Victoria's mistress of the robes during Whig governments. In 1853 she and other leading British women composed a public protest against American slavery. Julia Tyler, daughter of a New York family, had married the recently widowed president in June 1844. After Tyler's term ended eight months later, the couple relocated to his Virginia plantation and had seven children there. In her rebuttal to Sutherland, Julia Tyler skillfully derided British women for entering the political sphere, defended the institution of slavery, and reminded the remonstrants of pressing social problems in their own nation. Tyler described "the separation of husband and wife, and parents, and children, under our system of negro slavery—a thing . . . of rare occurrence among us, and then attended by peculiar circumstances. . . ." *New York Times,* February 4 and 5, 1853; James, *Notable American Women,* 3:494–96; *DNB,* 11:1031–32.

17. In the late fall of 1853 a white woman, Margaret Douglas of Norfolk, Virginia, had been sentenced to six months of imprisonment for breaking state laws against teaching free black children to read and write. *New York Daily Times,* December 2, 1853; Boston *Liberator,* December 23, 1853.

18. While a reporter in New York City in the early 1850s, Redpath had been a close friend of British-born dramatist and novelist William North. North took his own life in November 1854. Albert Parry, *Garrets and Pretenders* (New York, 1933), 49, 54–55.

19. Redpath alludes to the passage of the Kansas-Nebraska Act of 1854, which effectively repealed the earlier prohibition of the Missouri Compromise of 1820 against slavery in the portion of the Louisiana Purchase north of the 36° 30' latitude. P. Orman Ray, *The Repeal of the Missouri Compromise: Its Origins and Authorship* hCleveland, 1909), 16, 182–87.

20. Irish nationalist John Mitchel (1815–75) was deported to Tasmania in 1850 by British authorities for advocating violent means to gain Ireland's independence. He escaped to the United States in 1854 and established a newspaper, the *Citizen,* in New York City. While still agitating for Irish causes, Mitchel also battled editorially with abolitionists. He eventually moved to the South, where he briefly owned a plantation and then returned to journalism. William Dillon, *Life of John Mitchel,* 2 vols. (London, 1888); Arthur Webb, *A Compendium of Irish Biography* (Dublin, 1878), 340–42.

MY THIRD TRIP.

I.

LYNCHING AN ABOLITIONIST.

BEFORE proceeding on my third trip to the sea board slave States, let me narrate one scene that I witnessed in the Far West: On the 18th of October, 1855, I was at Parkville, Missouri.[1] It is one of the little towns on the Missouri River, and acquired some celebrity during the troubles in Kansas.

It is built on rugged and very hilly ground, as almost all the towns on this unstable river are. It was founded by Colonel Park,[2] a citizen of Illinois, twenty years, or more, before my visit to it. A mild, kind, hospitable, law-abiding man: one would naturally think that he—the founder of the town, the richest of its citizens, and a slaveholder, albeit, who had never once uttered an abolition sentiment—would not only have escaped the enmity, but even the suspicion, of the border ruffians of the State. But he did not escape. He owned the press and office of the *Parkville Luminary,* a paper which supported the party, or the wing of the party, of which Benton[3] was the peerless chief. In one number of the *Luminary* a paragraph appeared condemning the course of the invaders of Kansas.

Enough! The press was destroyed and thrown into the river by a mob of pro-slavery ruffians. Col. Park also got notice to leave, and was compelled to fly for his life.

I went over to Parkville from Kansas city, Missouri, to attend to some business there. I had previously made the acquaintance of several of its ruffian citizens. I rode into the town about one o'clock.

After stabling my horse, and getting dinner at the hotel, I walked leisurely through the town. I saw a crowd of about twenty men before the door of "Col." Summers' office. The Colonel—everybody in that region has a military title—is a justice of the peace, and has never, I believe, been engaged in any martial strife. I went over to the office.

"Hallo! Mr. R.," said a voice from the crowd, "here's an item for you.— Let's liquor."

It was Mr. Stearns, the editor of the *Southern Democrat*,[4] the pro-slavery successor of the *Parkville Luminary*.

After the usual salutations, he informed me that an Englishman, named Joseph Atkinson, had been arrested by his honor, Judge Lynch,[5] charged with the crime of attempting to abduct a negro girl, and that the crowd were awaiting the arrival of a witness before deciding how to punish the accused.

I looked into the office to see the doomed abolitionist.

"It's the way of the world," I thought; but I did n't speak my thought aloud! "Here am I, whose sins, in the eyes of Southrons—if they only knew it—are as scarlet of the reddest sort; free, a spectator, nay, even honored by being specially invited to drink by a band of ruffians, who, in a few minutes, will tar and feather this man, guilty only of a single and minor offence!"

I held my tongue; for, says not the sage that though speech be silvern, silence—divine silence—is golden?[6]

There were about fifteen persons in the room, which had the ordinary appearance of an out-West justice's office, with a green-covered table before the magistrate's desk, a home-manufactured book-case, with the usual limited number of sheep-bound volumes on its shelves, forms around the sides close to the walls, a few second-hand chairs here and there, a pail of water in the corner, a bottle redolent of "old rye" near his honor's seat, and dust, dirt and scraps of papers everywhere about the floor.

I closely scrutinized the persons in the room, but signally failed to recognize the prisoner.

He was pointed out to me. He was sitting on a low form, leaning slightly forward, his legs apart, whirling his cap, which he held between his hands, round and round in rapid revolution. He kept up, at the same time, a very energetic course of chewing and expectoration. No one would have suspected his critical situation from his demeanor or the expression of his face. I never saw a man more apparently unconcerned.

He was a fair complexioned, blue eyed, firmly knit, rather stupid looking man, about twenty-five years of age. He was a ropemaker by trade, and had worked near Parkville for five or six weeks past.

It appears that he tried to induce a negro girl, the "property" of Widow

Hoy, to go with him to St. Louis, where he proposed that they should spend the winter, and then go together to a Free State. This programme shows how stupid he must have been, or how totally ignorant of Southern institutions, and the manner in which they are supported by their friends. The girl agreed to go, but wished to take a colored couple, friends of hers, along with them. He did not seem at first to like the proposition, but finally agreed to take them with him. The day of flight was fixed. The colored trio's clothes, it is said, were already packed up. They intended to have started on Saturday, but the secret came to the knowledge of a negro boy—another slave of Mrs. Hoy's to whom also the girl's married friends belonged—who instantly divulged "the conspiracy" to his mistress. Measures were taken, of course, promptly and effectually to prevent the exodus. A committee of investigation was appointed to watch the movements of the ropemaker, and to procure evidence against him from the implicated negroes.

Atkinson's colored mistress and the married couple were privately whipped, and the punishment was relentlessly protracted, until they openly confessed all they knew.

The committee of investigation—all men "of property and standing"[7] in the county—patrolled the streets for two successive nights, watching the steps of the girls and Atkinson. Has *Freedom* such devoted friends in the Free States?

The Englishman was then arrested, and sternly interrogated. He gave evasive and contradictory versions of his connection with the girl: which was criminal both in point of morals and in the Southern social code.

He said enough, his self-constituted judges thought, to criminate himself—and such extorted testimony, however perverted, however contradictory, is as good as gospel (and, indeed, a good deal better) in all trials for offences against the darling institution of the Southern States.

Thus the matter stood when I joined the crowd.

After a private conversation between the members of the committee, the rabble entered the office, and soon filled the forms and the vacant chairs.

RUFFIAN LYNCH LAW PLEAS.

Col. Summers opened the meeting, by alluding to the circumstances that had called them together. There was a kind of property in this community (he said), guaranteed to us by the Constitution and the laws, which *must not* be tampered with *by any one.*

"Dammed if it must," whispered a hoarse, brutal voice beside me.

"It was as much property to us," he continued, warming with his glorious theme, "as much property to us as so many dollars and cents—it was our dollars and cents in fact—and so recognized by the statutes of Missouri and the Constitution of the United States. Evidence had been obtained against the prisoner," he added, after this eloquent and learned exordium, "*from negroes* which agreed with his own statement minutely enough to convince him"—the speaker—"that Atkinson was GUILTY. What is to be done with him, gentlemen?" he asked, "shall we merely drive him out of our *city*"—population 600—"and thus let him go unpunished? I'm opposed to that course, gentlemen, for one," he said; but with adroit non-committalism, he added, "I would like this meeting to decide what to do with him."

Major Jesse Summers was next called on. A very "solid" man is Major Jesse Summers. Weight, I should judge, about ten tons avoirdupois! No military reputation hath the fleshy Jessie; never did he head a bold brigade; never did he drill a gallant company; but the rank and the title—or the title less the rank—of a major, no less, hath the ponderous Jesse Summers. Not having resided very long among them, he said, he had not wished to appear prominently in this matter. A judicious man, you see, is Major Jesse Summers. "But," he continued, "as his opinion on this subject was expected, he thought that if all the committee were satisfied that the person arrested was guilty of this *crime,* of which"—said Jesse—"I have no doubt myself individually," he, Jesse, was of opinion, "that they ought to give him a coat of tar and feathers, and let him go."

Murmurs of applause greeted Jesse, as he resumed his seat: which he received with a greasy smile.

Mr. Stearns—*his* title I have forgotten—then called on every one of the committee to express their opinion of the prisoner's innocence or guilt.

Each of the committee, one by one, every one—for no dodging is permitted when slavery's interests are at stake—arose, and pronounced him, in their opinion, guilty of the crime with which he stood charged.

GUILTY! "Proclaim liberty throughout all the land, to all the inhabitants thereof."[8] We read that GOD thus spoke. Did he order, then, the commission of a crime? No doubt of it, the ruffians would insist!

When the committee sat down, Mr. Stearns again rose. Stearns is a lawyer. This, he said, is an extra-judicial case! It is not provided for in the statute book. It devolves on the meeting, *therefore,* to—

Set him free, if no law is violated? No. "To say," said Stearns, "what punishment shall be inflicted on the prisoner. The major had suggested that he be tarred and feathered, and started out of town. What had they to say to that? He moved that the prisoner be so punished."

The motion was seconded, and put.

It was carried, of course, as a harder punishment would as easily have been, if the major or any other solid citizen had made the suggestion.

Mr. Stearns—"The meeting has decided that the prisoner be tarred and feathered."

Mr. Hughes, a brutal ruffian, added—"*And lighted.*"

Another hoarse voice exclaimed: "Let's hang him; it's too good for him."

[Does the reader know what *lighted* means? The proposition was to set the tar on fire, after it covered the body of the prisoner. A mind that could conceive so devilish a suggestion, is a fit and worthy champion of slavery.]

"Hang him!" shouted several voices.

Mr. Stearns interposed. "No, no, gentlemen!" he said. "Tar and feathering is quite enough on *nigger evidence.*"

This adroit phrase satisfied nearly all, but several still seemed disposed to maintain that negro evidence, as against abolitionists, was as good as good need be.

Up jumped Capt. Wallace, a fierce, very vulgar-looking bully, with a pistol stuck conspicuously in his belt. "I move," he shouted, "that he be given fifty lashes."

Another fellow moved that it be a hundred lashes.

By the influence of Mr. Stearns, these motions were defeated.

During all this discussion the prisoner still chewed his tobacco, and twirled his cap, as careless, apparently, as if it was of no interest or consequence to him.

He never spoke but once—when the sentence was announced—and then he had better held his tongue.

"D—n me!" he said quietly, "if ever I have anything to do with a negro again!"

"Better not!" was the captain's fierce suggestion.

An executive committee was appointed, and the meeting adjourned.

THE LYNCHING DONE.

Some of the committee went for tar, and some for feathers, while the rest of them stood sentinels at the door of the roam. Tar enough was brought to have bedaubed the entire population of Parkville, including the women, the little children and the dogs; feathers enough to have given the prisoner a dozen warm coats, and left sufficient for a pair of winter pantaloons.

"Now!" said Capt. Wallace to Atkinson, in a savage tone, "now, stranger, to save trouble, off with your shirt!"

With imperturbable coolness, and without opening his lips, the prisoner doffed his linen and flannel. As he wore neither vest nor coat, this ceremony was speedily concluded.

"He's obedient!" said one of the crowd; "it's best for him!"

"He's got off too d—d easy," said a second.

"That's a fact," chimed a third.

By this time the prisoner was entirely naked, from the loins upward.

"Come out here," said Captain Wallace, "we don't want to smear the floor with tar."

Silently and carelessly Atkinson followed him.

A ruffian named Bird, and the wretch who proposed to burn the prisoner—*birds* of a feather[9]—then cut two paddles, about a yard long (broad at one end), and proceeded slowly, amid the laughter and jests of the crowd, which Atkinson seemed neither to see nor care for, to lay the tar on, at least half an inch deep, from the crown of his head to his waist; over his arms, hands, cheeks, brow, hair, armpits, ears, back, breast, and neck. As he was besmearing Mr. Atkinson's cheeks, one of the operators, bedaubing his lips, jocularly observed, that he was "touching up his whiskers," a scintillation of genius which produced, as such humorous sparks are wont to do, an explosive shout of laughter in the crowd. All this while the only outward sign of mental agitation that the prisoner exhibited, was an increased and extraordinary activity in chewing and expectorating.

"Guess you've got enough on—put on the feathers," said an idle member of the executive committee.

"You're doing it up brown," said a citizen encouragingly to the operators.

"Yes, *sur,*" chirruped Bird, as he took hold of the bag of feathers, and threw a handful on the prisoner's neck.

"Pour them on," suggested a spectator.

"No, it's better to put them on in handfuls," said another voice.

Four ruffians (all men of social position,) took hold of the ends of two long poles, of which they made a rude St. Andrew's cross.[10]

"Sit on there," said Mr. Hughes, pointing to the part where the poles crossed, and addressing the prisoner.

"Why, they're going to ride him on a rail," said a voice beside me.

"Serves the d—d scoundrel right," returned his companion.

"Yes," replied the voice, "he ought to be hanged."

"He's very right to do as he's bid," observes a man near the prisoner, as Atkinson calmly put his legs over the poles. "Best for him."

The tarred-and-feathered victim was then raised in the air; each of the four citizens putting the end of a pole on his shoulder, in order to render the prisoner sufficiently conspicuous. They carried him down the main street, which was thronged with people, down to the wharf, back again, and through several of the smaller streets.

Just as the grotesque procession—which it would require the graphic pencil of a Bellew[11] to do justice to—was passing down the main street, amid the laughter and jeers of the people, a steamer from St. Louis stopped at the wharf, and I ran and boarded her. When I returned, the prisoner had been released. He was put over the river that night.

NOTES

1. Redpath draws upon his own dispatch to the *St. Louis Daily Missouri Democrat,* October 24, 1855, for the bulk of this chapter. He had traveled by horseback from Kansas City to Parkville, Missouri, on October 17, 1855.

2. George S. Park relocated from Vermont to Missouri and taught school in Callaway County. After serving in the Texas War for Independence, he returned to Missouri and founded the town of Parkville at the juncture of the Platte and Missouri Rivers in 1837. A Free Soil advocate, Park launched the *Parkville Luminary* in 1853. Two years later, after the Kansas-Nebraska Act had intensified local sentiment regarding slavery, a mob wrecked the *Luminary*'s office and ordered Park out of the state. He moved to Illinois and became wealthy through land investments there. Howard L. Conrad, ed., *Encyclopedia of the History of Missouri,* 6 vols. (New York, 1901), 5:49, 60.

3. One of the dominant political figures in antebellum politics, Thomas Hart Benton (1782–1858) became one of Missouri's U.S. senators when the state was admitted to the Union in 1821 and held that seat for thirty years. A supporter of Jacksonian democracy and westward expansion, Benton eventually lost the support of militant proslavery politicians in his state. He remained a major political force in the state until his death, supported by (among others) Frank Blair, Jr., and Gratz Brown of St. Louis, who later launched the Republican party in the state. Elbert B. Smith, *Magnificent Missourian: The Life of Thomas Hart Benton* (Philadelphia, 1958); *DAB,* 2:210–13.

4. After another visit to Parkville, Redpath described Stearns as "an able writer as well as a most hospitable gentleman and agreeable companion." *St. Louis Daily Missouri Democrat,* July 28, 1855.

5. The personification of the lynch law: The origin of the phrase "Judge Lynch" is traceable to the execution of alleged horse thieves in the 1780s by a group of South Carolina settlers led by Capt. William Lynch (1742–1820). Mathews, *Dictionary of Americanisms,* 1:914.

6. Scottish philosopher Thomas Carlyle, in *Sartor Resartus,* book 3, chapter 3, attributed this expression to a Swiss inscription.

7. A contemporary cliché to describe the wealthy urban elite of the antebellum period, the phrase "gentlemen of property and standing" was used by abolitionists when condemning northern professionals and businessmen for supporting slavery in general, and for condoning mob attacks on abolitionists in particular. Leonard L. Richards, *"Gentlemen of Property and Standing": Anti-Abolition Mobs in Jacksonian America* (New York, 1970), 132–33.

8. The biblical injunction found in Lev. 25:10, "Proclaim liberty throughout *all* the land unto all of the inhabitants thereof," also is inscribed on the famous Liberty Bell in Philadelphia. Victor Rosewater, *The Liberty Bell: Its History and Significance* (New York, 1926), 6–16, 144–45.

9. Generally attributed to Robert Burton, *Anatomy of Melancholy,* part 3, section 1.

10. St. Andrew was the patron saint of Scotland. He was crucified on a cross composed of two diagonals, called a saltire. The Scottish flag, later incorporated into the British flag, features a white saltire against a blue background. James Flag, *The Book of Flags* (London, 1965), 14–15.

11. Redpath alludes to Frank H. T. Bellew (1828–88), a New York City–based illustrator and caricaturist for numerous publications. The son of an English officer stationed in India, Bellew had emigrated to the United States at nearly the same time as Redpath. *DAB,* 2:165–66.

II.

BOSTON TO ALEXANDRIA.[1]

ALEXANDRIA, *May, 14.*—I left our quiet Boston on Monday evening by the steamboat train; spent Tuesday in hurrying to and fro, in the hurly-burly city of New York; on Wednesday afternoon, I paced the sombre pavements of the Quaker City; while to-day I have visited the City of Monuments, and the City of Magnificent Distances and of innumerable and interminable perorations and definitions of positions. I intended to stay for a time in Washington; but ran through it, like Christian out of Vanity Fair,[2] praying to be delivered from the flocks of temptations, which hover, like ghouls, in and around the executive mansion and the capitol of our republic.

SAIL TO ALEXANDRIA.

Having thus, with expeditious virtue, resisted all offers of official position, I entered the ferry boat—George Page, by name—which plies between the capital and the city of Alexandria. It rained heavily and incessantly all the forenoon. Alexandria is ten miles from Washington, by water, but I saw very little of the scenery. What I did see was in striking contrast to the banks of the Delaware. Freedom has adorned the Delaware's sides with beautiful villas, and splendid mansions, surrounded by gardens and fields, carefully and scientifically cultivated; while slavery, where the national funds have not assisted it, has placed negro cabins only, or ordinary country-houses, to tell of the existence and abode of Saxon civilization.

After doling out to the captain of the boat, each of us, the sum of thirteen cents, we were landed at the wharf of Alexandria; and our feet, ankle deep in mud, stood on the here miry, ill-paved, but sacred soil of the Old Dominion.

FIRST IMPRESSIONS.

Presently, we entered a Virginia omnibus—of Virginia manufacture—lined and with seats of the very coarsest carpeting—with panels dirty, glass dirty, and filthy floor drove through dirty, ill-paved streets, seeing dirty negro slaves and dirty white idlers—the only population visible— and were halted in front of the City Hotel. The omnibus and its surroundings had so affected my physical organization, that I immediately called for a bath. But I found that there is not a public bath in all Alexandria. It rained heavily still. Blue-spirited, I sat down in the bar-room, and read the papers.

THE COUNTY PAPERS.

Alexandria supports two daily papers, the *Sentinel* (Democratic) and *Gazette,* (American).[3] Both languish so decidedly that a "consolidation," would not make one flourishing journal. Of a number of paragraphs, significant as indications of the overwhelming success of slave society, the present state of Virginia and its cause, or as curiosities of the Southern press and people, I subjoin the extracts following:

REASONS FOR DECLINING.

In the Northern States, when a candidate declines to run, it is generally because he believes he would be beaten if he did. J. W. Patterson, of this county, has declined from a very different motive—because popularity, prosperity and hospitality, are incompatible in Virginia. He says:

To the Voters of Fauquier Co.—I am induced by a number of considerations, to withdraw from the position I occupy as candidate for a seat in the next House of Delegates of Virginia. In the first place, I find that a man has to quit all private business, if he would become popular. Secondly, that every small deed of kindness, the loaning of money even as a business transaction, or any act that good citizenship and good neighborship imposes, is entirely perverted, and attributed all to selfish motives, for electioneering purposes, etc. . . . I have many warm friends, I believe, but I hope they will excuse me for declining *now;* but I am at all times ready to serve the public and private interests of the country when called on.

Your most obedient servant,
J. W. PATTERSON.

A SLAVE GIRL'S REVENGE.

Conceal or deny it as they may, the slaveholders must feel the truth of Mr. McDowell's declaration, that "slavery and danger are inseparable."

Such evidences as this paragraph gives, are too serious to be sneered at or overlooked:[4]

"Nancy, slave of Mr. Seth Marsh, has been arrested in Norfolk for attempting to poison the family of Mrs. Reid, milliner, residing on Church street, by whom she was hired. It was shown that oxalic acid had been mixed in with some food which the girl had been cooking for the family."

There are evidences, also, in every paper I pick up, of the beneficial effect of Northern free emigration. Wherever the free colonists settle, up goes the price of land forthwith. Here is an illustration:[5]

"RISE OF REAL ESTATE.

"Mr. Seth Halsey, a few days since, sold his farm of 600 acres near Lynchbury, Va., to Mr. Barksdale, of Halifax, for $45 per acre. He purchased it several years ago of S. M. Scott, for $27 per acre."

In the county of Prince George, land, it appears, is equally valuable.

The *Planter's Advocate* notices the sale of a farm in Bladensburg District, consisting of one hundred and ninety-one acres of unimproved land, for $3,247—seventeen dollars per acre.

Another farm, near Patuxent City, Charles County, near the dividing line, was sold for $8,000; another still, in the same neighborhood, for $41 per acre.

The *Advocate* contains another paragraph, which I cheerfully subjoin, as illustrative of the happy effects of the extension of slavery over virgin territories, in raising the price of Personal Estate in the Southern section of the Republic. The price of slaves in Fairfax County is the same as here given.

"SALE OF SERVANTS.—A. H. Chew and R. B. Chew, administrators of the late Leonard H. Chew, sold, on Thursday last, part of the personal estate belonging to the deceased, consisting of several servants. The sales were as follows:

"One woman and two small girls sold for $1,450, and were purchased by E. G. W. Hall, Esq.

"Boy, about 15 years of age, sold for $915, and was purchased by Wm. Z. Beall, Esq.

"Small boy sold for $700, and was purchased by Daniel C. Digges, Esq.

"Girl, about 14 years of age, sold for $900, and was purchased by John F. Pickrell, Esq., of Baltimore.

"Two small girls sold, one for $880, and the other for $550, and were purchased by Mrs. A. H. Chew."

MY ROOM.

Tired with the bar-room and the county papers, I asked to be conducted to my room. It is one of a series of ten, contained in the upper part of a wing, one room deep, the lower or ground part of which is either the cooking establishment or the negroes' quarters. It runs into a spacious yard, and my window commands an exhilarating view of the stables and out-houses. No. "35" is painted on the door, apparently by some ingenious negro, who, unprovided with a brush, conceived and executed the happy idea of putting his fingers into a pot of white paint, and then inscribing the desired figures on the panels. As a work of art, it is a great curiosity.

The black man who conducted me to my room, as soon as I permitted him—which I did not do until my soul had drank in the beautiful *chef d'oeuvre* of the unknown and perhaps unhonored artist—opened the door, and presented the interior of No. 35 to my astonished vision, and its multitudinous odors to my indignant olfactory organs.

Like Moses, I am a meek man.[6] It requires a powerful combination of circumstances to excite indignation in my heart. This view—these odors—I confess, excited me.

"This is infernal," I mildly remarked.

The room is of good size, nearly square, with two windows and a high ceiling—as excellent, in these respects, as nine-tenths of the hotel rooms, or hotel cells, in the city of Boston. But in every other respect, I believe that all Boston—I even venture to say New England—cannot match it or approach it.

The window that looks into the balustrade has evidently been undisturbed by water, cloth or brush for several months past. By placing your hand, flat, on the outside, you can secure an accurate delineation of it, quicker than a daguerrean artist could take it. Inside, it is embellished with innumerable indications of the transient visits of last year's flies—little dots, like periods, you know, which are familiar, I doubt not, to all good housewives, and their industrious helps. There are rollers inside to hang the curtains on, but no cords with which to pull them up or down. The curtain—an oil painted one—adorned with an old chocolate-colored castle, pea-blue hills, yellow rocks, and trees and shrubberies, with foliage like Joseph's coat—of many colors[7]—*pinned* on the rollers, and irregularly at that; its base describes an acute angle, and it is so hung as to leave one-half of a bottom pane of glass uncovered; for the purpose, I presume, of enabling the darkeys to watch the conduct of visitors when they feel so inclined.

The first object that presented itself to my astonished gaze on entering the room, was a nameless vessel, appropriate to sleeping apartments, which the servants had placed in as conspicuous a position as if it had been a glass globe containing gold-fish. The papering of the room was variously bedaubed and torn; the window opposite the door was nearly as dirty as its mate; a dirty, old, sun-stained curtain, of colored calico, *un-hemmed,* and torn in *seventeen* different places, hung mournfully over it. I went over to put this curtain to one side, in order to look out, but found that there was no means of holding it. I have had to stick my penknife into the window-frame, in order to hold it back, and get light, as the other curtain is hopelessly beyond my efforts. Were I to put it up, or tear it down, it would be necessary to clean the window for light to penetrate its present thick, sombre covering of dirt.

The window-frames and mantel-piece, *once,* I faintly guess, painted of a light color, are in keeping with their dirty surroundings.

The fire-place holds a little, rusty grate; the plastering immediately around it is nearly all knocked off; and the rest of it is covered with tobacco juice, and bears the marks of dirty boots. I do n't know but I'll buy the fender, and send it to Kimball. It is of copper, weighing about two pounds, but is so bent up, covered with verdigris and tobacco juice, that, until one lifts it up and examines it, it is impossible to tell what manner of metal it is of.

A dirty slop-pail, with a broken wire handle, a dirty mirror hung like the curtain, a couple of the cheapest kind of chairs, a good bedstead and wardrobe (locked, however), a cheap dressing-table, and a dirty little pine table to hold the washbowl, completes the inventory of this room in a Virginia hotel. There is a tradition, the negro tells me, that the ceiling was once whitewashed. I do n't believe it.

After looking at the other rooms, I found that I had better, after all, remain content with No. 35.[8]

TALK WITH A SLAVE GIRL.

"How much do girls hire for here?"

"I gets six dollars a month."

"How old are you?"

"Don' no."

"Are you free?"

"No, I b'longs to Miss——."

"Have you any children?"

"Yes, I's got two."

"How old are they?"

"Sal, she's six, and Wash, he's three."

"Where is your husband?"

"I'se not married."

"I thought you said you had children?"

"So I has."

"Is your mistress a member of the church?"

"Yes, course she is."

"Did n't she tell you it was wrong to get children, if you were not married?"

"No, ob course not," was the simple and rather angry answer.

"What did she say, when your children were born?"

"Did n't say nuthin'."

I presume Miss——, acts on the precept, "Judge not, that ye be not judged."[9] Her charity for her slaves is great, and verily it covereth a multitude of sins![10]

ELI THAYER'S SCHEME.

May 15.—I have had a conversation with a prominent politician of the town, on the plan of Eli Thayer,[11] to colonize Virginia by free white laborers.[12] He launched out into an ocean—or perhaps mudpuddle would be the apter phrase—of political invective against the "black republicans and abolitionists of the North." He regarded Mr. Thayer as a braggadocio—a fool—or a political trickster—who merely threatened Virginia for effect at home. He could n't think he was in earnest. I told him that Stringfellow[13] and Atchison[14] had said that had it not been for Mr. Thayer, and his Emigrant Aid scheme, Kansas ere this would have been a slave State.[15]

"Then, sir," said the politician, sternly, "if he comes to Virginia with such a reputation, he will be met as he deserves—expelled instantly or strung up."

He did not believe that a single responsible citizen of Virginia would aid or countenance his scheme of colonization. He did not believe that Virginia had contributed $60,000 of stock to the Company. Mr. Underwood[16] was an impertinent intermeddler; he had been always kindly treated in Virginia, although his free-soil sentiments were known; but, not content with that, he must go to Philadelphia, pretending to be one of us, and, if you please, sent by us to the black republican convention, and make a speech there, indorsing a party whose single idea and basis of organization was hostility to the Southern people and to Southern institutions. Did I suppose the Southern people would endure that? "They repelled him, justly," said the politician, "as justly as our forefathers would have punished by death a traitor who should go from their camp to assist the British in their efforts to conquer the colonies."

VIRGINIA POLITICAL SOCIETY.[17]

"He had as little patience with a free soiler as an abolitionist. One had done as much as the other to excite the just indignation of the South. The Black Republicans talked of hemming slavery in, and making it sting itself to death, like a serpent. Why should the southern man be prevented from going to the common play-ground of the nation with his—(I thought he would have said toys for slaves, but he called them)—property? The North might force the South to dissolution, but never to non-extension of slavery.

"He was often amused, he said, in reading the Black Republican papers. They would talk about the limited number of slaveholders, and ask whether this little oligarchy should rule the nation. Why, sir, the non-slaveholders are more opposed to abolitionism and Black Republicanism than the slaveholders. And they have cause. Liberate the negroes, and you put them on a level with the white man. This result might not disturb the nerves of a Northern man, because there were so few negroes in their section; but here, where they constituted a great class, it was a different thing. The two races could not live in harmony; one must rule the other. Put Theodore Parker,[18] or any other fanatic, in a society where the two races were nearly equal in numerical force, and you would soon make a good pro-slavery man of him. Where there is freedom, there must be disputes about superiority. There is no dispute between the two races here. I own a nigger. There can be no dispute about our rank. So of the non-slaveholder. *He's white,* and not owned by any one. He does n't wish that condition disturbed by any intermeddling northerner.

"There has been a great change in the sentiments of the people of Virginia on the subject of slavery, within the last few years: but not in favor of emancipation. No, sir! All the other way. I recollect my father going about with a petition in favor of giving the government—the National Government—the power to abolish it. Any man who would attempt that now would be tarred and feathered. The intermeddling of the North has caused us to look more deeply into this subject than we were wont to do. Sir, we hold that servitude is the proper and legitimate condition of the negro; it is evidently the position His Maker designed him for; and we believe, sir, that he is happier, more contented and more developed in slavery—here in the southern States—than in any other part of the world, whether in Africa, Europe, or the Northern States.

"This change in public sentiment is continually going on—always in favor of perpetuating the institution as it is. You will find my statements verified in every county you may travel in."

This gentleman is a respectable and prominent citizen of Alexandria. I call him a politician, because our conversation was of that character, rather than on account of his profession. His views are very generally diffused among all classes here.

I asked him whether, if Northern people were to settle here—from the New England States—they would be likely to be annoyed on account of their sectional birth?

He said that numbers of New England people were settled here; and, as they were sound on the slavery question, or quiet, they were not disturbed. If Northerners were sensitive, he thought that they would often be annoyed by the conversational remarks—for, especially during times of election, *denunciation of the North had become a habit of conversation.* He made the remark I have italicized as if it was a matter of course— nothing surprising, nor a circumstance to be lamented.

He said that if persons from the North, with free soil sentiments, came here to settle, they must certainly refrain, even in conversation, from promulgating their ideas, as they would undoubtedly be lynched or banished if they did.

Inly querying whether this was a liberty, and whether Virginia was a State of a Republic, I turned the conversation, and went from his presence.

ALEXANDRIA

Was originally in the District of Columbia; but, within a few years, has been organized, with a few miles adjoining, into the county of Alexandria.[19] The county is the smallest in the Commonwealth, and is almost exclusively held in small lots, on which market produce is raised.

Alexandria contains a population of from seven to ten thousand,[20] as nearly as I can guess; for it is impossible to learn anything accurately here. Several men whom I have asked, have variously stated its population at from six to thirteen thousand inhabitants.

The first characteristic that attracts the attention of a Boston traveller in entering a southern town, next to the number, and the dull, expressionless appearance of the faces of the negroes—is the loitering attitudes, and the take-your-time-Miss-Lucy style of walking of the white population. The number of professional loafers, or apparent loafers, is extraordinary.

TALK WITH A SLAVE.

In coming from Washington, on the ferry-boat, I had a talk with one of the slaves. I asked him how much he was hired for.

"I get $120—it 's far too little. The other fellows here get $30 a month—so they has $21, and they only pays $10 for me."

"Why do you work for so little, then?" I asked, supposing, from what he said, that he was a freeman.

"I's a slave," he said.

"Are the others free?"

"No, sir, but they hires their own time. Their mass'r takes $120 a year for them, and they hires out for $30 a month, and pays $9 for board—so they has $6 a month to themsel'es. I works as hard as them and I does n't get nothin'. It's too hard."

"Why do n't you hire out your time?" I asked him.

"Kase my missus won't let me. I wish she would. I could make heaps of money for myself, if she did."

"Why won't she let you hire your time?"

"Oh, kase she's a queer ole missus."

"What do your companions do with their money when they save it?"

"Oh, guess they *sprees.*"

"Would you if you had money?"

"No, sir."

"Do any of your friends save their money to buy their freedom?"

"Some on them as has a good chance has done it."

"What do you call a good chance?"

"When our owner lets us hire our time reasonable, and 'lows us to buy oursel'es low."

"What is the usual pay for laborers?"

"$120 or so—we as follows the water gets more. I won't foller it another year, 'kase it's too confinin'; but I'd allers foller it if my missus 'lowed me to hire my own time."

"What is paid to white laborers?"

"Same as colored, unless they's a boss, or suthin' extra."

"Suthin' extra," I presume, meant mechanics, who receive, in Alexandria, $1 50 a day; carpenters $2: printers get from $8 to $10, by the week. Over at Washington, they are employed by the piece, but work, they say, is precarious and fluctuating.[21]

NOTES

1. This chapter originally was published by Redpath as a letter to the *Boston Daily Evening Traveller.* It appeared in the May 23, 1857, issue under the headline "FROM VIRGINIA. *Special Correspondence of the Traveller*" and was signed with the pen name "Jacobius."

2. An allusion to the character Christian in John Bunyan's *Pilgrim's Progress* who fled the allegorical Vanity Fair after being imprisoned and tortured by its residents. Frank N. Magill, *Cyclopedia of Literary Characters* (New York, 1963), 882–83.

3. This and other characteristics of Alexandria, Virginia, in the mid-1850s are confirmed by contemporary descriptions. Edwards, *Statistical Gazetteer,* 161.

4. This paragraph did not appear in the John Ball, Jr. letter published in the *Boston Daily Evening Traveller* on May 23, 1857.

5. This paragraph did not appear in the John Ball, Jr. letter published in the *Boston Daily Evening Traveller* on May 23, 1857.

6. Redpath adapts Num. 12:3.

7. An allusion to the multicolored garment that Jacob gave to his son Joseph in Gen. 27:3.

8. In his original letter, Redpath published this paragraph in a slightly different fashion and then followed it with two sections omitted from the *Roving Editor:*

> After looking at other rooms, I found that I had better, after all, remain content with No. 35; and here I have slept and am now addressing you and your million-bodied patron.

STATISTICS.

Alexandria is in Fairfax county. By the last census of Virginia, this county contained a population of 10,682; of whom 3260 were slaves, and 507 free persons of color. 1329 were born in other States; 274 were of foreign birth. There were 1380 dwellings and families; there were 195 pupils at "colleges, academies and private schools," having an annual income of $15,880; only sixty pupils attended the public schools, having an income of $418; 2465 whites over five and under twenty years of age were unable to read, and 387 over twenty years were equally ignorant. The county has church accomodations for 7400 persons. There are 610 farms in Fairfax, containing 89,694 improved, and 96,650 unimproved acres, the aggregate value of which, with improvements and implements, is estimated at $9,345,319. It owns 2988 horses, asses and mules, 7635 neat cattle, 2727 sheep, 11,588 swine. It raises 56,150 bushels of wheat, 82,656 bushels of rye and oats, 207,531 bushels of Indian corn, 28,181 bushels of Irish and sweet potatoes, 603 bushels of peas and beans, 422 bushels of barley, 2,253 bushels of buckwheat, 144,872 lbs. of butter and cheese, 4,490 tons of hay, 21 lbs. hops, 181 lbs. grass seeds, 16,502 lbs. wool, and 2,544 lbs. beeswax and honey.

The value of animals slaughtered is estimated at $80,452, the value of market garden produce at $3,168, and of orchard produce at $3,547.

Forty-five thousand dollars are invested in manufacturing establishments, which employ 32 hands, of which the annual produce is $97,279. $4,674 worth of manufactures are produced in families.

ALEXANDRIA.

Alexandria impressed me at first very unfavorably. This morning—the sun is out—it appears to greater advantage. It is, at best, an old, dull, unenterprising town. The suburbs relieve it. The trees resound with the melody of birds; the warm earth, car-

peted with flowers and grass, is everywhere beautiful. The residences, too, surrounded with fruit trees, white with blossoms or green with foliage, look very snug.
and homelike. [*Boston Daily Evening Traveller,* May 23, 1857]

9. Matt. 7:1.

10. Redpath slightly misquotes 1 Pet. 4:8.

11. Born in Mendon, Massachusetts, Eli Thayer (1819–99) was a pioneer in the collegiate
education of women. One of the originators of the New England Emigrant Aid Society,
Thayer was dedicated to making Kansas a free state. He served two terms as a Republican in
Congress (1857–61). *DAB,* 9:402–3.

12. After playing a leading role in the effort to encourage northerners to settle in Kansas,
Eli Thayer turned his attention to a similiar emigration program for Virginia. By early 1857
Thayer was recruiting financial and journalistic support for this scheme. New York State
incorporated the American Emigrant Aid and Homestead Company, but the new business
had trouble raising adequate capital. The company managed to sponsor the founding of only
one community of northern emigrants, at Ceredo in western Virginia, before the Civil War.
Otis K. Rice, "Eli Thayer and the Friendly Invasion of Virginia," *Journal of Southern History*
37 (November 1971): 575–96.

13. A Virginian who moved to Missouri to practice medicine, John H. Stringfellow (1819–
1905) moved to Atchison, Kansas, in 1854. He served in the proslavery territorial legislature
and militia as well as editing the *Atchison Squatter Sovereign.* After service in the Confederate army Stringfellow returned to Atchison but moved to St. Louis in 1877. Walter Williams
and Floyd C. Shoemaker, eds., *Missouri: Mother of the West,* 5 vols. (Chicago, 1930), 4:389.

14. David Rice Atchison (1807–86) migrated to Missouri from his native Kentucky in 1830.
He quickly rose in Democratic party politics until obtaining a U.S. Senate seat in 1840. After
losing that position in 1855, Atchison played a leading role in "Border Ruffian" activities in
the Kansas Territory. He supported the Confederacy during the Civil War and retired to
farming after that conflict. Theodore C. Atchison, "David R. Atchison: A Study in American
Politics," *Missouri Historical Review* 24 (July 1930): 502–12; *DAB,* 1:402–3.

15. In the spring of 1854, Eli Thayer had been one of the founders of the New England
Emigrant Aid Society that financed free state settlements in the Kansas Territory. This and
similar northern organizations hoped to use the popular sovereignty provision of the Kansas-Nebraska Act, authorizing organization of the territory, to ensure that it would enter the
Union as a free state eventually. James A. Rawley, *Race and Politics: "Bleeding Kansas" and
the Coming of the Civil War* (Philadelphia, 1969), 84–85, 88.

16. New York–born John Curtiss Underwood (1800–1873) graduated from Hamilton College in 1832 and briefly tutored in Virginia. In 1839 he married and began farming in Clarke
County, Virginia. A Free Soiler, Underwood served as a delegate to the first Republican
National Convention at Philadelphia in 1856. Resultant unpopularity forced Underwood to
leave the state, but he again represented Virginia at the 1860 Republican convention. *DAB,*
19:113–14.

17. This subheading read "VIRGINIA POLITICAL PHILOSOPHY" in the original *Boston
Daily Evening Traveller* letter.

18. Unitarian minister Theodore Parker (1810–60) presided over a large and diverse Boston congregation. In many sermons, he opposed slavery after arguing that black emancipation would prepare the way for further Anglo-Saxon dominance. Parker supported active
resistance to the Fugitive Slave Act and John Brown's plans to raid Harpers Ferry, Virginia.
Henry Steele Commager, *Theodore Parker* (Boston, 1960); George M. Fredrickson, *The Black
Image in the White Mind* (New York, 1971), 119–21, 157–58; *DAB,* 14:238–41.

19. In the original letter in the *Boston Daily Evening Traveller* of May 23, 1857, this paragraph instead began: "I find that I erred when I stated that Alexandria is in Fairfax county.

Colton's pocket map misled me. It was originally in the District of Columbia; but, within a few years, has been returned organized, with a few miles adjoining, into the county of Alexandria." The retrocession of Alexandria to Virginia had occurred in 1846. Edwards, *Statistical Gazetteer,* 161.

20. The population of Alexandria, Virginia, in 1850 was 7,917. DeBow, *Seventh Census,* xcv.

21. The original published letter concluded with the following paragraphs:

KANSAS WHITE TURNED UP!

The celebrated Mr. J.W. White, the Southern drummer-up of recruits for Kansas, who absconded from Georgia with the funds of the company he collected, has re-appeared and re-absconded in Virginia! The Alexandria Sentinel of Wednesday, has the following paragraph, copied from an alphabetic (a-b—ab) exchange:

A FLASH IN THE PAN.—Mr. J.W. White, of Kansas, was here at our last Court, drumming up emigrants for that far-off territory. He raised a goodly number here as well as at other places, who were to rendezvous at Wytheville the first of this week. They assembled, but no Mr. White appearing, they disbanded on Wednesday last.—*Ab. Virginian.*

So disband all Queen Liberty's enemies!

—To-morrow, by sunrise, I will start on a pedestrian tour through the rural inland districts.

Good-bye.   JACOBIUS.

Boston Daily Evening Traveller, May 23, 1857.

III.

FAIRFAX COURT HOUSE, *May* 17.[1]—I left Alexandria this morning, on foot, to see how the country looked, how the people talked, the price of land, the mode of living, and the system of agriculture now in vogue in this very fertile section of Virginia.

I regret to state that repeated walks through the city of Alexandria compel me to adhere to my first impressions of that lazy town. It is a dull, dismal, dirty, decrepit, ill-paved, ill-swept, ill-scented place. It has slowly increased in population, and its real estate has greatly risen in value, since the opening of the railroads which now terminate there, and since the incorporation of another line now in course of construction.

With one-tenth of the natural advantages it possesses, if Alexandria had been situated in a Northern State, one hundred thousand souls would now have been settled there.

SUBURBS OF ALEXANDRIA.

For three or four miles around Alexandria, the country is as beautiful as beautiful can be. I walked through it "like a dream." The day was exceedingly pleasant—a soft, warm zephyr was blowing from the south—almost ponderous, at times, with the perfume of blossoms, shrubbery and flowers; the clear blue sky, variegated with fleecy clouds, in every variety of combination as to color and form—the shining waters of the apparently tranquil Potomac, visible and beautiful in the distance—cultivated fields in the valley and running up the hill-slopes, studded with houses, and interspersed with innumerable strips of forest in full foliage—made a landscape, a terrestrial picture, of almost celestial charms and other-worldly perfection.

A SMALL FARM.

For two or three miles on the road I travelled, the land is chiefly held in small sections, and devoted to the culture of market produce.

I entered the house of one of these small farmers. It was a one-and-a-half-story frame, old, and in need of repair; it *had been* whitewashed, and had rather a shiftless looking aspect generally.

The farmer's wife—a bustling Yankee-ish woman—was at home; the old man was in town with the produce of his fields.

I asked her how many acres there were in her farm, and whether she would sell it?

She said there were fifty-nine acres, of light sandy soil; that they cultivated sweet potatoes and market produce, almost exclusively. She did n't believe her old man would sell it; certainly not less than $100 an acre. Land had risen in value very much indeed within the last few years. Her brother William, however, had a farm on the Leesburg road, that he wanted to sell—"Well, he war n't in any hurry about it, either," but she reckoned he mowt come to terms with me—it were a first-rate farm, too, and she believed it would just suit me.

"How many hands do you employ to keep your farm in order?"

"Well, my husband, he keeps four hands besides himself; he's in town a good deal, but we employ three niggers and a white foreman, all the time on the farm."

"And you keep a woman to assist you?"

"Yes."

"What do you pay for your negroes?—do you hire them, or do you own them?"

COST OF SLAVE LABOR.

"Oh, no, we do n't own none: we hire them from their owners, by the year. Field hands—first rate hands—get from $110 to $128; and we pay about from eighty to ninety dollars for boys."

"What do you call a boy?"

"Well, a nigger from—say seventeen to twenty-two; pretty much, often, according to their strength. We count some hands, men, younger than others."

"What do you have to pay for women?"

"I pay seventy-five dollars for this gal, and then her doctor's bill, if she gets sick, and her clothes."

"What do you reckon her clothes worth?"

"Well, we have to give them, both field hands and house-servants, two summer suits and a winter suit. That's what's allowed them by law, but most of them have to get more. We most always have to give them four suits a year."

"How much does it cost you to clothe a house-servant?"

"Well, about fourteen or fifteen dollars a year, or so."

"And field hands?"

"Field hands cost about the same, or not much more than women. Their summer suits cost very little, and we clothe the niggers in winter in what we call Virginny cloth; it's coarse stuff, does very well, and do n't cost a great deal."

"Their pants, vest, and coat are all made out of the same stuff, are they?"

"Yes."

"What do you manure your farm with?"

"Guano, stable manure, and lime."

I asked her a great many other questions—quite enough, and a few to spare, to show that I had lived in Boston[2]—but she could not give me any reliable information in relation to agricultural subjects.

She showed me her garden. Tulips and a great many other flowers are in full bloom; the cinnamon rose is bursting its buds; gooseberries are as large as a bean, or larger; nearly all the apple trees have cast their blossoms. Every tree, without exception, is covered with foliage; grass is a foot high, and in some places two or three feet. Every grove is vocal with birds.

AN ABSENTEE FARM.

Further on—three miles and a half from Alexandria—is the farm of Mr. David Barber, of New York, an absentee proprietor, which is rented from year to year, by Mr. Leesome, a Virginian, who was also the agent, I ascertained, to sell it to the highest or the earliest bidder.

After mature reflection, I concluded that it might pay me to buy it, if I could spare the money, and the price was reasonable. I accordingly went up to the house to make the usual preliminary investigations.

It is an old, large, once-whitepainted house, which, like the edifice we read of in sacred writ, is set on a hill that it cannot be hid.[3] It is built on what a Yankee would call, "quite" a knoll—to-wit, a high knoll, and commands a most beautiful prospect of hill, and dale, and water.

A country portico—I had nearly said *shed*—extends along the entire front of the dwelling. The Venetian blinds on the room windows were shut, and, judging from the thick deposit of dust upon them, had been shut for several months past.

I modestly rapped on the door which stood hospitably open. A young negro girl, six or seven years old, came out of an adjoining room, looked at me steadily but vacantly, did not condescend to open her sombre-colored lips, but retired as she entered, without warning, and silently as death.

In a moment or two afterwards a young mother entered, a woman of twenty-six or twenty-seven, pale, rather pretty, blue-eyed, modest-seeming, and, as conventional writers phrase it, very lady-like in her deportment.

"Good morning, madam—here your polite correspondent, as in duty bound, "doffed his tile," with most "exquisite" grace.

"Good morning sir."

"I understand that this estate is for sale?"

"Yes, sir."

"I've called to make some inquiries about it."

"Please sit down, sir."

Your correspondent did so—first glancing around the room, and wondering whether or not it is not quite as easy to keep everything in order as to cultivate untidiness; but he could not reply, having never studied Heaven's first law himself—only seen it in successful operation in New England households.

"How many acres have you?"

"Two hundred and fifty-three."

"How much do you ask for it?"

"It is n't ours; we only rent it; it belongs to a New York gentleman; he offers to sell it for ten thousand dollars."

(I inly whistled, as my plan of buying it vanished into thinnest air at this tremendous announcement.)

"What rent do you pay for it?"

"$250 a year."

"How many acres of wood have you?"

"Fifty, or thereabouts—most of it is swamp."

"How many rooms are there in this house?"

"Seven and a kitchen."

I asked her some other questions, but she referred me to an old man who was working—planting corn—down in a field near the line of railroad.

I went down to him.

There are two high knolls on the farm, which are formed of a gravelly soil. On the knoll south of the master's house, is an old, large log hut—an Uncle Tom's cabin—of three rooms; at the bottom of the knoll is a stable, requiring renovation, capable of holding eight horses and two tons of hay, and a barn which is calculated to accommodate fifteen cows and twenty tons of hay. The soil, except on the knolls, is a light, rich, clayey loam.

It would take at least $500 to renovate the farm-buildings and the house; while the fences are sadly dilapidated. The whole farm requires refencing.

I went down to the field. A young negro man was ploughing, and a black boy of fourteen, very small of his age, was assisting the old man in planting.

I asked him several questions about the farm, which it is unnecessary to repeat here. He said he kept ten cows; might keep twenty if he "choosed ;" but there was no spring on the farm, and water was n't quite handy.

I thought, what a very insurmountable obstacle that would have been to a Yankee—a good swamp near at hand, and a chance to double his profits—but declined "because water was n't quite handy!"

FARMING IN VIRGINIA.

He said he had only a rent from year to year; Mr. Barber would n't give him a lease, because he calculated to sell it, and only allowed him to cultivate twenty-five acres a year, in this order—corn, oats, clover, pasture.

The swamp was valuable, but the farm was n't fenced near the railroad, or it would be worth fifty dollars more rent a year. Sometimes he raised fifty bushels of corn to the acre, but he did not average over thirty-five bushels. It took two men and a boy to cultivate these twenty-five acres and attend to the cows. He gave $80 a year for the young man—he was worth more than that, though—and twenty-five dollars for the boy. First rate field hands, that could cradle and mow, and good teamsters, brought as high, in this neighborhood, as $130 a year.

Between this farm and Alexandria, he said, land was selling as high as one hundred dollars an acre. He considered this farm the cheapest in this part of the country, the way land appears to be going now. It took four horses to cultivate this farm.

His estimate of the cost of clothing slaves was the same as the lady's of the other farm. Virginia cloth, he said, cost eighty-seven and a half cents per yard.

TALK ABOUT FREE LABOR.

I asked him if he would not prefer free labor? He said if he had a farm of his own, and everything as he wanted it, he would not employ a single slave.

I asked him if he could not get free laborers here?

"Yes," he said; "you can hire Irishmen, as many as you want, from ten to twelve dollars a month."

"Why do n't you employ them, then?"

IRISHMEN IN VIRGINIA.

"Well, for several reasons. First, there are too many slaves, and that induces us to hire *them*. It's the custom, and *you can order slaves about.* You can make them do a job on Sunday, or any time when you want to; but the Irish, when they come to this country, get above themselves— *they think they are free, and do just as they have a mind to!!* Then, again, they are very much given to drink, and they're very saucy when they're in liquor."

"What about the Virginians?"

"They'll not submit to be hired by the year."

"Why not?"

"Well, I do n't know; it's the custom, some how."

"Is n't it because slaves are hired by the year, and they do n't want to appear to be bound like slaves?"

"Very probable. Now, you can't hire a Virginia girl to do any house-work."

"How do the Virginian free laborers work?"

"Some of them," he said, "work very well; but, as a general thing, you can't hire them to work on a farm."

I told him that if any of my friends came down here to settle, I should advise them to bring their Northern laborers with them. He said it would be the best and most profitable thing they could do, and advised me to go and see a Mr. Deming, a New York farmer, who had come into this neighborhood recently, and employed free laborers only.

I asked the lady of the house if she could hire white servants.

IRISH GIRLS AS HELPS.

She said, "Yes, you can hire Irish girls for four and five dollars a month."

"Cheaper than slaves?"

"Yes."

"Why don't you hire them, then?"

"Because, when you hire a slave, if *you* like *her,* you can hire her from her master for seven or eight years, or as long as you like; but, if you hire an Irish girl, if *she* do n't like *you,* she will leave sometimes in less than a month, or stay all winter and leave you in the spring, just as your busy time is about commencing."

NORTHERN EMIGRANTS.

I visited Mr. Deming's farm, and walked over it. He has been here about four years. He paid $27 per acre for the farm, which contains a long one-and-a-half story house, a barn and other outbuildings, a good orchard and a garden. He had devoted his attention chiefly to a nursery, which he planted when he first came here.

This farm was one of the run-out estates, which Eli Thayer & Co. propose to "rejuvenate, regenerate and redeem." This experiment augurs well for Eli's great enterprise. It costs less—Mr. Deming says—to redeem worn-out estates than to hew down the aboriginal forests; and their value, after that, very seldom approaches an equality. Nearer markets, nearer civilization, the Virginia farms are much more valuable than Western claims.

Mr. Deming had found the experiment of free labor to work well; he finds little difficulty in procuring it; and it is much more profitable in every respect. In every direction around him the same experiment is in course of trial.

I am indebted to Mr. Deming and his wife for hospitable entertainment and much valuable information.

NOTES BY THE WAY.

After dinner at Mr. Deming's, I rode back to Alexandria, for a valued casket I had forgotten, but immediately returned and resumed my journey afoot and alone. The further you leave Alexandria behind, the land becomes less beautiful and less cultivated. I subjoin these notes as the results of my talks and observations on the road to Fairfax Court House.[4]

Northern farmers first began to settle in this county in 1841.[5] At that time, this section, now one of the most fertile in the State, was desolate and sterile, and the question was seriously discussed whether it could ever again be cultivated. The Northerners bought up the run-out farms, and immediately began to renovate the soil. Fertility reappeared—the wilderness began to blossom as the rose.[6] Virginia farmers began to see that there was still some hope for their lands, and immediately commenced to imitate and emulate their Northern neighbors. The result is a beautiful and fertile country—fertile and beautiful, too, in exact proportion to the preponderance of Northern population.

At Falls Church,[7] seven miles from Alexandria, where a colony of Northern farmers settled, land is higher now than in any other part of the county at the same distance from the city.

The Northerners first introduced guano, now so usefully employed in redeeming and fertilizing the farms in this State.

This is the uniform testimony of every one, white or black, that I talked with.

The Virginians have a good deal yet to learn from the Northern farmer. I saw a large farm—of some two or three hundred acres—yesterday, which consisted of two fields only—the road running through the centre of the estate and thus dividing it. There were patches of different produce in these mammoth fields—pasture, wheat, oats and clover.

I asked how they managed to "bait" their cattle on the clover pasture, without endangering the wheat.

"*Why, send a nigger out to watch them!*"

Fifty acres of land, three or four miles from Alexandria, sold recently for $57 50 per acre.

TALK WITH A SLAVE.

When within two or three miles of this place, I met a stalwart negro, very black, of whom I asked the price of land.

He said that some was as low as $30 an acre, and that it ranged from that price to $100: that it had risen very high since the Northern folks came in. This he said without a leading question, but he added instantly—

"Dey soon learns Virginny's tricks."

"What do you mean?"

"Why, dey soon's hard on collud folks as Virginians."

"I have heard that," I said, "but was unwilling to believe it."

"Well, mass'r," he said, "it 's a fac; dey soon holds slaves, and sells him, too, after dey stays here a while."

"Are you a married man?"

"Yes; I'se gwane to see my wife now." [He told me she lived some five or six miles off.]

"Is it true that the Virginians sometimes separate families of colored people?"

"Oh," he said, vehemently, as if surprised at such a question, "it 's as common as spring water runs."

"Quite common?"

"As common as water flows," he said. "Why, dey'll sell a chile from its moder's breast, as it were—dey does do it; I'se seen it done, dat berry ting."

"What induced any one to do that?"

"Why, sometimes favorite collud woman's chile die, and missus will buy anoder of somebody else's."

"How much do they get for a sucking child?"

"A darkey's worth a hundred dollars as soon as he kin holler—dat's what de white folks say bout here."

"At the North," I said, "when your masters come there, they say they never separate families."

"Oh!" he ejaculated, "just you stay few month in Virginny, and you'll soon see it done hundords of times."

I *have* seen it done repeatedly—in Virginia, and many other Slave States.

I must add one remark of this negro, which is a sign of the times. Talking of the Northerners in this section, he said:

"Some on 'em, maybe, is agin slavery; but dey's on de *light side.*"

"What do you mean by that?" I asked.

"Why, de Constitution is in de oder scale agin us, and de Northern folks here's too light agin it."

This theory—Garrison's Ethiopianized—was probably gathered from some "Only" Wise politician's speech, or allusions to the Federal Constitution.[8]

NOTES

1. The material in this chapter, bearing the same dates and places of composition, first was published by Redpath (using the pen name "Jacobius") in a letter to the *Boston Daily Evening Traveller* on June 6, 1857, dated from "FAIRFAX COURT HOUSE, Saturday Evening, May 17, 1857."

2. After working as a correspondent in the Kansas Territory for a year and a half, Redpath settled in Boston, Massachusetts, in late 1856. In April 1857 he married Mary Cotton Kidder of that city. After working erratically as a free-lance reporter for a number of publications in New England and after making his third and final John Ball, Jr. tour of the South, Redpath

returned to Kansas in July 1857. Richard J. Hinton, "Pens That Made Kansas Free," *Kansas State Historical Society Collections* 6 (1897–1900):378; *Boston Daily Advertiser,* April 16, 1857.

3. Redpath substitutes "house" for the original "city" in Matt. 5:14.

4. The seat of Fairfax County, Fairfax Court House, Virginia, lies approximately twenty miles west of Alexandria. Edwards, *Statistical Gazetteer,* 231.

5. The trend of New Yorkers buying farmland in Fairfax County had been going on for more than a decade before Redpath visited the region. Rice, "Eli Thayer," 557–58.

6. Redpath slightly misquotes Isa. 35:1.

7. Actually, Falls Church, a community in Fairfax County, Virginia, named for the original Falls Church built in the 1760s at the Little Falls of the Potomac River. Eleanor Lee Templeman and Nan Netherton, *Northern Virginia Heritage* (Arlington, Va., 1966), 62–63, 102; Edwards, *Statistical Gazetteer,* 233.

8. Henry Alexander Wise (1806–76) served as governor of Virginia from 1856 to 1860. Before that he represented the state in the U.S. House of Representatives (1833–44). During the Civil War, Wise performed poorly as a Confederate general in western Virginia. Barton H. Wise, *The Life of Henry A. Wise, 1806–1876* (New York, 1899); *DAB,* 20:423–25.

IV.

AT A FARMER'S HOUSE IN FAIRFAX COUNTY, *May* 18.[1]—Fairfax Court House, from which I dated my last letter, is a village of four or five hundred inhabitants—of what the Western people, in their peculiar idiom, call the "one horse" order of municipalities. It contains a court house, built of brick, one or two churches, half a dozen houses, on the outskirts of the village, built in rather a tasteful style, three taverns of the most decrepit and dilapidated aspect, and several stores which present the same unsightly and haggard appearance.[2] It supports a paper, called the Fairfax County *News,* from the last but one issue of which I learn—and the fact is recorded as a thing to be proud of—that the people of the South, and especially of Virginia, abhor and detest that "sickly philanthropy" which seeks to abolish punishment by death. No doubt of it. For do n't they cherish and inculcate that healthy benevolence which sells husband from wife, and children from parents?

A WHITE SLAVE.

I arrived at Fairfax Court House, as the village is called, on Saturday evening, about sunset, and immediately put up at the best hotel. I noticed at supper, that the young man who waited on the guests, was so nearly white and fair in his complexion, that he might easily have passed for an

Anglo-Saxon, if his hair, which was light, but slightly curly, had not betrayed his demi-semi-African origin.

After supper, he showed me to my room—a large, high room, without a shred of carpet, and no other furniture than a chair, a very small washstand, a bed and a 9 × 12-inch Yankee looking-glass.

I asked my demi-semi-colored conductor if there were many Northern people settled in this vicinity?

He said: "Yes, there's a good many; two of the heirs to the estate are Northern men who married two of Mr. W——'s daughters; they are worse on us than the Virginians—one of them put me in jail once, and he was a great big abolitioner, too, when he come here."

This abrupt and slightly unintelligible answer and autobiographical incident, induced me to ask him to tell his story. He promised to come up after bed time, as he would probably be suspected if he staid with me now.

I was very tired with my walk and ride, and so I went to bed, and was soon sound asleep. And behold, I dreamed a dream. I was talking.

"Oh, sir! can't you invent some plan so that I need n't be a slave all my life?"

"A slave!"[3]

"Yes, sir," said a plaintive voice; "can't you invent some way so that I can get to be free?"

I awoke and found that the slave was kneeling over me, with his hand around my neck. I had been talking in my sleep, sympathizing with him, cursing the slaveholders, and had touched his heart, unconsciously to myself! He said I had been talking about him, as if I was speaking to somebody else. I was too tired to talk to him much. I only asked him—

"Who is your master?"

"I belong," he said, "to the Estate: but am going to be divided in June."

"Divided!"

"Yes, sir," he said, "we all on us is to be divided among the heirs—there's eight on 'em—in June, and *I's afeard I'll fall to one of the Northerners!*"

Next morning he told me his story, in reply to my questions. I took it down in stenographic notes. Here it is:

HIS STORY.

"I belong to the estate of W——. I will be twenty-one, I think it is in June. (I have seldom known a slave to know his age positively.) My mother was a light-colored mulatto; she was a house-servant with old Mr W——. His son R—— was my father. Old W—— died about a month before last Christmas. The estate holds me and my mother too. There are eight heirs—all children of old Mr. W——.

"W—— had twenty-four slaves. We are to be divided this coming June. I do n't know who I am going to. There are two on them I would n't like to go to, 'kase they would not let me be free. Some of the heirs gave me a note to go round among the heirs, to see if they would not set me free, and not be divided; bekase I was the old man's waiter all my life, and they knowed who my father was."

(This "note," he explained, was an agreement, intended to be signed by each of the heirs; and, if so signed by all, would have secured the poor boy's freedom.)

"——, one of the Northern men who married one of my master's daughters, proposed this plan when the old man was living; but after the death of the old man, they both changed their minds, thinking I might come to them. These Northern men used to talk to the old man that I ought to be free. After his death they 'posed it. All the Virginians, every one of them, are in favor of setting me free.

"I am hired to this man for a hundred and twenty dollars a year."

"Would you like to be free?"

"Yes, sir, I would that. I do not get any money—not a cent—'cept what gentlemen I wait on chooses to give me. I have hardly time to change my clothes, let alone anything else. If I was free I would like to stay here if the law 'lowed me, but it wo n't 'low me. I would have to go to Canada, or some'eres else. I could n't live in a slave State. My mother has no other child but me. She is rather browner than I am."

I would respectfully transmit and submit to our prominent anti-slavery politicians, the interrogatory, heart-broken and vital, of the poor white slave:

"Oh, sirs, can't you invent some plan so that the slave need n't be in bondage all his life?"

When I see slavery as it is, and hear the poor bondmen talk, I feel my republicanism rapidly going out of me, and radical abolitionism as rapidly flowing in.

PRICE OF (INANIMATE) REAL ESTATE.

Before leaving the village I was making some inquiries concerning the price of landed estate. A stranger came up to me and asked if I wanted to buy. I told him I wanted to find out the price of land, but did n't calculate to buy just at present. He said he had three or four farms for sale, on commission, of which he gave the following description:

No. 1 is within two miles of Fairfax Court House. It consists of 140 acres. Twenty-five acres are in timber. It is a stiff, red clay soil. There are several springs on the farm; a comfortable log house, containing five rooms, with a kitchen detached. The farm is divided into two or three fields. Fencing pretty good. No barn, but a stable. Price twenty-five dollars an acre.

(Fairfax Court House is fifteen miles from Alexandria.)

No. 2 consists of one hundred acres. It has fifteen acres of timber. Fifty acres are bottom land—a rich sandy loam: thirty-five acres of upland have a stiff, red clayey soil. A large creek runs through the farm, and it has about twenty different springs. It is divided into five fields. The outside fence is good; the inner fences need repairing. It has a good house on it, of seven rooms—kitchen in the basement—ten years old; and a good barn of 16 × 40 feet. It is nine miles from Georgetown, on the only road now passable. The bridges have been swept away on the others. Price, $35 an acre.

He has three other farms for sale, at from $15 to $40 per acre.

I asked him the reason why so many farms were for sale.

"Well, the emigration to Kansas and the South is one cause, and another reason is that a great many northerners who came down here, were too greedy to make money; they laid too much money out in buying land, and did n't leave a reserve fund to repair and improve on. They calculated to pay part out of the farm, but did n't keep enough to bring it up. Some Northerners are in as prosperous condition here as in any Northern State. Them that don't come here to speculate, but settle down, do n't buy beyond their means, and go to work, get on well. There's plenty round here who came down with small means, bought a small tract, and kept adding to it, that are independent. Others have been ruined by speculation."

"Are there many Northern families in this county?"

"Yes, there are eight or nine hundred families—chiefly from York State, now and then a few from Pennsylvania, and occasionally one from Vermont."

I asked the price of farm stock. He said good work horses ranged from $160 to $170, sometimes $150. He said that if Northern men came down to settle here they had better bring their horses with them—it would be economical for them to do it. Two wealthy men from the North had moved into this neighborhood a month ago, and brought all their stock with them.

Cows are worth thirty dollars, and oxen, one hundred and twenty-five dollars a yoke. It would pay to bring them from the North here to sell them. Northern cattle brought as high, he said, as from a hundred and fifty to a hundred and seventy-five dollars. They are better broke, and last better than Virginia-raised cattle; so are Northern horses—we feed too much grain to ours. He said Northern emigrants had better bring all kinds of agricultural implements, except heavy things—such as ox-plows, carts, and the like.

FREE LABOR AND SLAVE LABOR.

I asked whether free or slave labor was the most profitable here?

He said, "Slave labor, because you can get it whenever you want it. Some Northern farmers brought their laborers with them, but they soon got dissatisfied, and left. They found they had no one to associate with but those they came with, and they left. Then again, if you are pressed for work, you can't get white laborers, and have to employ slaves, and white men won't work with them. So you are brought down to the nigger again. Small farmers are working with white laborers, and do very well."

A VIRGINIAN ON YANKEES.

"When the Yankees come down, can't you get them to work?"

"The further," he said, "you go North, the more industrious the men are. They are obliged to work to get a living. *But when they come here they deteriorate*—in other words, they get lazy, and they are always inventing something or other to get shut of work. Now, a nigger has none of that inventive faculty, and you get work out of him by hard knocks and clumsiness."

"But the Germans," I remarked, "are industrious workers?"

"Yes," he said, "but you must get them that do n't know much—the greener the better—one that does n't understand the English language, and can't learn more than what you want him to do, is the best!"

SYSTEM OF FARMING.

Two or three miles from Fairfax Court House, on the road to Centreville, Virginia,[4] I met a man and a boy carrying pails of water. I found he was a farmer, and asked how many bushels they could raise to an acre. He said an average crop was five or six barrels. (They estimate by barrels here—a barrel is five bushels.)

"What is the average price of land between here and Centreville?"

"Wall," he drawled out, "say between fifteen and thirty dollars per acre."

I asked him what system of cultivation they adopted here.

"Wall, we take a crop of wheat, say, or oats, and then sow it with clover, and let it lay two or three years."

I asked him if they had never tried the system of rotation of crops and manuring.

"No."

"Do all cultivate in the way you describe?"

"Yes," said he, "most of them; they all ought to, but some take a crop every year, and run the land out. That has been the system in these parts until quite recently—within seven or eight years."

"Who introduced the change?"

"The Northern people," he said. "Since they came, they have carried up and restored a great deal of land, and taught us to do it, too."

"There are a good many Northern people coming in here—are there not?" I asked him.

"No," he answered, "not so many buyers as there used to be."

"Why?"

"Because a great many's sold out, and gone back agin."

He gave the same reason as the stranger at the hotel.

The country in this section (I am within a mile of the western line of the county) is beautiful in most parts, and apparently very fertile. All that it needs is men who know how to till the soil, without exhausting its strength. Centreville is a hamlet of twenty or thirty houses. As I entered it, yesterday afternoon, half-a-dozen negroes were playing at ball—Sunday is their holiday—and over twenty white loafers were congregated in different parts of the place. Of their domestic industry I saw not the faintest indication, excepting only several very handsome mulatto women and children. Every house in the hamlet looks as if it could recollect Noah,[5] when he was a sucking child, and had been inhabited by ladies of the Mrs. McClarty tribe from time immemorial.

On my way from Centreville hither, I saw rye in the ear. The woods look very beautiful.

AMALGAMATION.

The abolitionists, it is well known in Congress—I mean in the Democratic ranks—are, all of them, negro-worshippers and amalgamationists. If they alone, or chiefly, are the fathers of mulattoes, Fairfax county, Henrietta county, and every part of Virginia I have visited, are infested with these dangerous inhabitants. The number of semi-black children, men and women, that one meets with here, is extraordinary.

Colored children and white children play together in the street—openly in the light of day—and they associate without concealment in the house; whites and blacks talk together, walk together, ride together, as if they were men and brothers.

Why is Governor Wise[6] so silent on this dangerous indication of the amalgamation and equalization-ward tendency of Southern society? What say our Northern Democracy to these negro-fraternizing Southern brethren?

I pause for a reply.

NOTES

1. Under the pen name "Jacobius," Redpath originally published the material in this chapter in a letter to the *Boston Daily Evening Traveller* of June 13, 1857.

2. In the 1850s Fairfax Court House contained the county buildings and was home to two hundred to three hundred residents. Edwards, *Statistical Gazetteer,* 231.

3. The original letter included the following sentence at this point: "That wasn't exactly the language I expected to hear from the one I supposed I was with." *Boston Daily Evening Traveller,* June 13, 1857.

4. This community on the Warrenton Turnpike in Fairfax County was four miles northeast of the site of the Bull Run battles in the Civil War. Angelo Heilprin and Louis Heilprin, eds., *A Complete Pronouncing Gazetteer or Geographical Dictionary of the World* (Philadelphia, 1922), 372.

5. Noah was the patriarch of the only family that God permitted to survive the Great Flood. Gen. 5–8.

6. Henry A. Wise.

V.

PRINCE WILLIAM COUNTY.

WARRENTON, FAUQUIER COUNTY, *May,* 18.[1]—I have walked, to-day, across Prince William county, on the turnpike road, from Centreville to Warrenton.[2] Prince William county is a small one. It has a population of over 5,000 whites, 2,500 slaves, and 550 free negroes. It has a thousand dwellings. Its annual educational income is $695! Only 316 pupils attend the public schools. Seven hundred and eighty-four white adults can neither read nor write, and nearly two thousand youths, between five and twenty years of age, are in the same benighted state of ignorance. The county, however, has church accommodations for nearly five thousand souls. It is evident, therefore, that although the people's minds must be dark, their souls have a very fair chance for salvation. That's a great comfort.

The county is divided into 579 farms, valued, with improvements and implements, at $1,499,886; and containing 104,424 acres of improved, and

72,343 acres of unimproved land. It produced, when the last census was taken, 57,728 bushels of wheat, 59,549 of rye and oats, 161,248 of Indian corn; and 10,374 of Irish and sweet potatoes; 96,679 lbs. of butter and 2306 tons of hay, were the principal additional items in the list.[3]

So far Mr. Gradgrind.[4]

A FREE COLORED FARMER.

The first person I met, after crossing the line, was a hearty old man of color, who was engaged in repairing his neighbor's fence. Yankee-like, the first sentence I uttered, on seeing him, was an interrogation. I asked him the price of land. He said that a neighbor had recently bought a farm, adjoining his place, for $26 an acre. He would n't swap his even, no how, either as buyer or seller. If I wanted to buy, however, he would sell me his farm, of one hundred and fifty acres of excellent land, for $20 an acre.

I asked him if he was a free man, and why he wanted to sell. He said— Yes, he was a free man. His father was one of nine hundred and ninety-nine slaves, once the property of Mr. Carter, who liberated every one of them, and secured to them the right to remain in the county.[5] Slaves who are freed now, he added, have to leave the State, or go to Washington and remain there a year to get their papers.[6] His wife was there now. Her year was almost out, and he intended to go after her as soon as it expired.

I asked if she was a slave, or had he bought her. He said she had been a slave, but her master freed her by his will. The master was an old bachelor—never married—but had a lot of children by a black woman. His wife was one of these children. He offered him five hundred dollars for her when she was quite young, but he said he would never sell her—he knew what stock she came from—but would liberate her when he died. On this promise the relator married her, and had several children. Meanwhile her mother refused any longer to cohabit with the bachelor, and, to use the colored man's phrase, he took up with an *out* woman—a white woman— but he did not marry her. She, also, bore him several children. On his death, he left the narrator's wife and all her daughters free, but bequeathed her two sons—his grand-children—"to this outwoman," with the proviso that she should sell them to their father if he wanted to purchase his (and the testator's) own flesh and blood. The "out woman," however, sold them to the traders, who handed them over to their father in consideration of eighteen hundred dollars, one thousand of which had already been paid.

The old man said he wanted to sell his farm in order to raise the balance, and to pay some other debts, now due, that he had recently incurred.

I went up to his farm and looked over it. It is very good soil, indeed; commands a beautiful prospect, and is cultivated as well as Virginians know how.

I asked him if there were many Northerners settled here? "Yes," he added, "a good many;" and pointed out the farm of one gentleman from New Jersey. He said the Northerners, somehow, made more money, raised better crops, and worked less to do it, than "we Virginians." Somehow, he thought, after they were here awhile, they seemed to get an idée of the land, and make it do 'sactly as they wanted to. The Northerners didn't own slaves. They said slaves cost too much. You buy one, pay a thousand dollars for him; he goes off, and fights or sprees, and the first thing you know your thousand dollar 's dead!"

The old man did not think himself that slave labor paid, and believed it would be better for the white men, as well as the negro, if slavery was instantly and everywhere abolished.

I was too tired, when I talked with him, to report his remarks stenographically, as I generally do. I regret it now, for his idiom was exceedingly unique and humorous. If Mrs. Partington ever meets him she will have to hide her diminished head forever.[7]

IGNORANCE.

The ignorance of both the poor whites and blacks is almost incredible; even to the traveller who has daily and astonishing evidences of it. I have sometimes asked negroes who have lived near a village all their life, if they knew what its population was; and they could not understand what population meant nor—when explained to them—could they answer my question. Like Socrates, they seemed "only to know that they knew nothing."[8]

I asked an Irish woman and some poor whites, where a railroad—which passed by their cabins—terminated. They could not tell me. It was an uncompleted line, I afterwards found—this was in Fairfax county—which had been stopped for want of funds, although intersecting a very fertile region, and running into the mining districts.[9]

"Sir," said a gentleman in conversation on this subject, "if the road to heaven went by their front door, they could n't tell you the way there to save themselves from ——!"

NEGRO-DRIVING OF HORSES.

The country is less cultivated—along the turnpike, at least—wood is more plentiful, the fields far larger, and the scenery less beautiful, the nearer you approach to Fauquier county.

The first place I came to was a hamlet of a dozen houses, called Gainesville, on the Manassas Gap Railroad,[10] where I asked the price of land of a workman in a field close by. Another white man and a negro woman were working with him. He said, that in this part of the country, land ranged from eight to twenty-five dollars an acre, but advised me, if I wanted to buy, to go farther back into the country.

"How many bushels of corn do you raise to an acre?"

"Well, we don't average more than three barrels—nor that often." (Fifteen bushels.)

"Are there many northern people settled round here?"

"No, sir. Lots down at Brentsville,[11] though."

Let the traveller go to Brentsville, and he will find land higher, and crops more abundant there. So much for free labor.

It began to rain heavily, and I was induced to hasten my steps.

I soon overtook a wagon drawn by six horses, and driven by a negro. I never saw such a wagon in my life before. It was twenty feet long, broad and very deep. It was covered with a sailcloth, which partly protected it, and was higher at both ends than at the middle.

I got into the wagon first, and then into a talk with the negro.

In Fauquier county, he informed me, "most all de farms was big again as in Prince William; most on them was seven, eight or nine hundred acres."

His master holds eighteen slaves. "Our farm," as he proudly styled his master's plantation, "had seven hundred acres. They raised four or five hundred barrels of corn and two thousand bushels of wheat last year. Farms," he said, "were getting very high in ole Fauquer county. Mass'r bought forty acre las' year and he paid forty dollars an acre."

He rode the near horse, and held a heavy cowhide in his hand, with which, from time to time, he lashed the leaders, as barbarous drivers lash oxen when at work. Whenever we came to a hill, especially if it was very steep, he dismounted, lashed the horses with all his strength, varying his performances by picking up stones, none of them smaller than half a brick, and throwing them with all his force, at the horses' legs. He seldom missed.

The wagon was laden with two tons of plaster in sacks.

This is a fair specimen of the style in which slaves treat stock.

Thus it is that wrong begets wrong, and that injustice is unprofitable as well as unrighteous.

The wagon turned off the turnpike about three miles from Warrenton. We had passed through two or three hamlets—New Baltimore and Buckland[12] I remember—but they did not afford anything worthy of notice.

I walked, through a drenching rain, to Warrenton, which is a pleasant country village. In entering it, I asked for the best hotel. I was directed down the street. On looking up at the swinging sign, I read, with astonishment, this horrible announcement, equally laconic as impious and improper:

WARREN

GREEN

H EL.

[13]

Nothing daunted, I ventured, with perfect recklessness—or in the spirit of the Six Hundred of Balaklava[14]—into the very mouth—the open doorway—of this terrestrial "H EL." Astonished to find a room in it without a *fire,* I instantly ordered one, "regardless of consequences." And here I am, for once, in a very snug old room, with a blazing wood fire, as comfortable as a Boston traveller can be, at so great a distance from the old folks to hum and the mellifluous nasal melody of New England pronunciation.

RICHMOND, *May* 23.—Warrenton is a pleasant little village, situated in the centre of Fauquier county. I arrived there late in the afternoon, tired, drenched and muddy, and left by the early train on the following morning.[15] It was still raining when I took my departure; so I had no time to collect statistics of the price of land, or any incidents of social life and country customs. I had a talk with a Virginian at the hotel on politics, and Eli Thayer's scheme of colonization. He said that in Eastern Virginia, in consequence of the tactics of politicians and the ignorance of the country editors—who took for granted whatever figures or opinions their leaders advanced—Mr. Thayer would probably meet with resistance at the outset; but, in Western Virginia, where slavery was weak, and a free soil feeling had long been predominant,[16] he would be welcomed, he believed, with open arms, and realize his most sanguine hopes of pecuniary success, if the affairs of the organization should be managed by shrewd and experienced business men.

He said that white labor was becoming so scarce and high, that every emigration from the North was felt to be a blessing to the State. In the present canvass, he added, candidates were openly advocating the repeal of the law of expatriation against freemen of color. This was done, I gleaned, from no sense of justice, but owing solely to the scarcity of labor.

We waited at the junction nearly half an hour before the train from Alexandria came up. When I entered these cars, I found myself entirely blockaded, on every side, with gentlemen in black suits and snowy white cravats. It was a delegation of clergymen to a Denominational Convention. "A man is known by the company he keeps."[17] Fearing to be mistaken for a wolf in lamb's clothing[18]—in other words, for a pro-slavery divine—I got out at Gordonstown, and went on to Charlottesville,[19] instead, as I intended, of going to Richmond, by the nearest route and in the quickest time.

CHARLOTTESVILLE.

An accident detained me at Charlottesville two days. It is situated in a charming valley—fertile, wooded, watered well—with cultivated hills rising from the plain, and snow-capped misty mountains in the western background. The village, too, is the prettiest, it is said, and one of the most thriving in Virginia. The College founded by Jefferson is situated there.[20] It rained almost incessantly all the time I was there. The soil is exclusively a red stiff clay, which, when the rain subsided for an hour, rendered walking exceedingly unpleasant to attempt, and impossible when tried.

Yesterday I left the village for Richmond—distance, about ninety miles.[21] The fare is four dollars, and the time six hours. We passed miles adjoining miles of worn out land, producing only hedge broom, stunted shrubbery and grass, when, by scientific culture and a little labor, it might be heavy with tobacco or the cereal grains. There is a great field open here for Northern intelligence and Northern industry.

NOTES

1. Careful search of the surviving issues of the *Boston Daily Evening Traveller* for 1857 did not uncover an earlier published version of the material in this chapter.

2. Redpath traveled along the Warrenton Turnpike between Centreville and Warrenton, through the region that would be the scene of the First and Second Battles of Bull Run.

3. Contemporary sources confirm Redpath's statistics for Prince William County. There were thirteen churches identified in the county in the 1850s. Edwards, *Statistical Gazetteer,* 349–51.

4. The fictional character of "Mrs. Gradgrind" was the feebleminded wife of Thomas Gradgrind, the retired hardware merchant who operated a model school in Charles Dickens's *Hard Times* (1854).

5. Redpath probably refers to Robert Carter III (1728–1804) of Nomini Hall in Westmoreland County, Virginia, a descendant of one of the state's wealthiest families. After becoming a religious radical as well as a merchant and manufacturer, Carter gradually emancipated his more than five hundred slaves in the late eighteenth century. Roller and Twyman, *Encyclopedia of Southern History,* 185–86; Clifford Downey, *The Golden Age: A Climate for Greatness, Virginia 1732–1775* (Boston, 1970), 339.

6. In 1806 Virginia revised its slave codes regarding manumission to require freed slaves to leave the state within a year. Miller and Smith, *Dictionary of Afro-American Slavery,* 430–32.

7. Actually a reference to a literary character created by Boston journalist Benjamin Penhallow Shillaber (1814–90). Shillaber began publishing humorous sayings attributed to "Mrs. Partington" in the *Boston Post* in 1847. He continued the series in his own weekly newspaper, the *Carpet-Bag* (1851–53). Many of these witticisms were republished in the best-selling *Life and Sayings of Mrs. Partington* (1854). *New York Daily Tribune,* May 10 and 12, 1854; *DAB,* 17:109–10.

8. The expression "I know nothing except the fact of my ignorance" was attributed to Socrates by Diogenes Laertius in the third century A.D.

9. In 1862 this uncompleted railroad became famous as the scene of bloody fighting on the first day of the Second Battle of Bull Run. The line was intended to be a spur of the Manassas Gap Railroad, connecting Gainesville to Alexandria. Work on the line's right-of-way began in the mid-1850s, but the company eventually ran out of funds before laying track. John J. Hennessy, *Return to Bull Run: The Campaign and Battle of Second Manassas* (New York, 1993), 200–201.

10. Gainesville was a post office village on both the Warrenton Turnpike and the Manassas Gap Railroad in Prince William County, Virginia. Edwards, *Statistical Gazetteer,* 243.

11. Located in southeastern Fauquier County, Brentsville—originally named Brent's Town—was the site of a blockhouse erected in 1686. *Fauquier County, Virginia: 1759–1959* (Warrenton, Va., 1959), 12–15.

12. Originally named Ball's Store, the village of New Baltimore in Fauquier County was incorporated in 1822. Buckland, on Broad Run in Prince William County, was the site of a distillery and several other small manufacturing businesses. *Fauquier County,* 80, 126–27, 294.

13. Thaddeus Norris opened the three-story, wooden Warren Green Hotel in Warrenton, Virginia, in 1817. The building served as a headquarters for Union Army units at various times during the Civil War. *Fauquier County,* 173, 293, 294.

14. Made famous by Alfred Lord Tennyson's poem "The Charge of the Light Brigade," the Battle of Balaklava, which occurred on October 25, 1854, in the Crimean War, featured a hopeless charge by the approximately six hundred men of the British Light Cavalry Brigade on Russian entrenchments. Pemberton, *Crimean War,* 15–26.

15. The seat of Fauquier County with a population in 1850 of nearly fifteen hundred, Warrenton had a branch line to connect it with the Orange and Alexandria Railroad. By this route, Redpath would have traveled approximately one hundred miles to Richmond. Edwards, *Statistical Gazetteer,* 403.

16. Because of rugged terrain and poor transportation, the western counties of antebellum Virginia attracted a mere three hundred thousand white settlers, including slaveholders owning only about twenty thousand slaves. Early industrial development along communities on tributaries of the Ohio River created strong economic attachments between northwestern Virginia and the free-state economy. Rice, "Eli Thayer," 577–78, 585–86; Miller and Smith, *Dictionary of Afro-American Slavery,* 806–9.

17. A Greek proverb first recorded in Euripides, *Phoenix,* frag. 809.

18. An allusion to the fable by Aesop.

19. A railroad junction and trading center in Orange County, Virginia, Gordonsville lies eighteen miles northeast of Charlottesville. Seltzer, *Columbia Lippincott's Gazeteer,* 697.

20. Attended by about four hundred students in the mid-1850s, the University of Virginia had been founded in 1819 by the state legislature at the urging of former president Thomas Jefferson. Charlottesville at the time of Redpath's visit had a population of approximately 2,600 and was the seat of Albemarle County, Virginia. Edwards, *Statistical Gazetteer,* 205.

21. Redpath would have traveled on the Central Railroad for eighty-one miles between Charlottesville and Richmond, Virginia. Edwards, *Statistical Gazetteer,* 205.

VI.

RICHMOND.

RICHMOND, *May* 24.[1]—Charleston excepted, and also, perhaps, Montgomery in Alabama, "Rome-hilled Richmond " is the most charming in situation or in outside aspect, of all the Southern cities that I have ever visited.

It is a city of over 20,000 inhabitants—the political, commercial, and social metropolis of the State—well laid out, beautifully shaded, studded with little gardens—has several factories, good hotels, a multiplicity of churches, a theatre, five daily papers, a great number of aristocratic streets, with large, fashionable, but not sumptuous residences; and, to crown all, and over and above all, it has four or five negro pens and negro auction-rooms.[2]

A SLAVE SALE.

I saw a slave sale to-day. The advertisement subjoined, announcing it, appeared in the *Richmond Enquirer* and *Richmond Examiner.*

AUCTION SALES.

THIS DAY.

BY DICKINSON, HILL & CO., Auctioneers.

----

10 NEGROES.—Will be sold by us, this morning at 10 o'clock, 10 likely negroes.

may 24   DICKINSON, HILL & CO., Aucts.

AUCTION SALES.

BY PULLIAM & DAVIS, Auctioneers.

8 NEGROES.—This day, at 10 o'clock, we will sell 8 likely negroes, Men, Boys, and Girls.

may 24.   PULLIAM & DAVIS, Aucts.[3]

Dickinson, Hill & Company, body-sellers and body-buyers, "subject only to the Constitution," carry on their nefarious business in Wall street—I believe its name is—within pistol shot of the capitol of Virginia and its executive mansion.[4] Near their auction-room, on the opposite side of the street, is the office of another person engaged in the same inhuman traffic, who has painted, in bold Roman letters, on a sign-board over the door:

E. A. G. CLOPTON,
AGENT,
For Hiring Out Negroes,
AND
Renting Out Houses.

Both negroes and houses, by the laws of Virginia, are "held, adjudged and reputed" to be property! This is Southern Democracy!

At ten o'clock there was a crowd of men around the door of the auction-room, but it was nearly eleven when a mulatto man came out, and vociferously shouted—"This way, gentlemen, this way—sale 's 'bout to begin—sale 's 'bout to begin—gentlemen wishin' to buy, please step into the room inside."

I entered the auction-room. It is a long, damp, dirty-looking room, with a low, rough-timbered ceiling, and supported, in the centre, by two wooden pillars, square, filthy, rough-hewed, and, I assure you, not a little whittled. At the further end of it, a small apartment was partitioned off, with unpainted pine boards, and the breadth which it did not cover was used as a counting-room, divided from the larger one by a blue painted paling.

The walls of the auction-room were profusely decorated with tobacco stains, which, by their form, number and variety, indicated that they had been hastily ejected from the human mouth—sometimes, by poets, styled divine. Handbills, which plainly showed that—"Negro clothing," "Servants' wear," "Negro blankets," and other articles of servile apparel, were for sale by various merchants in town, served, with the tobacco stains, to render the walls exeeedingly attractive to a Northern eye. Rough, and roughly used pine forms extended around the room, and partly into the body of it, too. In the centre, four steps high, is a platform—a Southern platform, a Democratic platform, a State Rights platform—where men, women, children, and unweaned babes are daily sold, by Dickinson, Hill & Co., "for cash," or "on time," to the highest bidder.

I saw a number of men enter the inner room, and quietly followed them, unnoticed. The slaves—the males—were there. What do you think, my conservative reader, is the object of the little room? I will tell you what was done. The slaves were stripped naked, and carefully examined, as horses are—every part of their body, from their crown to their feet, was rigorously scrutinized by the gallant chivalry Who intended to buy them. I saw one unfortunate slave examined in this way, but did not care to see the mean, cowardly and disgusting act performed on any other.

After a time they were brought out. The auctioneer—a short, thick-set, gross-eyed, dark, and fleshy fellow—who was dressed in black, opened the sale by offering a boy of twelve or fourteen years of age.

"Gentlemen,"—he said, in accents that seemed to be very greasy—"I offer you this boy; he is sound and healthy, and title warranted good— What d'ye offer, gentlemen?"

"Eight hundred dollars."

"Eight hundred dollars bid—eight hundred dollars—(he talked very fast)—eight hundred dollars—eight hundred dollars—eight hundred and fifty—thank you—eight hundred and fifty dollars bid—eight"—

"Nine hundred."

"Nine hundred dollars bid—nine hundred dollars—nine hundred dollars—nine hundred dollars—gentlemen, he 's a first-rate boy"—

"Come down here," said the mulatto, who is Dickinson's slave, I believe, "come down."

The boy came down.

"Please stand out of the way, gentlemen," cried the mulatto, to a number of men who stood between the platform and the counting-room.

They did so.

"Now you walk along to the wall," said the slave to the other article of commerce—"now hold up your head and walk *pert*."

The boy did as he was directed.

"Quick—come—pert—only there already?—pert!" jerked out the mulatto, to hasten the boy's steps.

The crowd looked on attentively, especially those who had bid. He mounted the President—I mean the platform—again, and the bidding was resumed with greater activity.

"Well, gentlemen," said the body-seller, "you see he's a likely boy— how much do you bid?"

"Ten," said a voice.

"Nine hundred and ten dollars bid—nine hundred and ten—nine hundred and ten—nine hundred and TEN—nine hundred and ten—nine hundred and ten dollars bid—nine hundred and ten"—

"Twenty."

"Nine hundred and twenty dollars bid—nine hundred and twenty dollars—nine THIRTY—nine hundred and thirty dollars—nine hundred and FORTY—nine forty 's bid—nine hundred and forty dollars—nine forty—nine forty—nine FIFTY—nine fifty—nine hundred and fifty—nine hundred and fifty—nine hundred and fifty—nine hundred and fifty—nine hundred and fifty dollars—nine hundred and SIXTY—nine hundred and sixty dollars."

"Seventy," said a voice.

"Nine hundred and seventy dollars—nine hundred and seventy dollars"——

"Five."

"Nine hundred and seventy-five dollars," said the auctioneer.

"He 's an uncommon likely boy," chimed the auctioneer's mulatto.

A chivalrous Virginian mounted the steps of the platform. "Open your mouth," he said. The Article opened its mouth, and displayed a beautiful, pearly set of teeth.

"You all sound?" asked the white.

"Yes, massa," said the boy.

"Nine eighty," said the white.

"Five," said another, who stood beside him.

"Ninety," said the other white.

"Nine hundred and ninety," exclaimed the auctioneer—"nine hundred and ninety dollars—nine hundred and ninety dollars"——

"D—n it," said a man at my side, "how niggers has riz."

"Yes, sir," said his old white-haired companion, "I tell you, if a man buys niggers now, he has to pay for them. That's about the amount of it."

"Nine hundred and ninety dollars—all done at nine hundred and ninety dollars?—nine hundred—and—nine-ty dollars—go-ing at nine—hundred *and* nine-ty dollars—and—gone—if no one bids—nine hundred and ninety dollars—once—nine hundred and—ninety, a-n-d"

He looked round and round in every direction, but no one moved, and he plaintively added—

"Gone!"

This boy was one of those unfortunate children who neber *was* born, but are raised by the speculators, or are the offspring of illicit connections between the Saxon and African races. He was of a brown complexion—about one-third white blood. He was dressed in a small check calico trowsers, and a jacket of a grey color. The whole suit would not cost more than three dollars; but it was new, clean and looked very tidy.

The next Article disposed of was a young man, of similar complexion, twenty years old, muscular, with an energetic and intelligent expression. One thousand dollars was the first bid made. He was sold to "Jones & Slater,"[5] who are forwarding agents, I was told, of animated merchandise to New Orleans. I hunted up their office after I left the auction-room. It was shut. It is situated in the congenial neighborhood of a cluster of disreputable houses.

The third article offered was a very black, low-browed, short, brutal looking negro, for whom nine hundred dollars only was bid. He was not sold. So also with several others.

A woman, with a child at her breast, and a daughter, seven years old, or thereabouts, at her side, mounted the steps of the platform.

The other sales did not excite my indignation more than the description of such a scene would have done; certainly—had I never visited a slave auction-room before—a great deal less than some narratives would have done. These men and boy were too brutal in their natures to arouse my sympathies. Besides, they were men, and could escape by death or flight, or insurrection; and it is a man's duty, I hold—every man's duty—to be free at every hazard or by any means.

But the poor black mother—with her nearly white babe—with the anxiety of an uncertain future among brutal men before her—and the young girl, too, now so innocent, but predestined by the nature of slavery to a life of hard labor and involuntary prostitution—I would have been either less than a man, or more, to have looked on stoically or with indifference, as she and her little ones were sold.

Twelve hundred and fifty dollars were bid for her, but she was not sold. She was worth, a Virginian told me, "fifteen hundred dollars of any man's money." I do n't doubt it. The Christian Theology tells us that she was once, vile and lowly as she may be, deemed worthy of an infinitely greater price than that. She was "warranted sound and healthy," with the exception of a female complaint, to which mothers are occasionally subject, the name and nature of which was unblushingly stated.

She was taken into the inner room, after the bidding commenced, and there indecently "*examined*" in the presence of a dozen or fifteen brutal men. I did not go in, but was told, by a spectator, coolly, that "they 'd examined her," and the brutal remarks and licentious looks of the creatures when they came out, was evidence enough that he had spoken the truth.

The mother's breast heaved, and her eye anxiously wandered from one bidder to another, as the sale was going on. She seemed relieved when it was over—but it was only the heart aching relief of suspense.

A young girl, of twenty years or thereabouts, was the next commodity put up. Her right hand was entirely useless—"dead," as she aptly called it. One finger had been cut off by a doctor, and the auctioneer stated that she herself chopped off the other finger—her forefinger—because it hurt her, and she thought that to cut it off would cure it. This remark raised a laugh among the crowd. I looked at her, and expected to see a stupid-looking creature, low browed and sensual in appearance; but was surprised, instead, to see a woman with an eye which reminded me of Margaret Gardiner (whom I visited in Cincinnati),[6] but more resolute, intelligent and impulsive. She was perfectly black; but her eye was Saxon, if by Saxon we mean a hell-defying courage, which neither death nor the devil can terrify. It was an eye that will never die in a slave's socket, or never die a natural death in so unworthy an abode.

"Did n't you cut your finger off," asked a man, "kase you was mad?"

She looked at him quietly, but with a glance of contempt, and said:

"No, you see it was a sort o' sore, and I thought it would be better to cut it off than be plagued with it."

Several persons around me expressed the opinion that she had done it willfully, "to spite her master or mistress, or to keep her from being sold down South."

I do not doubt it.

A heroic act of this kind was once publicly performed, many years ago, in the city of St. Louis. It was witnessed by gentlemen still living there, one of whom—now an ardent Emancipationist—narrated the circumstance to me.

These scenes occurred, not in Russia or Austria, or in avowedly despotic countries, but in the United States of America, which we are so fond of eulogizing as the chosen land of liberty!

LIBERTY!

"Oh Liberty! what outrages are committed in thy name!"[7]

These verses, penned in Richmond after a slave sale, by a personal friend of the present writer,[8] although bitter, sectional, and fanatical, when viewed from a conservative position, more faithfully and graphically than any poetry that I have ever read, express the feelings of a man of compassionate and impulsive nature, when witnessing such wicked and revolting commercial transactions as the public auction of immortal human beings:

A CURSE ON VIRGINIA.

Curses on you, foul Virginia,
   Stony-hearted whore!
May the plagues that swept o'er Egypt—
   Seven—and seventy more,
Desolate your homes and hearths,
   Devastate your fields,
Send ten deaths for every pang-birth
   Womb of wife or creature yields:
     May fever gaunt,
     Protracted want,
Hurl your sons beneath the sod,
Send your bondmen back to God!
     From your own cup,
     Soon may you sup,
The bitter draught you give to others—
Your negro sons and negro brothers!
     Soon may they rise,
     As did your sires,
     And light up fires,
     Which not by Wise,
Nor any despot shall be quenched;
   Not till Black Samson, dumb and bound,
   Shall raze each slave-pen to the ground,
Till States with slavers' blood are drenched.

NOTES

1. A careful search of the surviving issues of the *Boston Daily Evening Traveller* for 1857 did not uncover an earlier published version of the material in this chapter.

2. The capital of the state of Virginia and the seat of Henrico County, Richmond had a population of 27,570 in 1850. Edwards, *Statistical Gazetteer,* 355–65.

3. Advertisements identical to these, with the exception of slightly different numbers of slaves to be auctioned off, appeared in the *Richmond Enquirer* on May 24, 1858.

4. The slave trading firm of Dickinson, Hill, & Co. of Richmond had its office on the corner of Franklin and Wall Streets. Robert Hill of the firm boasted that its sale of slaves grossed two million dollars in 1856. Bancroft, *Slave Trading,* 96–99, 116–17.

5. The slave trading firm of Jones & Slater was located at Locust Alley in Richmond where several similar firms also had headquarters. Bancroft, *Slave Trading,* 97.

6. A fugitive slave from Kentucky, Margaret Garner (1833–61), not Gardiner, and her family had just reached Ohio when an armed band attempted their rendition. Seeing capture as inevitable, Garner stabbed all four of her children, killing one. While being returned to her

master, Garner attempted a second escape, which tragically resulted in the drowning death of another child. During a trip east in February 1856, Redpath had reported on a visit with Garner in her Cincinnati prison cell for the *St. Louis Daily Missouri Democrat,* February 23, 1856: Julius Yanuck, "The Garner Fugitive Slave Case," *Mississippi Valley Historical Review* 40 (June 1953):47–66.

7. Reportedly the last words of Jeanne Mason Roland before her death on the guillotine in 1793. Alphonse de Lamartine, *Histoire des Girondins* (n.p., 1847).

8. Possibly written by Francis Jackson Merriam (1837–65), nephew of leading Garrisonian abolitionist Francis Jackson. Merriam accompanied Redpath on part of his third tour of the slave states. Through Redpath, Merriam became involved with John Brown and was a member of the party that raided Harpers Ferry in 1859. *Boston Atlas and Bee,* October 30, 1859; Jeffrey Rossbach, *Ambivalent Conspirators: John Brown, the Secret Six, and a Theory of Slave Violence* (Philadelphia, 1982), 211; Villard, *John Brown,* 421.

IN MY SANCTUM

I.

GENERAL RESULTS.

I DID not originally visit the Slave States for the purpose of writing a book. Hence the preceding notes of travel are much less minute than they would otherwise have been made. I shall make yet another journey South—*Down the Mississippi;* which (if the sale of this volume shall warrant it) I shall narrate at much greater length, and make more comprehensive and various—relating as well the effects of slavery on agriculture, trade and education, as on the morals of the subjugated people, and the humanity of the ruling race.[1]

Let me here subjoin the general results and miscellaneous incidents of my travels and conversations, without any especial regard to rhetorical order or intrinsic importance of topic.

I. I do not believe that the progress of physical science, the extension of railroads, or the exhausting effects of involuntary labor, will ever induce or compel the peaceful abolition of American slavery. Worn out lands will be recuperated by scientific skill, by guano, rotation of crops, the steam plough, and the knowledge—now rapidly diffusing—of agricultural chemistry. Railroads raise both the price and value of slave labor, by rapidly conveying the rural products of it, to the Northern and European markets. Slave labor, although detrimental to the State, is profitable to the individual holders of human "property." Hence, this powerful class of criminals will ever oppose its speedy extinction. I do not believe, also, that—unless conducted on a gigantic scale—the emigration of free white laborers will ever extinguish slavery in any Southern State. I except

Missouri, where the active interference of the abolitionists would undoubtedly prolong the existence of bondage; but where, owing to its peculiar geographical position, slavery will soon be drowned by "the ad-
vancing and increasing tide of Northern emigration."[2] Neither will the
mere prevention of the extension of slavery kill it. Within its present
limits, it may live a thousand years. There is land enough to support the
present races, and their increase, for that length of time there. Unless
we strike a blow for the slaves—as Lafayette and his Frenchmen did for
the revolutionary sires[3]—or unless they strike a blow for themselves, as
the negroes of Jamaica and Hayti, to their immortal honor, did[4]—American slavery has a long and devastating future before it, in which, by the
stern necessities of its nature, Freedom *or* the Union must crouch and die
beneath its potent scepter of death and desolation.

II. The field negroes, as a class, are coarse, filthy, brutal, and lascivious;
liars, parasites, hypocrites, and thieves; without self-respect, religious aspirations, or the nobler traits which characterize humanity. They are almost as degraded intellectually as the lower hordes of inland Irish, or the
indolent semi-civilized North American Indians; or the less than human
white-skinned vermin who fester in the Five Points cellars,[5] the North
street saloons,[6] or the dancing houses and levee of New Orleans or
Charleston. Not so vile, however, as the rabble of the Platte Region,[7] who
distinguished themselves as the champions of the South in Kansas. Morally, they are on a level with the whites around them. The slaveholder
steals their labor, rights and children; they steal his chickens, hogs and
vegetables. They often must lie, or submit to be whipped. Truth, at such a
price—they seem to think—is far too precious to be wasted on white
folks. They are necessarily extremely filthy; for their cabins are dirty,
small and uncomfortable; and they have neither the time nor the conveni-
ences to keep them clean. Working from morn till night in the fields, at
the hardest of hard labor, under a sultry sun, is quite enough for the poor
women to do—especially as they have also to cook their provisions—
without spending their leisure hours in "tidying up" their miserable and
unhome-like huts. The laws forbidding the acquisition of knowledge, and
the fact that slavery and intelligence are incompatible, keep them, as
nearly as possible, as ignorant and degraded as the quadrupeds of the
fields. Chastity is a virtue which, in the South, is entirely monopolized by
the ladies of the ruling race. Every slave negress is a courtesan. Except
one per cent. of them, and you make ample deduction. I have talked on
this subject with hundreds of young men in different Southern cities, and
the result of my observations and information is a firmly settled conviction
that not one per cent. of the native male whites in the South arrive at the
age of manhood morally uncontaminated by the influences of slavery. I

do not believe that ten per cent. of the native white males reach the age of *fourteen* without carnal knowledge of the slaves. Married men are not one whit better than their bachelor brethren. A Southern lady bears testimony to this fact:

"This subject demands the attention, not only of the religious population, but of statesmen and law-makers. It is one great evil hanging over the Southern Slave States, destroying domestic happiness, and the peace of thousands. It is summed up in a single word *amalgamation*. This, and this only, causes the vast extent of ignorance, degradation and crime, that lies like a black cloud over the whole South. And the practice is more general than even the Southerners are willing to allow. Neither is it to be found only in the lower order of the white population. It pervades the entire society. Its followers are to be found among all ranks, occupations and professions. The white mothers and daughters of the South have suffered under it for years—have seen their dearest affections trampled upon—their hopes of domestic happiness destroyed, and their future lives embittered, even to agony, by those who should be all in all to them, as husbands, sons, and brothers. I cannot use too strong language in reference to this subject, for I know that it will meet with a heartfelt response from every Southern woman."

This lady is Mrs. Douglas,[8] a native of Virginia, and a pro-slavery woman, who was imprisoned in a common jail at Norfolk, for the heinous crime of teaching free colored children TO READ THE WORD OF GOD! At the time of the Revolution, pure blacks were everywhere to be seen; now they are becoming, year by year, more and more uncommon. Where do they go to? The white boys know—the census of mulattoes tells! I suppose it is indecorous to speak so plainly on so delicate a subject; but if the report is revolting, how much more appaling must be the crime itself?

I have given instances enough to show that deception is the natural result of slavery. Of course, as the slaves are entirely at the mercy of the whites, they are forced to be parasites and hypocrites in their intercourse with them. And how can the poor people have self-respect? "I'se only a nigger" is the first note they are taught in the sad funereal dirge of their existence. It is repeated in ten thousand forms, and in every variety of method, from the time they are born till they draw their last breath. How can they respect themselves, when they know that their mothers are ranked with the beasts that perish—sold, exchanged, bought, forced to beget children, as cows and sheep are bartered and reared for breeding purposes?

As for the religious negroes—"the pious slaves"—I have no patience with the blasphemous and infernal ingenuity which breeds and preserves these unfortunate creatures. Dr. Johnson praised the youth, who, having seduced a young girl in a fit of animal excitement, on being asked by her, after the fact, "Have we not done wrong?" promptly replied, " Yes." " For," he said, " although I ravished her body, I was not so bad as to wish to ravish her mind." Our slavemasters are not so generous. The perpetrators of the most tyrannical despotism that the world ever saw, still, not content with degrading the body of their bondmen into real estate, they seek, by the same priestly machinery that other tyrants have found so effective, to enslave their souls also—a task which they try to make the more easy by the ignorance in which they assiduously keep them. I have investigated the character of too many of the "pious negroes," to feel any respect either for their religion or their teachers. Church membership does not prevent fornication, bigamy, adultery, lying, theft, or hypocrisy. It is a cloak, in nine cases out of ten, which the slaves find convenient to wear; and, in the excepted case, it is a union of meaningless cant and the wildest fanaticism. A single spark of true Christianity among the slave population would set the plantations in a blaze. Christianity and slavery cannot live together; but churchianity and slavery are twins.

That slavery alone is responsible for the peculiar vices of the plantation negroes, the condition and character of the city bondmen attest. Wherever you find a negro in the Southern cities who has had the chance to acquire knowledge, either from reading by stealth, or from imitation, or the society of an educated class, you will find, in a majority of instances, the moral equal—often the superior—of the white man of the same social rank and educational opportunities. In manners, the city slaves are the Count D'Orsays of the South.[9]

III. Slave preachers are usually men of pliant and hypocritical character—men who are easily used by the ruling race as *white-chokered chains*. The more obsequious that they are—the more treacherous to their own aspirations—the more they are flattered and esteemed by the tyrants whose work they do. I attended a colored church at Savannah.[10] The subject of discourse was the death of John the Baptist: "Bredren, de 'vang' list does not tell us 'bout anoder circumstance 'bout de text, but de legions ob de church has unformed us. When Herodeyus got hold ob de plate dat da put de head ob John de Baptis' in, she war so mad at him, de legions tell us, dat she tuk a handful ob pins and stuck 'em in de tongue ob de Apostle![11] Ah"——

The preacher, from whose discourse I selected this remarkable biblical information, was a great favorite with the white population, who (if I mistake not) addressed him as a Doctor of Divinity. When he died I read a paragraph from a Savannah paper, in which his virtues and *learning* were eulogized!

IV. At Augusta, Georgia,[12] I knew a boy of between sixteen and seventeen years of age, who supported a mulatto girl mistress. Her mother was a free woman, and the daughter was about his own age. He took up a peck of meal to their house, and some bacon, every Saturday night, and for this weekly allowance he was permitted, as frequently as he pleased, to cohabit with the girl. The pernicious effect of slavery on children I have frequently heard parents lament. And yet these same parents would favor the extension of slavery into virgin territories!

V. The poor whites suffer greatly from the existence of slavery. They are deprived by it of the most remunerative employment, and excluded from the most fertile lands. I once heard a poor Alabama farmer lament that he would soon have to move, as they were beginning to "close him in again." I asked what he meant? He said that, years and years ago, he and several of his poor neighbors had moved far away into the wilderness, in order to be out of and beyond the influence of slavery. They had selected a spot where they thought they would be secure; but the accounts of the extraordinary fertility of the soil soon brought the wealthy slaveholders to their paradise. They bought up immense tracts of land bordering on the poor men's farms, which, one by one, they soon managed to possess. Sickness, bad seasons, poor harvests, and improvidence, and other causes, soon compelled or induced the petty farmers to borrow from their wealthy neighbors, who, knowing the result, were ever willing to lend. All had gone now, excepting him. "But," he said, "you see they have bought all around me; my only way of getting to the road is by the side of that marsh, and in wet weather I can 't take a team out there. The laws give me the right of buying a passage out through ——'s plantation; but he wants my land, and would charge so high a rent for the passage that I could not afford to pay it." (In Alabama and most Southern States, the land is not laid out as in many of the Northern and the Western States— multiplication-table fashion; the roads are crooked, the farms irregular in size as in extent, and the whole arrangement of roads is entirely different.) "Again," the farmer said "I am feeding his niggers. They steal my chickens and eggs and vegetables. I complained to the overseer about it: 'D—n it,' he said, 'shoot them—we won't complain.'" But then, if he shot them, he would have to pay their market value; and, besides, he had been hungry himself often, and had not the heart to interfere with the poor starving slaves. He was soon obliged to sell out. I met him in Doniphan county, Kansas.[13] He is a Republican now, and thanks God for the opportunity of belonging to an open anti-slavery party. The accounts often published of the condition of the poor whites of the South are not exaggerated, and could not well be. There is more pauperism at the South than at the North: In spite of the philosophy of the Southern socialists, who claim that slavery prevents that unfortunate condition of free society.[14] So, also, although Stringfellow claims that black prostitution prevents white harlotry,[15] there are as many, or more, public courtesans of the dominant race, in the Southern cities I have visited, than in Northern towns of similar population. Slavery prevents no old evils, but breeds a host of new ones. The poor whites, as a class, are extremely illiterate, ruffianly, and superstitious.

VI. No complaints are ever made of the indolence or incapacity of the negroes, when they are stimulated by the hopes of wages or of prerogatives which can only be obtained in the South by hard work. It is the *slave,* not the *negro,* that is "lazy and clumsy."

VII. Overseers are generally men of the lowest character, although I have met with some, the managers of extensive estates, who were men of culture and ability. Yet these few instances are hardly exceptions, as such men employ subordinates to do the grosser work. I have often been told that overseers are frequently hired *with special reference to their robust physical condition;* and this told not in jest, as to a Northerner, but in conversation between wealthy slaveholders, who, for aught they knew, supposed me to be a Southerner and a friend of their "peculiar" or "sectional" crime. The *Southern Agriculturist,* published at Charleston, South Carolina, thus faithfully describes this class of persons:

"Overseers are changed ever year; a few remain four or five years; but the average length of time they remain on the same plantation will not exceed two years. They are taken from the lowest grade of society, and seldom have the privilege of a religious education, and have no fear of offending God, and consequently no check on their natural propensities; they give way to passion, intemperance, and every sin, and become savages in their conduct."—Vol. IV., p. 351.

VIII. Such, by the confession of the Southerners themselves, being a faithful description of the character of overseers, is it necessary to produce negro testimony to prove that cruelty and crime are of frequent occurrence on the large plantations? The negro is entirely in the power and at the mercy of our race. Supposing—to take an extreme case by way of illustration—a planter or overseer, in the presence of five hundred negroes, was to arrest a slave, tie him hand and foot, and cut him to pieces, inch by inch, no legal punishment could reach him, and no legal body investigate the crime, unless a white man was a witness of the barbarity. The laws refuse to accept negro evidence in any case, whether it be against or in favor of a white man. Judge Lynch, alone, of all Southern jurists, relaxes this rule; and that only in the case of abolitionists! This fact effectually destroys the efficacy of all the laws—few in number as they are—which have been passed in some States for the protection of the bondmen. Whipping women, beating boys with clubs—innumerable cruel and unusual punishments—are circumstances of daily occurrence in every Southern State.

IX. I heard a planter one day sneering at the ladies who advocated woman's rights. He was shocked that women should attempt to go out of their sphere. On his plantation, near Savannah, I saw women filling dung carts, hoeing, driving oxen, ploughing, and engaged in many other similar employments. Is it within woman's sphere to perform *such* labors?

X. One of the proprietors of the Montgomery (Alabama) *Mail,* at the period of my visit to that town,[16] described to me the execution by a mob of a negro *by fire at the stake.* He had either killed a white man or ravished a white girl—I have since forgotten which—but one sentence of his account, for its characteristic Southern inhumanity to the negro, I shall never forget to my dying day. "They piled pretty green wood on the fire, to make it burn slow; he gave one terrible yell before he died; and, every time the wind blew from him, there was the d——dest stench of burnt flesh. D—n it, how it did smell." This was said, laughingly. Several well authenticated cases of the same fiendish torture have occurred within the last five years. Parson Brownlow, as I have already stated, eulogized the barbarity in one instance.[17]

XI. As against whites, in courts of justice, the negro has not the faintest chance of fairness. I could illustrate this statement by citing examples; but, as a South Carolina Governor has confessed the fact, it will suffice to quote his admission. Says Governor Adams[18] in his message for 1855:

"*The administration of our laws, in relation to our colored population,* by our courts of magistrates and freeholders, as these courts are at present constituted, *calls loudly for reform. Their decisions are* RARELY *in conformity with justice or humanity.* I have felt constrained, *in a majority of the cases* brought to my notice, either to modify the sentence, or set it aside altogether."

XII. Colonel Benton, in a lecture that he delivered in Boston,[19] had the audacity to assert that slaves are seldom sold by their masters, *excepting* for debt or faults, or crimes. Granting, for the sake of argument, the truth of this falsehood, these exceptions are sufficient grounds, I think, for the overthrow of slavery at any cost. Debts are so common, among the unthrifty Southrons, that this cause alone must separate hundreds of families every year. The sale of one slave mother, in my view, is enough to justify the slaughter of a race. Much more, then, the separation of thousands. "Faults!" great heavens! supposing that every white Virginian, who has "faults," was to be sold by public auction—where would the slaveholders, the first families, and the future Presidents be? Not in free homes, I know. "Crimes!" Does the reader know that, by the laws of Virginia, if a slave commits a capital offence, he may be pardoned *by being sold out of the State,* the owner of him pocketing the proceeds of the auction? But statistics refute Colonel Benton's statement. It is capable of demonstration that twenty-five thousand negroes are annually sold from the Northern or slave-breeding to the Southern or slave-buying Slave States. See Chase and Sanborn's "North and South," and the authorities they cite.[20] I have seen families separated and sold to different masters in Virginia; I have spoken with *hundreds* of slaves in the Carolinas, who were sold, they told me, *from their wives and children* in the same inhuman State; and I have seen slave-pens and slave-cars filled with the unhappy victims of this internal and infernal trade, who were travelling for the city of New Orleans; where, also, I have witnessed at least a score of public negro auctions. Everybody who has lived in the seaboard Slave States—women, politicians and clergymen excepted—well know that to buy or to sell a negro, or breed one, is regarded as equally legitimate in point of morals with the purchase of a pig, or a horse, or an office seeker.

I can corroborate Mr. Olmsted, therefore—(from whose book, as this volume was passing through the press, I have already made several extracts), and can fully indorse him when he says:

"It is denied, with feeling, that slaves are often reared, as is supposed by the abolitionists, with the intention of selling them to the traders. It appears to me evident, however, from the manner in which I hear the traffic spoken of incidentally, that the cash value of a slave for sale, above the cost of raising it from infancy to the age at which it commands the highest price, is generally considered among the surest elements of a planter's wealth. Such a nigger is worth such a price, and such another is too old to learn to pick cotton, and such another will bring so much, when it has grown a little more, I have frequently heard people say, in the street, or the public houses. That a slave woman is commonly esteemed least for her laboring qualities, most for those qualities which give value to a brood-mare, is, also, constantly made apparent. A slaveholder writing to me with regard to my cautious statements on this subject, made in the *Daily Times,* says: 'In the States of Maryland, Virginia, North Carolina, Kentucky, Tennessee and Missouri, as much attention is paid to the breeding and growth of negroes as to that of horses and mules. Further South, we raise them both for use and for market. Planters command their girls and women (married or unmarried) to have children; and I have known a great many negro girls to be sold off, because they did not have children. A breeding woman is worth from one-sixth to one-fourth more than one that does not breed.'"[21]

XIII. The lower classes of the Southern States hate and affect to despise the negro in exact proportion to their own intellectual and moral debasement.

XIV. The assertion that without slave labor, cotton, rice and sugar could not be grown in the Southern States—that these staples would not and cannot be cultivated by white men—that "the choice," to use the language of Senator Douglas, is "between the negro and the crocodile,"[22] is utterly without foundation, and is refuted by facts. There is nothing more common in Georgia and Alabama than to see white men, *and white women too,* at work in the fields at every hour of the day. Of course, these persons belong to the class of "poor white trash." But, granting that the Southern staples would perish without slavery—what then? Down with the staples, rather than criminally cultivate them. Perish the products whose roots are watered by inhumanity.

XV. SLAVERY IS THE SUM OF ALL VILLAINIES.[23]

NOTES

1. Redpath did not make his fourth southern trip.

2. Redpath made this claim in a John Ball, Jr. letter that he wrote on February 1, 1857, while in St. Louis, Missouri. That letter was published in the Boston *Liberator* on February 20, 1857. Redpath did not reproduce that letter in the *Roving Editor;* its text can be found in appendix 9.

3. Marie-Joseph-Paul-Yves-Roch-Gilbert du Motier, marquis de Lafayette.

4. Weakened white power in the French colony of Saint-Domingue (Haiti) due to the revolution in the mother country allowed slaves to revolt against both the French planters and the mulatto Creoles in 1789. Despite French attempts to reassert authority, the revolutionary blacks eventually won their freedom and the island's independence. There had been a series of unsuccessful slave revolts in northwestern Jamaica in 1831–32, which heavily influenced the British Parliament's decision to abolish slavery in its colonies. Philip D. Curtin, *Two Jamaicas: The Role of Ideas in a Tropical Country* (1955; New York, 1970), 40, 61–72, 81–89; Rice, *Rise and Fall of Black Slavery,* 157, 187, 221, 252, 259.

5. Named for the intersection of Worth, Baxter, and Park Streets, this neighborhood on the lower end of Manhattan in New York City had a reputation for crime and poverty. Mathews, *Dictionary of Americanisms,* 621.

6. Possibly Redpath alludes to the North End district of Boston, which in the 1850s was a crowded neighborhood where recently arrived Irish immigrants lived and sought out cheap entertainment. Pease and Pease, *Web of Progress,* 4.

7. An allusion to Platte County in western Missouri, the home of many of the Border Ruffians of the mid-1850s. *Columbia Lippincott Gazetteer,* 1484.

8. Margaret Douglas.

9. Albert Guillaume Gabriel, count d'Orsay (1801–52) was among the fashion leaders of his generation. Son of French nobility, d'Orsay had resigned his army commission and spent most of his youth in England, where he had befriended the exiled Louis Napoleon. When the latter became leader of France he made d'Orsay, a minor painter, his director of fine arts. *New York Times,* August 19, 1852; *DNB,* 5:1156–58.

10. Redpath resided in Savannah, Georgia, from mid-April to June 1854, working as a reporter for the *Savannah Daily Morning News.*

11. Described in Mark 6:16–29 and Matt. 14:1–12.

12. As described in chapters 16 and 17, Redpath spent most of November and December 1855 in Augusta, Georgia.

13. Redpath began reporting in Kansas in June 1855. From December 1857 to May 1858 he operated a newspaper (the *Crusader of Freedom* in Doniphan) and might have reacquainted himself with the Alabamian at that time.

14. Possibly an allusion to the writing of proslavery propagandist George Fitzhugh (1806–81), a South Carolina lawyer and planter. A critic of capitalism and laissez-faire economics, Fitzhugh championed a mixture of slavery and socialism. His books *Sociology for the South* (1854) and *Cannibals All!* (1857) and his journal and newspaper articles made him a nationally known figure. Ironically he later opposed secession and served as an agent of the Freedmen's Bureau. Harvey Wish, *George Fitzhugh, Propagandist of the Old South* (Baton Rouge, 1943); Miller and Smith, *Dictionary of Afro-American Slavery*, 244–45.

15. Probably John H. Stringfellow, coeditor of the proslavery *Atchison Squatter Sovereign.*

16. Probably J. J. Hooper, editor of the *Weekly Montgomery Mail,* who hired Redpath to work for his paper as a New Orleans correspondent. Redpath to Sydney Howard Gay, January 23, 1855, Gay Papers; *New Orleans Daily Picayune,* March 16, 1855.

17. In September 1857 the Reverend William G. Brownlow wrote a letter to the editor of the *New York Times* protesting an editorial that had condemned the burning of a slave by a mob in eastern Tennessee. Brownlow defended the mode of execution as "perfectly right" because the slave had murdered his master and mistress in their sleep. *New York Times,* September 17 and 22, 1857.

18. South Carolina native James Hopkins Adams (1812–61) graduated from Yale College before entering politics. He served in both houses of the state legislature prior to his election as governor in December 1854. A states-rights Democrat, Adams advocated reopening the slave trade and expanding slavery into the western territories. Sobel and Raimo, *Governors of the United States,* 3:1409–10; *DAB,* 1:71–72.

19. Thomas Hart Benton lectured before the Mercantile Library Association of Boston on November 25, 1856. His talk was entitled "The Union." *New York Times,* November 27, 1856.

20. An allusion to *The North and South: A Statistical View of the Condition of the Free and Slave States,* a travel account of the slaveholding states by Henry Chase and Charles W. Sanborn. Published in 1856, this account used a variety of statistical sources to validate its observations regarding slavery and the South. Miller and Smith, *Dictionary of Afro-American Slavery,* 737.

21. Olmsted, *Seaboard Slave States,* 1:60–61.

22. Stephen A. Douglas.

23. A reference to John Wesley's description of the slave trade as "that execrable sum of all villanies." *The Works of the Rev. John Wesley, A.M.,* 14 vols. (London, 1872), 3:453.

II.

THE INSURRECTION HERO.

WE were talking about slavery, and its probable duration, in the office of the *Leavenworth Times.*[1] I expressed my doubts of the efficacy of political action against it, and stated that I was in favor of a servile insurrection. I believe I found no one who approved of such a scheme of abolition.

John C. Vaughan[2] was in the room. He told us of the terror which such events inspired in Southern communities, whenever it was believed that the negroes intended to revolt.

He told the story of Isaac. It made an indelible impression on my mind. Subsequently, I desired him to furnish me with a written account of the death of the heroic slave.

This chapter is the result. After a preliminary word on slave insurrections, Mr. Vaughan proceeds:

THE STORY OF ISAAC.

All other perils are understood. Fire upon land, or storm at sea, wrapping mortals in a wild or watery shroud, may be readily imagined. Pestilence walking abroad in the city, making the sultry air noisome and heavy, hushing the busy throng, aweing into silence heated avarice, and glooming the very haunts of civilization as if they were charnel-houses, can be quickly understood. But the appalling terror of a slave revolt, made instinct with life, and stunning as it pervades the community—the undescribed and indescribable horror which fills and sways every bosom as the word is whispered along the streets, or borne quickly from house to house, or speeded by fleetest couriers from plantation to plantation— "an insurrection"—"an insurrection"—must be *felt* and *seen* to be realized.

Nor is this strange. The blackest ills are associated with it. Hate, deep and undying, to be gratified—revenge, as bitter and fiendish as the heart can feel, to be gloated over while indulged—lust, unbridled and fierce, to be glutted—death, we knew not how or where, but death in its basest and most agonizing form; or life, dishonored and more horrible than most excruciating death—these are the *essence* of an insurrection. Could worse forms of evil be conjured up? Can any human actions—the very darkest that walk at midnight—excite equal terror? We pity slaveholders who are startled by the dread of it, and wonder at their want of manhood in exposing the gentler sex to this human whirlwind of fury, and revenge, and lust and death.

But to our story. I remember, when a boy, going out one bright day on a hunting excursion, and, on returning in the evening, meeting at the bridge, a mile or more from the town I lived in, a body of armed men. The road turns suddenly, as you approach the spot from the south, and is skirted, on either side, by deep swamps. I did not see them, consequently, until I came directly upon them.

"Where have you been?" was the abrupt question put to me by the captain, without offering the usual salutation.

"I have been hunting," I replied, "along the banks of the river, and up by the old Hermitage."

"Did you see or meet any one?" continued my questioner, no man else saying a word.

"No one."

"Go home instantly," he said, imperatively, "and keep up the main road. Do n't cross over by the swamp, or the old ford"—two nearer footpaths to the town, skirting heavily timbered land.

I cannot recollect now whether I had heard before of an insurrection. I had not, certainly thought much about it, if at all. But I knew, instantly, why these armed citizens were at the bridge. The low, compressed, yet clear voice of the captain—the silence of his men—their audible breathing as they waited for my replies to his questions—their military order—with sentries in advance—told me all, and I experienced a dread which chilled me through; and the deepening shade of the forest, under which I had so often whistled merrily, served now to add to the gloom of the hour. I asked no questions. With quickened pace I pushed up the main road, and was not long in reaching my father's house. I wished to know the worst, and to help in meeting it.

I found all alarm at home. Guns were stacked in the passage, and men were there ready to use them. Two friends were in the parlor informing the household of the place of rendezvous for the women and children, and the signal which was to be given if the town should be fired, or an attack be made upon it by the negroes. I inquired and learned here the cause and extent of the danger.

That morning a negro had informed his master of the plot, and had represented to him that it reached plantations over a hundred miles off, and embraced the thickest negro settlements of the State.

The first step taken was to arrest the leaders named (some thirty in number) by the informer. The second, to inform the town and country of the impending danger. Armed patrols were started out in every direction. Every avenue to the town was guarded, and every house in it made a sort of military fort. The apprehension was, that the plantation negroes would rise and sweep all before them with fire and sword; and the "white strength " was prepared, in all its force, to meet the contingency.

The master, if he be kind to his bondmen, is apt to believe that they will never turn against him. We hear planters say, "I would arm my slaves," whenever this subject is broached. This is a strong expression, and to be received with "grains of allowance," as the sequel will illustrate. Yet, boy-like, I felt as if no soul in our yard could strike a blow against one of the family. I went to the servants' quarter. Not one of them was out—a strange event—and not a neighbor's domestic was in—a still stranger circumstance! They were silent as the grave. "Even "Mamma," privileged to say and do what she pleased, and who could be heard amid the laughter and tongue clatter of the rest, had nothing to tell me. I asked a few questions; they were simply answered. It was evident that the servants were frightened; they knew not what they feared; but they were spell-bound by an undefined dread of evil to them and harm to us. Indeed, this was the case with the blacks, generally; and while the excitement lasted, the patrol did not arrest one slave away from his quarters! An honest Irishman remarked at the time, "it was hard to tell which was most frightened, the whites or the negroes."

The proposed revolt, as regards territory, was an extended one. It embraced a region having over forty thousand male slaves. But the plot was poorly arranged, and it was clear that those who planned it knew little or nothing of the power they had to meet and master. For six months the leaders of it had been brooding over their design, and two days before its consummation they were in prison and virtually doomed as felons. Then seizure arrested the insurrection without bloodshed; but not without a sacrifice of life! That was demanded by society and the law. Thirteen of the negroes arrested were declared guilty and hung. They had, according to all notions then, a fair trial; lawyers defended them, and did their best; an impartial and intelligent jury determined their fate; and by the voice of man, not of God, this number of human beings was "legally" sent out of existence!

The leader of the insurrection—ISAAC—I knew well. He was head man to a family intimate with mine. Implicit confidence was placed in him, not only by his master, but by the minister of the church and everybody who knew him. The boys called him Uncle Isaac, and the severest patrol would take his word and let him go his way.

He was some forty years old when he first planned the revolt. His physical development was fine. He was muscular and active—the very man a sculptor would select for a model. And yet, with all his great strength, he was kind and affectionate, and simple as a woman. He was never tired of doing for others. In intellect he was richly gifted; no negro in the place could compare with him for clear-headedness and nobleness of will. He was born to make a figure, and, with equal advantages, would have been the first among any throng. He had character: that concentration of religious, moral, and mental strength, which, when possessed by high or low, gives man power over his fellows, and imparts life to his acts and name.

His superiority was shown on the trial. It was necessary to prove that he was the leader, and counsel were about taking this step. "I am the

man," said Isaac. There was no hesitation in his manner—no tremulous-
ness in his voice; the words sounded naturally, but so clear and distinct
that the court and audience knew it was so, and it could not have been
otherwise. An effort was made to persuade him to have counsel. His
young masters pressed the point. The court urged him. Slaveholders were
anxious for it, not only because they could not help liking his bearing, but
because they wished to still every voice of censure, far or near, by having
a fair trial for all. But he was resolute. He made no set speeches—played
no part. Clear above all, and with the authoritative tone of truth, he repeated, "I am the man, and I am not afraid or ashamed to confess it."

Sentence of death was passed upon him and twelve others.

The next step, before the last, was to ascertain all the negroes who had
entered into the plot. Isaac managed this part wisely. He kept his own
counsel, and, besides his brother, as was supposed, no one knew who
had agreed to help him at home or from a distance. The testimony was
abundant that he had promise of such help. His declaration to the colored
informer, "The bonfire of the town will raise forty thousand armed men
for us," was given in evidence. He admitted the fact. But no ingenuity, no
promises, no threats, could induce or force him to reveal a single name.
"You have me," he said; "no one other shall you get if I can prevent it. The
only pain I feel is that my life alone is not to be taken. If these," pointing
to his fellow captives, "were safe, I should die triumphantly."

The anxiety on this point naturally was very deep, and when the usual
expedients had failed, the following scheme was hit upon: Isaac loved his
minister, as everybody did who worshipped at his altar, and the minister
reciprocated heartily that love. "Isaac will not resist him—he will get out
of Isaac all that we want to know." This was the general belief, and, acting
upon it, a committee visited the pastor. An explanation took place, and
the good man readily consented to do all he could.

He went to the cell. The slave-felon and the man of God confronted
each other.

"I come, Issac," said the latter, "to find out from you everything about
this wicked insurrection, and you"—

"Master," hastily interrupted Isaac, "you come for no such purpose. You
may have been overpersuaded to do so, or unthinkingly have given your
consent. But will you, who first taught me religion, who made me know
that my Jesus suffered and died in truth—will you tell me to betray confidence sacredly intrusted to me, and thus sacrifice others' lives because
my life is to be forfeited? Can you persuade me, as a sufferer and a strug-
gler for freedom, to turn traitor to the very men who were to help me?
Oh, master, let me love you:" and, rising, as if uncertain of the influence
of his appeal, to his full stature, and looking his minister directly in the
face, he added, with commanding majesty, "You know me!"

I wish that I could repeat the tale as I heard the old minister tell it. So minute, yet so natural; so particular in detail, yet so life-like! The jail, its inner cell, the look and bearing of Isaac, his calmness and greatness of soul. It was touching in the extreme. I have known sternest slaveholders to weep like children as they would listen to the story. But I can only narrate it as I remember it, in briefest outline. The old divine continued:

"I could not proceed. I looked at Isaac; my eye fell before his. I could not forget his rebuke; I acknowledged my sin. For the first time in my ministerial life, I had done a mean, a base act; and, standing by the side of a chained felon, I felt myself to be *the* criminal."

A long silence ensued. The minister was in hopes that Isaac would break it; he did not. He himself made several attempts to do so, but failed. Recovering from his shock at length, and reverting in his own mind to the horrors which the revolt would have occasioned, he resumed the conversation thus:

"But, Isaac, yours was a wicked plot; and if you had succeeded, you would have made the very streets run blood. How could you think of this? How consent to kill your old master and mistress? How dream of slaying me and mine?"

"Master," Isaac quickly responded, "I love old master and mistress. I love you and yours. I would die to bless you any time. Master, I would hurt no human being, no living thing. But you taught me that God was the God of black as well as white—that he was no respecter of persons—that in his eye all were alike equal—and that there was no religion unless we loved him and our neighbor, and did unto others as we would they should do unto us.[3] Master, I was a slave. My wife and children were slaves. If equal with others before God, they should be equal before men. I saw my young masters learning, holding what they made, and making what they could. But master, my race could make nothing, holding nothing. What they did they did for others, not for themselves. And they had to do it, whether they wished it or not; for they were slaves. Master, this is not loving our neighbor, or doing to others as we would have them do to us.[4] I knew there was and could be no help for me, for wife or children, for my race, except we were free; and as the whites would not let this be so, and as God told me he could only help those who helped themselves,[5] I preached freedom to the slaves, and bid them strike for it like men. Master, we were betrayed. But I tell you now, if we had succeeded, I should have slain old master and mistress and you first, to show my people that I could sacrifice my love, as I ordered them to sacrifice their hates, to have justice—justice for them—justice for mine—justice for all. I should have been miserable and wretched for life. I could not kill any human creature without being so. But, master, God *here*"—pointing with his chained hand to his heart—"told me then, as he tells me *now,* that I was right."

"I do n't know how it was," continued the old minister, "but I was over-powered. Isaac mastered me. It was not that his reasoning was conclusive; that, I could have answered easily; but my conduct had been so base and his honesty was so transparent, his look so earnest and sincere, his voice so commanding, that I forgot everything in my sympathy for him. He was a hero, and bore himself like one without knowing it. I knew by that instinct which ever accompanies goodness, that the slave-felon's conscience was unstained by crime even in thought; and, grasping him by the hand, without scarce knowing what I was going to do, I said, 'Isaac, let us pray.' And I prayed long and earnestly. I did not stop to think of my words. My heart poured itself out and I was relieved."

"And what," I asked, "was the character of your prayer?"

"What it ought to have been," energetically replied the old divine. "I prayed to God as our common Father. I acknowledged that he would do justice; that it was hard for us, poor mortals, to say who was right and who was wrong on earth; that the very best were sinners, and those deemed the worst by us might be regarded the best by Him. I prayed for Isaac. I prayed God to forgive him, if wrong; to forgive the whites, if he was right; to forgive and bless all. I was choked with tears. I caught hold of Isaac's hand and pressed it warmly, and received his warm pressure in return. And with a joy I never experienced before or since, I heard his earnest, solemn 'Amen' as I closed.

We stood together for some time in silence. Isaac was deeply moved. I saw it by the working of his frame, and the muscles of his face and his eye. For the first time tear-drops stood on his eyelids. But, stilling every emotion, he began, as calmly as if he were going to rest:

"'Master, I shall die in peace, and I give you a dying man's blessing. I shall see you no more on earth. Give my love to old master and mistress, and'—for a moment he faltered, but with concentrated energy choked down instantly his deepest emotion as he continued, more solemnly than I ever heard mortal speak—'and, master, if you love me—if you love Jesus—lead my wife and children as you have led me—to heaven. God bless you forever, master.'

"We parted. I saw him no more. I could not see him hung, or pray for him, as requested to do by others in the last dying hour. I had been with him long. For four hours we were together in his narrow, noisome cell. How indelibly are the events which occurred in them impressed upon my memory! Oh! slavery—slavery!"

The citizens outside awaited anxiously the good minister's egress from the jail, and, when he appeared, crowded round him to know the result. He looked like one jaded with a long journey. He was worn down. "It is useless—it is useless—let him die in peace," was all he said; and, seeing that he was deeply moved, and taking it for granted that he had been engaged in devotional exercises with the dying, silence pervaded the group, and he was allowed to depart in peace. And never in public or in a mixed audience, would that minister refer to Isaac, or the hours he spent with him!

No other effort to elicit information from the leader was made, and none who promised him help were discovered through him.

The death-day came. A mighty crowd gathered to witness the sad event to which, in that place, it was to be devoted; and the military, with gleaming swords and bright bayonets, stood under the gallows, to guard against escape or difficulty. Six "felons" were upon the gallows—it could hold no more—and Isaac was put on the list. "Be men," said he, when one of the number showed some timidity, "and die like men. I'll give you an example: then, obey my brother." That brother stood next him. Isaac gazed intently upon the crowd—some thought he was looking for his wife and children—and then spoke his farewell to his young masters. A few words passed between him and his brother, when, saying audibly, "I'll die a freeman," he sprung up as high as he could, and fell heavily as the knotted rope checked his fall. Instantly his frame was convulsed, and, in its muscular action, his feet reached the plank on which he had stood, looking as if he sought to regain it. His brother, turning his face to his comrades, deliberately put his hand upon his side, and, leaning forward, held the body clear with his elbow, as he said: "Let us die like him."

The authorities perceived that the terrors of the law would be lost and none of "the good" they anticipated be secured among the blacks, especially, who filled up the outer circle of the dense crowd, if this lofty heroism were witnessed. They proceeded rapidly with the execution, and, in a few moments, Isaac and his brother and their felon comrades were asleep together.

The bodies of the blacks, after dangling in the air the usual time, as if in mockery of heaven and earth, were cut down, coffined, and carted away to their burial-place. That was an out-of-the-way old field, with a stagnant lagoon on three sides of it, and a barren sand-waste, covered with a sparse growth of short pines, on the other.

Beneath the shade of one of these pines which skirted the field, and not far off from the felons' graves, a colored woman and a cluster of little ones might have been seen. These were Isaac's wife and children. They stood where they were, until all, save one white man, had departed. He made a signal, and they approached the burial spot. He pointed to a particular spot, and left. None know, save our Father, how long the widowed one and the fatherless remained there, or what were their emotions. But, next morning, a rough stake was found driven into the earth where Isaac lay, and, ere the next Sabbath dawned, a pile of stones with an upright memorial, was placed at the head of his grave. How these stones were obtained—for none like them were to be seen within thirty or forty miles—no one could say, though all knew *who* put them there. The rude memorial still stands! The grave of Isaac is yet known! And that widowed one, while she lived—for she, too, has departed—kept the lone burial spot free from weeds, and covered it with the wild rose, as if the spirit which had once animated the cold clay beneath, loved a robe of beauty and sweetness!

As not the least remarkable feature in Isaac's conduct, was the course he pursued towards his family, we cannot close without referring to it. He was an exemplary husband, and a wise as well as kind father. His wife was not superior, intellectually, but she was affectionate, and he so moulded her character as to make her worthy of him. His children were well-behaved, and remarkable for their polite manners. His very household gave evidence of all this. Everything was in order; the furniture was neat; in all the arrangements he had an intelligent eye to comfort and taste; he had a watch, and some tolerable scripture engravings; and his little garden was well stocked with the best vegetables, the best fruit, and the rarest flowers.

Of the plot, Isaac's wife knew nothing. He had evidently thought of his failure, and committed no women, and as few married men as he could. He meant, let what might happen to him, that his partner should suffer no harm. This was evident enough from his conduct. For, the first thing he did after his arrest, was to desire an interview with his master. That was denied him. Not that the old gentleman was cruel or angry—for he loved Isaac—but because, as he said, "He could not stand it." The next thing was to send for his young master. He came, and to him he said: "Massa Thomas, I have sent for you to say that my wife does not know anything about the insurrection, or any of my action. I wanted to see old master to beg of him not to sell or separate her and the children. I must get you to do that. And, Massa Thomas, when your father dies, I want you to promise that you will help them." The young man promised (and we rejoice to say his word was kept), and then Isaac, the slave and the felon, blessed him. Never again, until near his last hour, when conversing with his minister, did he refer to his family, and the only message he sent them was a torn Bible, with this sentence rudely writ down on one of the leaves: "We shall live again, and be together." So deep was his affection for his family, and so careful was he to ward off every suspicion from them.

I met, last summer, the slaveholder—an intelligent and humane man—who commanded the military the day Isaac was hung.

I referred to the scene. He spoke of it as one of the most moving that he

had ever witnessed, and to my surprise, though very much to my gratification, remarked:

"I never knew what true heroism was until I saw Isaac manifest it upon
his seizure, trial and death. I felt my inferiority to him in every way, and I
never think of him without ranking him among the best and bravest men
that ever lived."

The record below tells of his crime, and he will be remembered on
earth as a felon; but the record above will contain his virtues, and in
heaven the good will know and love him—for ISAAC was a MAN.

NOTES

1. Redpath frequently used Leavenworth as his base while a reporter in the Kansas Territory. This conversation probably occurred in Leavenworth in September 1857 after the
founding of the free state weekly newspaper, the *Times,* there by John C. Vaughn. See *St.
Louis Daily Missouri Democrat,* October 26, November 9, 27, and 28, and December 5, 8, 10,
12, and 27, 1855, January 29 and February 4 and 6, 1856, September 21, 1857; *Chicago
Tribune,* May 22, 1856; *New York Daily Tribune,* January 5, 1857.

2. The editor of the *Leavenworth Times,* John C. Vaughn was a free state partisan active
in both political and military clashes with the proslavery forces in Kansas. His father, John
A. Vaughn, had edited the *Louisville Examiner* in the 1840s and the *Chicago Tribune* in the
mid-1850s. While in charge of the latter paper in 1856, Vaughan Sr. had hired Redpath to
report on events in the Kansas Territory. *Chicago Tribune,* May 22, 1856; Lloyd Wendt,
Chicago Tribune: The Rise of a Great American Newspaper (Chicago, 1979), 63, 65, 72–73,
78–79; Richard J. Hinton, "Pens That Made Kansas Free," *Kansas State Historical Society
Collections* 6 (1897–1900): 372.

3. A paraphrase of the biblical Golden Rule: Matt. 7:12.

4. Ibid.

5. Often mistakenly attributed to the Bible, this phrase came from Algernon Sidney's *Discourse Concerning Government,* part 2.

III.

THE UNDERGROUND TELEGRAPH.

THE thriving condition of the Underground Railroad,[1] establishes conclusively the existence of secret and rapid modes of communication
among the slave population of the South. Many extraordinary stories are
told by the Southrons themselves of the facility with which the negroes
learn of all events that transpire in the surrounding country. In spite of
strict surveillance on the plantation, and careful watching abroad, by
means of numerous and well mounted patrols, the slaves pass freely over
large tracts of country. More especially does this state of things exist

among the plantations of the cotton growing States. The dense forests, swamps and morasses, which the negroes alone can tread with impunity, enable them to avoid the highways and beaten paths wherein they would be likely to meet the patrol.

This system of secret travel originally grew out of the social desires of the slaves—their love of gossip and wish to meet their friends and relatives; but, as the tyranny of the system grew more insupportable, in the natural course of events, and the yearnings after freedom became stronger in the minds of the negroes themselves, it was used for other and far more dangerous purposes. The preceding chapter will show how an earnest man can use this power.

I remember an incident narrated to me at Charleston,[2] which illustrates this point. In conversation upon various subjects with Col. ——, a fine specimen of the Southern planter, with whom I had formed a slight acquaintance, various traits and peculiarities of the negro character were alluded to; and, among others, the extraordinary facilities possessed by the slaves in communicating with each other.

Col. —— said it was impossible to prevent it. No matter how rigid the laws might be, or how strictly they were enforced, the *evil* (as he called it) still continued to grow. He related the following incident as a proof of this rapid inter-communication:

"Several summers since, I was in the interior of the State, visiting the plantation of a friend. While there, one morning, the news arrived of a dreadful murder that had been committed, a short distance from the estate, by a poor white man who kept a small grocery at the cross roads near the boundary of several estates. He was supposed to be a receiver of the various articles which plantation slaves are in the habit of stealing. In a fit of insane jealousy, he had brutally murdered a woman who lived with him as his wife. He had immediately decamped, and was supposed to have gone in the direction of Charleston. I was about returning to my home; and my friend, an active magistrate, proposed that we should endeavor to overtake the murderer; or, by reaching the city at an early hour, cause his arrest. The distance was about eighty miles, and we did not start till late in the afternoon. We rode rapidly, changing our horses twice, and about two o'clock in the morning, reached the banks of the river a few miles from the city. My companion had alluded, during the ride, to the knowledge that our servants were generally possessed of all intelligence and offered to bet any amount of money that 'Old Harry' (the black ferryman), already knew everything about the murder. I was incredulous; for we had ridden fast, and, by no possibility, did it seem to me, could he have learnt anything relating to the tragedy.

"'Well, Harry,' said my companion to the old fellow, 'what 's the news up country?'

"'I dun'no know, mass'r,' was the hesitating reply; 'you gentlemen has jest come down, and probable knows more 'bout it dan I does.'

"About what?" I asked.

"'Why sah, de murder ob Abe Thomas' wife las' night.'

"The murder was discovered by the patrols about three o'clock in the morning!

"We both expressed our ignorance of the event, and old Harry, after some hesitation, gave us the particulars very accurately, stating that he had heard of it that night from a plantation hand.

"Here was an extraordinary proof of what my companion had stated. We had travelled rapidly; no one had left the neighborhood before us; yet this old man had learnt of the event some hours previous to our arrival. It had been passed from plantation to plantation, and thus it had reached him."

I listened to the story, and treasured up its facts. It seems to me that here lies a power, by means of which a formidable insurrection, directed by white men, can safely be formed and consummated. And the slaves *know this fact.* The Canadian fugitives understand it; and are thoroughly systematizing this Underground Telegraph. Many of them are constantly passing to and fro in the Slave States with perfect impunity. Through it, hundreds of the relatives and friends of men, who have already secured their freedom, have been informed of the means by which they can obtain the liberty so eagerly desired. By its operations, when the appropriate hour for sounding the alarm shall have come, speedily, surely and swiftly, will the news spread southward, and reach, in the silent hours of the night, thousands of eager souls now awaiting, in trembling anxiety, for the terrible day of deliverance.

NOTES

1. The term "Underground Railroad" was popularly used to describe the network of sympathetic individuals who aided fugitive slaves in their escapes. While white abolitionists participated in this activity, most of the Underground Railroad "agents" were fellow slaves and free blacks. Roller and Twyman, *Encyclopedia of Southern History,* 1259–60.

2. Redpath resided in Charleston in April 1854 while covering the commercial convention described in chapter 7.

IV.

THE DISMAL SWAMP.

THERE is a Canada in the Southern States. It is the Dismal Swamp. It is the dreariest and the most repulsive of American possessions. It is the favorite resort of wild animals and reptiles; the paradise of serpents and poisonous vegetation. No human being, one would think, would voluntary live there; and yet, from time immemorial, it has been the chosen asylum of hundreds of our race. It has been the earthly heaven of the negro slave; the place "where the wicked cease from troubling, and the weary are at rest."

For the following account of life in the Swamp, I am indebted to the courtesy of Mrs. Knox, of Boston.[1] It was narrated by a fugitive slave in Canada, whose words, as he uttered them, she reported *verbatim.* She purposes to publish, a volume of autobiographical sketches of the Canadian fugitives; and it is from her manuscript collection that this narrative is taken.

The uniform testimony of the runaways she conversed with, as well as of all the fugitives whom Mr. Drew[2] examined, is that slavery is the sum of all villainies[3]—"Cousin of Hell," as one of them phrased it—and that the bondmen everywhere are discontented with their lot.

This is the Canadian runaway's narrative of

LIFE IN THE DISMAL SWAMP.

. . . . "Thirty-five miles I was sep'rated from my wife, buildin' house for overseer. 'Casionally I was permitted to go home. De las' time (I remember it 'stinctly) when I seed her, I telled her I would come back agin in four weeks. Arter I had worked four weeks, de overseer would n't let me go; so I waited and axed him sever'l times. I knowed my wife would keep 'spectin' me and 'spectin' me till I comed. I begged de overseer one dey to jist let me go home; for I had n't seen my wife den for seven weeks. He got orful vexed at me, and writed to my mass'r 'bout me.

"Arterward de overseer's wife was mad wit Charity, an my brudder hearn her treaten to send Charity to Richmond, whar my mass'r was agoin' to send me to be selled. My brudder telled me now was my time to make clar, or else I'd be hussled off 'fore I knowed it.

"Dat mornin' de overseer comed whar I be, an' axed me: 'Charlie, I want ye to come to de house an' work; cellar steps need 'pairin', as da 'bout given way, and old Charity fell down dem to'der day, and like to have broken her ole thick skull; 'specks she will, yet, boy, less ye impair dem. Ye better come right up, Charley, and dood it.'

"Now I jist knowed dat ole coon was tryin' to lay wait to ketch me, to tie me so he 'd sell me down Souf. I did n't live wid old Hunker for not'in', I tort; and as I did n't never 'spect much else but my larnin' from him, I bet ye I laid out to make all my larnin' tell. Slavery teaches some t'ings you does n't find in books, I tell ye. Well, I knowed dem ar cellar steps would be a long time 'fore da ketched impairs by my fixin's. . . . I telled de overseer 'Yes, sah,' an' he went struttin' 'bout, 'spectin' every minnit to make a grab at me when I comed out. But he did n't t'ough, bet ye.

"Arter he sot down to dinner, I jist tort, dem are heels 'longed to me, and so I jest let my legs be 'sponsible for my heels, till da bringed me and my heels to de woods. . . . I runned all dat arternoon, and in de nex' night I got whar my brudder lived, 'bout five miles off my wife. . . . Lizzie was a good wife to me, and I did n't know how I could leave her. Slavery asunders everyting we love in dis life, God knows. . . . Den I walked fifteen mile to my mudder's. I knocked at her winder, and telled her I was her own Charley in great 'stress. She comed right to de door, grieved most to def, when I tell'd her mass'r gived overseer commission to sell me. Oh! I didn't know what to do. My poor ole mudder! . . . .

"I started off an' lef' her frettin' mightily. Dat's de las' I knowed 'bout my wife or ole mudder, or any ob my 'lations. . . .

"I went to a friend ob mine. He was gone away. His wife knowed I was hungry, and so she ga'en me a right smart supper, and arterwards I intired. In de night her husband comed home. He 'mediately called me. I 'peared. He say he knowed folks in de Dismal Swamp, and p'raps he might 'ceed for me, an' get me 'casion to work dar. He keeped me six days, whar I was hided away an' would n't be 'sturbed. Den I hired into de Juniper Swamp for two dollars a month.

"I 'spect you've heern good deal 'bout dat swamp, ma'am? Da calls it Dismal Swamp; and guess good name for it. 'Tis all dreary like. Dar never was any heaven's sunshine in some parts orn't.

"I boarded wit a man what giv me two dollars a month for de first one: arter dat I made shingles for myse'f. Dar are heaps ob folks in dar to work. Most on 'em are fugitives, or else hirin' dar time. Dreadful 'commodatin' in dare to one anudder. De each like de 'vantage ob de odder one's 'tection. Ye see dey's united togedder in'ividually wit same interest to stake. Never hearn one speak disinspectively to 'nut'er one: all 'gree as if dey had only one head and one heart, with hunder legs and hunder hands. Dey's more 'commodatin' dan any folks I's ever seed afore or since. Da lend me dar saws, so I might be 'pared to split my shingles; and den dey turn right 'bout and 'commodate demsels. Ye ax me inscribe de swamp?

"Well: de great Dismal Swamp (dey call it Juniper Swamp) 'stends from whar it begins in Norfolk, old Virginny, to de upper part ob Carolina. Dat's what I's told. It stands itse'f more 'n fifty mile north and souf. I worked 'bout four mile 'bove Drummond Lake, which be ten mile wide. De boys used to make canoes out ob bark, and hab a nice time fishin' in de lake.

"Best water in Juniper Swamp ever tasted by man.* Dreadful healthy

---

* It is stated to have medicinal properties.

place to live, up in de high land in de cane-brake. 'Speck ye've heern tell
on it? There is reefs ob land—folks call de high lands. In dar de cane-
brake grow t'irty feet high. In dem ar can-brakes de ground is kivered wit
leaves, kinder makin' a nat'ral bed. Dar be whar de wild hogs, cows,
wolves, and bars (bears) be found. De swamp is lower land, whar dar's de
biggest trees most ever was. De sypress is de handsomest, an' anudder
kind called de gum tree.

"Dismal Swamp is divided into tree or four parts. Whar I worked da called
it Company Swamp. When we wanted fresh pork we goed to Gum Swamp,
'bout sun-down, run a wild hog down from de cane-brakes into Juniper
Swamp, whar dar feet can 't touch hard ground, knock dem over, and dat's
de way we kill dem. De same way we ketch wild cows. We troed dar bones,
arter we eated all de meat off on 'em up, to one side de fire. Many's de time
we waked up and seed de bars skulking round our feet for de bones. Da
neber interrupted us; da knowed better; coz we would gin dem cold shot.
Hope I shall live long enough to see de *slaveholders* feared to interrupt us!

". . . . I tort a sight 'bout my wife, and used allers be planin' how I get to
see her agin. Den I heern dat old mass'r made her live wid anudder man,
coz I left her. Dis 'formation nearly killed me. I mout 'spected it; for I
knowed de mass'rs neber ingard de marriage 'stution 'spectin' dar slaves.
Dey hab de right to make me be selled from my wife, and dey had de right
of makin' her live wid anudder man if she hated him like pisin. I do n't
blame Lizzie; but I hoped she would b'lieve dat I was dead; den she would
n't fret herself to def, as I knowed she would if she reckoned I was livin'.
She loved me, I knowed, but dat warn't no 'count at all. De slaves are
ingarded as dey must marry jist for dar mass'r's int'rest. Good many on
dem jist marry widout any more respect for each oder den if dey was
hogs. . . . . I and my wife warn't so. I married Lizzy, and had a ceremony
over it, coz I loved her an' she loved me. Well, arter I heern dat she was
livin' wid 'nudder man, dat ar made me to come to Canada.

"Ole man Fisher was us boys' preacher. He runned away and used to
pray, like he's 'n earnest. I camped wid him. Many 's been de 'zortation I
have 'sperienced, dat desounded t'rough de trees, an' we would almos'
'spect de judgment day was comin', dar would be such loud nibrations, as
de preacher called dem; 'specially down by de lake. I b'lieve God is no
inspector of persons;[4] an' he knows his childer, and kin hear dem jest as
quick in de Juniper Swamp as in de great churches what I seed in New
York, whar dey don't 'low a man, as I'm told, to go in thar, if he hasn't
been allers customed to sit on spring bottomed cheers, and sofas and
pianners and all dem sort of tings. Tank de Lord, he don 't tink so much
'bout spring-bottom cheers as his poor critters do—dat's a fac'. I was
fered to peep inside dem ar rich churches, and I 'spects de blessed Lord

hisself dunno much more 'bout dar insides dan I does. . . . . Oh, dey were nice prayers we used to have sometimes, an' I donno but de old preacher is dar now.

"Dar is families growed up in dat ar Dismal Swamp dat never seed a white man, an' would be skeered most to def to see one. Some runaways went dere wid dar wives, an' dar childers are raised dar. We never had any trouble 'mong us boys; but I tell you pretty hard tings sometimes 'cur dat makes ye shiver all over, as if ye was frozed. De master will offer a reward to some one in de swamp to ketch his runaway. So de colored folks got jist as much devil in dem as white folks; I sometimes tink de are jist as voracious arter money. Da 'tray de fugitives to dar masters. Sometimes de masters comes and shoots dem down dead on de spot. . . . I saw wid my own eyes when dey shot Jacob. Dat is too bad to 'member. God will not forget it; never, I bet ye. Six white men comed upon him afore he knowed nothin' at all 'bout it most. Jist de first ting Jacob seed was his old master, Simon Simms, of Suffolk, Virginny, standing right afore him. Dem ar men—all on em—had a gun apiece, an' dey every one of dem pointed right straight to de head of poor Jacob. He felt scared most to def. Old Simms hollored out to him—'Jake! You run a step, you nigger, and I'll blow yor brains out.' Jacob didn't know for de life on him what to do. He feared to gin up: he too scared to run; he dunno what to do. Six guns wid number two shot, aimed at your head is n't nothin', I tell ye. Takes brave man to stand dat, 'cordin' to my reck'nin'.

"Jacob lifts up his feet to run. Marcy on him! De master and one ob de men levelled dar guns, and dar guns levelled poor Jacob. His whole right side from his hip to his heel was cut up like hashmeat. He bleeded orfull. Dey took some willow bark—made a hoop orn't—run a board trough it— put Jacob on it like as if he war dead; run a pole t'rough de willow hoop, and put de poles on dar shoulders.

"Dreadful scenes, I tell ye, 'sperienced in de Dismal Swamp, sometimes, when de masters comes dar. Dey shoot down runaways, and tink no more sendin' a ball t'rough dar hearts and sendin' dar hearts into 'Ternity dan jist nothin' at all. But de balls will be seen in 'Ternity, when de master gets dar 'spectin' to stay; 'spect dey'll get dispinted a heap!

"I feared to stay dar arter I seed such tings; so I made up my mind to leave. . . . 'Spect I better not tell de way I comed: for dar's lots more boys comin' same way I did."

NOTES

1. No book meeting this description was ever published.
2. Benjamin Drew, a Boston abolitionist, interviewed fugitive slaves in Canada for the

1856 book *The Refugee,* variously subtitled *A North-Side View of Slavery* or *The Narratives of the Fugitive Slaves in Canada.* Jason H. Silverman, *Unwelcome Guests: Canada West's Response to American Fugitive Slaves* (Millwood, N.Y., 1985), 57, 135, 144, 159; Miller and Smith, *Dictionary of Afro-American Slavery,* 697.

3. Redpath quotes John Wesley, *Works of the Rev. John Wesley,* 3:453.
4. A mangled version of Acts 10:34—"God is no respecter of persons."

V.

SCENES IN A SLAVE PRISON.

[From a private letter to Charles Sumner, by Dr. S. G. Howe,[1] of Boston.]

I HAVE passed ten days in New Orleans—not unprofitably, I trust—in examining the public institutions, the schools, asylums, hospitals, prisons, etc. With the exception of the first, there is little hope of amelioration. I know not how much merit there may be in their system, but I do know that in the administration of the penal code, there are abominations which should bring down the fate of Sodom upon the city.

A man suspected of a crime and awaiting his trial, is thrust into a pandemonium filled with convicts and outlaws, where, herding and sleeping in common with hardened wretches, he breathes an atmosphere whose least evil is its physical impurity; and which is loaded with blasphemies, obscenities, and the sound of hellish orgies, intermingled with the clanking of the chains of the more furious, who are not caged, but who move about in the crowd with fettered legs and hands.

If Howard[2] or Mrs. Fry[3] ever discovered a worse administered den of thieves than the New Orleans prison, they never described it.

In the negroes' apartment I saw much which made me blush that I was a white man. Entering a large paved courtyard, around which ran galleries filled with slaves of all ages, sexes and colors, I heard the snap of a whip, every stroke of which sounded like the sharp crack of a small pistol. I turned my head and beheld a sight which absolutely chilled me to the marrow of my bones. There lay a black girl, flat upon her face on a board, her two thumbs tied and fastened to one end, her feet tied and drawn tightly to the other end, while a strap passed over the small of her back, and fastened around the board, confined her closely to it. Below the strap she was entirely naked; by her side, and six feet off, stood a huge negro with a long whip, which he applied with dreadful power and wonderful precision. Every stroke brought away a strip of scarf skin and made the blood spring to the surface. The poor creature writhed and shrieked, and, in a voice which showed alike her fear of death and her dreadful agony, screamed to her master, who stood at her head, Oh! spare my life—do n't cut my soul out!" But still fell the horrid lash; still strip after strip was broken from the skin; gash after gash was cut in her flesh, until it became a livid and bloody mass of raw and quivering, muscle.

It was with the greatest difficulty that I refrained from springing upon the torturer and arresting his lash. But, alas! What could I do but turn aside, to hide my tears for the sufferer, and my blushes for humanity.

This was in a public and regularly organized prison. The punishment was one recognized and authorized by the law. But, think you, the poor wretch had committed a heinous offence, and been convicted thereof, and sentenced to the lash? Not at all! She was brought by her master to be whipped by the common executioner, without trial, judge, or jury, to gratify his own whim or malice. And he may bring her day after day, without cause assigned, and inflict any number of lashes he pleases, short of twenty-five, provided only he pays the fee. Or, if he choose, he may have a private whipping-board on his own premises and brutalize himself there.

A shocking part of this horrid punishment was its publicity. As I have said, it was in a courtyard, surrounded by galleries which were filled with colored persons of all sexes: runaway slaves; slaves committed for some crime, or slaves up for sale. You would naturally suppose they crowded forward, and gazed, horror-stricken, at the brutal spectacle below. But they did not; many of them hardly noticed it; and some were entirely indifferent to it. They went on in their childish pursuits, and some were laughing, outright in the distant parts of the galleries! So low can man, created in God's image, be sunk in brutality! So much is he the creature of circumstance, that, by a degrading and brutalizing system of slavery, every distinguishing trait of humanity may be effaced, and he be made happy as the stalled ox; while a Christian and civilized people can be found, who, from the mere love of lucre, will fasten their system, and urge, in their defence, that he is as happy as a brute, and is incapable of any higher enjoyment.

S. G. Howe.

NOTES

1. Born into a prominent Boston family, Samuel Gridley Howe (1801–76) graduated from Harvard Medical School and then went to Greece to assist the rebels there fighting against Turkish rule. Returning home, he pioneered the education of the deaf and blind. An avid opponent of slavery, he contributed generously to the free state cause in Kansas and later to John Brown's raid on Harpers Ferry. *DAB*, 9:296–97.

2. John Howard.

3. A middle-class English Quaker, Elizabeth Fry (1780–1845) devoted herself to improving the conditions of incarcerated females in Newgate Prison. She also visited Ireland, France, and Prussia investigating prison conditions there. *DNB,* 7:734–36.

VI.

MY OBJECT.

THE reader must have noticed that I took particular pains to ascertain the secret sentiments of the Southern slaves. He must have seen, also, that I never stepped aside to collate or investigate any cases of unusual cruelty, or to portray the neglect of masters in the different States, to provide their bondmen with the comforts of a home or the decencies of life. That I had material enough, my summary will show.

I did not go South to collect the materials for a distant war of words against it. Far more earnest was my aim.

I saw or believed that one cycle of anti-slavery warfare was about to close—the cycle whose correspondences in history are the eras of John Ball, the herald of the brave Jack Cade;[1] of the Humble Remonstrants who preceded Oliver Cromwell,[2] and the Iconoclastic Puritans; and of the En-cyclopaedists of the age of Louis the Sixteenth, whose writings prepared the way for the French Revolution.[3] I believed that the cycle of action was at hand. I considered it, therefore, of importance to know the feelings and aspirations of the slaves. I cared little, comparatively with this object, to ascertain their physical condition. I never even read a book on the sub-ject—a volume of fiction alone excepted—until the manuscripts of the preceding pages were placed in the hands of the printer. I knew that irrepressible power must, from its very nature, corrupt men, and make them cruel, heartless, and licentious. It would have been useless to travel South to corroborate that truth.

My object was to aid the slaves. If I found that slavery had so far de-graded them, that they were comparatively contented with their debased condition, I resolved, before I started, to spend my time in the South, in disseminating discontentment. But if, on the other hand, I found them ripe for a rebellion, my resolution was to prepare the way for it, as far as my ability and opportunities permitted.

I believed that a civil war between the North and South would ultimate in insurrection, and that the Kansas troubles would probably create a military conflict of the sections. Hence I left the South, and went to Kan-sas;[4] and endeavored, personally and by my pen, to precipitate a revolution. That we failed—for I was not alone in this desire—was owing to the influence of prominent Republican statesmen, whose unfortunately conservative character of counsel—which it was impossible openly to resist—effectually baffled all our hopes: hopes which Democratic action was auspiciously promoting.

Are we, then, without hope?

No! and, while slaves live, and the God of justice is omnipotent, never will we be discouraged. Revolutions never go backward.[5] The second American Revolution has begun. Kansas was its Lexington: Texas will be its Bunker Hill, *and South Carolina its Yorktown.*[6]

It is fashionable for our animalculae-statesmen to lament or affirm that slavery cannot speedily be abolished. It is so wrought and interwoven with the social system of the South—with its commercial, political, and religious organizations—that to root it out at once, they maintain, would be disastrous to the country and to the slave himself. Perish the country, then, and woe to the slave! Whatever falls, let slavery perish. Whoever suffers, let slavery end. If the Union is to be the price of a *crime,* let us repent of the iniquity and destroy the bond.

Do you desire to aid in overthrowing slavery? There is work for you to do, whatever may be your talents or ideas of policy.

—Shall I venture to predict? It may be that I am not a prophet—but, as far as we believe in humanity, and right, and an overruling God, we have the power of foreseeing results. All fanatics are prophets to the extent of their vision—for fanaticism is the ardent worship of a truth; and by its light we can—nay, must—see the sequences of acts performed in accordance or in violation of it. And I am a fanatic.

Slavery will be speedily abolished. That I see. I think, by violence; nay, I know by bloodshed, if the present spirit long pervades the South. "Unless it repents it shall utterly perish."[7]

Slavery will soon be driven east of the Mississippi.

Missouri—already surrounded by free communities; with friends of the slave, from the adjoining territory, ever active on her borders; with the money of the merchant, the selfishness of the laborer, and the ambition of the politician arrayed against her domestic institution, and the fear of the slaveholder justly aroused for the safety of his property in man—this State, so recently the champion of the South, will be the first to succumb to the spirit of the North, and realize the truth that they who take the sword shall perish by it.[8]

South of Kansas lies a fertile region already darkened by the curse of slavery. It is the Indian Territory. It will soon be thrown open for the settlement of the white race. Another struggle will ensue—and another victory for freedom; for the men who, at Yellow Stone, fired at Federal troops,[9] and, at Osawattomie—seventeen against four hundred—made the embattled marauders bite the dust,[10] will be there to avenge the martyrs of Lawrence[11] and the Marais des Cygnes.[12] Will they have no other aid? Yes; for there are negroes enslaved in the Indian Territory: the descendants of the bravest warriors America has produced—the hunted maroons, who, for forty years, in the swamps of Florida, defied the skill and armies of the United States.[13] They hate slavery and the race that upholds it, and are longing for an opportunity to display that hatred. Not far from this territory, in a neighboring province of Mexico, live a nation of trained negro soldiers—the far-famed Florida Indians, who, after baffling and defying the United States, and after having been treacherously enslaved by the Creeks, incited thereto by Federal officials, bravely resisted their oppressors and made an Exodus, the grandest since the days of Moses, to a land of freedom.[14] Already have their oppressors felt their prowess; and their historian tells us—*"they will be heard from again."** Mark the significant warning!

Arrizonia is a mining country. There is gold, silver and copper there. It requires skilled labor to extract them from the ore. Free laborers will flock to these regions as soon as it is profitable to go, and overwhelm, by mere numerical force, the champions of the Southern system. The wild Indians, too, are the friends of the negro. The diplomacy of the Florida Indians has made them the eternal enemies of the South. *The nation will see this fact when the Texan struggle begins.*

Slavery can never be extended into Northern Mexico. The people hate it. Through all the multitudinous mutations of their history, this hatred has been the only established principle which pervaded the entire nation. If color is to be the badge of bondage, they know that they must succumb to it, if the Southern "Norman" obtains dominion in their land. For the Mexicans of the frontier provinces are of mixed Indian, Negro and Spanish origin. There are numbers of fugitives from American slavery among them, who superadd to a deadly national animosity, a still stronger hatred of a race of tyrants.[15]

Texas is a tempting bait for the North; the greatest territorial prize of the age. By the terms of its admission, it may be divided into five States. What shall the character of those States be? There are numbers of resolute pioneers in Kansas who have sworn that Texas shall again be free— as it was under Mexican domination—before the "flag of the *free*" waved over it. They have declared that a line of free States shall extend, southward, to the Mexican Gulf; that slavery shall, westward, find the bound which it cannot pass. Within the borders of Texas there is already a nu-

* See "The Exiles of Florida," by Joshua R. Giddings.

merous free-labor population, whose numbers, by the organized emigration movement, will speedily be increased and presently preponderate. The wealth of the North, which would shudder at the idea of a servile insurrection, is already pledged to the programme of anti-slavery emigration—which, as surely as to-morrow's sun shall rise, will ultimately and rapidly drive slavery to the eastern shore of the Mississippi.

Thus far, the programme will be essentially pacific—at most, a conflict of sections and rival civilizations. Thus far, but no further, political action may benefit the slave. The Republican party, the champion of white laborers, will plead their cause and insure them success. To this extent, therefore, the friend of the slave can consistently aid the Republican party; but, this end gained, it will be his duty to desert and war against it. For it is publicly pledged never to interfere, by political action, with slavery where it already exists; but, on the contrary, to preserve and defend whatever may be "protected by the aegis of State sovereignty."*

West of the Mississippi and in the State of Missouri, therefore, the friend of the slave, from the inevitable operation of potent political and commercial forces, may leave, to a great extent, the fate of slavery to peaceful causes or other than distinctively abolition movements.

Westward, slavery cannot go. Northward, its influence daily diminishes. The sentiment of the Eastern world is hostile to it always. Can it extend Southward? It will look in vain to Central America. The same mixed races who hate the modern "Norman" in Mexico inhabit those regions, and are animated by the same true spirit; and the attempt, if ever made, to subdue this people, in order to extend the area of bondage, will justly precipitate a war with the powers of Europe. The South does not dare to hazard a war with such great powers on such an issue.

The islands of the American Archipelago are to-day almost exclusively in the hands of the liberated African race. *The first serious attempt at annexation will put them entirely in the possession of the blacks.* Cuba has already, within her borders, seven thousand self-emancipated citizens; and it is a fact, well known in our State Department, that the Spanish rulers of that island would unhesitatingly arm the black population, both slave and free, in the event of any serious attempt at conquest.[16]

But I would not fear the extension of American slavery, even if the neighboring nations were more friendly to it. *The South will soon find enough to do at home.* Canada has hitherto been the safety valve of Southern slavery.[17] The bold and resolute negroes, who were fitted by their character to incite the slaves to rebellion, and lead them on to vic-

---

* See J. C. Fremont's Letter of Acceptance, and the Republican Campaign Documents, passim.

tory, have hitherto, by the agency of the underground railroad, been triumphantly carried off to a land of freedom. The more sagacious Southrons have seen this fact, and congratulated themselves on it. They forget that the same qualities which induced these slaves to fly, would enable them, in their new home, to accumulate riches; and that to men who have endured the tyranny of slavery, there is nothing so much coveted as the hope of revenge. There are thousands of dollars in the Canadian Provinces which are ready for the use of the insurrectionists.[18]

But is insurrection possible?

I believe that it is. The only thing that has hitherto prevented a universal revolt, is the impossibility of forming extended combinations. This the slave code effectually prevents. To attain this end, therefore, the agency of white men is needed.

Are there men ready for this holy work?

I thank God that there are. There are men who are tired of praising the French patriots—who are ready to *be* Lafayettes and Kosciuskos[19] to the slaves.

Do you ask for a programme of action?

The negroes and the Southrons have taught us. The slaves of the Dismal Swamp, the maroons of Florida, the free-state men of Kansas, have pointed out the method. The South committed suicide when it compelled the free squatters to resort to guerilla warfare, *and to study it both as a mode of subsistence and a science.* For the mountains, the swamps and morasses of the South, are peculiarly adapted to this mode of combat, and there are numbers of young men, trained to the art in the Kansas ravines, who are eager for an opportunity of avenging their slain comrades, on the real authors of their death, in the forests and plantations of the Carolinas and Georgia.

Will you aid them—will you sustain them? Are you in favor of a servile insurrection?

Tell God in acts.

Farewell.

NOTES

1. The original John Ball was a fourteenth-century English priest executed by Richard II for seditious preaching. His death encouraged the peasants' insurrection led by Wat Tyler and Jack Cade. *DNB,* 1:993–94, 19:1347–48.

2. Redpath refers to the English Puritans and parliamentarians whose religious and political quarrels with the authoritarian King Charles I escalated into civil war in the 1640s. Oliver Cromwell (1599–1658) led the parliamentary forces to victory and effectively ruled as "Lord Protector of England, Scotland, and Ireland" for the final five years of his life. *DNB,* 5:155–86.

3. Redpath alludes to French intellectuals such as Denis Diderot (1713–84) and Jean le Rond d'Alembert (1717–83), editors of the seventeen-volume *Encyclopédie,* whose utilitarian and physiocratic philosophy was used to question many of the bases for the ancien régime and indirectly contributed to the French Revolution, beginning in 1789, that overthrew King Louis XVI. R. J. White, *The Anti-Philosophers: A Study of the Philosophes in Eighteenth-Century France* (London, 1970), 4, 91–120; John Viscount Morley, *Diderot and the Encyclopaedists* (London, 1923), 6–7, 115–18.

4. Redpath left New Orleans in late May 1855. He traveled to St. Louis, where that city's *Daily Missouri Democrat* hired him as its "special correspondent" to cover the political developments in the Kansas Territory. Jim Alee Hart, *A History of the St. Louis Globe-Dispatch* (Columbia, Mo., 1961), 2–15; Hart, "James Redpath," 70–71.

5. Redpath quotes a widely reported controversial statement by Republican politician William H. Seward. *The Irrepressible Conflict: A Speech by William H. Seward, Delivered at Rochester, Monday, Oct. 25, 1858* (New York, [1860]), 7.

6. An allusion to three battles in the American Revolution: Lexington on April 19, 1775, Bunker Hill on June 17, 1775, and Yorktown in September and October 1781.

7. Redpath garbles Luke 13:3.

8. Matt. 26:52.

9. In the spring of 1858, free state militia leader James Montgomery determined to use his "Jayhawkers" to chase proslavery settlers from southeastern Kansas. When his men neared Fort Scott in March, the U.S. cavalry intervened. Montgomery's eight men resisted, killing two and wounding four of the cavalry at a small stream known as Yellow Paint. Nichols, *Bleeding Kansas,* 223–25.

10. A party of approximately 250 Border Ruffians led by John W. Reid set out to attack the free state settlement at Osawatomie, Kansas, on August 30, 1856. The small town was the home of John Brown and his sons and had only forty male settlers. Osawatomie residents ambushed the attackers as they approached, but the Border Ruffians ultimately captured and burned much of the settlement. Among the free state casualties in the fighting was John Brown's son, Frederick. Malin, *John Brown,* 1:28; Nichols, *Bleeding Kansas,* 140–41.

11. In May 1856 a "posse" of approximately 750 proslavery Kansans and Missourians led by Sheriff Samuel J. Jones seized control of the principal free state settlement of Lawrence. Jones arrested the key leaders of the free state territorial government on warrants for treason. His men destroyed the presses of two antislavery newspapers and burned the town's Free State Hotel and several other buildings. The outnumbered free staters made no effort at resistance, and the only death that occurred in the "sacking" of Lawrence was accidental. Rawley, *Race and Politics,* 130–31; Nichols, *Bleeding Kansas,* 96–101.

12. On May 23, 1858, nine Kansas free state settlers were massacred by proslavery guerrillas led by Charles A. Hamilton at a gulch on the Marais des Cygnes, as the upper Osage River was popularly known. Nichols, *Bleeding Kansas,* 225–28.

13. Since the early eighteenth century, slaves from southern colonies had been fleeing to Spanish Florida where they sought protection from the Seminole Indians. Although reenslaved by the Seminoles, the black fugitives found their status much higher than back in the United States. In the 1830s and 1840s the United States military took action against this alliance of fugitive slaves and Indians in the first and second Seminole wars. Of the nearly four thousand Florida Indians transplanted westward as a consequence of these wars, perhaps 10 percent were fugitive slaves or their descendants. Edwin C. McReynolds, *The Seminoles* (Norman, Okla., 1957), 250, 253, 258–60; Miller and Smith, *Dictionary of Afro-American Slavery,* 663–65.

14. Despite Seminole protests, the tribe had been resettled by the federal government in the 1840s among the Creek and Cherokee lands in Oklahoma rather than on a separate tract.

As a consequence, the Seminole chief Coacoochee (known as Wild Cat to whites) advocated that his people move to Mexico to escape exploitation. In 1849 Coacoochee led a small group of Seminoles, Creeks, and Cherokees, including many of African ancestry, to the remote Texas-Mexican border region. Local Indians attacked Coacoochee's band and attempted to kidnap the blacks for sale to southern whites. Finally the Mexican government granted land in Coahuila Province to the refugees. McReynolds, *Seminoles*, 248–81 [Writers' Program of the Works Progress Administration], *The Seminole Indians in Florida* (Tallahassee, Fla., 1940), 57–61.

15. By the end of the 1820s the Mexican government had emancipated all children born to slaves and outlawed the slave trade. Miller and Smith, *Dictionary of Afro-American Slavery,* 466.

16. The importation of slaves from Africa to Cuba continued until 1870. The Cuban slave population surpassed a quarter of a million by midcentury. A mainly urban free black population numbered only a few thousand. The institution was ended by royal decree in 1886. Rice, *Black Slavery,* 278–86, 382–89.

17. Never an economically viable institution in Canada, slavery had been under legal assault there since the 1790s. The final prohibition of the institution, however, came in 1834 when the British government abolished slavery in all its imperial colonies. Even before then, fugitive slaves from the United States had sought refuge in Canada. British officials rejected legal as well as diplomatic efforts to compel Canadians to extradict American fugitive slaves. Besides the runaway slaves, hundreds of free blacks also emigrated to Canada to escape oppressive racial discrimination in the United States. Despite growing negrophobia in parts of Canada, its population of fugitive slaves and their descendants reached forty thousand by the 1850s. Silverman, *Unwelcome Guests,* 8–13, 23, 26–27, 40–41, 151; Miller and Smith, *Dictionary of Afro-American Slavery,* 276–81.

18. By the time the *Roving Editor* manuscript was being published, Redpath had become a close friend of John Brown and probably knew that the abolitionist placed great hope in Canadian black support for his planned effort to incite an armed slave insurrection. Oswald Garrison Villard, *John Brown, 1800–1859: A Biography Fifty Years After* (1910; New York, 1943), 331–36.

19. Tadeusz Andrzej Kościuszko (1746–1817) was a member of the gentry and a captain in the Royal Polish Army. He came to the United States to aid the revolutionary cause and rose to the rank of brigadier general. He returned to Poland and fought in Poland's unsuccessful struggle to resist Russian annexation. *DAB,* 5:497–99.

SLAVERY IN KANSAS.

I.

THE FIRST SLAVE IN KANSAS.

I WAS one day in an office where I occasionally called. A colored woman entered the room, inquired for me, and presented a note of introduction from an eminent reformer. She told me her sad story. She had been a slave, but had been liberated. She had a son in slavery. Having tasted the bitter draught of bondage, she was working, night and day, to save her son from the curse.

He was in Parkville, Missouri. His master or masters had offered to sell him for eleven hundred dollars. She had nearly raised the sum, when she wrote to him again. Instead of receiving an encouraging reply, the following inhuman note was sent to the gentleman who wrote in her behalf:

PARKVILL *sept. 9th* 1857

sir I recived yours of the 28 of August you say that the Mother of Miller is verry anxious to Buy him. I have rote some too or three Letter in relation to the time and Price now all I have to say is if you want him you must come by the fust of Oct or you will have to come to Texs for him & I will not consider my Self under any obligation to take the same price after the first of Oct. if you can get here by the 20 of this Month per haps it would be better for you for I want to start soon as I can & by the 1 of Oct is the out Side time

your in hast

JOHN WALLIS

Mr HENRY MOR—*

---

* Illegible in the MS.

The poor mother did not think that Mr. Wallace* had the remotest intention of removing to "Texs;" but believed that it was a pretext to raise the price of her boy; and, as she was nearly worn out already with anxiety and travel, she was beginning to despair of rescuing him from bondage.

Could I do anything for her? Could I not run him off? I told her I would try. Shortly after this interview I went out to Kansas. It was some months before I could see any hope of successfully attempting to liberate her boy. The weather was so unusually mild that the river was not frozen over until some time after New Year's Day. I then made a trip to Parkville; carefully, of course, concealing my intention.[1]

I saw the boy at the livery stable and spoke to him privately. He refused to try to escape. He would not run the risk of recapture. He appeared, in fact, indifferent to his fate. I afterwards spoke to him, in the presence of a slaveholder, of the efforts of his mother to secure his freedom. He did not think, he said, that she could do it. She had written about it so often that he had given over all hope. He did n't keer much about it, nohow. He had n't, he said, much feelin' for his kinsfolks. He had seen his father the other day—the first time for a number of years. The old man ran to meet him, and put out his hand; but he would n't take it, would n't call him father— only "that man!" He said that his father was living with another woman now, and had a family not very far off; but he had never called to see them, and never intended to go near them. He made another remark that shocked me so much that I determined to leave him to his fate.

He told me that he had a brother, the property of Mr. Pitcher, who lived in the town of Liberty. I mounted my horse and went there. I soon saw Pitcher. He was sitting in the public room of the hotel, with his feet against the dirty stove. His talk was of bullocks and blooded horses, with which, in all their varieties—with their genealogical history, and the various *faux pas* of their different branches—and other interesting equestrian information, he was as familiar as the thorough bred cockney is with the scandal of the Green Room,[2] or the bed-room mysteries of the leading houses of the British aristocracy. As I rode a splendid steed, I was soon, to all outward appearance, as deeply interested in horse-history as he was. From horses to slaves the transition was easy. He had come from the North, he said, with anti-slavery sentiments. But he soon saw his error. He was a slaveholder now; and thought that it was not only right, but best for the nigger, for the white man to hold him as property. "My niggers, sir," he said, "are well fed; they 've got plenty of good clothing; if they 're sick, I have to foot the doctor's bill; I work as hard as they do—and harder too; only, they work with their hands and I work with my head!"

---

* This is the Capt. Wallace mentioned in the chapter on Lynching an abolitionist.

I could not help laughing. For I never saw a lazier-looking fellow in my life; and, if there is any truth in phrenological science, it might easily be disputed whether he had got any head to work with. I asked him how much he would sell Georgy for? Georgy was the brother of Millar. "He would take," he said, "one thousand dollars down. Nary cent less. No, sir, nary cent; he was a right smart boy and would bring that any day."

I waited in Liberty two or three days[3] in the hope of meeting the boy. I would have waited some days longer, but my departure was hastened by an act of carelessness. Liberty had distinguished herself, during the Kansas troubles, by her ultra devotion to "Southern Rights." She sent out bands of brutal men to vote and fight for slavery in Kansas. When in my room, at the hotel, I perpetrated the following atrocity:

ON LIBERTY IN MISSOURI.

As maids (or *un*maids), if you'll pardon the new phrase,
Who ne'er have trodden Virtue's straight and narrow ways,
    But sell their foul desires,
Whose path (says Solomon), leads downward to the grave
    And the infernal fires,
Are styled by bacchanals and rakes, *Nymphs* (of the pave!)
    So, on slave soil, we see
A town, renowned for despot deeds and ruffian bands,
Self-styled by men with Freedom's life-blood-dropping hands
    The Town of—LIBERTY![4]

With my usual carelessness, I left this poetical abortion on the table. When I returned, it was gone. Now, as, upon reflection, I saw that the execution of these lines gave sufficient warrant and excuse for my own execution, I determined to depart without delay, which—saddling up my horse at once—I forthwith did, leaving the "right smart boy" in slavery— in Liberty.

I heard nothing of the slave mother or her children, until, coming to New York to correct the final proofs of this volume, I met her and her son at the house of a gentleman of color. As the publisher required more copy still, I determined to narrate the history of this slave. It is subjoined. I reported her own language, as she replied to my questions. The arrangement of it, therefore, is all that I can claim.

This woman has never seen the harshest features of slavery; for she lived in the State, where, of all others, it exists in its mildest form; she had, also, as she says, a kind old master, until the marriage of his children; and Mr. Hinckley, as is evident, although a Haynau[5] and petty despot, never punished her with unusual severity or frequency. This, then, is a picture of slavery in its most pleasing aspects.

Of many of the facts she relates I have personal knowledge; and her character for veracity is vouched for by every one who knows her.

Another word, before her narrative begins. She was the first slave, or one of the first slaves, ever held in Kansas. She was kept there in bondage, in a Military Reservation, under the immediate shadow of the Federal flag.[6] The North, whether accountable for or guiltless of slavery in the South, is morally responsible for its existence in the Federal forts. Will the Republicans see that their Congressional Representatives shall instantly withdraw this Federal protection, and instantly abolish slavery, wherever—according to their own theories—they have the power to reach and extinguish it? Unless the *People* compel them, they will never attempt it. But, to the slave mother's narrative:

AN OLD KENTUCKY HOME.

"I was born and raised in Madison county, Kentucky. I will be thirty-nine next August. I belonged to Mr. William Campbell. I was raised in the same family as Lewis Clarke, who has written a book about his life.[7] My master lived on Silver Creek, about eight miles from Richmond. He owned nineteen or twenty slaves. My mother belonged to him; my father to Mr. Barrett, who lived about three miles off. My mother was always the cook of the family. I lived in Kentucky till I was about fourteen years of age, when old master moved off to Clay county, Missouri, carrying my mother with him, and all her children, excepting Millar, who had been sold to one of Mr. Campbell's cousins. She had thirteen children at that time, and had one more in Missouri. One daughter died on the journey.

A KIND MASTER.

"They parted my father and mother; but, when in Indiana, old master went back and bought him. He left us in charge of a son-in-law, and rejoined us with my father in Missouri. My poor mother! It seems to me too bad to talk about it. You have no idee what it is to be parted; nobody knows but them that's seen it and felt it. The reason that old master went back to Kentucky and bought my father, was because my mother grieved so about being separated from him. She did not think about running away. Slaves did n't long for freedom in those days; they were quiet and had plenty of privileges then.

"We were treated pretty well in Kentucky. Mr. Campbell was a kind master; one of the best there was. He had between six and seven hundred acres of land, but he did not push his hands; he was well off and did not seem to care; so we did pretty much as we pleased.

"Millar, who was left in Kentucky, was sold South; none of us have ever heard of him since."

THEORY OF THE MARRIAGE OF SLAVES.

"We girls were all unmarried when we moved to Missouri, and excepting Millar, we all lived together till old master's family began to set up for themselves. I was the first that got married. It was the next year after we went to Missouri that I was married to Nathaniel Noll. There was about three hundred people at my wedding. When a respectable colored girl gets married, it is the custom there, and in Kentucky, for all the neighbors, white and black, to come and see the ceremony. Colored people and whites associate more in the South than in the North. They go to parties together, and dance together. Colored people enjoy themselves more in the South than in any other part of the world, because they do n't know their condition.

"We were married by Mr. Chandler, at my master's house. I remember the words he said after I was married; says Mr. Campbell, says he, 'You join these people together; *that is, till I choose to make a separation.*' I heard it myself. He went up to the minister just as soon as the ceremony was over, and said it aloud, in presence of everybody in the room. I was young and happy, and did n't think much about it then, but I've often, often thought about it since."

PRACTICE AT THE MARRIAGE OF SLAVEHOLDERS.

"Sam was the first of my master's family married. When he married, the old man gave him Ellen and Daniel, my sister and brother. Daniel was twelve or thirteen; Ellen ten years old. She died soon after, from the effects of a cold, brought on by insufficient clothing. Otherwise she was well treated.

"My husband belonged to Mr. Noll, who lived about seven miles below our place. *He was half-brother to his master.* His mother was his father's slave. After we were married, he used to come up every Saturday night, and leave before daylight on Monday morning. He was treated pretty well.

"I staid about four years with old master, until his daughter, Miss Margaret Jane, was married to Mr. Levi Hinkle. Then the old man gave me and two of my children to her. My oldest boy he kept. I had had a pretty easy life till I got with them. Hinkle lived at Fort Leavenworth; he was a forage master. It was about fourteen years ago. I was taken immediately to Fort Leavenworth, with my two little children, and have never seen my husband since, excepting twice, both times within six months after Mr. Hinkle's marriage. Nathaniel came up to Fort Leavenworth three months after our separation; and then, again, three months from that visit. Last time his master told him that he would never allow him to leave the State again. That is fourteen years ago; I have never seen him since. My boy, Millar, says that he saw him recently, and that he lives with another woman, and has a family by her."

THE OLD FOLKS' FAMILY.

"Daniel, my brother, was sold by Sam. Campbell to a man in Clay county, and lives there yet.

"Mahala, my oldest sister, was given to Mr. Green White, who was married to Mary Ann Campbell. She got married after she went home with them. She had five children by her husband, and then she was sold away from them. Her husband, Joe Brown, was driven out of the house some three or four years before she was sold; he belonged to another master, and Mr. White did not like him about his house. I know nothing about Joe; his wife was sold somewhere up in Andrew county, and I have heard nothing of her since. I do not think she has ever seen her children from that time. I know that four of them are with Mr. White yet, and that she is not there; and that, about two months after she was taken away, her oldest boy, Henry, was sold down South. My son has kept track of them.

"Mahala told me she was treated very badly by her mistress. She often tried to whip Mahala; but as she was sickly she could n't do it—for we girls never would allow a woman to strike us—and so she had to get her husband to do it. He often whipped her; sometimes stripped her, and sometimes not."

A GREAT MISFORTUNE.

"Serena and Manda, my other sisters, were both sold out of the family, privately, to a man of the name of Elisha Arrington,* of Platte county, Missouri. He lives on the prairie between Fort Leavenworth and Clay county, near the dividing line of Platte. I cannot say much of the life of Mandy, as I have only seen her once since. Mr. Arrington owned two men also. Both of my sisters were married while they belonged to him. Mr. Arrington met a great misfortune, and sold all his slaves, and swore he would never keep another nigger about him, but compel his daughter to do the kitchen work herself."

* Or Errington, Malinda did not know how it was spelt.

"What do you mean," I asked, "when you say a great misfortune?"

She hesitated, but finally told me that "his daughter bore a child to one of his slaves. The boy was frightened, and ran away to Kansas, but was brought back in chains and sold. Manda was sold to a Mr. Jacks. Mr. Jacks is a very nice sort of man, but his wife treated Manda very badly. Our family are all high-spirited, and would never let a woman strike them. *That's the reason why we've been sold so often.*

"Serena was sold to a man named Yates, who lived up in Savannah. He bought her husband too. Mr. Yates kept her about seven years. None of us knew where she was all the time. She had two or three children. Then he sold her, but *kept her children.* She has been sold twice since; each time with her husband, *but each time away from her children.* He belongs now to a man named Links, who lives somewhere in Platte county."

THE OTHER SISTER SOLD.

"Maria (another sister) was sold by Mr. Campbell next winter after I was married. Poor little thing! she was taken out of the yard, one day, as she was running about—so young and happy-like. It almost broke old mother's heart. Campbell was an old villain, he was, although he did not whip us often, and fed us well. Nobody but an old villain would have treated poor old mother so, after she had worked for him so long and faithful. Campbell would always make us take our own part, even against his own young one, or anybody else's: he would n't allow anybody to whip us except himself. Maria was sold to a man named Phelps."

"The Congressman?" I asked.

"No," she said, sneeringly, "not that old Phelps: he was not smart enough: this Phelps lived north of Estelle's Mills, near Clinton. She was not treated like human—she was treated like a dog by both of them. I saw her once at Phelps's; she was twenty-one or twenty-two then. But we did not get much chance to talk; I staid there only a few minutes. She told me she was treated very badly; she looked broken-hearted, poor thing; she was n't clad decent; She had not a shoe to her feet. I saw the marks of the whip on her neck, and shoulders and arms. Poor child! it made me sad to see her. She had two young ones: but I do n't know whether she was married or not."

FATE OF HER BROTHERS.

"Howard, my brother, the old man gave to his son John, who took to gambling and horse-racing, and got into debt; then he mortgaged him to a man by the name of Murray, of Platte city. He is a very good master, I hear. Howard is with him now.

"Lewis ran away into Kansas six or seven years before the wars there; but they brought him back in irons, and he is there yet. Lewis was married to a girl that belonged to another man, and had two children by her. Then Mr. Williams, who owned her, moved into Jackson county, and took her and her young ones with him. Lewis has never seen them since."

THE OLD AND YOUNG FOLKS.

"My youngest sister, I do n't know anything about.

"Angeline, another sister, was sold to Col. Park, of Parkville. She is with him yet. He is a kind master; but you know more of her than I do.

"My old father is dead. The separation of our family broke the hearts of my father and mother. It was dreadful to see the way my old mother took on about it. You could hear her screaming every night as she was dreaming about them. It seemed so hard. No sooner was she beginning to get sort-of reconciled to one child being gone, than another was taken and sold away from her. My poor old mother! It was awful to see her. And yet they say we have no feelings!"

The relation of these facts so excited Malinda, that it was with difficulty that she could compose herself to conclude the narrative. I told her to confine herself now to her personal history.

SLAVERY IN KANSAS.

"I was taken to Fort Leavenworth some two or three years—it may be more—before the Mexican war. My oldest boy was three years old then; now he is twenty-two.

"My oldest boy, as I said, was kept at home. My youngest child, Julia, was about three years old; she died about two years afterwards. Georgy was but a boy.* Oh! how I used to worry! Oh! I was n't nobody. It did n't seem as if I keered for anything or anybody in the world. I was worrying about my husband and boy. Then he treated me badly, and she treated me badly. I was well clothed, and well fed; they couldn't have starved me if they had wanted to; for I was their body servant and housekeeper, and had everything to look after. They allowed me everything. We got along pretty well the first two or three years. She did not begin to get ugly till she began to have children. Then she began to get ugly. They were bad and it worried her. She did not bring them up right. She never was pleasant after she began to have children. You would not have thought it was the same woman."

---

* He is still in slavery.

SLAVERY IN THE HOUSEHOLD.

"*She seemed to be very jealous of me.* She seemed to think her husband liked me too well. She could not bear him to give me anything, or to say anything in my favor. When he went to Weston and got anything for me, she would fight about it; and, sometimes, she would get hold of it, and not let me have it; then he would insist on her giving it up; and then they would fight. I attended to my work well, and he treated me well; but she could not bear to hear me praised. *This sort of tyranny, occasioned by jealousy, is one of the most common causes of the bad treatment of the domestic servants of the South.* It is far more common than anybody knows of; for Southern gentlemen, generally, are very partial to colored girls. This makes a continual feud in families."

"Does not the church take notice of these things whenever they become public?" I inquired.

"No! Southern clergymen are no better than worldly folks. I know of my own self about them. I have known Southern ministers, my own self, make impudent advances to me in the very Sunday schools. Colored women know what *they* are.

"My mistress used to go home every two or three months. She always took me with her; she would not trust me alone at the Fort. She never tried to strike me at Fort Leavenworth, because her husband would not allow it. When she got home to her father's, she tried to get him to whip me. He refused. One day, when I had her child in my arms, she came up behind me, and struck me with a broom over the head. I had a good mind to throw her child into the fire, but I restrained my temper, and didn't say a word to her. When we got back to Fort Leavenworth, she boasted to Aunt Jennie (her husband's other slave), that she had struck me once and would keep it up now. I heard her, and said, loud enough for her to hear me, that if she ever laid her hand on me again, she would not get off so easy as she did before. After that, she seemed afraid to try. But, one morning, she got angry at me, seized a broom, and attempted to strike me with it. I seized hold of another, and made at her. She did n't dare to strike. She told her husband about it. He tied me up, stripped me, and lashed me, till the blood rained off my back and arms. Then he put handcuffs on me and threatened to sell me South. I talked back to him, and told him that I wished he *would* sell me. It makes me mad to think about it. When these Yankees come out to be slaveholders, are n't they fiends?"

"Was Hinkle," I asked, "a New Englander?"

"No," she said, "he was a Pennsylvanian. Well: after he got through, I told him that if his wife ever tried to strike me, I would half kill her. She never did try again. But of all the devils that ever lived, she was the worst.

She tormented me in every way she could, and make me right miserable, I tell you.

"I found out that Hinkle was trying to sell me, and sought secretly to find a master to suit me. A gentleman who knew me—a Missouri slave-holder—offered to buy me, take me with him to California, and liberate me after two years. When Hinkle found out that I had a chance to be free, he refused to sell me, and he and my friend had a regular row about it. The way Col. E—— did abuse him, and Northern men who held slaves, made him terrible angry. Hinkle then tried to make me contented; denied that he had intended to sell me, and told me he would never part with me if I would be a good girl. I told him I would never be contented in his service again, and he had better find a purchaser as soon as he could do it.

"Soon after this quarrel, he went to Pennsylvania to see his folks and his wife placed me in the care of Mr. White, her brother-in-law. They treated me like a lady, excepting that they watched me like a dog. They were afraid that I would run away, and never trusted me a minute out of their sight. They took me to meeting in their own carriage, and made me come back in the same way. They made me sleep in their bedroom, on a mattress on the floor, but paid no regard to my feelings, any more than if I was a cat.

"When they found that I would not be contented nohow, they agreed to sell me. Major Ogden knew me at the Fort; and, when he heard I was for sale, came down and asked me if I was willing that he should buy me. He said that he would only keep me until I paid for myself in work. He would allow me ten dollars a month. But he could not buy my children.

"I agreed to go with him. He would not have bought me unless I had been willing to go. I led a first-rate life. I had more work to do than ever in my life before; but I had plenty of privileges, and did not complain when I was treated so well. I was thirteen years at Fort Leavenworth, eight years with Hinkle, and five years with the Major's family.

"Before my time was out, the Major took me to Connecticut. He was ordered West with his regiment, and died at Fort Riley. I did not try to run away; I was willing to work my time out. But, if he had wished me to return to a Slave State, I would not have gone with him. I would not trust any one with my freedom. 'A bird in the hand,' I thought, 'was worth two in the bush.'[8] These Northern people, when they taste slavery, like it as well as anybody. When they change, they are *so* different.

"I have been free, in every way, for two years now."

Here the narrative of the mother ends. The first thing that she did, after having faithfully carried out her contract with the Major's family, was to work till she saved the sum of fifty dollars. That amount she placed in the bank, as the first installment for the purchase of her son at Parkville. It heads the long list of subscriptions which ultimately enabled her to buy him. I find that the fourth name on the list is the Editor of the *Journal of Commerce*.[9] The world does move after all![10]

She travelled from city to city, and from State to State, receiving pecuniary aid from hundreds of persons—in sums varying from twenty-five cents up to five and ten dollars. The master of her boy unfortunately heard of her zeal and success, and, with truly characteristic barbarity, raised the price of his slave to $1,200. That this amount was duly paid, this copy of his certificate of freedom will show:

FREE PAPERS.

Know all Men by these Presents, That we, John H. Nash, and William Nash, of Platte County, Missouri, for and in consideration of twelve hundred dollars, to us in hand paid by Henry Rawles, of New York city, through his agent, John S. Andrews, the receipt of which is hereby acknowledged, do by these presents grant, bargain and sell unto Malinda Noll, his mother, her executors, administrators and assigns, a negro man, slave for life, named Miller Noll, now of the age of about twenty-two years, together with all our right, title and interest in and to said slave. To have and to hold said negro slave, above bargained and sold, to the said Malinda Noll, her executors, administrators and assigns forever.

In testimony whereof we have hereunto set our hands and seals, this eleventh day of November, 1858.

JOHN H. NASH, ******

·SEAL·

****

WM. NASH. ******

·SEAL·

******

PLATTE COUNTY, }
State of Missouri. }

Be it Remembered, That on this eleventh day of November, 1858, before me, William McNeill Clough, a Notary Public, within and for the County of Platte, and State of Missouri, personally appeared the above-written John H. Nash and William Nash, who are personally known to me to be the same persons whose names are subscribed to the above instrument of writing, as their voluntary act and deed for the uses and purposes therein contained.

In testimony whereof I have hereunto set my hand and affixed my official seal, at office in Parkville, this 11th day of November, 1858.

********   WILLIAM MCNEILL CLOUGH,

* SEAL *   *Notary Public.*

****

"All men," says a great American State paper, "are endowed by their Creator with certain inalienable rights, and among these are life, liberty and the pursuit of happiness."[11]

What a comment on this specious declaration is this American bill of sale of a son to his own mother!

NOTES

1. In December 1857 Redpath had launched his own newspaper, the *Crusader of Freedom,* in Doniphan, Kansas, a town approximately fifty miles up the Missouri River from Parkville, Missouri. In his newspaper, Redpath described the winter of 1857–58 in the Kansas Territory: "The weather is mild, and the air as balmy as that of a spring morning." *Doniphan Crusader of Freedom,* December 19, 1857, and March 6, 1858; P. L. Gray, *Gray's Doniphan County History* (Brenda, Kans., 1905), 15–16, 68; Nichols, *Bleeding Kansas,* 20–21.

2. The "green room" was a term for a place in a theater meant to accommodate costumed actors and actresses waiting to go on the stage. "Cockney" was a derisive term for a native Londoner. *Oxford English Dictionary,* 2:575–76, 4:404.

3. The precise date of this trip to Liberty, Missouri, a town in Clay County northeast of Kansas City and approximately forty miles from Doniphan, cannot be determined. The trip must have taken place before Redpath closed the *Crusader of Freedom* at the end of May 1858 and left Kansas for good that July. Gray, *Doniphan County History,* 37–38, 68.

4. Redpath published many of his own poems in the *Doniphan Crusader of Freedom.* Only a few issues of this newspaper have survived, and none contains this poem. See *Doniphan Crusader of Freedom,* March 6, 1858.

5. Probably the same biblical figure, Haman, referred to in chapter 5.

6. An allusion to Fort Leavenworth, established in 1827 as a garrison for U.S. Army personnel in the Indian Territory. Nichols, *Bleeding Kansas,* 23.

7. Lewis Garrard Clark[e], *Narratives of the Sufferings of Lewis and Milton Clarke, Sons of a Soldier of the Revolution, During a Captivity of More Than Twenty Years Among the Slaveholders of Kentucky* (Boston, 1846).

8. John Heywood, *Proverbs and Epigrams* (London, 1546), part 1, chapter 11.

9. A reference to Gerald Hallock (1800–1866), a Williams College graduate who edited several newspapers in Boston in the 1820s. Hallock purchased the *New York Journal of Commerce* in 1828 and operated it until 1861, when the federal government indicted him for

encouraging pro-Confederate sympathy. Despite Hallock's vehement antiabolitionist senti-
ments, he purchased more than one hundred slaves for the purpose of sending them to
Liberia. Joseph P. McKerns, *Biographical Dictionary of American Journalism* (Westport,
Conn., 1989), 305–7; *NCAB,* 11:193.

10. Generally attributed to Italian astronomer Galileo Galilei (1564–1642). Stillman Drake,
"Galileo: A Biographical Sketch," in *Galileo: Man of Science,* ed. Ernan McMullin (New York,
1967), 52–66.

11. Redpath quotes from the Declaration of Independence.

II.

FELONS IN FODDER.

KANSAS, for four years past, has held up the mirror to modern Democracy; and in its history the true character of this subtile and stupendous
despotism—very hidden and hideous feature of it—is faithfully and un-
erringly delineated. Whatever, elsewhere, its partisans and supporters
may pretend or say, there, by the pressing exigencies of the pro-slavery
cause, and the frequent necessity for prompt, decisive and energetic action, Democracy—as represented by its chosen and honored Federal Ex-
ecutives—has stood forth undisguisedly and boldly as the special and
zealous champion of the Southern Aristocracy.

Let us briefly review the history of its most prominent officials in Kansas—the unerring mirror of its secret aims and hidden aspirations.

Mr. Reeder,[1] the first governor, a conservative among conservatives—a
Democrat to whom the Fugitive Slave Law, even, was neither repulsive in
character nor in any feature unconstitutional—a devout worshipper at
the shrine of Squatter Sovereignty[2] and of its high priests Messrs. Pierce
and Douglas[3]—was promptly disgraced and dismissed from office, as
soon as it was found that he would not become a servile and passive
instrument of iniquity in the bloodstained hands of Atchison[4] and his Missouri cohorts.*

Mr. Shannon,[5] his successor, who signalized his disembarkment by pro-
claiming, from the door of a common tavern in Westport, that he was in
favor of slavery and "the laws" of the Missourians, as represented by the
Shawnee Territorial legislature,[6] was retained in office and sustained by

* I may mention here that after Reeder was dismissed, Kansas, until recently—as long as
the pro-slavery party had the remotest hopes of success—was permitted to have only
two even *nominally* Free State officers; one of whom (Day) was murdered and a ruffian
appointed in his place, and the other (Shoemaker) was first supplanted by a ruffian and then
murdered.

the party, although notoriously incapable and a sot, until the record of his innumerable misdemeanors and follies, official and personal, endangered the success of the Democracy in pending State elections; or, rather, until he resolutely and publicly declared at Lecompton that he would not any longer be deceived and used by the ruffians.

Mr. Woodson,[7] the Secretary of State, thrice the Acting Governor of Kansas—a man who never faltered in sustaining the Missouri mobs—who hounded on the Carolina and Alabama robbers to the sack of Lawrence[8] and the desolation of the Free State settlements—was retained in office, and with honor, until, on the acceptance of Geary,[9] it was necessary to replace him by Dr. Gihon,[10] whose appointment that gentleman insisted on as an indispensable "condition precedent" to it. Was Woodson dismissed? No! the faithful—the *unfalteringly* faithful—are never so disgraced; except, indeed, at rare intervals and for a brief period only. He is now one of the chiefs of the land office at Kickapoo—a faithful town and a well-rewarded one![11]

To Geary's administration, the Democracy, sometimes, in free-soil districts—never in their Southern strongholds!—attribute the freedom of Kansas, and the election of Buchanan! His fate is familiar to every one. The moment that he dared to resist the secret will of the Slave Power, as uttered by its faithful instrument Lecompte;[12] when he said that a Missourian should *not* be bailed for murdering a poor Yankee cripple,[13] the signal was given from the windows of the White House, and the remorseless axe fell! Such heterodoxy was not to be tolerated. "By God!" said Mr. Kelley,[14] a Kansas postmaster, once, "when it comes that a man can be hanged for only killing a d—d Yankee abolitionist, I'll leave the country."* This sentiment seems to have received high official indorsement; for Lecompte was sustained, and Geary—*was permitted to retire.*

After Geary came Walker:[15] and when *his* eyes were opened and *his* tongue spake against the too transparent frauds of the party in power, his name at once became the prophet of his fate: and his name was Walker!

Stanton[16] entered Lawrence with threats on his tongue and the spirit of slavery—the desire of domination—in his heart; but when he mingled with the people, heard the story of their wrongs, saw the efforts, unjust and violent, of his party to continue their oppression, the scales fell from *his* eyes[17] also, and he ceased to kick against the pricks. What then? "Off with his head," said the South. "Let Alabama howl," said Buchanan. "Off with his head"—again did the South repeat the order, but this time in a sterner tone. Buchanan did not dare to disobey—"he winced beneath the Southern thunder," as Mr. Bigler[18] phrased it—and Mr. Stanton was dismissed.

---

* He did leave—in a hurry, too.

The next governor was Denver,[19] a Platte County man, recently from California, a noted duellist there, whose character and conduct in that country secured for him the terrible title of the Butcher. The Butcher, however, came too late, and had sense enough to see it. There was an odor of fight around the country, too, that somewhat alarmed him; visions of duels haunted his uneasy slumbers; he thought, upon the whole, that to attempt to enslave such a people might be, and probably would be, an unhealthy operation. So, we find, that he confined his exertions to the pocketing of important bills, charters, and resolutions. A sort of mincemeat butcher, this; afraid of the ox's horns, indeed, but willing enough, if need be, to stand behind a fence and goad it gently.

His successor is Mr. Sam. Medary,[20] a Democratic midwife of territorial governments, who was thus rewarded for his attempt, in Minnesota, to swamp the ballots of American citizens by the fraudulent and literally "*naked* votes" of semi-civilized and unnaturalized Indians.

If the history of their *executive* officers demonstrates that the Democracy are the special champions of slavery, no less clearly is the fact apparent and transparent in their judicial appointments for Kansas.

Lecompte, Elmore, and Johnson[21] were the first supreme judges. Judges Elmore and Johnson were discharged, with Governor Reeder, nominally for land speculations; but Elmore, really, as he himself declared in his letter to Mr. Cushing,[22] in order that the dismission of two acknowledged Free State officials might not give it the appearance of pro-slavery championship. This occurred in the earlier history of the Territory, before the Democracy had entirely thrown off their disguises.

Lecompte holds office still. No man doubts his professional incapacity for the high position of Chief Justice, but no one can ever doubt his eminent ability to advance the iniquitous designs of the Slave Power. Of all Judges, since Jeffrey[23] disgraced the bench, he has probably been the most subservient to the will of tyranny. He neither falters nor revolts at its utmost demands. One specimen of his legal erudition will suffice. Judge Wakefield[24] was arrested by Titus[25] and his men and brought before Lecompte. He demanded that the writ of arrest should be read to him. Lecompte examined the books, and inquired of his clerk, but could find neither record of complaint nor note of the issue of any writ. He informed Mr. Wakefield of this fact, and *then advised him to take out a writ of habeas corpus!*[26]

A brief examination of Judge Lecompte's record in Kansas will explain why he has retained his place of honor so long and undisturbed, notwithstanding the incessant and angry remonstrances of the people of the Territory.

Here is a brief and incomplete chronological note of it:

Judge Lecompte, Chief-Justice, April 30, 1855, addresses and takes prominent part in a border ruffian meeting at Leavenworth, by which a Vigilance Committee is appointed, who notify all "Abolitionists" to leave Kansas, and drive several of the Free State men out of the city.[27] He subsequently appointed Lyle,[28] one of these ruffians (who participated in the tar and feathering of Phillips),[29] clerk of his court, and refused to strike his name from the roll of attorneys, when a motion to that effect was made by Judge Shankland. He appointed Scott Boyle and Hughes,[30] two brutal ruffians engaged in the transaction, to other minor offices in his court.

July, 1855. Published a letter to the Legislature, indorsing their action, and declaring (before any case was before him, and, therefore, extra-judicially), that their conduct and enactments were legal in every respect— thus, without precedent, prejudging a point of law which might subsequently have involved, as it did involve, the legal rights and titles of thousands of citizens.[31]

Aug. 30. Invited the Legislature, by special letter read in the House, to a grand collation, or, rather, what the Indians style "a big drunk," and then addressed the inebriated assembly, eulogizing them for their patriotism and wisdom, and indorsing their infamous code of laws.[32]

Nov. 14. Attended a "law and order meeting" of ruffians, held at Leavenworth,[33] and declared his determination to enforce the laws *at all hazards:* and this after the delivery of the most sanguinary speeches by Calhoun[34] and other office-holders, in the course of which Judge Perkins (one of the most conservative of them all—*subsequently a District Judge*), told them to "Trust to their rifles, and to enforce the laws, if abolition blood flowed as free as the turbid waters of the Missouri."[35]

May 15. Lecompte made a violent partisan speech to the Grand Jury (reported by Mr. Leggett, who was one of them), in which he earnestly urged the conviction of the Topeka Free-State officers for high treason, but uttered not a syllable about the murderers of Barber[36] and other Northern martyrs.[37] This jury was packed by Sheriff Jones[38]—thirteen pro-slavery to three Free-State men. The jury became a caucus, the pro-slavery members making abusive speeches against all the Free-State leaders as Massachusetts paupers; and then found indictments against several prominent citizens for the crime of high-treason and usurpation of office.

Lecompte (at the same time) issued writs for the destruction of the Free-State Hotel as a nuisance. The only evidence brought against it, according to Mr. Leggett, was the fact that it was the property of the Emigrant Aid Co.,[39] and had been the head-quarters of the people who assembled at Lawrence, when it was threatened (in December) by a Missouri mob.[40]

Issues writs, also, for the destruction of the *Herald of Freedom,*[41] and *Free-State*[42] newspapers, and against a bridge over the Wakarusa River, built by a Free State man named Blanden, because he refused to take out a charter for it, and thereby acknowledge the validity of the Territorial laws.[43]

Nov. 8th. Releases the murderer of Buffum on *straw bail.*[44] Geary has him re-arrested. Lecompte again liberates him. He is sustained by Buchanan.

Liberates, also, on straw bail (both bondsmen, Federal office-holders in these cases), the scalper of Mr. Hops, the notorious *Fuggitt,*[45] who bet and won a pair of boots on the wager that he would have an abolition scalp in six hours.

Last summer, he liberated Jack Henderson when arrested under the Territorial laws, for stuffing ballot-boxes at the Delaware Crossing.[46]

To fancy that such a man, so faithful and so prompt, could ever be disgraced by the Democracy, was an indication, on the part of the people of Kansas, of the existence of extraordinary powers of imagination.

Elmore was dismissed by Pierce, it is true, but has been reinstated by Buchanan. He has been, and still is, I believe, the largest slaveholder in the territory. Although conservative both by nature and education, he was the captain of a company of ruffians during the civil wars. At Tecumseh, during Geary's administration, he perpetrated a most cowardly outrage on the person of Mr. Kagi, the correspondent of the *National Era.*[47] The store of a Free-State man had been robbed at Tecumseh. Law there was none. The boys of Topeka threatened vengeance unless the case was examined. A committee was appointed by the ruffians at Tecumseh. It consisted of the person suspected of the robbery! proslavery; Judge Elmore, pro-slavery, and a Free-State man. The evidence, full and positive, was given in. The robber, of course, objected to restitution, and the Free-State man was in favor of justice! the decision, therefore, devolved on Judge Elmore. He said he could not make up his mind about it. Mr. Kagi remarked, after recording the decision in the Topeka *Tribune,* that, although Pierce had dismissed Mr. Elmore for land speculations, he evidently might have assumed the stronger ground of incompetency; for surely a man who could not decide, after explicit testimony and on mature reflection, whether a convicted robber should be punished or make restitution, was hardly qualified for a seat on the Supreme Bench of any Territory! A few days after the publication of the paper, Mr. Kagi again visited Tecumseh, for the purpose of reporting the proceedings of the court, then in session there. Judge Elmore advanced towards him, and asked—just as the assassin Brooks asked Massachusetts' great senator on a memorable occasion,[48] when prepared to perpetrate a similar outrage— "Is your name Kagi?" Hardly had the word "Yes," been uttered, before Kagi was rendered nearly insensible, stunned and blinded by a savage blow on the head from a bludgeon in the hands of Elmore. From an instinct familiar to Kansas men—hardly knowing what he did—he groped for his pistol. Before he could draw it, several shots were fired at him by Elmore, and one shot by the United States Prosecuting Attorney, who was perched at a window overhead. Kagi rewarded the cowardly assassin by one shot—fired at random—which rendered him, it is said, a eunuch for life![49]

Elmore was a member of the Lecompton Constitutional Convention.[50] At first, he opposed the more radical pro-slavery features of the constitution and insisted on its submission to the people. But he suddenly faltered, and made a speech in favor of the Calhoun dodge.[51] It was understood—openly said at the time—that for this service he would be rewarded and deserved to be rewarded by a seat on the Bench; for, if he had adhered to his original plan, the dodge would undoubtedly have been defeated, and the constitution buried beneath an Alps-on-Apeninnes of freemen's votes. The prediction is fulfilled. Elmore is again a judge of the Supreme Court of Kansas. He has received the reward of consenting to endeavor to impose a fraudulent constitution on an unwilling people.

Johnson has *not* been reinstated. *He opposed Lecompton.*[52]

When Lawrence was surrounded by a Missouri mob, in December, 1856, a peaceful and good man was going homeward with his brother and two neighbors. He was pursued, shot at, and fell from his horse a pale, bleeding corpse. "I hit him; you ought to have seen the dust fly," said an office-holder, speaking of the murder. The murdered man was Barber; the office-holder Clark.[53] For so meritorious a servant of the Slave Power one lucrative office did not suffice. His brother-in-law (a person who can neither read nor write) was appointed to a high position in the Land Office at Fort Scott—the murderer drawing the salary of it.[54] When he became obnoxious to the people there, by his frequent marauding excursions and persecutions of the Free-State men, and was obliged to flee for his life, Buchanan opened his arms to receive him, and gave him the fat berth of a purser in the navy—a life-long office.*

Jones—faithful sheriff—whose recent presence, when the war raged, was indicated by sacked villages or desolated farms, has been recently rewarded still further for his services in Kansas by the Marshalship of Arrizonia Territory.

Clarkson, notorious as a bully and ballot-box stuffer, long held the office of Postmaster of the city of Leavenworth.[55]

Col. Boone, of Westport, who made himself conspicuous, in 1856, in

---

* Since the above was in type, Clark has been found dead on the prairie! He met his fate in returning to Lecompton to close up his business there.

raising ruffian recruits in Missouri, for the purpose of invading Kansas, was Postmaster of that place until he retired from business.[56]

He was succeeded by H. Clay Pate,[57] the correspondent of the Missouri *Republican,* a man publicly accused by his own towns-people of robbing the mail, who is known to have sacked a Free-State store at Palmyra, and to have committed numerous other highway robberies. But, although these facts were notorious, he obtained and still holds the appointment of Postmaster (*at a point convenient for the surveillance of the interior of the Kansas mails*), in order to compensate him for his disgraceful and over-whelming defeat by old John Brown at Black Jack.[58]

Mr. Stringfellow,[59] the most ultra advocate of pro-slavery propagandism in the West, at the instance of the friends of the Administration, was elected to the Speakership of the House of Representatives; and the Rev. Tom Johnson,[60] of the Shawnee Mission, who enjoys the unenviable noto-riety of having first introduced negro slavery into Kansas proper—long before the Territory was opened—was elected by the same influence President of the Council. It is said that his sons are provided for, also.

Mr. Barbee,[61] an ignorant and debauched drunkard—a man hardly ever seen sober—having been effectually used as a tool in a military capacity, was appointed U. S. District Attorney, a position he retained till the day of his death. One instance of his aptitude for such a post may be recorded as a specimen of Democratic appointments to legal positions in Kansas. At Tecumseh, one day, after vainly endeavoring, in thick, guttural ac-cents, to open a case, he exclaimed—"Move-'journ—please—move"—

"Gentlemen," said Judge Cato,[62] "I adjourn the case, as you will notice that the United States is drunk."

Cato himself, when in power, frequently left the bench for the purpose of "taking a smile," as western people phrase the practice of imbibing watered strychnine at the bar of a low grocery; and more than once the Counsellors, Sheriff and Jury, weary of waiting for his Honor's return, left the Court for the purpose of rejoining him, and indulging in his habits also.

The mention of bar-rooms naturally reminds us of another celebrated Kansas official, whose name, quite recently, was in all men's mouths. I refer to Mr. John Calhoun. He has been a faithful servant of both Adminis-trations. As early as November, 1856, he distinguished himself, at the Law and Order Convention at Leavenworth, as an ultra and blood-thirsty member of the pro-slavery party. On that occasion he hastened to inform the people that—

"I,"—this Prince of political forgers—"I could not trust an abolitionist or a free-soiler out of sight."

That—"They"—the Free-State men—"would kneel to the devil and call him God, if he would only help them to steal a nigger."

And again that—"I"—this veracious chief of the tribe, of Candlebox—"I would not believe one of them under oath more than the vilest wretch that licks the slime from the meanest penitentiary."

He "declared himself ready," too, to "enforce the laws"—the enactments of the Missouri mob—and "to spill his life's blood if necessary to do it."[63]

Unluckily he did not deem it necessary to shed his blood—as the future historian and probably Calhoun's own posterity will record with regret. With Falstaff's valor and Falstaff's prudence,[64] he kept himself distant from the battle-field—reserving his strength and ability for another day. His services to slavery, in the Lecompton Constitutional Convention, are known to every one. By adroit management, and the skillful use of Federal money, he procured the passage of the fraudulent constitution, without a "submission clause," and so arranged the subsequent proceedings to be had under the instrument, that, had it passed through Congress "naked," the Legislature might have met at Fort Leavenworth and elected two pro-slavery United States senators. The political complexion of that assembly was in his own hands. The defeat of the conspiracy in Congress prevented the completion of the plot.[65]

Jack Henderson, his creature—he whose action in the matter of the Delaware crossing put everything in Calhoun's power—United States Senators, State Government and Legislature—the continuance or the abolishment of slavery in Kansas—as far, at least, as political power, under the peculiar circumstances, could have affected slavery, was received at the White House with honor, closeted with Buchanan, and appointed a *Secret* Territorial Mail Agent.

Buford's marauders were presented with arms, and paid by the day for sacking Lawrence and desolating the surrounding region; and one of their number, a Mr. Fane, was appointed by the President United States Marshal.[66]

Titus was made a Colonel of Militia, and he and his men were promptly paid; while Captain Walker and his Free-State company, organized at the same time and in the same manner, under the same arrangement, have never been remunerated for their services to this day.[67]

General Whitfield,[68] bogus delegate, the leader of several gangs of the invaders of Kansas—on whose hands rests the blood of many martyrs, slain by his ruffians—after failing to be returned to Congress, was made a chief in the Land Office at Kickapoo, where he now resides.

Mr. Preston,[69] a Virginian, for overhauling a peaceful emigrant train, abusing the Northern people who composed it, and throwing their bedding and clothing on the miry soil, to be trodden on by the cavalry, has also been rewarded with a lucrative position in the same establishment.

Who has not heard of Colonel Emory[70]—a man notorious—the husband of a woman who once offered to a company of South Carolina ruffians, to marry any one who would bring her the scalp of a Yankee! Rich as she was, and poor and ruffianly as they were, not one of them accepted the offer. Emory was Secretary of State in General Walker's ragamuffin "State" of Southern California. In Kansas, after his appointment as mail contractor, he signalized his devotion to Democracy by ordering a quiet Free-State German to be shot down, like a dog, in the streets, for expressing his disapprobation of the murder of Phillips, that noble and heroic martyr whom, also, he had so brutally massacred. For these services, and for loaning his horses—for he kept a livery stable—to the South Carolina ruffians, he was appointed the comptroller of the Land Office at Ogden. Thus: the murderer of Phillips, as well as every man who had outraged his person a year before, has been rewarded with government offices.

The press has not been forgotten. Three Free-State offices in Kansas have been destroyed by violence—two by order of Judge Lecompte and the official *posse* of the United States Marshal; one (the Leavenworth *Territorial Register,* a Douglas Democratic paper), by a legally organized Territorial militia company—the same men who so savagely butchered R. P. Brown—the infamous Kickapoo Rangers.[71]

The pro-slavery press, on the other hand, has also been rewarded for *its* success. The *Squatter Sovereign,* once published in the town of Atchison, was edited by Mr. Speaker Stringfellow, already mentioned, and Mr. Robert S. Kelley.[72] This Kelley has always advocated the most bloodthirsty measures against the Free-State men—urging their expulsion always, and often their extermination. He advocated, also, a dissolution of the Union, and the formation of a Southern Confederacy. In the pro-slavery camp once, he entered the tent where a young Free-State man, a prisoner, lay dangerously ill, and savagely yelled, "I thirst for blood," an expression which, in the debilitated condition of the invalid's health, superinduced a brain fever, from which he did not recover for many months. This man, also, was the leader of the mob which tarred and feathered the Rev. Pardee Butler, and then put him on a raft on the Missouri River—for presuming, in a private conversation, to deprecate the lynching of a man who had suffered there a few days before for his political belief, and also for saying that he himself was in favor of making Kansas a Free State.[73] This man was appointed postmaster at Atchison; his brother-in-law is postmaster still at Doniphan; his paper received the government patronage, and printed the United States laws.

The *Herald,*[74] published at Leavenworth, although neither so honest in expression, nor violent in policy, was equally Satanic in its conduct. It slandered the murdered Free-State martyrs and the Free-State cause; and by its insidious misrepresentations and appeals did more than any other journal to prolong the troubles in Kansas. Its editor-in-chief was appointed Brigadier-General of the militia; its associate editor and Washington correspondent was rewarded with a consulship; and the paper has been the official organ of the administration in Kansas, the publisher of its laws and its bribery advertisements, from its establishment till now.

Its present associate in these advantages is the *Herald of Freedom,* which has been rewarded with the government patronage ever since its attacks on the Republican party.

It is to the credit of the Free-State men that since they obtained the power, both political and of the mob, no paper has been disturbed, nor the freedom of speech assailed, although the pro-slavery press and pro-slavery stump still echoes the foulest slanders on their creed, their leaders, and their party.

I might prolong to an unendurable extent this list, black—and still blackening as it lengthens—of the ruffianly recipients of official rewards for vile deeds done in the unhappy territory, which has so long been the victim of the Slave Power's lust; but which, recently—thank God—proved itself not unworthy of its illustrious and free Puritan descent, by spurning so unceremoniously and so firmly the bribe that was held up beneath a threat to reduce it! But with another instance I will close it, referring those of you who would learn the entire length, and the depth, and the breadth of it, to consult the ensanguined chronicles of Kansas, which are strewed with similar and even more deplorable outrages.

There was, and yet is, a wealthy firm in Leavenworth, who have thousands of men in their employ. They established a branch of their business in the city when it was still a straggling village, and wealth thus contributed greatly to its rapid increase in population. Lawrence was surrounded with ruffians. It was dangerous at Leavenworth to be known as a Free-State man. This in 1856. Suddenly every man was asked by the chief of the firm what party he belonged to. Every man who was in favor of a Free State, and every man who was not emphatically pro-slavery, without any regard to his merits as a workman, was instantly cashiered. A handbill appeared in Lexington and other Missouri towns a few weeks afterwards, telling workmen that this firm needed help; but it contained this ominous, and in view of the author's connection with the Government, this significant postscript: "N.B. None need apply who are not sound on the Southern question."

Months elapsed and the war was resumed. The territory was covered with guerillas, gangs of highwaymen, horse-thieves, and house-breakers from Missouri, Georgia, Alabama, and South Carolina. An immense *posse* was gathering at Lecompton to sack the town of Lawrence. The firm had about a hundred men at their establishment preparing to start across the prairies. They were told to go and fight the Yankees, furnished with arms and powder, and had the same pay that they received for their services at their ordinary work.

This same firm appealed, with Atchison, to the South for men and arms; one of them acted as the treasurer to the Southern contributors, and disbursed the treasury of desolation and civil war as the exigencies of their guerilla forces and armies required.

This firm has made *millions* by the government contracts.

For a specimen of the manner in which they have been rewarded, I refer you to the last report of the Secretary of the Treasury, from which you will see that they have been paid at the rate of $187 per barrel for transporting each and every barrel of flour forwarded to the army at Utah.[75]

If, then, as Charles Sumner says, "he who is not for freedom in her hour of peril, is against her," be true, and be equally true of slavery, how will the South and her oligarchy ever be able to defray their indebtedness to the Democracy? and how, too, will New England and the North ever be able to square *their* accounts, even when the terrible day of reckoning does come?

NOTES

1. Pennsylvania lawyer Andrew Horatio Reeder (1807–64) was an active Democrat but never held any elective political office. President Franklin Pierce appointed Reeder the first territorial governor of Kansas in June 1854. When Reeder objected to the participation of Missourians in the first election for a congressional delegate, Pierce removed him on the bogus charge of illegal land speculation. Thomas A. McMullin and David Walker, eds., *Biographical Directory of American Territorial Governors* (Westport, Conn., 1984), 161–62.

2. In the political debates of the 1850s, "squatter sovereignty" was used synonymously with "popular sovereignty," the doctrine that local settlers should determine whether new territories entered the Union as slave or free states. Rawley, *Race and Politics,* 33–34.

3. Franklin Pierce and Stephen A. Douglas.

4. David R. Atchison.

5. A lawyer from St. Clairsville, Wilson Shannon (1802–77) won the Ohio governorship in 1838 and again in 1842 as a Democrat. He resigned that office to accept appointment as U.S. ambassador to Mexico from President John Tyler. In 1849 Shannon migrated to California, which chose him for a term in the U.S. House of Representatives (1853–55). President Franklin Pierce appointed Shannon territorial governor of Kansas to replace Andrew Reeder in August 1855. Shannon's proslavery views and ineffectual leadership encouraged an escalation of the guerrilla warfare in the territory. After a year in office, Shannon resigned and took up the practice of law in eastern Kansas. McMullin and Walker, *Territorial Governors,* 163–64.

6. Redpath had originally reported on Governor Wilson Shannon's proslavery speech in Westport, Missouri, on August 31, 1855, for the *St. Louis Daily Missouri Democrat.* Shannon

later contested the accuracy of that report. Redpath also covered the meetings of the territorial legislature in Shawnee Mission in summer of 1855, where the fraudulently elected proslavery majority expelled its opponents and enacted a slave code for Kansas. *New York National Anti-Slavery Standard,* September 22, 1855; *St. Louis Daily Missouri Democrat,* July 23, August 15, October 22, and November 10, 1855; Daniel W. Wilder, *Annals of Kansas* (Topeka, Kans., 1875), 113; Rawley, *Race and Politics,* 96.

7. A Virginia native, Daniel Woodson (1824–94) operated a vigorous Democratic party newspaper in Lynchburg, Virginia, before his appointment as Kansas's first territorial secretary in 1854. He held that post for three years and often served as acting governor in the absence of that official in the territory. Afterward he became a farmer in Leavenworth County and later a printer in Montgomery County. Blackmar, *Kansas,* 2:937; Wilder, *Annals of Kansas,* 165.

8. The first "sack" of Lawrence had occurred on May 21, 1856, but territorial secretary Daniel Woodson did not play a significant role in that attack. Redpath probably refers to events of later that year. Before John W. Geary arrived to take the office of territorial governor in September 1856, Woodson—as acting governor—had declared the free staters to be in a state of rebellion. A force of more than twenty-seven hundred Missourians led by David R. Atchison, John W. Reid, and John H. Stringfellow rallied to attack free state settlements, particularly Lawrence. Geary hurried to Lawrence and ordered the volunteer militia disbanded before the fighting had gone beyond skirmishing. Wilder, *Annals of Kansas,* 108; Rawley, *Race and Politics,* 159–69; Nichols, *Bleeding Kansas,* 140–44, 152–58.

9. John White Geary (1819–73) pursued a number of professions in western Pennsylvania before heroic conduct in the Mexican War prompted President James K. Polk to appoint him postmaster of San Francisco. A Democrat, Geary won election as San Francisco's first mayor in 1850, but he returned to Pennsylvania two years later. Appointed to succeed Wilson Shannon as Kansas's territorial governor, Geary tried to end the fighting in the territory through impartiality on the crucial issue of slavery. Feeling unsupported by President Franklin Pierce, Geary resigned in March 1857. Geary served as a brigadier general in the Union Army during the Civil War and then held the Pennsylvania governorship for six years. McMullin and Walker, *Territorial Governors,* 164–66; William Alan Blair, ed., *A Politician Goes to War: The Civil War Letters of John White Geary* (University Park, Pa., 1995).

10. Territorial Governor John W. Geary selected a physician, John W. Gihon, to act as his personal secretary. Gihon later wrote a book detailing Geary's and his own careers in Kansas. Nichols, *Bleeding Kansas,* 145–53, 156–57, 159, 173–76, 180.

11. President James Buchanan appointed Daniel Woodson as receiver of public monies for the Delaware Land District. His office was at Kickapoo, Kansas. Wilder, *Annals of Kansas,* 165.

12. Samuel D. Lecompte (1814–88) practiced law in Carroll County, Maryland, and served in that state's legislature in the 1840s. After a defeat in a congressional election as a Democratic candidate, he removed to Baltimore. In 1854 President Franklin Pierce appointed Lecompte chief justice of the Kansas Territory, an office he filled until his resignation on March 9, 1859. Lecompte used his judicial position to support the proslavery faction in the territory. Ironically, Lecompte became a Republican after the Civil War and sat in the Kansas state legislature (1867–68). Blackmar, *Kansas,* 128.

13. John W. Geary resigned as Kansas governor on the day of James Buchanan's inauguration after failing to convince the president-elect of the guilt of Missourians and proslavery Kansans for the breakdown of law and order in the territory. The specific murder to which Redpath refers was that of David C. Buffum (described later in this chapter). Rawley, *Race and Politics,* 176–79, 182, 203; Nichols, *Bleeding Kansas,* 162–63.

14. Possibly the Robert S. Kelley discussed by Redpath later in this chapter, who was one of the attackers of the Reverend Pardee Butler. Kelley also was the junior editor of John H. Stringfellow's proslavery *Atchison Squatter Sovereign.* For a time Kelley held the office of postmaster of Atchison. [A. Morrall], "Brief Autobiography of Dr. A. Morrall," *Kansas State Historical Society Collections* 14 (1915–18): 130; Nichols, *Bleeding Kansas,* 102, 214.

15. Pennsylvania lawyer Robert John Walker (1801–69) migrated to Mississippi in 1826, where he became a land and cotton speculator. Democrats elected him to the U.S. Senate and he served there from 1835 to 1845. After duty as President James K. Polk's secretary of the treasury, Walker practiced law in Washington, D.C. President James Buchanan appointed him territorial governor of Kansas in March 1857. Walker angered proslavery Kansas settlers by insisting on a fair application of "popular sovereignty" principles to the slavery question there. He resigned his post in December and returned to Washington to assist Stephen A. Douglas in battling against the admission of Kansas as a state under the proslavery Lecompton constitution. James P. Shenton, *Robert John Walker: A Politician from Jackson to Lincoln* (New York, 1961); McMullin and Walker, *Territorial Governors,* 166–68.

16. The territorial secretary, Frederick P. Stanton, had arrived in Kansas in April 1857. He immediately angered free staters by dismissing their complaints about unfair apportionment in the election to choose delegates to the constitutional convention at Lecompton, causing them to boycott the vote. Stanton became acting governor in December 1857 while Territorial Governor Robert Walker was in Washington. On this occasion, he outraged proslavery opinion by calling the newly elected legislature—with its free state majority—into special session to deal with the rising tide of violence. President James Buchanan quickly removed Stanton and replaced him with James W. Denver. Nichols, *Bleeding Kansas,* 190, 194, 204–5; Rawley, *Race and Politics,* 226, 231–32; *DAB,* 17:523–24.

17. A paraphrase of Acts 9:18.

18. Pennsylvania Democrat William Bigler (1814–80) rose through state politics to the office of governor (1851–55); in 1856 he won election to the U.S. Senate. Bigler patched earlier quarrels with fellow Pennsylvanian James Buchanan and worked for his nomination and election as president. After a visit to Kansas, Bigler dropped his original objections to Buchanan's position in favor of the territory's admission as a state under the proslavery Lecompton constitution. Rawley, *Race and Politics,* 156, 245; *DAB,* 2:264.

19. James William Denver (1817–92) was an Ohio lawyer and Democratic politician who relocated to Missouri and then California after service in the Mexican War. Following a single term as a U.S. congressman, Denver accepted appointments from President James Buchanan as U.S. commissioner of Indian affairs (April–December 1857) and then as territorial secretary (December 1857–February 1858) and territorial governor (February–November 1858) of Kansas. Denver quarreled with the free staters who controlled the territorial legislature but unsuccessfully tried to convince Buchanan that the majority of Kansans opposed the Lecompton constitution. After resigning as governor, Denver again served as Indian commissioner and later as a Union Army general in the Civil War. McMullin and Walker, *Territorial Governors,* 168–70; *DAB,* 5:242–44.

20. Samuel Medary (1801–64) migrated to Ohio from eastern Pennsylvania in 1825 and through his journalistic talents soon became a major force in his adopted state's Democratic party. President James Buchanan appointed Medary as governor of the Minnesota Territory in 1857 and then of Kansas the following November. He held that post until Lincoln's election, after which he returned to Ohio and became a leading Peace Democratic editor during the Civil War. McMullin and Walker, *Territorial Governors,* 170–72; *DAB,* 12:490–91.

21. President Franklin Pierce named Alabamian Rush Elmore (?–1864) as an associate justice of the Kansas territorial supreme court. Before moving to Kansas, Elmore had served

as a captain in the Mexican War and practiced law in his home state. He was dismissed along with Governor Andrew Reeder and fellow justice Saunders W. Johnston, originally of Ohio, in the fall of 1855 by Pierce on the fraudulent charge of illegal speculation in Indian land. In the spring of 1857 President James Buchanan restored Elmore to his judicial post. In the interim, he served as a delegate representing Shawnee County at the Lecompton constitutional convention. Elmore unsuccessfully advocated a popular referendum on the controversial proslavery document. "Executive Minutes of Governor John W. Geary," *Kansas State Historical Society Collections* 4 (1886–88): 704; James C. Horton, "Business Then and Now," *Kansas State Historical Society Collections* 8 (1903–4): 148; "Biographical Sketch of Judge Rush Elmore," *Kansas State Historical Society Collections* 8 (1903–4): 435.

22. Massachusetts politician Caleb Cushing (1800–1879) left his Newburyport legal practice to occupy seats first in the state legislature and then in Congress as a Whig. After service in the Mexican War, Cushing failed in two bids for the governorship as a Democrat. President Franklin Pierce appointed Cushing his attorney general, a post Cushing used to lash out at abolitionists. Claude M. Fuess, *The Life of Caleb Cushing,* 2 vols. (1923; Hamden, Conn., 1965); *DAB,* 4:623–30.

23. An allusion to English judge George Jeffreys, first baron of Wem (1648–89), who was twice censured by Parliament for his judicial excesses. He held several high offices under James II and died in the tower after the Glorious Revolution overthrew the Stuarts. *DNB,* 10:714–21.

24. John A. Wakefield (?–1874) lived west of Lawrence and was a leading delegate at the free state convention that wrote the Topeka constitution in the fall of 1855. He was the unsuccessful free state candidate in the first election for territorial delegate to the U.S. Congress. In 1856 free staters elected him treasurer of their extralegal territorial government. *St. Louis Daily Missouri Democrat,* November 9, 1855; *Chicago Tribune,* May 22, 1856; James C. Horton, "Reminiscences," *Kansas State Historical Society Collections* 8 (1903–4): 199–200, 205.

25. A Kentucky native, Henry T. Titus (?–1881) had served in Narcisco Lopez's unsuccessful filibustering expedition to Cuba in 1850. He arrived in Kansas in April 1856 as part of a party of southern emigrants headed by Col. Jefferson Buford. Titus was active in the proslavery territorial militia's skirmishing with free staters. In 1857 he joined William Walker's Nicaraguan expedition, and he later settled in Florida. William O. Scroggs, *Filibusters and Financiers: The Story of William Walker and His Associates* (New York, 1916), 237; Blackmar, *Kansas,* 2:809; Nichols, *Bleeding Kansas,* 89, 130–31, 137–39.

26. In May 1856 proslavery military leader Henry T. Titus arrested free stater John A. Wakefield without producing a writ. Titus brought Wakefield before territorial supreme court chief justice Samuel D. Lecompte. The exchange that Redpath describes occurred before Lecompte relented and released Wakefield. *New York Tribune,* June 9, 1856.

27. After free stater Cole McCrae shot a proslavery settler named Malcolm Clark, a mass meeting in Leavenworth on April 30, 1855, which Samuel D. Lecompte attended and addressed, formed a vigilance committee. George W. Martin, "The First Two Years of Kansas," *Kansas State Historical Society Collections* 10 (1907–8): 135; Wilder, *Annals of Kansas,* 100.

28. A lawyer and clerk of the first session of the Kansas territorial legislature in 1855, Georgia native James M. Lyle (?–1857) also served as clerk for state supreme court justice Samuel D. Lecompte. He also participated in the lynching of free stater William Phillips. *St. Louis Daily Missouri Democrat,* December 12, 1855; Wilder, *Annals of Kansas,* 100; Nichols, *Bleeding Kansas,* 195.

29. An active free state lawyer, William Phillips (?–1856) was kidnapped by a proslavery vigilance committee in Leavenworth and taken to Weston, Missouri, on May 17, 1855. There

he was subjected to numerous indignities including a tarring and feathering. The following year, he was murdered in his home by proslavery gunmen. C. E. Cory, "Slavery in Kansas," *Kansas State Historical Society Collections* 7 (1901–2): 233; John B. Dunbar, "The White Man's Foot in Kansas," *Kansas State Historical Society Collections* 10 (1907–8): 61; Nichols, *Bleeding Kansas,* 30, 149.

30. D. Scott Boyle and Thomas C. Hughes are listed as two members of the vigilance committee formed by proslavery settlers in Leavenworth, Kansas, in April 1855. Hughes is known to have been one of the attackers of William Phillips. He later served as one of the secretaries of the constitutional convention held at Lecompton. Wilder, *Annals of Kansas,* 100, 162.

31. The March 1855 election for the territorial legislature was the scene of major voting fraud when thousands of Missourians entered Kansas to vote for proslavery candidates. The legislature proceeded to expel practically all of the free state minority elected to it and quarreled with Governor Andrew Reeder about its meeting site. In a letter read to the Kansas House of Representatives on August 8, 1855, Chief Justice Samuel D. Lecompte gave the territorial legislature his sanction despite Reeder's declaration that all of its enactments were illegal. Nichols, *Bleeding Kansas,* 33–36; Rawley, *Race and Politics,* 91–92; *St. Louis Daily Missouri Democrat,* August 14 and 15, 1855.

32. Redpath was present at this dinner in Shawnee Mission, which took place on August 23, not August 30, 1855. Lecompte thanked the legislators for honoring him by deciding to move the territorial capital to the settlement named for him, Lecompton, in Douglas County. *St. Louis Daily Missouri Democrat,* August 30, 1855.

33. Redpath's own report for the *St. Louis Daily Missouri Democrat* noted that Justice Samuel D. Lecompte attended and addressed a "Law and Order" convention held in Leavenworth on October 14–15, 1855. *St. Louis Daily Missouri Democrat,* November 21 and 26, 1855.

34. A New Yorker who migrated to Springfield, Illinois, in 1830, John Calhoun (1806–59) had been a friend of the young Abraham Lincoln and had trained him as a surveyor. A Democrat, Calhoun had been elected a state legislator and mayor of Springfield but failed at aspirations to hold higher office. President Franklin Pierce appointed Calhoun as surveyor general of Kansas and Nebraska in 1854. Calhoun made the speech at the evening session of the "Law and Order" convention in Leavenworth on November 15, 1855, threatening free state settlers with violence. He served as presiding officer of the territorial convention at Lecompton in 1857 that framed the controversial proslavery state constitution for Kansas. *St. Louis Daily Missouri Democrat,* November 26, 1855; *DAB,* 3:410–11.

35. At the "Law and Order" convention in Leavenworth on November 15, 1855, Judge George W. Perkins followed John Calhoun and Samuel Lecompte and made the remarks Redpath quotes. A Virginia native, Perkins had been an unsuccessful proslavery candidate in the fall 1855 election for territorial delegate to Congress. *St. Louis Daily Missouri Democrat,* November 24 and 26, 1855; Wilder, *Annals of Kansas,* 114.

36. A migrant from Ohio, Thomas J. Barber (1813–55) was a private in the Kansas Volunteers, a free state militia. A band of proslavery gunmen shot Barber as he rode near Lawrence on December 6, 1855. U.S. Indian agent George W. Clarke as well as Missourian James Burns claimed credit for Barber's killing; neither was ever convicted. O. N. Merrill, *A True History of the Kansas War* (Cincinnati, 1856), 24–28; Wilder, *Annals of Kansas,* 120; Villard, *John Brown,* 126.

37. In May 1856 Chief Justice Samuel Lecompte of the territorial supreme court ordered the grand jury of Douglas County to issue bills of indictment against leading free staters as traitors. He also instructed the grand jury to indict the Free State Hotel of Lawrence for

being "regularly parapeted and port-holed for use of small cannon and arms" and the *Lawrence Herald of Freedom* and *Kansas Free State* for their "inflammatory and seditious language." Nichols, *Bleeding Kansas,* 101–2.

38. Samuel J. Jones migrated to Kansas from Virginia and became sheriff of Douglas County in August 1855. The following May he led the proslavery "posse" that sacked the free state settlement of Lawrence. He subsequently relocated to New Mexico. Buchanan later appointed Jones to be collector of the district of Paso del Norte in West Texas. Blackmar, *Kansas,* 2:37; Nichols, *Bleeding Kansas,* 50, 53–55, 96–101, 234.

39. Begun in April 1854 by Eli Thayer as the Massachusetts Emigrant Aid Society and reincorporated the following year as the New England Emigrant Aid Company, this organization encouraged and assisted free staters to settle in the Kansas Territory. Wealthy Massachusetts industrialist Amos Lawrence served as treasurer of the New England Emigrant Aid Company, and the leading free state town in the territory was named for him. The organization owned mills and hotels, including Lawrence's Free State Hotel, which it hoped to operate at a profit to support its other emigrant aid activities. Rawley, *Race and Politics,* 84–85.

40. As part of the "Wakarusa War," Sheriff Samuel J. Jones raised a "posse" of nearly fifteen hundred proslavery Kansans and Missourians in December 1855 with the intention of attacking Lawrence and arresting the leaders of the free state party there. The free staters made the nearly completed Free State Hotel their military headquarters in this crisis. Governor Wilson Shannon managed to persuade the two sides not to engage in fighting at this time. Nichols, *Bleeding Kansas,* 53–79.

41. Founded in the spring of 1855 by George W. Brown thanks to a loan from the New England Emigrant Aid Company, the *Lawrence Herald of Freedom* was a strong free state voice in the territory until its destruction by Sheriff Samuel J. Jones's "posse" in May 1856. The paper resumed publication in November with a more conservative free state tone, causing antislavery radicals such as Redpath to charge that it had been "bought" by a contract from Governor John W. Geary for public printing. Malin, *John Brown,* 63–65, 68, 170, 176–77.

42. One of the earliest antislavery newspapers in the territory, the *Lawrence Free State* was started by Josiah Miller. It was one of the targets of Sheriff Samuel Jones's attack on Lawrence in May 1856. Unlike the *Herald of Freedom,* the *Free State* was never revived. Malin, *John Brown,* 32–33, 69, 74; Nichols, *Bleeding Kansas,* 26, 29, 107–8, 213.

43. Actually Blanton's Bridge on the Wakarusa Creek in Douglas County, which Justice Samuel Lecompte condemned as a nuisance. *New York Tribune,* June 9, 1856; Rawley, *Race and Politics,* 2.

44. A free state settler with a crippled leg, David C. Buffum of Douglas County was murdered on February 15, 1856, by Charles Hays of Atchison, a member of a squad of the proslavery Kickapoo Rangers. Governor Geary offered a five hundred dollar reward, and Hays finally was arrested in November. Judge Samuel Lecompte released Hayes on bail. Geary called this a "judicial outrage" and ordered his rearrest, but Lecompte issued a writ of habeas corpus and again released Hayes. "Executive Minutes of Governor John W. Geary," *Kansas State Historical Society Collections* 4 (1886–88): 571, 629, 631; "A Defense by Samuel D. Lecompte," *Kansas State Historical Society Collections* 8 (1903–4): 393n; Wilder, *Annals of Kansas,* 151–53; Nichols, *Bleeding Kansas,* 159–63.

45. Stung by accusations of bias in his acquittal of Charles Fuggitt for the murder and scalping of a free state settler named Hoppe, Judge Samuel Lecompte denied all previous acquaintance with Fuggitt and argued that the prosecution witnesses had failed to identify him as the perpetrator. "A Defense by Samuel D. Lecompte," *Kansas State Historical Society Collections* 8 (1903–4): 396–97.

46. Investigations of territorial elections in Kansas on December 21, 1857, and January 4,

1858, found that John D. "Jack" Henderson of Delaware Crossing had added 336 fraudulent proslavery ballots to the total. Martin, "First Two Years in Kansas," 143n; "The First Free State Territorial Legislature of 1857–58," *Kansas State Historical Society Collections* 10 (1907–8): 172n.

47. Ohio-born John Henri Kagi (1835–59) had worked as a journalist in the Kansas Territory during the same period as Redpath had. Among the newspapers hiring Kagi was Gamaliel Bailey's antislavery *National Era*, published in Washington, D.C. Kagi joined the free state militia in Kansas and soon became a follower of John Brown. Designated "secretary of war" under Brown's "Provisional Constitution" for the liberated South, Kagi died in the raid on Harpers Ferry. John W. Wayland, *John Kagi and John Brown* (Strasburg, Va., 1961); Oates, *To Purge This Land*, 200, 246, 266–68, 280, 290–96.

48. An allusion to Representative Preston Brooks's attack on Senator Charles Sumner.

49. In February 1857 Rush Elmore had confronted John Henri Kagi on the street in Tecumseh, Kansas. After Elmore began to cane him, Kagi drew a pistol and wounded his assailant in the leg. Elmore then shot Kagi in the side. Neither man's wounds proved serious. "Executive Minutes of Governor Geary," 704; Nichols, *Bleeding Kansas*, 184.

50. Chosen in an election called by the proslavery territorial legislature and boycotted by most free staters, the delegates to the convention at Lecompton had responsibility for drawing up a constitution to govern Kansas after its admission to the Union as a state. Former territorial supreme court justice Rush Elmore was one of the few well-known men elected to the convention, which drew up a proslavery constitution. Despite pressure from territorial governor Robert J. Walker, the Lecompton convention took the controversial step of calling for a referendum on the constitution in which either a positive or a negative vote would make Kansas a slave state. Nichols, *Disruption of American Democracy*, 120–21, 125, 129–33; Rawley, *Race and Politics*, 213–17.

51. The majority of delegates to the Lecompton convention had opposed putting their constitution to a referendum before submitting it to Congress. Eastern Democratic leaders pressured John Calhoun, the territorial surveyor, to take the lead in convincing the convention to agree to a form of referendum that did not jeopardize slaveholding. The referendum passed by twenty-seven to twenty-five votes—only after the convention charged Calhoun, not territorial governor Robert J. Walker, with supervision of the election. Almost alone, Rush Elmore had initially favored a referendum on the slavery issue; but ultimately he supported Calhoun's measure. Nichols, *Disruption of American Democracy*, 129–33; Nichols, *Bleeding Kansas*, 201–3, 207.

52. After his removal as territorial supreme court associate justice, Saunders W. Johnson of Leavenworth (an Ohio native and a Democrat) gravitated to the free state camp and opposed the Lecompton constitution. *New York Tribune*, January 19, 1856; *Doniphan Crusader of Freedom*, March 6, 1858.

53. A U.S. Indian agent and active leader of proslavery guerrillas, George W. Clarke from Georgia claimed credit for the murder of Thomas W. Barber but never was charged. *Lawrence Herald of Freedom*, December 15, 1855; John Speer, "Accuracy in History," *Kansas State Historical Society Collections* 6 (1897–1900): 61; Martin, "First Two Years of Kansas," 135.

54. George W. Clarke was the receiver of public monies for the Fort Scott land office. Albert R. Greene, "United States Land Offices in Kansas," *Kansas State Historical Society Collections* 8 (1903–4): 9.

55. J. J. Clarkson, a colonel in the proslavery Kickapoo Rangers, was rewarded with the postmastership of Leavenworth, Kansas. William H. Coffin, "Settlement of Friends in Kansas," *Kansas State Historical Society Collections* 7 (1901–2): 351.

56. The grandson of famed frontiersman Daniel Boone, Albert G. Boone had been a to-

bacco merchant in Missouri. In 1848 he established a warehouse in Westport, Missouri, that profited from outfitting settlers heading to California. The federal government often hired Boone as a translator in negotiations with Indian tribes in the region. He was one of the prominent leaders of the Missouri Border Ruffians who sacked Lawrence in May 1856. William R. Bernard, "Westport and the Santa Fe Trade," *Kansas State Historical Society Collections* 9 (1905–6): 565; Nichols, *Bleeding Kansas,* 63, 71–72, 105.

57. Henry Clay Pate (1832–64) worked as a correspondent for the *St. Louis Missouri Republican* in the Kansas Territory in the mid-1850s. Pate also was a deputy U.S. marshal and a Missouri militia captain who fought in several engagements in Kansas on the proslavery side. Pate returned to Virginia in the late 1850s and served as a colonel in the Confederate army. Oates, *To Purge This Land,* 143, 152–56, 159; Villard, *John Brown,* 200–208.

58. On receiving news of the Pottawatomie massacre in May 1856, Henry Clay Pate led a band of thirty Missourians to capture John Brown. He succeeded in arresting two of Brown's sons. The senior Brown and eight followers attacked and captured Pate's band at the "battle" of Little Jack Creek. U.S. cavalry troops soon liberated the Missourians. Redpath provides an eyewitness account of this fight in the next chapter. Wilder, *Annals of Kansas,* 188–201; Oates, *To Purge This Land,* 143, 152–56, 159; Villard, *John Brown,* 200–208.

59. John H. Stringfellow.

60. A Virginian who migrated to Missouri in his youth, Thomas Johnson (1802–65) became a missionary to the Shawnee Indians in Kansas for the Methodist Episcopal church during the 1830s. He returned to his missionary labors in 1847 and was generally thought to have introduced slaves into the Kansas Territory. Johnson was a proslavery member of the first territorial legislature but later supported the Union cause in the Civil War. Blackmar, *Kansas,* 2:35–36.

61. William Barbee of Bourbon County, Kansas, commanded the Second Brigade of the proslavery territorial militia until his death in 1856 or 1857. "Correspondence of Governor Geary," *Kansas State Historical Society Collections* 4 (1886–88): 420; "Executive Minutes of Governor Geary," 628.

62. Territorial supreme court associate justice Sterling G. Cato was a proslavery partisan, often riding with Border Ruffian raids on free state settlements. Cato resisted Governor John W. Geary's attempts to pressure him to try proslavery guerrillas for assaults on free staters and later refused Governor Robert Walker's requests for writs to ensure fair territorial elections. Nichols, *Bleeding Kansas,* 127, 157, 160–63, 182, 198.

63. Redpath reported John Calhoun's remarks at the "Law and Order" convention in Leavenworth on November 15, 1855, for the *St. Louis Daily Missouri Democrat* on November 26, 1855.

64. An allusion to Sir John Falstaff, a ribald fictional character in William Shakespeare's plays *Henry IV, Part I, Henry IV, Part II,* and *The Merry Wives of Windsor.*

65. The Lecompton constitution was written and ratified in a fashion that perverted the popular sovereignty doctrine of the author of the original Kansas-Nebraska Act of 1854, Democratic senator Stephen A. Douglas. Douglas and a small number of northern Democrats broke with President James Buchanan and the rest of the party and joined Republicans in resisting congressional admission of Kansas to the Union under that constitution. The Senate narrowly accepted the Lecompton constitution, but the House rejected it in April 1858. A compromise measure resubmitted the entire constitution to Kansas voters, who rejected it by a six-to-one margin in an August 1858 referendum. Nichols, *Disruption of American Democracy,* 159–80; Rawley, *Race and Politics,* 223–34, 244–56.

66. William F. Fain was a deputy U.S. marshal for the Kansas Territory. He is most famous for his failure to arrest John Brown, whom he had apprehended after the Battle of Black Jack. Fain released Brown because he had lost the arrest warrant. Wilder, *Annals of Kansas,* 127, 130; Nichols, *Bleeding Kansas,* 103, 123.

67. Probably a reference to free state leader Samuel Walker. At the request of Governor Wilson Shannon after the Battle of Black Jack in 1856 Walker had mobilized the Bloomington Rifles, which he commanded as captain. Later that summer Henry Titus led an attack by proslavery gunmen on Walker's home, but the latter's free state friends drove off Titus. In August, after a fight near Leavenworth, Walker's men captured Titus and exchanged him for free state prisoners. The following year, Governor John W. Geary mobilized the companies and commanded Titus and Walker to arrest Charles Hays, the murderer of David C. Buffum. Walker eventually rose to the rank of brigadier general of militia when free staters won control of the territorial government. Nichols, *Bleeding Kansas,* 115, 123, 130–31, 136–39, 143, 162–63, 207–8, 227–29.

68. Kansas Territory's first delegate elected to Congress, John Wilkins Whitfield (1818–79) migrated to Tecumseh, Kansas, from Tennessee in the early 1850s. A spokesman for the proslavery cause, he lost his race for reelection in October 1855 to former territorial governor Andrew A. Reeder. In subsequent territorial politics, Whitfield remained a proponent of the proslavery party and was appointed register of the Doniphan land office by President James Buchanan. During the Civil War, he served as a captain in the Confederate cavalry. Blackmar, *Kansas,* 2:909–10; Nichols, *Bleeding Kansas,* 22, 123, 157; *Biographical Directory of the American Congress, 1774–1961* (Washington, D.C., 1961), 1915.

69. In October 1856 Deputy Marshal William J. Preston and a detachment of the U.S. cavalry halted a free state party of twenty wagons entering the Kansas Territory near Archer. Citing Governor John W. Geary's recent proclamation as authority, Preston searched the wagons for arms and munitions and arrested the group. The cavalry soon released the settlers and gave them rations to continue their journey. "Correspondence of Governor Geary," 584.

70. Col. Thomas Emory led the proslavery unit known as the Leavenworth Regulators. Emory's group was responsible for the murder of free stater William Phillips. A "Frederic Emory," possibly the same man, served as secretary of state for William Walker's short-lived filibuster government of Lower California in 1853–54. Scroggs, *Filibusters and Financiers,* 40; Wilder, *Annals of Kansas,* 147; Nichols, *Bleeding Kansas,* 135, 148–49.

71. On January 17, 1856, proslavery Missourians and Kansans attacked free staters in Leavenworth while the latter were conducting an election. The press of the free state *Territorial Register* was thrown into the nearby Missouri River. Fighting between groups of pro- and antislavery settlers in the vicinity continued over the next few days. A free state militia captain named Reese P. Brown was shot and killed by the proslavery band known as the Kickapoo Rangers. *St. Louis Daily Missouri Democrat,* January 29 and February 6, 1856; *New York Tribune,* February 4, 1856; Nichols, *Bleeding Kansas,* 82–83.

72. Founded in late 1854 and edited by John H. Stringfellow and Robert S. Kelley, the *Atchison Squatter Sovereign* followed an ardently proslavery course until sold to free stater Samuel Pomeroy in late 1856. *St. Louis Daily Missouri Democrat,* February 1856; *Doniphan Crusader of Freedom,* January 16, 1856; Nichols, *Bleeding Kansas,* 25–26, 213–14.

73. On April 30, 1856, Robert S. Kelley and other militant proslavery residents of Atchison, Kansas, had tarred and feathered the free state Campbellite minister Pardee Butler (1816–88) and expelled him from the town. The previous summer, Butler had been seized by an Atchison mob and sent down the Missouri River on a raft as punishment for his antislavery opinions. Butler eventually returned to his Kansas settlement. *Chicago Tribune,* May 15, 1856; [A. Morrall], "Brief Autobiography," 130; David Edwin Harrell, Jr., "Pardee Butler: Kansas Crusader," *Kansas Historical Quarterly* 34 (Winter 1968): 386–408; Nichols, *Bleeding Kansas,* 40–41, 102, 118.

74. The *Kansas Weekly Herald* was launched in Leavenworth in September 1854. After a change of ownership, Lucian J. Eastlin became editor the following year. Under Eastlin, the

Herald adopted a strongly proslavery position. He also served as a member of the proslavery territorial legislature and a brigadier general of militia. *St. Louis Daily Missouri Democrat,* November 9 and 21 and December 8, 1855; Elmer L. Clark, "Southern Interest in Territorial Kansas, 1854–1858," *Kansas State Historical Society Collections* 15 (1919–22): 350; Nichols, *Bleeding Kansas,* 25–26.

75. Redpath alludes to the shipping firm of Majors and Russell, which had relocated its depot from Westport, Missouri, to Leavenworth in early 1855. The firm employed more than one thousand men to drive its supply wagons to widely scattered western army bases and settlements. Nichols, *Bleeding Kansas,* 19, 31; Malin, *John Brown,* 545.

III.

SLAVE-HUNTING IN KANSAS.

THE most romantic passages of Kansas history have never yet been penned. I will relate two authentic incidents, as specimens of these narratives suppressed; and will give them, as nearly as I remember, in the language of a noble friend,[1] who related, and participated in the scenes described.

I had been speaking of the first slave who escaped from Missouri by the Kansas and Nebraska Underground Railroad, and remarked that I was proud of the fact that I had armed them, and otherwise assisted them to continue their heroic and arduous journey.[2]

"That railroad," my friend said, "does a very brisk business now. I'll tell you an incident of its history."

CLUBBING SLAVE-HUNTERS.

"A slave, named —— ——, escaped from Rates County, Missouri, and succeeded in reaching Lawrence. There, he was put in the track of the Underground Railroad, and was soon safely landed in Canada. He wrote to our President, announcing his arrival, and urging him to tell his wife of it and to aid her to escape.

"Next morning after the letter arrived, our mutual friend—left Lawrence for Missouri. He went to the woman, told her of her husband's wish, and, after sunset, started her for Lawrence. They reached it in safety, and were beyond Topeka, when the slave-hunters overtook them, overpowered them and arrested the woman. She had two children with her. They put them in their covered wagon, and drove rapidly towards home. They gagged her; but, in passing H——'s house, she tore off the bandage and shouted for help. He happened to be out of doors at the time—it was night—and instantly mounted his horse. He came down to Lawrence, and roused us from our beds. We dressed ourselves hastily, (there were three of us,) ran to the stable, and put after the Missourians. We rode at full speed for nearly four hours, when, shortly after midnight, in turning a bend of the road in the woods, we came up right suddenly on the slave-hunters. There were three of them on horseback, and one driving the wagon. They had heard us coming, and waited for our approach, and fired simultaneously as soon as we saw them. Crack, crack, crack, went our pistols in return! One fellow tumbled from his horse, which ran away, dragging him along as it went.

"'Charge!' shouted Col.——. 'Club them!'

"We were mounted on splendid large horses, while the slave-hunters were on shabby little Indian ponies. This gave us a great advantage over them in charging. I seized my navy pistol by the barrel; rode straight upon one fellow; and, raising the weapon, brought it down with all my strength on his head. The colonel did the same with the other man. I supposed that we killed them, for they fell and never moved again. The first man who had been shot, was badly wounded; but, I supposed at the time, not fatally. Yet, I do n't *know* it; for we did n't wait to see!

"When the fellow who was driving the wagon saw the first man tumble, he lashed his horses and tried to keep them at a gallop. But the negro woman sprang up, caught hold of him by the neck, and tried to pull him over into the wagon. —— rode after the fugitives, overtook them, cocked his revolver, and put it close to the slave-hunter's head. He shouted savagely:

"'Surrender! d— you, or here goes!'

"He did n't need to repeat the order. The fellow cried for mercy, jumped out of the wagon, and ran off as fast as his legs could carry him.

"'I'm cursed sorry he surrendered!' said ——, 'my mouth was watering for a shot at him!'

"We turned round the wagon, let the horses of the slave-hunters go, left the bodies of the Missourians lying on the prairie, and drove back as rapidly as we came from Lawrence. —— drove the wagon a couple of hundred miles. It is now regularly employed in the service of the U. G. R. R.

"The fire of the Missourians injured a hat, and a cravat; a ball went through them; but that was all the damage done."

"All?" I asked.

"Yes, that's all."

"But, the Missourians?"

"Oh! yes; we heard that they were found on the prairie, *dead;* but, then, the woman and her two children, once mere property, are now human beings, and alive. I guess they will answer instead of the Missourians, when the great roll of humanity is called!

"No one but we three (with H—— and the woman), ever heard of this affair. We reached Lawrence before sunrise, put our horses up, slipped quietly to our rooms in the hotel, and no one supposed we had been out of bed."

FATE OF THE —————— GUARDS.

"But that scene was nothing when compared with the charge on the —————— Guards. Oh, God!"

My friend shuddered violently.

Everybody who is familiar with the history of Kansas has heard of the —————— Guards. They were a gang of Missouri highwaymen and horse-thieves, who organized under the lead of ——— ——— ———, the Kansas correspondent of a leading pro-slavery paper,[3] when the Territorial troubles first broke out in the spring of 1855.

After sacking a little Free-State town on the Santa Fé road, and committing other petty robberies and misdemeanors, they were attacked, in the summer of '56, by a celebrated Free-State captain, and defeated by a force of less than one-half their numerical strength.[4] They were kept as prisoners until released by the troops. Capt. ——, satisfied with his laurels, then retired from the tented field. But the company continued to exist and still lived by robbery. Shortly after the Xenophon[5] of the Kansas prairies left them, they elected, as their captain, a ruffian of most infamous character and brutal nature. He presently was known to have committed outrages on the persons of three Free-State mothers.

I will now report the narrative of my friend:

"Capt.—— and the boys, when they were convinced of the crimes these marauders had committed, resolved to follow them and fight them until the very last man was either banished or exterminated. We heard one night that they were encamped in a ravine near ——. We cleaned our guns, filled our cartridge boxes with ammunition, and left our quarters with as stern a purpose as ever animated men since hostilities were known.

"It was about midnight when we began our march. A cold, misty, disagreeable night. We marched in silence until we came within a mile of the ravine. Then the captain ordered us to halt. There were thirty men of us. He divided us into two companies or platoons in order to get the highwaymen between a cross fire. We could see their camp lights twinkling in the distance. We then made an extended detour and slowly approached the ravine. Not a word was spoken. Every man stepped slowly and cautiously and held in his breath as we drew near to the camp of the enemy. We knelt down until we heard a crackling noise among the brush on the opposite side, which announced the presence and approach of our other platoon.

"The ——— Guards heard it also, and sprang to their feet. They numbered twenty-two men.

"Our captain, then, in a deep, resounding voice, gave the order:

"'*Attention!* COMPANY!'

"The ——— Guards, hitherto huddled together around the fires, tried to form in line and seize their arms.

"But it was too late.

"'*Take aim!*'

"Every man of us took a steady aim at the marauders, whose bodies the camp fires fatally exposed.

"'FIRE!'

"Hardly had the terrible word been uttered ere the roar of thirty rifles, simultaneously discharged, was succeeded by the wildest, most unearthly shriek that ever rose from mortals since the earth was peopled.

"I saw two of them leap fearfully into the air. I saw no more. I heard no more. That shriek unmanned me. I reeled backward until I found a tree to lean against. The boys told me afterwards that I had fainted. I was not ashamed of it.

"'March!'

"I obeyed the command mechanically. We marched back in truly solemn silence. I had walked a mile or two before I noticed that the other platoon was not with us.

"I asked where it was.

"'*Burying them,*' was the brief and significant response.

"'Were they all killed, then?'

"'Every one of them.'

"I shuddered then: I can 't think of it yet without shuddering."

My friend did not speak figuratively when he said so; for he shuddered in earnest—in evident pain—as he related these facts. But it was not an unmanly weakness that caused it, for he instantly added:

"That scene haunts me. It was a terrible thing to do. But it was right—a grand act of retributive justice—and I thank God, now, that I was 'in at the death' of those marauders. No one ever missed them; they were friendless vagrants. God help them! I hope the stern lesson taught them humanity!

"What do you think of it? Do n't you think it was right?"

"It was the grandest American act since Bunker Hill," I said.

THE END.

NOTES

1. While impossible to identify conclusively, the friend who took part in both events probably was John Henri Kagi, one of John Brown's closest lieutenants.

2. Redpath did not relate this incident in any of his other writings on Kansas.

3. Redpath appears to be referring to Henry Clay Pate, the Kansas correspondent of the proslavery *St. Louis Republican* and a Border Ruffian captain. Some sources state that Pate's unit was the Shannon Sharp Shooters. Wilder, *Annals of Kansas,* 131.

4. Probably a reference to the Battle of Black Jack in June 1856, where John Brown's band defeated and killed or captured most of Pate's "Sharp Shooter" militia company. Wilder, *Annals of Kansas,* 199–201; Nichols, *Bleeding Kansas,* 120–23.

5. Xenophon (c. 428–c. 354 B.C.), an Athenian, led an expedition of Greek mercenaries to fight in a civil war in Persia. After its side lost, Xenophon's band had a harrowing retreat back to safety in Greece. M. C. Howatson, ed., *The Oxford Companion to Classical Literature* (New York, 1989), 601–2.

APPENDIXES

APPENDIX 1.
ITINERARY OF JAMES REDPATH'S
TOURS OF THE SOUTH

First Tour

Late March 1854	Departs New York, N.Y.
March 30, 1854	Richmond, Va.
March 31–April 1, 1854	Wilmington, N.C.
April 4–late April 1854	Charleston, S.C.
Late April–early June 1854	Savannah, Ga.

Second Tour

Mid-September 1854	Departs New York, N.Y.
September 20–23, 1854	Richmond, Va.
September 23–24, 1854	Petersburg, Va.
September 26–29, 1854	Weldon, N.C.
Early October	Wilmington, N.C.
Mid-October 1854	Manchester, N.C.
Late October 1854	Columbia, S.C.
November 6?–25, 1854	Augusta, Ga.
December 1854	Atlanta, Ga.
Mid- to late December 1854	Montgomery, Ala.
Late January–late May 1855	New Orleans, La.
Late May 1855	Departs for St. Louis, Mo.

Third Tour

May 11, 1857	Departs from Boston, Mass.
May 14–15, 1857	Alexandria, Va.
May 17, 1857	Fairfax Court House, Va.
May 18–19, 1857	Warrenton, Va.
C. May 20, 1857	Charlottesville, Va.
May 23–24, 1857	Richmond, Va.

Appendix 2

List of All Known

John Ball, Jr., and

Jacobius Letters

Date of Composition	Original Publication: Place and date	Location in the original Roving Editor	Location in the edited Roving Editor
1. July 20, 1854*	Boston *Liberator*, August 4, 1854	pp. 4–10	pp. 20–25
2. April 1, 1854*	Boston *Liberator*, August 11, 1854	pp. 11–24	pp. 28–36
3. April 4, 1854*	Boston *Liberator*, September 1, 1854	pp. 25–35, 39–48	pp. 39–45, 49–56
4. April 10, 1854*	Boston *Liberator*, September 8, 1854	pp. 50–60, 62–67	pp. 58–67, 69–74

Appendix 2 (*continued*)

	Date	Source		
18.	March 10, 1855	*New York National Anti-Slavery Standard*, March 31, 1855		pp. 162–65
19.	March 15, 1855	*New York National Anti-Slavery Standard*, April 7, 1855		Appendix 6
20.	March 16, 1855	*New York National Anti-Slavery Standard*, April 14, 1855		Appendix 7
21.	March 10, 1856	*New York National Anti-Slavery Standard*, March 22, 1856		Appendix 8
22.	February 1, 1857	*Boston Liberator*, February 20, 1857		Appendix 9
23.	February 25, 1857	*New York National Anti-Slavery Standard*, March 7, 1857	pp. 179–84	Appendix 10
24.	May 14 & 21, 1857	*Boston Daily Evening Traveller*, May 23, 1857	pp. 199–212	pp. 180–88
25.	May 17, 1857	*Boston Daily Evening Traveller*, June 6, 1857	pp. 213–25	pp. 191–99
26.	May 18, 1857	*Boston Daily Evening Traveller*, June 13, 1857	pp. 226–35	pp. 200–206

*Probably a fictitious date.

Appendix 3. White Slaves South.

Liberty Lodge, Far South,
Nov. 25, 1854.

William Lloyd Garrison:

Dear Sir,—I have just read a letter, signed C.K.W., on the 'Unwritten Articles' in our National 'covenant with death and agreement with hell,' which was copied from a recent number of *The Liberator* by the *Anti-Slavery Standard* of Nov. 18. I wish to make a few strictures on its sentiments. You know that I am a radical Abolitionist. Born a member of a disfranchised class, I have always opposed oppression, in every form in which I have encountered it. Therefore, I have never subscribed any formula of doctrines, religious or political, and never shall enlist myself under the banners of any party—even any pro-liberty party—unless freedom of individual opinion, and its public expression, are willingly permitted by its leaders. The party of which you are the honored chief allows of such dissent. Of this privilege, I purpose at present to avail myself.

After narrating the incident, of which the 'damned plain' Theodore Parker, of Boston, was the hero—or otherwise, your valiant correspondent, C.K.W., thus expresses his opinion of his conduct, and of the conduct of Abolitionists in these Southern States:—

'Now, this particular incident may be a mere joke, manufactured from no other real material than the resemblance between the names, and Mr. Theodore D. Parker may never have conducted in *the shabby manner* imputed to him in the story; but I refer to it, because it is the exact type of many real conversations which are constantly taking place throughout the Southern States; because all slaveholders assume the right to make this sort of impertinent inquisition; and because the great majority of Northern men who travel at the South quietly submit to it, in many cases, without even a suspicion that they are degraded by so doing.

'It has happened to me frequently, in debate with both Northern and Southern men on the subject of slavery, to be told that Abolitionists would have no difficulty in travelling or residing at the South, if they would keep their opinions to themselves, and be careful not to talk to the colored people, nor take anti-slavery newspapers, nor let themselves be publicly known as Abolitionists, and the minds of these persons had become so accustomed to the requisition of this subserviency by Southern men, and its concession by Southern doughfaces, that they really saw nothing objectionable in it; really failed to perceive that such conduct is an arbitrary annihilation on one side, and *a cowardly surrender* on the other, of that indispensable safeguard of liberty, freedom of speech and of the press.

It is refreshing, in contrast with the demeanor of *these white slaves,* to read the eminently perpendicular letter recently addressed, through the newspapers, to the Rev. Nehemiah Adams, of Boston, by Henry A. Wise, of Virginia.'

The italics are my own.

After thus stigmatizing the *silent* Abolitionists of the South as cowards and white slaves, he proceeds to eulogize the 'manhood' of the foolish Mr. Wise, and his fellow-cowards, the slaveholders of the Old Dominion, in this wise:—

'It must be admitted that, however the slaveholders may fall short of being just, humane, democratic or Christian, they possess, eminently, this element of manliness; that

'"They know their rights, and, knowing, dare maintain." However erroneous may be their assumption of a right to buy and sell human beings, they understand the real right of manfully expressing their own opinions, and would scorn the idea of submitting to be gagged.'

The word italicised was so distinguished by the writer.

I most cordially endorse the concluding sentiments of your correspondent's letter, that 'there needs a reeducation of this whole people in the principles of freedom, and as a preliminary step towards this, an understanding that such traitors to liberty as Dr. Adams and Pres. Lord cannot be true teachers of Christianity'; but I nullify the arguments (or sneers rather) which preceded this, his concluding opinion.

C.K.W. is evidently one of those gentlemen of New England, who live at home at ease, and therefore little does he think about the dangers that are braved by those Abolitionists of the Southern States, who remain true to their principles. He does not seem to be aware that there is a masterly as well as a slavish silence.

I have lived in this State for nearly three months in succession, without any of my acquaintances suspecting me of being an Abolitionist. Placed in similar circumstances, I would again act as I have hitherto acted. What has been the result of my silence policy? I have done more, I believe, to disseminate Abolitionism among the slaves, than any 'fanatic' who ever visited this State. *How* I have done so, it would be imprudent to relate. I have seen evils, springing out of the slave system, of which few Northern men even suspect the existence. I have seen, also, in how many different methods our cause may be advanced in the Southern States. I have listened to confidential lamentations and curses—excuse the phrase—uttered by prominent pro-slavery men, as they spoke of the progress of Garrisonian ideas at the North. I have learned facts which will yet crush many of the false assertions that at present are so boldly advanced as truths by pro-slavery preachers and politicians North. I will yet attain a position here that will enable me to give a *succession* of well-aimed stabs at the Southern Baal.

Had I acted as C.K.W. seems to advise, what would have been the result? Probably, I would have been shot or hanged, or tarred and feathered, or ridden on a rail; certainly, I would speedily have been compelled to leave the slave States, and been 'passed round' by the pro-slavery press.

Wherever I have gone, however, I have argued the question of slavery with several persons—argued it as a friend of the negro? What has been the result? A narrow escape once; fruitless exertion always. Sir, the heart of the public of the South is HARDENED; slavery, when it is abolished, will be ended by fear of revolt or by Northern influence. The South cherishes the wrong. It will not listen to arguments. It answers them by falsehood always, and sometimes with personal insult also. The tyranny of the majority in the slave States is the most terrible despotism that the world has ever seen. Liberty of speech does not exist here. The press is enslaved as effectually as the negro. The pulpit is simply a forger of spiritual chains for the planter's interests.

It is because I know these facts that I am silent. I fear nothing. If my sense of duty told me to speak, I would speak in spite of every danger. But, as I can *work* in silence, and not otherwise, I shall remain yet, for a season, as Abolitionist 'citizen of the great Empire of Silence.'

Pray, C.K.W., what 'manliness' is manifested by Mr. Wise in publishing his letter? Does it require any courage to utter the opinions of the powers that be, or of the majority of the people? I think not. Slaveholders are NOT manly. Slaveholders are a race of cowards—for none but cowards would live by robbing the poor of the fruits of their industry. They are *bullies,* not 'braves.'

No Union with Slaveholders; no eulogium of their imaginary manliness!

Ever, yours and the slave's,
JOHN BALL, JR.

Boston Liberator, December 8, 1854.

Appendix 4. A Letter from the South

In Georgia, Nov. 25.

Farewell, my favourite Southern City! Willingly would I spend a few years of my life in Charleston; for I love its old customs; its pleasant suburbs; its beautiful promenade by the river; its proud-souled sons; and, above all, its warm-hearted and beautiful daughters. I hate its hatred of Liberty, and all its embodiments of that spirit—the *Mercury,* for example, and the Sugar House, the night-watchmen and the Mayor's Court, where iniquity is daily enacted in the forms of law; but, in spite of all these and other of its offences against Justice, I love the high-spirited city of Calhoun.

But I dare not sacrifice my principles to my happiness, and therefore I have taken my departure in peace—not caring, also, to leave it in costumes of other's choosing.

I sailed from Charleston to Savannah. The bay of Charleston is a beautiful bay. Nature has evidently designed it as the entrance to a metropolitan city. Charleston, I believe, is destined to be the New York of the Southern States. Perhaps it may yet be the rival of that city—but not before Slavery is abolished, not in South Carolina alone, but in every State of the North American Continent. The day is rapidly approaching when that event shall be consummated. "When the task of brick is doubled"—say the Mystics—"Moses is near." If this saying be true, the Southern Moses is not far off! Emancipation is coming—of that I am assured—but whether it will come from the North, clad in the robes of peace, or from the cabins of the South, armed with the terrors of a servile war—that it is impossible to forsee. My earnest prayer is—"Emancipation, peacefully if possible; but, at any cost—Emancipation."

Charleston supports four daily newspapers. The *Courier* has the largest circulation. It prints about ten thousand copies. The Charleston *Evening News*—a semi-literary sheet—claims to be second in rank of popularity; its proprietors say that its circulation is only one-sixth less that of the *Courier.* I believe that this assertion is false—the *Standard,* if I am correctly informed, is the second in point of circulation. The *Mercury*—the

celebrated fire-eating journal and the organ of the Southern Disunion-
ists—is reported to print about six or seven thousand copies daily. If the
proprietors of the *Evening News* speak truly of *their* circulation, the celebrated *Mercury* has the smallest circulation of the journals of Charleston!

The *Mercury* is owned by Messrs. Heart & Taber. Taber is the Editor;
Heart the man of business. It is Taber who writes those ultra pro-slavery
leaders, that are so often quoted by Northern journals. Taber is a true
type of the South Carolinian. He is an aristocrat worthy of High Tory
adoration. He is a despiser of Compromises. He deserves to be admired
for his consistency. A few years ago, when the subject of education was
agitated in his State, he said, in the South Carolina legislature, that the
poor had no more right to education than the slaves. This remark produced great excitement out-of-doors. Democracy started in surprise! His
opponents seized the opportunity of increasing his unpopularity—and
succeeded. He has never regained the popularity he lost by that *consistent*
remark. How long will the working class refuse to see that Democracy is
incompatible with the Institution of Slavery? In the slave States there is
no Democracy.* The slave States are *Republics;* the free States are alone
democracies. Newspapers South never speak of the PEOPLE; politicians seldom engage or try to win favour of the working men; they talk of 'the
public'—just as English journals do—and court the favour of Planters,
who form the Ruling class. In the South the People are secretly feared or
secretly despised; they are seldom courted or flattered. By People I mean
the Lower Million and the Mechanics; by Public I mean the privileged
classes.

Charleston has several good hotels and a handsome theatre. Its public
edifices are built in the old English style.

Charleston has also produced—"a poet!" So is Mr. John Russell styled
by the Charleston *Mercury.* A slavish rhymer—that, in my opinion, is his
true definition. I once read, in your journal, a poem on Nebraska, by, I
believe, the late unhappy William North, which, I thought, truly "defined
the position" of a *real* Poet on the subject of Slavery. Here is the stanza—
it has often been repeated by me in the forests and cotton fields of the
South:

> Let the Irish Renegade,
>   Born a Slave of Slavish Race,
> Bow before the Southern Baal,
>   In his mantle of Disgrace,
> He who turned his back on Honour,

* Of course, I do not allude to the political party, so-called.

Well may cringe to slavers grim,
Well may volunteer to rivet
    Fetters on the Negro's limb.

But the Poet has no pity,
    For the human beast of prey;
Boldly speaks he, though the Heaven
    And the Earth should pass away;
Aye—tho' thrones and Empires crumble,
    Races perish in the strife,
Still, he speaks the solemn warning,
    Live for the Eternal Life.

Mr. John Russell, however, is "a poet" of a very different class. He is an ally of the Parole-breaker; not his antagonist. The *Mercury* published the subjoined extract from his forth-coming poem. It is entitled "the Hireling and the Slave." The *Mercury* introduces its extract with these extremely eulogistic remarks:

"The author, who has acted an honoured part in the literature and politics of South Carolina, has improved the leisure of his retirement from public life, by taking up the most tangled social and political question of our times, and treating it in the true spirit of Pope, and with a grace of expression, a pungency of satire, a fullness of knowledge, and a richness of fancy that would not have discredited that great moralist. We have read this brilliant Poem with almost unmixed gratification. It recalls the time when English poetry was something more than feathery fancies, heartless sentimentalities, crooked conceits, and the small bubbles of vanity; when the Poet was a teacher, who fearlessly explored the great problems of life, and allowed fancy only to choose the dress, while reason furnished forth the body of his effusions.

The author has three main topics—the Philanthropists, the Peasantry of Europe, and Slaves of America. The two former form the subject of the first part, and the latter of the second. We might quote many passages to illustrate the force and grace and truthfulness of this work, but we prefer to make a single extract from the opening of Part 2d. It presents a scene equally true and beautiful."

Where hireling millions toil, in doubt and fear,
For food and clothing, all the weary year,
Content and grateful if their Masters give
The boon they humbly beg—to work and live,
While dreamers task their idle wits to find

A short hand method to enrich mankind;
And Fourier's scheme and Owen's deep device,
The drooping hearts of list'ning crowds entice
With rising wages, and decreasing toil,
With bounteous crops from ill-attended soil;
If, while the anxious multitudes appear,
Now glad with hope, now yielding to dispair,
A Seraph form, descending from the skies,
In mercy sent, should meet their wond'ring eyes,
And smiling, promise all the good they crave,
The homes, the food, the clothing of the Slave;
Restraint from vice, exemption from the cares
The pauper Hireling ever feels or fears;
And, at their death, these blessings to renew,
That wives and children may enjoy them too;
That, when disease or age their strength impairs,
Subsistence and a home should still be their's;
What wonder would the promised boon impart,
What grateful rapture swells the Peasant's heart;
How freely would the hungry list'ner give
A life-long labour, thus secure to live!

And yet the life, so unassailed by care,
So blessed with moderate work, with ample fare;
With all the good the pauper Hireling needs,
The happier Slave on each plantation leads;
Safe from harassing doubts and annual fears,
He dreads no famine in unfruitful years;
If harvests fail, from inauspicious skies,
The Master's providence his food supplies;
No paupers perish here for want of bread,
Or lingering live, by foreign bounty fed;
No exiled trales of homeless peasants go,
In distant climes to tell their tales of woe;
Far other fortune, free from care and strife,
For work or bread, attends the Negro's life;
And Christian Slaves may challenge as their own,
The blessing claimed in fabled States alone—
The cabin home not comfortless, though rude,
Light daily labour and abundant food,
The sturdy health that temperate habits yield,
The cheerful song that rings in every field;

The long, loud laugh, that freemen seldom share,
Heaven's boon to bosoms unapproached by care,
And boisterous jest and humour unrefined,
That leave, though rough, no painful sting behind;
While, nestling near, to bless their humble lot,
Warm, social joys surround the Negro's cot;
The evening dance its merriment imparts,
Love, with his rapture, fills their youthful hearts;
And placid age, the task of labour done,
Enjoys the summer shade, the winter's sun;
And, as through life, no pauper want he knows,
Laments no poor-house penance at its close.

   His too Christian privilege to share
The weekly festival of praise and prayer;
For him the Sabbath shines with holier light,
The air is balmier, and the sky more bright;
Winter's brief suns with warmer radiance glow,
With softer breath the gales of Autumn blow;
Spring with new flow'rs more richly strew the ground,
And Summer spreads a fresher verdue round.
The early shower is past; the joyous breeze
Shakes pattering raindrops from the rustling trees,
And with the sun, the fragrant offerings rise,
From Nature's censers to the bounteous skies.
With cheerful aspect in his best array,
To the far forest church he take his way;
With kind salute the passing neighbour meets,
With awkward grace the morning traveller greets;
And joined by crowds, that gather as he goes,
Seeks the calm joy the Sabbath morn bestows.

   There no proud temple to devotion rise,
With marble domes that emulate the skies;
But bosomed in primeval trees, that spread
Their limbs o'er mouldering mansions of the dead,
Moss tinctured oaks and solemn pines between,
Of modest wood, the house of God is seen,
By shaded springs, that from the sloping land
Bubble and sparkle through the silver sand;
Where high o'er arching laurel blossoms blow,
Where fragrant bays breathe kindred sweets below;
And elm and ash their blended arms entwine

With the bright foliage of the mantling vine;
In quiet chat, before the hour of prayer,
Masters and Slaves in scattered groups appear;
Loosed from the carriage, in the shades around,
Impatient horses neigh and paw the ground;
No city discords break the silence here,
No sound unmeet offend the listener's ear;
But rural melodies of flocks and birds,
The lowing, far and faint, of distant herds;
The mocking bird, with minstrel pride elate,
The partridge whistling for its absent mate;
The thrush's soft solitary notes prolong,
Bold, merry blackbirds swell the general song;
And cautious crows their harsher voices join,
In concert, cawing, from the loftiest pine.

When now the Pastor lifts his earnest eyes,
And hands outstretched, a suppliant to the skies;
No rites of pomp or pride beguile the soul,
No organs peal, no clouds of incense roll.
But, line by line, untutored voices raise,
Like the wild birds, their simple notes of praise;
And hearts of love, with true devotion bring,
Incense more pure to Heaven's eternal King;
On glorious themes their humble thoughts employ,
And rise transported with no earthly joy;
The blessing said, the service o'er, again
Their swelling voices raise the sacred strain;
Lingering, they love to sing of Jordan's shore,
Where sorrows cease and toil is known no more.

The first stanza is a rhythmical repetition of Calhoun's absurd assertion that Slavery is a practical realization of the problem which French philosophy has been trying to solve for the last eighty years. It is so—with a difference! The difference, namely, between churchyard order and Christian harmony!

The argument in favour of Slavery drawn from the *supposed* condition of the people of Europe and the actual state of the English lower class is a favourite one in the Southern States. I have often heard pro-slavery men assert that Southern slaves are uniformly better off than even the Northern working-classes! Admitting these assertions to be true, for the sake of argument, as I often have done—I have frequently annoyed them by adding—

"Well, what of it? Does that prove Slavery to be a good?"

"Why, of course, it does. Why don't the Abolitionists abolish Pauperism before they try to abolish Slavery?"

"They do. All the prominent anti-slavery leaders are prominent pauperism Abolitionists also. They do all that lies in their power to abolish the curse of the North as well as the crime of the South. What Church has done so much to alleviate the condition of the poor as the New York *Tribune?* All the churches of the North put together have done less to root out Pauperism than the anti-slavery men and journals."

I have frequently advanced these facts; but *cui bono?* They 'know better'—they cherish error.

SAVANNAH!

I passed through Savannah. It presents a very desolate appearance. The shade-trees blown down; the ruins of the recent hurricane and flood everywhere visible; the melancholy-creative colour of the Autumnal leaves; the immeasurable new-made graves in the Cemeteries—all conspired to cast a gloom around the city (or my spirit) which made me glad to depart from it as speedily as possible.

In walking along the pleasantly-shaded road that leads to the Catholic Cemetery, I met an aged negro. It was on Sunday.

"Good day, Uncle."

"Good mornin', mass'r."

"Who do you belong to?"

He told me.

"Hired out?"

"No, mass'r, I works on the boss's plantation."

"What's your 'lowance?"

"A peck of meal, mass'r."

"What else?"

"Nothin', mass'r, at all; we has a little piece of ground that we digs and plants. We raises vegetables and we has a few chickens. We sells them (vegetables and eggs) on Sunday and buys a piece of bacon with de money when we kin, mass'r."

"That pretty hard 'lowance."

"Yes, mass'r, it is dat; but we can't help dat."

* * *

"Did you ever know a slave who would rather be in bondage than free?"

"I neber *did,* mass'r."

You may have noticed the extraordinarily small number of coloured people who died from the yellow fever, in comparison with the list of its white victims. Ludicrous and curious are the reasons advanced to account for this difference. "No care on their minds," say some; "come from a warm climate," says another—"two centuries ago?" inquired I, ironically. The *true* Reason is that the whites are effeminate and enfeebled by idleness, debauchery and drunkenness, while the blacks are industrious, temperate and *as virtuous as their constitution admits of.* Of course, I do not mean to infer that the coloured female slaves are chaste: *for it is utterly impossible for chastity and slavery to exist in the same city or State.* Coloured females *must* submit either to their masters or to others. For almost every young man in a southern city, there is somewhere around a little coloured child uncommonly like him! I have jocularly talked "on a certain subject" with hundreds of young boys in the slave States;* but I *never yet* met or heard of any boy of above 14 years of age who had not violated at least *one* of the commandments. Guess which one! Let clergymen think of this fact: let Gardiner Spring pray for its continuance.

Savannah is a city of some 20,000 inhabitants.

How many policemen, do you think it requires to keep the peace there? *Eighty-one mounted Guards.*

There are larger cities in the Northern States with but *one* constable, and he engaged only occasionally in performing his official duties!

Who pay the expenses of this Guard—for the salaries of the eighty-one, for the purchase, and feed, and accoutrements of the horses?

Chiefly, *the non-slaveholding population.*

Let "Democratic" supporters of slavery reflect on this fact!

In all slaveholding cities, the Lawyers form the richest and most influential class.

Let the People think of this fact; let them remember, too, that Lawyers are the leeches of the body politic.

JOHN BALL, JR.

New York National Anti-Slavery Standard, December 16, 1854.

---

* The writer is a young working-man.—ED.

APPENDIX 5. A PERSONAL LETTER FROM OUR SOUTHERN CORRESPONDENT.

NEW ORLEANS, Feb. 10, 1855.

EDITORS STANDARD: I have resided in this city for two weeks past, but have not yet found time to reply to your private note or to write a letter for the *Standard.* I shall soon resume my regular correspondence. In the meantime, permit me publicly to allude to several circumstances, in relation to my published letters, of which my friends have informed me by post, since you commenced to print my correspondence.

My *travelling* individuality and veracity have been doubted, I am informed. I can only reply to these charges, that I have actually travelled over the routes mentioned by me and in the manner indicated; and that I wrote all the letters you published, in the city or State from which each is dated. Every conversation that I have recorded was an accurate report of my talks with slaves. Every question and every answer published in the *Standard* was asked by me and answered by the slaves in the Southern States.

On my honour as a gentleman, I declare that not one false statement or fictitious incident is contained in any of my letters. If they contain any errors of fact—and I do not believe they do—I am not responsible for these mistakes.

One of my friends states that the faith of some good people in my veracity has been shaken by my statements concerning the pedestrian journey I have made. They cannot understand, says he, how any man should prefer to go on foot rather than by rail. Did these good people never hear of the post-Collegiate pedestrian journey of the students of Germany? Every educated youth of that great nation makes a grand tour on foot after finishing his Collegiate Education. Every English aristocratic youth of fortune is fond of similar excursions. Young America is too busy money-making to follow their example. But I am not engaged in doing so; money is my aversion—knowledge is my wealth. I have sought it in the cotton fields of the South as well as in the libraries of the North. Walking is one of my greatest pleasures. Goldsmith, the pedestrian as well as poet, justly observed that a country could not be seen from a carriage window.

I know this fact from previous experience; and accordingly I adopted the only mode of travelling in a country by which accurate information of it can be gathered—"I footed it."

Another friend advises me to be more sober-phrased; because my want of sobriety detracts from the moral weight of the facts I furnish. Our good leader, Wm. Lloyd Garrison, was the original advancer of this argument. There is some truth in it; but still I cannot act on it, simply because my letters are a faithful mirror of my feelings at the time of writing them. When I am older, I shall be sober enough. I expect; but, at present "I'm one of the boys and cannot be anything else."

I defy the united slavocracy of the South to prove that I have spoken falsely. Many facts that I have advanced will be doubted or denied; but whoever will follow in my footsteps and speak with the slaves as I spoke to them, and as frequently as I did, will find that I have been a most truthful chronicler.

Yours truly,   JOHN BALL, JR.

New York National Anti-Slavery Standard, March 17, 1855.

Appendix 6. From Our Southern Correspondent.

Woman and Slavery—Slave-children as Servants—Marital Rights and Slavery—Northern Women and Slavery—A Young Southern Authoress on Slavery and Woman's Sphere, &c.

New Orleans, March 15, 1855.

Editors of the Anti-Slavery Standard:

I HAVE explained why it is that Northern Travellers in the slave States so often return with pro-slavery opinions. How comes it that Southern Women who suffer so much by slavery, should support and defend it? That is the question to which I shall devote this letter—or as much of it as is necessary for a reply.

I lately sent you a copy of the *Daily Delta,* in which appeared an anti-Abolitionist article.* The writer quoted a paragraph from Mrs. Swisshelm's journal, in which that Editress, on the authority of a Presbyterian clergyman, made one of the most extraordinary statements relative to the women of the South, that I ever read or heard of. She writes that a young Southern lady, in speaking of the several rival candidates for her hand, said, that she did not think that one of them would make a good husband because he had no slave-children! On being interrogated by this unnamed theologian as to her meaning, she answered, it is said, that it is usual for Southern gentlemen, before marriage, to have children by their slaves, whose destiny or duty it was to attend on their wives! It is added that the lady made this statement as if it was a matter of course rather than a startling assertion. I believe, sir, that nine out of every ten persons who read that anecdote instantly muttered that they did not believe it, or ejaculated that it was a falsehood of that class of lies that are frequently preceded by an adjective which is the anthesis of *blessed.* None of your

---

* See last week's *Standard,* first page, first column.—ED.

readers will be apt to class me with pro-slavery writers. Even Mrs. Swiss-helm, if she peruses my correspondence, must acknowledge that I am an uncompromising Abolitionist. Yet I believe that the statement she published is *untrue*. She owes it to her own reputation and to the cause of Abolition, to compel the clergyman she refers to, to endorse his statement with his name, and to mention at least, the city and State in which the "Southern lady," who made amalgamation the test of masculine amiability, resides. At present, such an anecdote is a pro-slavery argument. Publicly endorsed by its original narrator it will be an equally powerful anti-slavery ally. The public are always willing to believe a personal statement, rather than an anonymous assertion.

I believe that it is untrue, because I have studied Southern society with patient industry, for the special purpose of ascertaining the influence of slavery on the relation of the sexes of the dominent and subjugated races; and, although I have acquired knowledge which it would be neither expedient nor possible to print in a journal with a general circulation, I never once heard of such a practice or even seen symptoms of such a laxity of ethical opinions as would result in so unnatural a toleration of the unlegalized indulgence of the passions. If woman's nature is the same everywhere, Mrs. Swisshelm's anecdote is untrue. I don't profess to understand the better half of humanity—in point of fact, the dear creatures who compose it have always been a puzzle to me—but this I do know, that, for one sin, there is no forgiveness with them. The noblest of them, cannot endure any evidence of the previous pure love or impure passions of their liege lords—unless, indeed, that love was sanctioned by the laws of the land. We have known good step-mothers but what man ever saw a wife cherish the illegitimate child of her husband? What man who always attentively watches the "Unspoken utterances" of the eye, has not heard its "soundless voice" tell of a woman's soul's pang when the name of a previous "lady love" of her husband was accidentally alluded to? It is, I think, ridiculous, to believe that any matron, North or South, could see with indifference the illegitimate offspring of her husband around her, especially when their mothers are still in his power. The anecdote may be true; but the inference drawn from it is not so.

Mrs. Swisshelm says, also, that experience has shown that southern woman are even more earnest opponents of Emancipation than Southern men. I think so, too. It is the case, everywhere. Women as a class are conservatives. A woman has said that her sex cannot reason; that they "are persuaded because they *feel* that a truth exists."* Perhaps this is the reason of their conservative tendencies; for prejudice is often mistaken

---

* Marian Harland.

for truth—and reason and observation alone can distinguish the false from the apparently true.

On this question of slavery, reason is silent in the Southern States. Argument on one side is prohibited alike by public opinion and legal enactments. The friends of Freedom are forced to cherish their political ideas in secret; or are publicly punished by the most ignominious insults if they dare to avow them. The prophets of the olden time were stoned; the Abolitionists of to-day are tarred-and-feathered. In the true sense they are not insulted but honoured, for "it is the crime and not the scaffold that is a disgrace." But such honours are not generally coveted, and the voice of truth is silent in the Southern land.

On this question of slavery, observation, also, is denied to the woman of the South. If the ladies of the Southern States saw slavery as it is, "our Harriet" would instantly be acknowledged as the leader of the most invincible "Light Brigade" that the world ever saw. Slavery would be swept from the face of the earth in less than a year. This glorious South, instead of being the chosen land of obsolete ideas, would gladden the whole world with its sunny philosophy; it would no longer cherish a theology worthy of its birth-places—the damp, subterranean, unhealthy, God's light-excluding cells of the ignorant, bigoted and diseased bachelor-monks of a dark and barbarous age—but would cheer the human race with its heart-felt reiteration of that celestial truth which was announced at the birth of the holy Founder of Democracy—GOD IS LOVE. That classic State which gave Washington to the world, instead of being a second rate political power; instead of presenting the appearance of a decaying land; instead of being the property of a small clique of haughty aristocrats, who still speak of the People as if Jefferson was yet to be born; instead of deriving its chief revenues from robbing the poor and weak of their wages, of their toil and—oh! shame, thou nurse of this People's Saviour from oppression!—of the fruits of their *love,* too; instead of electing orators to defend her sins and denounce the opponents of her criminal endeavours to extend the plague that so long has weakened and is now prostrating her—instead of this, the proud old mother of States and statesmen would once more be equal to her sisters in the National Council, not in right of an ancient compact, but in consequence of her inherent power; her wilderness would bloom with civilization again; her unsightly homesteads would be replaced by houses fit for the residence of her lovely daughters; her indolent feudal landed proprietors would be obliged to give place to the industrious, democratic farmers that are now hewing out States in our far Western Territories; the doctrines which her Jefferson proclaimed would be believed and practiced at home and abroad, and her men of intellect would be the Vanguard of Liberty throughout the world. Virginia would not profit more by the eradication of her cancer, than her sister States of the South.

But the ladies of the South see slavery as it is *not;* and these desirable changes are yet to be effected. Justly, said William North, that the life of man to woman is one long hypocrisy. Every man knows this truth—or, if he does not, let him read the lady novelist and be convinced! The ladies of the South have no idea of the immense immoral influences that the institution of slavery exercises over man. They know that it does not injure *their* morals—they imagine that men also escape its influences. Men have not the manliness to undeceive them. Men only know that chastity in the South is a virtue entirely monopolized by the ladies of the ruling race. Very few men would have the manliness simply not to *deny* this fact if it was utterred—"which it could n't well be"—in the presence of a Southern woman. But, denied or not, it is a *fact.* I defy any young boy to live in the South and remain ignorant (I use ignorant in its ante-diluvian sense) till the age of manhood.

Mrs. Douglass would not stand alone in her womanly protest against slavery if her sisters had seen as much of its domestic effects as she. For young unmarried men are not the only sinners whom slavery creates in the Southern States. Married men South, like Benedicts everywhere, oftener do evil in the sight of the Lord than we young bachelors, who are erroneously supposed to be the chief of sinners in that respect.

Southern ladies never see the most obnoxious features of slavery. They see only its "South-Side View." They never'attend auctions, nor are they ever present in the prison yards when slaves are sold by private bargain.

They are confirmed in all of their educational prejudices, by pro-tyranny slavish-souled Northern men, and especially by the violent anti-Abolitionism of Northern women, more ignorant than themselves when travelling in the South.

What they defend as slavery is an ideal thing, which they suppose to be a peculiar institution of the South. What they denounce as Abolition is an ideal creed of error—a sum of all moral villanies—which they imagine to form our articles of faith.

Women, as a class, are believers. They dislike scepticism. They seldom doubt. This peculiarity makes Southern ladies pro-slavery in politics. They seldom see the hidden evils of slavery; they are informed, day after day, in their parlours, by their papers and from their pulpits, that it is a Divine Institution, and productive of unalloyed good. They believe. Thus it is that they make such astounding assertions when they write of it—assertions which every man who has personally investigated the subject reads with mingled feelings of amazement and deep sorrow. Mrs. Tyler, for example, in her reply to that—don't erase my epithet, Mr. Editor!—

that tyrannical representative of a class of hateful oppressors, the Duchess of Sutherland,* boldly asserted that females were seldom or never separated when sold into slavery. I have no doubt that she believed her statement to be true. Yet, a greater falsehood was never written. I have spoken with at least one hundred Virginia slaves in the Carolinas, Georgia and Alabama, who were sold from their wives—often from their wives and families, in the very city from which Mrs. Tyler's letter was dated.*

Southern women, as a class, defend oppression because they know not what they do. There are exceptions—as the following paragraph which I clip from the city news department of the *New Orleans Delta* will prove:

"ATTEMPTED SUICIDE.—A slave girl, named Henrietta, was arrested at the request of her mistress, Mrs. Julia Mardi, and brought to the guard-house for safe keeping, she having attempted to drown herself in the well of the yard. She is badly bruised and cut, and says that her mistress did it."

I shall conclude my letter by illustrating my position by a quotation from a Virginia novel, written by a young lady of Richmond, which is selling very rapidly in the South and England, although it is comparatively unknown at the North. It is entitled, "ALONE: By Marian Harland." It is said to be her first attempt at authorship. Its sketches of life in Virginia are correct and vivid pictures. Its characters are ably described. It does Honour to her heart and head; and gives promise of a future of great usefullness—or evil. For Marion Harland is too earnest in her opinions to be silent; and too strong, intellectually, to be a powerless advocate of truth or error. Shall this noble young spirit—for such her book proves her to be—be an ally of the rich and powerful oppressor, or a champion of the poor and unfriended slave? We fear. Ida, the heroine of "Alone," is a noble ideal of womanhood—but the authoress describes her as a slaveholder and tacitly defends the peculiar misfortune of her State. "'Tis true, 'tis pity, pity 'tis, 'tis true," that the sophisms which are unceasingly scattered into the soul of every Southerner and resident of the South, have sadly dulled her naturally delicate perception of the Right and Noble. It is melancholy to see how infinitely higher than the "common herd of mankind's" morality is Ida's sense of honour as exhibited in her indignant rejection of Richard Copley's scheme of revenge over her successful rival in love, and then to find her at the *denouement* "settling down" for life to

---

* [No, we let the epithet stand if only to correct, what we believe is, the error into which our correspondent has fallen. He undoubtedly confounds, as many have done before him, the present Duchess of Sutherland with her late mother-in-law the Countess of Sutherland, who inflicted so much wrong and suffering upon her Highland peasantry by banishment. EDS. *STANDARD*.]

* Richmond.

subsist in luxury—without even the suspicion that it is *mean* to do so—on the profits of the compulsory and unrequited toil of her slaves.

—But I find that I have already filled more than my allotted space. In my next communication I shall return to the subject, and criticise this young authoress's defence of slavery.

JOHN BALL, JR.

New York National Anti-Slavery Standard, April 7, 1855.

APPENDIX 7. FROM OUR SOUTHERN CORRESPONDENT.

NEW ORLEANS, March 16, 1855.

A PRO-SLAVERY NOVEL, BY MARION HARLAND.

Editors of the Anti-Slavery Standard:

THE rapid growth of an anti-slavery literature in the North is one of the most gladdening signs of the times. The immense sale of Abolition novels and their great popularity is also cheering evidence of the progress of the true "American principle"—of Equality in judicial and political Rights without respect of sex, or race, or religion. It shows that the days of despotism in America are numbered. I do not wonder that our party should rejoice when they see so many authors arranging themselves in the ranks of the friends of Freedom.

I would have them to remember, however, that we are not the monopolists of the power of the pen. A Southern Literature is springing up. In the periodical issues of the muzzled press of the slave States, sectionalism is taught under the name of patriotism; and the standard of a man's worth as a citizen is measured by his devotion to the interest of the slavocrats. Within the past year, three authors, residents of the South, have defended slavery in books—Sims, Russell, and Marion Harland. I intend to expose the errors and sophistries of each of these writers. I shall begin with the youngest and best-intentioned of them—the last Southern authoress "out."

Marion Harland, I learn from the New York *Leader,* is a young Southern lady, a resident of Richmond, Virginia. She is the authoress of "Alone," which is heralded as the "great Virginia novel of the season." I have already given my opinion of it. I dislike its theology, disapprove its ethics, and detest its politics—but still I think that it deserves the great success it has met with. Although published in a provincial city, by a person without tact or enterprise, unpuffed and unadvertised, it has already reached its tenth American edition; ten thousand copies of it have been printed in England; it has been superbly illustrated by celebrated artists; its poetry has been set to music, and it has been translated into French. I like the book because its fervid style is the sign of an earnest soul. Earnest in my own opinions, I have a friendly feeling for every earnest thinker—however widely our creeds may differ. But for practisers of Paley's degrading doctrine of Expediency—as it is popularly *mis*understood—I have only denunciation and scorn for answer when they speak of the blessings of slavery. I would not stoop to argue with such men as the traitor Douglas, or the demagogue Wise; but I will willingly devote an afternoon to point out the erroneous statements of Marion Harland, or of the authoress of the Planter's Northern Bride.*

Marion Harland defends slavery rather by inference than statement. Here is the paragraph I intended to quote in my last communication:

"The house was a princely pile, rearing its towers from the midst of a finely wooded park. The architecture was Gothic, and perfect in all its parts, even to the stained windows, imported, at an immense expense, from abroad. A village at the base of the hill was peopled by the negroes, of whom there were more than a hundred connected with the plantation. The equestrians rode up the single street. Good humour and neatness characterized the simple inhabitants; children drew to one side of the road with smiles and courtesies; the aged raised their bleared eyes to reply to the respectful salutations of the young riders; through the open doors were seen clean, comfortably-furnished rooms—in most, the tables were spread for the evening meal, and the busy housewives preparing for their husband's return from field or forest.

"'There are thy down-trodden children, O Africa!' said Ida, sarcastically.

"Lynn fired up." [Lynn is the hero of the novel—an enthusiastic, poetic character—a Virginia R.B. Haydon; or, as the authoress calls him, a "modern Raphael." Mr. Lacy, a serious, uncomfortably pious young man, was intended as the hero; but the authoress, in attempting to improve human nature, was unsuccessful.] "'They are the happiest beings upon the globe,' said Lynn.

"'As far as animal wants are concerned,' subjoined Arthur.

"'I do not accept that clause. They are happy! They have a kind and generous master; every comfort in health; good nursing when ill; their church and Bible, and their Saviour, who is also ours. What the race may become I do not pretend to say. These are far in advance of the original stock; but their intellectual appetite is dull, and I dare affirm that in nine cases out of ten it is satisfied. I never knew a master who denied his

---

* I say, Messrs. Editors, if I write a fiction, *per contra*, entitled the Fanatic's Southern Sweetheart—will you publish it? It will be "nothing if not"—spicy!

servants permission to read, and many have them taught by their own children. The slave lies down at night, every want supplied, his family as well cared for as himself; not a thought of tomorrow! He is secure of a home and maintenance, without disturbing himself as to the manner in which it is to be obtained. Can the same be said of the menial classes in any other country under the sun?'

"'American as ever!' smiled Cary.

"'And Virginian as ever. The Old Dominion is my mother! He is not a loyal son who does not prefer her, with her infirmities and foibles, to a dozen of the modern "fast" belle States. The dear old creature has a wrinkle or two that do not improve her comeliness, and adheres somewhat pertinaciously to certain obsolete ideas, but Heaven bless her! the heart is right and sound.'

"Ida's eyes sparkled:

> "'Where is coward would not dare
> To die for such a land.'"

It is easy to condense into one paragraph, errors which could not be logically or even statistically refuted in less than a large quarto volume. To answer the various inferences of the preceding extract, it will be necessary to notice each sentence separately.

I affirm, at the commencement, that if the description of the "princely pile" referred to in the paragraph, and the picture given of the homes of the slaves attached to it, are intended as Representatives of the "Master's Houses" and of life in the "Uncle Tom's Cabins" of the Southern States, the passage is simply—*ridiculously* unfaithful. I believe that such a princely pile exists; that a generous master lives in it; that his negroes are well cared for; but, in behalf of the poor slaves of the Carolinas, Georgia, Alabama and Louisiana, I emphatically deny that such masters are common in the South.

To begin with the sentences:

"The respectful salutations of the young riders." Gentlemen and ladies are the same all the world over—but the majority of the human race, of the "respectable" as well as of the "lower" classes, are not entitled to that name. I have no doubt that William Shakespeare, the first gentleman of Europe in his age, or George Washington, the first gentleman of America in his time, spoke as courteously to the poorest man whom they addressed as to the proudest aristocrat they ever conversed with. I am certain that Marion Harland and her friends would address a slave respectfully; but I deny that it is the general custom to speak to them with gentleness. The least symptom of independence in a man of colour is instantly extinguished by a shower of abusive epithets, in nine cases out of every ten. The last time I dined at a Virginia hotel—in Petersburg—I was asked by the coloured waiter if I would like a certain dish he named. I said, "no, thank you." A well-dressed fellow, at the other side of the table, gave me a contemptuous glance—which I returned with interest—and then growled to his companion, in an audible tone, "Who the —— is that, speaking *so* to the niggers!" He then turned round and called out to the boy—"I say, *Buck,* bring me," &c. This was a sort of challenge, which I accepted by asking the waiter—"Will you have the kindness, *sir,* to hand me, &c." The bully "looked daggers," but was silent. In my opinion, a greater misfortune arising out of slavery than even the separation of families is the annihilation in the slaves of the glorious Right of *striking back.* (Dr. Brown, I believe, terms it the sixth sense, or the sense of Resistance.) Probably I would think differently if I was a father; but I would now prefer death to deprivation of the Right of resenting insults.

"Neatness" in dress is not a characteristic of country slaves, as a class.

"Through the open doors were seen clean, comfortably furnished rooms; in most, the table were spread for the evening meal, and the busy house-wives preparing for their husband's return from field or forest." Those who have read my previous letters will not need any words in which to answer this couleur-de-rose picture of a model plantation. If this planta-tion has been selected by the authoress as a Representative, I need only say of it, as has been said of each of our great philosopher's Representa-tive Men, that it does not represent. Good heavens! when I remember the comfortless, womanless, pig-sty huts of the African race in the Carolinas, and the negro villages I have seen in Georgia and Alabama, and then read Marion Harland's fanciful description of "slavequarters," and think how many will peruse it as if it was a faithful picture of Southern life, and when I further reflect how many writers are engaged in promulgating the same dangerous delusion, I confess that I lose all hopes of a bloodless termination of the battle between slavery and freedom at present in prog-ress throughout the Union.

"They are the happiest beings in the world." That's false; but if it was true, it would not prove that they are happy in consequence of being slaves.

"They have a kind and generous master." True—when they have *not* a cruel and ungenerous owner!

"Every comfort in health." What do you mean by comfort, Marion? Is a husband a comfort? You must be a very eccentric young lady if you think that he is not; and that you do think so is proved by the fact that you have married all your female favourites and left Ida's enemies and the coquette to live "Alone." Now, Marion, I have seen men sold into slavery *from their wives and families* in your own city, and I have spoken to "any quantity" of slaves in the Carolinas, who had suffered the same fate, many years ago. Education is a source of comfort. Music, also, is. Hope is the soul of comfort. The country negroes are all ignorant—the city slaves learn to read by stealth. The negro enjoys music—but his taste is as uncultivated as is that of the admirer of Buntline, or as was the critical ability of the young lady who styled Fanny Fern (the father-slanderer) "a woman of immense genius." Hope is a white! You "never knew a master who denied his servant permission to read?" Did you never hear of Mrs. Douglass? Are you ignorant of the fact that, in Virginia, it is a penitentiary offence to teach coloured persons to read? If you are not, read Mrs. Douglass's book and the statutes of your State.

"Can the same be said of menial classes in any other country under the sun?" Perhaps not—but a great deal more ought to be said—it ought to be said that there is *no* "menial" class—and a sin is not less criminal in Virginia because there are other sins practiced elsewhere.

What shall we say of the authoress's eulogy of Virginia? As a lover of that classic State, I shall only say that I wish Virginia did not deserve it. "Dear old creatures" are very well in their way; but commend me to the "fast young belles"!

Yours, in the preference of youth, and vigour, and beauty, to age and "infirmities" and "wrinkles."

JOHN BALL, JR.

New York National Anti-Slavery Standard, April 14, 1855.

APPENDIX 8. AN ABOLITIONIST IN KENTUCKY.

NEWPORT, Ky., March 10, 1856.

MESSRS. EDITORS: I've been travelling in the manchattel States for several months past, kindling and relighting the flame of hope in the breasts of the hopeless blacks, and endeavouring, as far as possible, to aid the sacred cause of Abolition among the whites, by politico-economical arguments in favour of Free Labour and Free Soil. Not by the argument of a Higher Law—ah! no! Slavery has deadened the moral sense of this people too effectually, to render appeals to their humane or religious instincts effective. To reach their humanity, you must go through their purse. Their hearts are guarded by Dollars.

There is a paper published here which I wish to commend to the attention of your readers. I refer to the *Newport* (Ky.) *News*. It is a daily paper, anti-slavery "up to the hub, and all"—as uncompromising in its opposition to the "domestic" iniquity of the South; as fearless in its denunciations and expositions of the moral and pecuniary effects of the "peculiar" and "patriarchal" crime as *The Liberator* or the *Anti-Slavery Standard*. Mr. Bailey has sacrificed a great deal to keep up this journal. He is personally as well as morally a brave man; if he were timid, in either respect, his press would long ago have been immersed in the Ohio river. His whole family deprive themselves of the comforts of life, which are within their immediate reach, to sustain the cause of freedom of speech and advance anti-slavery sentiment in Kentucky. His son, two grown daughters and a young child-daughter, as well as Mr. Bailey himself, devote their whole time to the paper—editing, setting up type, and printing. By crossing the river into free Ohio they could live in comparative affluence, but they prefer to serve freedom, even with poverty, by living in Kentucky.

Newport has few slaveholders, but many pro-slavery men. In fact, it is the most ultra pro-slavery town in Kentucky. Here, as elsewhere, the meaner the white man the intenser is his hatred of the slave. Slaveholders, as a general thing, are more favourably inclined to Emancipation than the "poor whites of the South."

Bailey is doing a great deal of good here. They dare not throw his press into the river, because they are afriad of him; Abolition, therefore, can get an audience at this point.

Can't you do something to put the *News* on a firm pecuniary basis?

Let those who wish to read a Southern paper with a backbone, sub-scribe for the *News*. It costs only $2 per year.

Yours ever,   JOHN BALL, JR.

New York National Anti-Slavery Standard, March 22, 1856. Reprinted in Boston *Liberator,* March 28, 1856.

Appendix 9. Emancipation in Missouri.

St. Louis, Feb. 1, 1856.

To The Liberator:

The Free Soilers of Missouri have unfurled the glorious banner of Emancipation! Already they have won a victory! Already a prominent paper, of extended circulation and established position, has announced its determination to 'trust its fate and fortune' to this holy and invigorating cause! There *is* something good in Nazareth; and the world *does* move, after all!

St. Louis is anchored. Platte county and the frontier region of Missouri may heave and tug as they are able, but the ship of State is immovably anchored to the policy and creed of the mighty North. The propagandists are fighting Abolitionists in the prow, but a fire has been opened in their rear, and, please God, we intend to keep it up, till the last ruffian among them all is dead, conquered, or missing! No compromise our principle, and victory our motto, we will soon complete the repeal of the Missouri Compromise, by wiping out the criminal and disastrous institution which our fathers permitted the South to establish here.

I say *we;* but I must explain the expression. I rejoice at this auspicious movement, but have no fellow-feeling with its advocates.

You may have heard how this movement was inaugurated. It was the duty of the Legislature to elect a President and Director of the Bank. Mr. Palm, an Emancipationist, was a candidate. A border-ruffian, in the course of his remarks, announced that he had intended to vote for Mr. Palm, but, having learned since he came here that the gentleman was not 'sound on the goose,' he would now cast his vote for another candidate. Mr. Glover, of St. Louis, immediately arose and said:—

'The Senator from St. Clair (Mr. Mayo) has stated that when he took his seat this morning, it was his intention to vote for Mr. Palm, but that the developments since made, showing that gentleman to be unequivocally on the record in favor of the emancipation of negro slaves in Missouri, have not only altered that intention, but produced a contrary one, manifesting itself in his voting against Mr. Palm. I change parts in every particular with the honorable Senator from St. Clair. When I came here this

morning, it was my intention to vote against Mr. Palm; it is now my determination to vote for him. The change in my case is attributable to the
same cause which produced the change in the views of my friend from St.
Clair. I shall cordially vote for Mr. Palm, because he is an emancipationist; because, as I have learned from the honorable Senator from St. Gen-
evieve, who put him in nomination, sooner or later, as the good people of
Missouri shall determine, he will vote for ridding the State of slavery by
gradual emancipation.'

Mr. Palm was elected! The discussion which preceeded his election is
significant as a sign of public opinion, and is in some respects encouraging to the friends of equal and exact justice to all men. Mr. Brown, editor
of the Missouri *Democrat,* took part in the debate, and declared himself in
favor of free labor and free soil. Members of the three political parties
expressed themselves in favor of emancipation—and members of each, I
believe, declared themselves opposed to such a policy.

This discussion, I suspect, was foreordained by our Free Soil politicians. It was to act the part of Richard Roe. The case is in court now, and
Messrs. Doe and Roe will soon be forgotten.

It is easy to forsee that this debate will have a great and important
influence on our political parties. At this time, we are cursed with three
contending organizations—I can neither call them parties nor factions;
for principles and men are so strangely mingled in their creeds, that one
cannot be loyal to principles and support the men, or loyal to the men
and advocate the principles they profess! First comes the Benton party—
half of it free soil, part of it abolition, part of it pro-slavery, *sans* propagandism. Next comes the 'Antis'—Atchison party—border-ruffian propagandists chiefly, but partly composed of free-soilers in creed, who have a
personal antipathy to Benton. Lastly comes the American party—which,
dead in the Union, must bury itself here as soon as possible.

From these three organized political mobs, two parties will inevitably
spring, who will be loyal to their principles, regardless of Mr. Benton—
the Emancipationists, and the 'Blacks,' or pro-slavery propagandists. All
other issues will be buried by common and joyful consent.

My sympathies, of course, are with the advocates of emancipation; but
while I would hail with gladness the accomplishment of their object, I
cannot but recoil from the method by which they seek to secure it. They
are trying to serve God and the devil both: an unnecessary, unrighteous,
unprofitable undertaking. I have served God and the devil in my day and
generation; but I decidedly object to serving both at once.

Let me explain myself.

Slavery is a central crime—the centre of a system of vices and evils.

Slavery, like every other crime, casts a blight on the material condition
of the people who cherish it. This constitutes the *evil* of slavery.

To root out a crime, it is necessary, if you would eradicate the system of which it is a centre, to strike at the inward principle by which it is sustained and nourished. Will the Emancipationists do this? No. They are aristocrats themselves—these Democrats in creed! These advocates of emancipation are taskmasters themselves—the best, gentlest, most indulgent of taskmasters, it may be, but slaveholders, nevertheless, and upholders of this gigantic crime against the fatherhood of God and brotherhood of man.

Take, for example, the leader of this host—Mr. Francis P. Blair, the younger; a noble gentleman of generous impulses, incorruptible fidelity to his principles, afraid of no living man or organization of men. He might have been in Congress years ago; he might have sat in the Senate of the United States; he might have been the Governor of Missouri, if he had consented to pay the common price for such positions—sacrifice of manhood, abjuration of his real political faith. He valued the *honor* of place rather than the *position.* Jim Green is a Senator; so is our beloved Charles Sumner: but both seats are not places of honor. Sumner walked uprightly into his seat, while the demagogue of Missouri crawled into his place. 'Frank' won't crawl; he would never go upon his belly—so he kept out of Congress until he could walk there.

I honor him for it; but we Abolitionists cannot spare the rod even to men who are incorruptible themselves, if they uphold iniquity by example or by silence.

Frank Blair is a slaveholder—in the sight of God, a robber of men; and, until he washes his hands of this huge crime, we, at least, will have no communion with him. We must regard him as a time-serving politician merely, until he lets his slaves go free, and acknowledge manhood where he now sees chattelhood.

We must look on his part as a division of the army of the enemy. Beelzebub is trying to cast out Beelzebub. If good men, who hate wrong, not because it is *bad policy,* erroneous political expediency, but because it *is* wrong,—if they step in and stab the monster while its children are contending among themselves, glory be to God in the highest; but to these aristocratic advocates of Democracy none!

Stand forth, Frank Blair!

What is slavery? Listen to his answer. You will find it in the Missouri *Democrat,* of which, it is understood, he is part proprietor, and the 'inspiration.' Slavery is bad policy, says Mr. Blair. Why so? Because injustice is always impolitic? 'Because,' says Mr. Blair, 'it keeps out capital and free white labor from the State. It robs a State of political power. It seals up the earth and her hidden treasures; its spectre drives back prosperity, great cities, and manly intellect: it blights the soil; it impoverishes the State treasury; it depreciates the value of real estate; it degrades the condition of the poor white population. That's all,' adds Mr. Blair, 'and therefore I will root it out.'

God prosper you! I say; but *that's not all* about slavery, Mr. Blair.

Slavery is a crime, and the mother of a numerous brood of sins.

It crucifies the Christ afresh, in making merchandise of God's poor children, for whom His only Son died on the cross of Calvary.

It is a sin against the Holy Ghost, for it blasphemes it by ranking God's awful and sacred image among the things of worldly traffic.

It is *soul-murder*—the highest crime of man against man.

It is robbery. Every slaveholder is four times a robber. He robs his slaves of their sacred, civil, political and personal rights—their rights to hold and acquire property, to the wages of their labor, to self-government, and—holier than all—their right to themselves, their wives or husbands, and their children. Property in man is robbery of man.

It is piracy. The receiver is equally guilty with the thief. The forefather of every slave on this continent was a free man before our pirate-fathers who enacted the Constitution framed the iniquity into a law. Equally guilty are those who acknowledge the crime by selling, buying or holding men.

It is fornication and adultery—for, by destroying the self-respect of the female slave, by placing her in the power of her master, by putting the social brand upon her and her race, by annihilating marriage, by selling the little ones whom God has given her, it is guilty of these offences. Slavery, not Popery, is the true 'mother of harlots.'

It incites the slaves to revenge—an unholy passion, which manifests itself in petty thefts, lying, idleness, and occasionally, as at Southampton, in 'righteous insurrection.'

It disobeys the Divine law, saying, 'Whom God hath joined together, let not man put asunder'—for it forcibly separates fathers and mothers from their children, husbands from wives, brothers from sisters.

It is a vast machine for the production of Haynans.

It is the main pillar of heathenism in America.

It degrades the master as well as the slave, and the poor white man also is its victim.

It incites mobs to murder by hanging, burning at the stake, drowning and shooting.

It makes a holy duty a penal offence by its laws prohibiting the education of the slave, and divine sympathy with the suffering fugitive it punishes by fine and imprisonment and confiscation of property.

It defies Christ's command when he said—'Preach the Gospel to every creature'—for it refuses to permit the slave to study the Bible, by keeping him in ignorance.

It drives out Christianity from the pulpit, the Legislative chamber, the printed book and newspaper.

Slavery, in brief, is the sum of all villanies.

What does Mr. Blair say about these crimes?—This:—

'It will be asked—What will be done with the niggers? We answer, that charity begins at home; that we are only interested for the whites. You who are so much attached to the niggers could not fail to provide for them. We are not the Apostle of the Gentiles. We regret to say that we have very little Booraboolagha philanthropy in our nature; and even for the purpose of civilizing and Christianizing the Africans, we should not tolerate his presence, if we could lawfully and honorably dispense with it. We feel that our mission is not of that nature, but we do not object to those who are called to it. We will, nevertheless, suggest that our colored folks might be shipped to Liberia.'

See the effects of slavery on a noble mind! It causes it, in this case, to limit its sense of justice, its benevolence, to a class and a race. It gives up to party 'what was meant for mankind.'

All the cruel wrongs inflicted on the slave are justified, slighted, almost, as Clay said, 'sanctioned and sanctified,' by one word—*nigger.* Mr. Blair 'is not the apostle of the Gentiles.' I do not see why he should, therefore, suggest further wrongs on the 'Gentiles' of Missouri on this account. He proposes to expatriate them. What right has he to do this great and cruel wrong? Ship them off to Liberia, indeed! Suppose we reverse the process, and ship off the slaveholders? Try it, Mr. Blair, and see how you would relish this proposal. I would rather see the slaveholder expatriated than the slave. The negro, I know, would never have repealed the Missouri Compromise, or invaded Kansas, trampling on its rights and murdering its citizens. The negro may be a degraded race, but we *know* the border-ruffian is still more degraded. I 'will, therefore, suggest that our *un*colored folks of Platte county might be shipped to Liberia.' More anon.

JOHN BALL, JR.

Boston *Liberator,* February 20, 1857.

Appendix 10. Governor Geary, Sir!

"I am the Governor of Kansas, sir, and I intend to play the Governor's part."—JOHN W. GEARY, in a conversation with Gen. Higginson, Gov. Robinson and "John Ball, Jr."

BOSTON, Feb. 25, 1857.

Correspondence of The National Anti-Slavery Standard.

UNCLE JOHN was right. It don't pay. It is not only wrong to serve God and the Devil, but it don't pay in a worldly sense. No man can do it and prosper. "No, sir! It don't pay."

Gov. Geary is not the man to see an unembodied truth. He does not feel that unfaltering devotion to Eternal Truth is the highest policy for every one in every station. But he is now, it would seem, in a fair way to know it.

Forgetting, if he ever knew, that to be Governor of one's self is the only truly noble gubernatorial position, he came to Kansas a very slave to Self, hungering and thirsting, not for the applause of the holy monitor within, but for the pitiful huzzas of the unthinking mob. To satisfy this craving, and act with true manliness was an utter impossibility for Gov. Geary! He played double. His popularity was short-lived. For mobs have souls, which *will* be heard; even in spite of the wild huzza. In the long run, the man who fears God too much to fear the mob is the most popular with the people and most warmly loved by them.

Poor Gov. Geary did not feel the truth and coquetted with the "Peculiar" organization of Crime which the Free State men detest. He lost their favour. The Free State people look on him now as a man who is not to be trusted—but to be used, and paid for, if necessary, like any other tool, if he should come to their hand and serve their purpose. They might vote for him as Governor if he aided them to be admitted into the Union immediately. That is the price of the tool, and they are willing to settle the bill.

Crime, like virtue, likes sincerity. Gen. Stringfellow, I know, respects

Mr. Garrison, although he hates his doctrines—but he hates Mr. Seward's doctrines without respecting the man. Dr. Stringfellow, the brother of the General, respects Gov. Robinson while he hates his principles; but that he hates Gov. Geary without respecting him will be seen by the extract subjoined. I quote from *The Squatter Sovereign* of Jan. 27:

GOV. GEARY'S MESSAGE.—We are not disposed to become contentious at mere shadows; but when we discover their substance clearly developed, we are not content to retain passive attitude. It is thus that we have dealt with his Excellency John W. Geary—cautiously refraining from condemnation until something more tangible than shadows had loomed forth against him. We have watched, with an impartial eye, his every step, until *it has become our settled conviction that he is playing a double game—* that is, *favouring the Free State movement* to his utmost *without giving open offence to the "Democratic" party.* His message is a verification of this.

He assumes the credit of restoring peace with quite an egotistical flourish, and counsels our legislators to follow in his wake if they desire success. *We think they will decline his advice,* ungrateful as it may seem, especially as regards the repeal and amendment of certain portions of the statutes, a few of which we cite.

Investing the appointing power in the Legislative Assembly is objected to by the Governor and, as a *general* practice, is to be deprecated. Did his Free Soil prejudices permit, however, he must see that peculiar circumstances made unusual legislation necessary. At the time the statutes were framed, *and at the present period,* there are counties *where the popular majority* openly set the laws at defiance, and *could be viewed in no other light than that of outlaws.* To have placed the offices of sheriff, county commissioner, &c., within the grasp of such a population would have been to render the offices a nullity, or, what is worse, seen them prostrated to the most pernicious ends. The offices, thus far, have been well filled, and none have expressed dissatisfaction except outlaws and their sympathizers.

So far, so bad; thus far, Stringfellow. The italics are my own. Let us take breath, for a second, after this exhausting draught of modern democracy.

It will be noticed that Mr. Stringfellow, in the first paragraph, assumes, as an undeniable truth, that to favour Freedom openly would be treason to Democracy. Mr. Stringfellow is a leading Democrat; his journal was the official organ of the National Administration in Kansas; he was an honoured member of the Cincinnati Convention, and was in constant and close communion with Toombs and Douglas, Pierce and Mason during his recent visit to the National Capital. Is this his doctrine, true Democracy? I ask *The Post*. I hope that the popular proverb is false—that our Post is *not* deaf, and will condescend to make reply. Like Rosa Dartle, "I merely ask for information."

Again: "Investing the appointing power in the Legislative Assembly" is a very convenient and euphonious phrase to conceal a gigantic wrong—no less than the annihilation of the spirit and even form of American Freedom. Let us look back.

Under the heading of the *Squatter Sovereign,* in broad black letters, extending across the page, is printed conspicuously this sentence:

"The Squatter claims the same Sovereignty in the Territories that he possessed in the States."

'Twill do, I think, as a comment on these sad and undeniable facts:

On the 30th of March, 1855, the day appointed by the Governor of Kansas for the first election of members of the Territorial Legislature—6,307 votes were recorded. Of these ballots, 4,908 were cast by residents of Missouri, who came over in military companies, armed with cannon, rifles, shot guns, pistols, sabres, swords, knives and clubs, to enforce, if necessary, by physical force, their favourite theory, that a majority of men have the right to trample under foot the laws of Almighty God. They did not so phrase it. They called it "the right of the slaveholder to carry his property into the Territories."

Well, they elected every member in every District but one. The Legislative Assembly was theirs—altogether two-thirds, at least, of the people were in favour of Freedom.

To retain the power thus criminally obtained, it was necessary to heap iniquity on iniquity. They did so. It was necessary to deprive the *majority of the people* of all political rights in order to establish their power. They did so—

By disenfranchising every true Christian in Kansas without exception.

By closing the Court, the Jury-box, and all political offices from freemen.

In every free State, the people have the right to elect their civil officers. In Kansas the highest officers—Governor, Judges, Secretary of State—are appointed by the President. The members of both branches of the Legislature were elected by the lowest grade of the population of Missouri. These representatives of Missouri crime, re-elected, on their part, *every* officer in the Territory, not in the gift of the National Executive—from District Judges and County Commissioners down to Sheriffs, Constables, and managers of the House.

This will explain the startling admission of the *Squatter Sovereign* that "there are Counties where the *popular* MAJORITY **** are outlaws"! and it will show that when he says that none are dissatisfied with the present officers but outlaws, he intends to say—none *but* "the popular MAJORITY"! That's all, I admit.

Now, for another draught from the *Squatter Sovereign*'s vessel of Democracy:

"'Section eleventh' (it is quoting Geary's Message), 'requiring certain test oaths as prerequisites to the right of suffrage, is wrong, unfair and unequal upon citizens of different sections of the Union.' Then, is our Federal Constitution 'wrong, unfair and unequal.' The test oaths go no further than does that instrument; and the citizen who cannot swear allegiance to it has no claim to the right of suffrage—for he is a traitor and deserves to be marked as such."

—This section of chap. 66 of the "laws" of Kansas, which the *Squatter Sovereign* thinks so very constitutional, confirms the right of suffrage to every male citizen—*provided,* 1, That he is white and an adult; 2, That he shall pay one dollar before voting; 3, That he is not a soldier or marine, or United States officer, in the army or navy; 4, That, he shall never have trampled under foot the infamous and loathsome Fugitive Slave law; and 5, That he will swear to sustain the provisions of the Kansas-Nebraska act. Thus every Christian and every gentleman is disfranchised—for to respect the Fugitive Slave act he must violate the plainest and most sacred precepts of the Christian religion and the code of Chivalry, which teach us—both of them—to aid the unfortunate, to defend the helpless, to pity the oppressed and to resist the tyrant.

The *Squatter Sovereign* continues:

"The Governor has taken under his especial tutilage every Free Soil scheme that has been devised, doubtless moved by a tender commiseration for the weak and unprotected. His message abounds in recommendations that have in view the promotion and furtherance of plans and schemes concocted by the free Stateites, whilst any measures set on foot by the opposing party are not even noticed. Indeed, his Excellency seems to throw his whole Executive influence in favour of abolitionism; as if he desired, in a measure, to make up for the absence of all representation from that party in the Legislative body. Abolitionism will not acknowledge the legitimacy of the Legislature, even so far as to ask for Legislation in their favour; but, through Gov. Geary, they would obtain what they desire. A 'cute way of reaping benefits from a source they affect to despise and repudiate.'"

—Gov. Geary, it is known, *aspires to the Presidency.* Let him take truth by the forelock now, and learn that it is utterly impossible to serve Slavery and Freedom. Let him choose which of them he will serve. Let him see from this article of the *Squatter Sovereign* that it is bad policy to play a double game. You cannot serve God and Mammon, nor Liberty and Slavery. It is wrong to try. But, above all, Oh ye politicians be warned by the example of Gov. Geary that if you truckle to crime, you will find, in the language of Uncle John, that *It don't pay.*

JOHN BALL, Jr.

New York National Anti-Slavery Standard, March 7, 1857.

INDEX

Hoppe, Mr. (Kansas murder victim), 271, 282 n. 45
Hopper, J. J., 227, 230 n. 16
House of Delegates (Va.), 96–101, 102 n. 2, 104–8, 181
Howard, John, 80, 83 n. 14, 246, 247 n. 2
Howe, Samuel Gridley, xii, xix, 246, 247 n. 1
Hoy, Mrs. (Missouri), 174–75
Hudson, Ontario, 95 n. 3
Hughes, Thomas C., 270, 281 n. 30
Hughes, Mr. (Missouri), 177
Huguenots, 76 n. 11

Illinois, 105, 173
immigrants, 7, 48 n. 5, 95 n. 3, 144 n. 8
  and slavery, xxiii, 55, 141
  See also German Americans; Irish Americans
Impending Crisis of the South, The (1856), xviii, 109
Indian Territory, 249, 253 n. 14, 266 n. 6
Indiana, 258
Indians, 118, 222, 269, 270, 279 n. 19
  in Kansas, 283 n. 56, 284 n. 60
  oppose slavery, 250, 253 n. 14
  See also individual tribes
internal improvements, 83 n. 16
Iowa, xvi, 25 n. 3
Ireland, 222
Irish Americans, 124
  economic status of, 143 n. 7, 196–97, 229 n. 3
  proslavery views of, xxiii, 56 n. 4, 141, 143 n. 7, 161 n. 11, 166, 304–5
  in South, 65 n. 4, 208, 233
Irish nationalism, 171 n. 20, 304–5
Isaac (slave rebel), 231–39

Jacks, Mr. (Missouri), 261
Jackson, Francis, 220 n. 8
Jackson County, Mo., 262
"Jacobius" (Redpath), xvii, 189 n. 1, 206 n. 1
Jamaica, 141, 222, 229 n. 4
James II, 280 n. 23
Jayhawkers, 253 n. 9
Jefferson, Thomas, 54, 83 n. 16
  biography of, 57 n. 7, 108 n. 3
  Kentucky Resolutions (1798–99) and, 147, 153 n. 10

political principles of, 66 n. 10, 139, 315
slavery and, 102 n. 1, 151 n. 6
University of Virginia and, 211, 212 n. 20
Jefferson County, Va., 97, 103 n. 9
Jeffreys, George, 269, 280 n. 23
John Ball, Jr., letters of, xv, xviii, xix–xx, xxiv n. 69, xxv, 25 n. 1, 27 n. 16
  in Boston Daily Traveller, xvii, 19, 180–88, 189 nn. 1 and 8, 190 n. 17, 191–206, 191 n. 21, 206 nn. 1 and 3, 211 n. 1
  in Boston Liberator, xvi, xxiv, 19–25, 25 n. 3, 26 n. 4, 27 nn. 8, 11, and 15, 28–36, 37 nn. 1 and 2, 38 nn. 3, 8, 10, and 12, 39, 46, 47 nn. 1 and 3, 48 nn. 5, 12, 13, and 15, 49–52, 53–56, 56 nn. 2, 3, and 4, 57 nn. 5, 6, 11, 12, and 14, 58–65, 58 n. 15, 65 n. 4, 66 nn. 13 and 14, 67 nn. 16 and 17, 68–74, 75 nn. 1 and 2, 76 nn. 3, 5, 9, 10, and 16, 77 n. 18, 299–301, 327–31
  in New York National Anti-Slavery Standard, xvi, xxiv, 85–90, 91–95, 91 nn. 14 and 15, 95 n. 1, 96–101, 101 n. 1, 104–8, 108 nn. 1 and 8, 109–14, 114 nn. 2, 3, and 5, 115–21, 115 n. 9, 121 nn. 1 and 3–6, 122–28, 122 nn. 7, 8, and 10, 130 n. 1, 131 nn. 6 and 11, 132–36, 132 n. 12, 136 n. 1, 137–41, 143 nn. 2–7, 144–50, 150 n. 1, 151 nn. 4 and 6, 152 n. 8, 153 nn. 16 and 20, 155 n. 21, 156–59, 159 n. 1, 160 nn. 4 and 8, 161–65, 161 n. 11, 169 nn. 7 and 8, 170 nn. 10, 14, and 15, 299–301, 311–13, 313–18, 333
John the Baptist, 224
Johnson, Andrew, xxiii
Johnson, Samuel, 224
Johnson, Thomas, 269, 272, 273, 284 n. 60
Johnston, Saunders W., 280 n. 21, 283 n. 52
Jones, James C., 78, 83 nn. 9 and 10, 169 n. 8
Jones, Samuel J., 253 n. 10, 270, 282 nn. 38 and 40–42
Jones and Slater (New Orleans, La.), 217, 219 n. 5
Juniper Swamp. See Dismal Swamp

Kagi, John H., xix, 271–72, 283 nn. 47 and 49, 290 n. 1
Kalamazoo County, Mi., 95 n. 3